Outsourcing, Insourcing and IT for Enterprise Management

Also by Prof. Dr. Ing. Dimitris N. CHORAFAS

Liabilities, Liquidity and Cash Management. Balancing Financial Risk,
Wiley, New York, 2002

The Management of Philanthropy in the 21st Century,
Institutional Investor, New York, 2002

Modelling the Survival of Financial and Industrial Enterprises.
Advantages, Challenges, and Problems with the
Internal Rating-Based (IRB) Method
Palgrave/Macmillan, London, 2002

Enterprise Architecture and New Generation Information Systems
St Lucie Press/CRC, Boca Raton, FL, 2002

Managing Operational Risk. Risk Reduction Strategies for
Investment Banks and Commercial Banks
Euromoney, London, 2001

Managing Risk in the New Economy
New York Institute of Finance, New York, 2001

Implementing and Auditing the Internal Control System,
Macmillan/Palgrave, London, 2001

Integrating ERP, Supply Chain Management, and Smart Materials
Auerbach/CRC Press, New York, 2001

Internet Supply Chain. Its Impact on Accounting and Logistics
Macmillan/Palgrave, London, 2001

Reliable Financial Reporting and Internal Control: A Global Implementation Guide
John Wiley, New York, 2000

New Regulation of the Financial Industry
Macmillan – now Palgrave, Basingstoke, 2000

Managing Credit Risk, Volume 1 Analyzing, Rating and Pricing the Probability of Default
Euromoney, London, 2000

Managing Credit Risk, Volume 2 The Lessons of VAR Failures and Imprudent Exposure
Euromoney, London, 2000

Credit Derivatives and the Management of Risk
New York Institute of Finance, New York, 2000

Setting Limits for Market Risk
Euromoney, London, 1999

Commercial Banking Handbook
Macmillan – now Palgrave, Basingstoke, 1999

Understanding Volatility and Liquidity in Financial Markets
Euromoney, London, 1998

The Market Risk Amendment: Understanding Marketing to Model and Value-at-Risk
McGraw-Hill/Irwin, Burr Ridge, IL, 1998

Outsourcing, Insourcing and IT for Enterprise Management

Dimitris N. CHORAFAS

First published 2003 by
PALGRAVE MACMILLAN
Houndmills, Basingstoke, Hampshire RG21 6XS and
175 Fifth Avenue, New York, N.Y. 10010
Companies and representatives throughout the world

PALGRAVE MACMILLAN is the global academic imprint of the Palgrave
Macmillan division of St. Martin's Press, LLC and of Palgrave Macmillan Ltd.
Macmillan® is a registered trademark in the United States, United Kingdom
and other countries. Palgrave is a registered trademark in the European
Union and other countries.

ISBN 1–4039–0345–X

This book is printed on paper suitable for recycling and made from fully
managed and sustained forest sources.

A catalogue record for this book is available from the British Library.

Library of Congress Cataloging-in-Publication Data

Chorafas, Dimitris N.
    Outsourcing, insourcing and IT for enterprise management / Dimitris Chorafas.
        p.   cm.
    Includes bibliographical references and index.
    ISBN 1–4039–0345–X
1. Contracting out.   2. Information technology.   3. Industrial management.
I. Title.

HD2365 .C47 2002
004'.068'7—dc21

                                                                    2002030703

10   9   8   7   6   5   4   3   2   1
12   11   10   09   08   07   06   05   04   03

Printed and bound in Great Britain by
Antony Rowe Ltd, Chippenham and Eastbourne

Contents

Preface   ix
List of Abbreviations   xii

Part I   Risk and Reward in the Economy of the Twenty-first Century

1   Enterprise Management in the Economy of the Twenty-first Century   3
1   Introduction   3
2   Definition of outsourcing and insourcing   5
3   The search for higher return in the new economy   9
4   The modern company is the network   13
5   Knowledge companies and supply chains   17
6   Business markets, consumer markets and the new economy   20

2   Outsourcing, Insourcing and Leveraging Business Operations   25
1   Introduction   25
2   Virtual companies and the sense of strategic outsourcing   26
3   Learning how to apply the practice of outsourcing   30
4   Outsourcing can focus on quality of service only when the deal is
     thoroughly planned   34
5   Outsourcing done for uplifting the balance sheet   39
6   Establishing the reasons for outsourcing and sorting out priorities   44

3   Operational Risk with Outsourcing and Insourcing   49
1   Introduction   49
2   Operational risk control in a service economy   51
3   How to play safe with operational risks from outsourcing   56
4   Measurement of operational risk through use of operating
     characteristics curves   59
5   Operational risks which require steady qualitative evaluation   64
6   Understanding the evolution of operational risk control policies
     and practices   68

**4   Supply Chain Integration and the Management of Time; What
       Outsourcing Should Learn from the Internet   71**
1   Introduction   71
2   The shift in paradigm with online supply chain   73
3   Living and working in Internet time   75
4   Fast flow mechanisms and dynamic pricing help in changing
     our culture   80
5   Client base, brand loyalty, and the security challenge   83

6   The management of technology requires clear objectives
    and lots of know-how   87
7   Understanding and avoiding the common hype about
    websites   91

**Part II   What's the Value Differentiation with Outsourcing and
            Insourcing?**

5   Being in Charge of Outsourcing Agreements   **97**
1   Introduction   97
2   Satisfaction and dissatisfaction with outsourcing agreements   99
3   Evaluating benefits and selecting contractual norms   102
4   Potential efficiencies and inefficiencies with outsourcing   106
5   Service level agreements with insourcers   109
6   Beware of outsourcing deals that turn sour   113
7   The JP Morgan example: an entity may be both outsourcer
    and insourcer   116

6   Can We Leverage R&D and Engineering through Outsourcing?   **120**
1   Introduction   120
2   Innovation is basic to every strategic plan   122
3   How Charles Kettering characterised the process of innovation 127
4   Acquisitions and development. Risks associated to outsourcing 130
5   Multisourcing design tools and being aware of pitfalls with
    linear thinking   133
6   Project management. Is it wise to outsource it?   136
7   Meeting the challenge of design reviews   139

7   What It Takes to Outsource the Pattern of Production   **143**
1   Introduction   143
2   Markets, products and the manufacturing industry   146
3   Doing away with wrong ideas about production and
    outsourcing   149
4   The changing face of production: cell-based manufacturing
    and offshore outsourcing   154
5   Both outsourcing approaches and inhouse solutions must be
    foolproof   157
6   The changing pattern of production and the role of services   161

**8   Outsourcing Information Technology and Managing
      IT Operational Risks**   **166**
1   Introduction   166
2   The role of information technology in expanding the frontiers
    of globalisation   168
3   Outsourcing the services of IT professionals and their wares 173

4 Using the Web for outsourcing 176
5 An outsourcing–insourcing partnership must satisfy several
prerequisites 181
6 Operational risk and the interruption of business continuity
at Cantor Fitzgerald 184

**Part III Advantages To Be Gained from Better Organisation and
High-grade Personnel**

9 The Prerequisite of Rigorous Organisation Studies 191
1 Introduction 191
2 Organisational studies, business objectives and span of control 192
3 Business continuity and other organisational responsibilities 197
4 Information technology investments and organisational change 202
5 Killing inertia and bureaucracy through better organisation 206
6 Why cutting organisational fat can be a rewarding exercise 209
7 Can outsourcing improve the efficiency of the organisation? 212

**10 Personal Characteristics and Cognitive Complexity
Required by the New Technologies 215**
1 Introduction 215
2 Both an analytical mind and a doer's personality are
important to success 216
3 Background reasons for personality traits and cognitive
complexity 220
4 Creativity, awareness and the saturation of input–output
channels 225
5 A company's growth, maturity, recovery and decay depend
on the personality characteristics of its people 229
6 Interpreting the results of qualitative measurement of
personality traits 233

11 Globalisation Needs Goals, Better Education and Life-long Learning 241
1 Introduction 241
2 Work environment and the challenge of staffing 242
3 Knowledge, paths of learning and the new economy 246
4 The shortfall of trained technologists 250
5 The new economy and the effect of the Internet on learning 254
6 Appreciating the role of Internet-based learning 257

PART IV Cost Control Helps the Bottom Line of Outsourcing

12 Extending Our Company's System of Cost Control to the Insourcer 265
1 Introduction 265
2 Standard costs and the measures needed for cost control 266

3   Profit centres, cost centres and the insourcer   271
4   The crucial role of overheads in financial results   275
5   Why cost control is a very serious business   281
6   Sharp and steady cost control separates the good insourcer
     from the rotten   286

**13   Innovation and Cost Control in Information Technology through
       Re-engineering   290**
1   Introduction   290
2   Re-engineering helps in promoting innovation and in improving
     efficiency   292
3   Without appropriate testing, re-engineering and downsizing
     are in no way 'sure bets'   295
4   The budget for outsourcing and for re-engineering must be tight   299
5   Cost awareness improves the strategic advantages gained
     with computer systems   302
6   Charge-backs and the auditing of IT applications   305

14   Return on Investment and IT's Impact on Outsourcing Agreements   309
1   Introduction   309
2   Assistance in innovation and benefits from fast response time   311
3   The need for increasing management's awareness of return on
     investment   316
4   Structural change is one of the channels of return on
     investment   319
5   Infrastructural interdependencies with IT outsourcing   322
6   The synergy between return on investment and streamlined
     organisational solutions   325

Epilogue   330
Notes   332
Index   336

Preface

In the history of mankind the processes of outsourcing and insourcing began with the first artisans. The evolution of the practice of outsourcing has not ended yet, as everyday there are new opportunities for both outsourcers and insourcers – and with them new risks. Some of these risks are financial, while others relate to functionality, timeliness and quality of deliverables.

Excellence in enterprise management, at the insourcer's and outsourcer's side, has an evident impact on results. One of the biggest mistakes people make in trying to diagnose and correct business problems is to blame others, or factors outside the system, for undesirable outcomes when in fact the system itself may be at fault. Determining the nature and frequency of problems involved in outsourcing agreements means, first of all, understanding the way business decisions may be playing themselves out in a complex process of cause and effect.

Written for executives responsible for outsourcing agreements and their immediate assistants, this text focuses on ways and means that allow them to be in charge of service-level contracts. It also concentrates on the evolving aspects of information technology and the way these have changed because of outsourcing. Based on an extensive research project, the book provides a common experience regarding objectives and deliverables in outsourcing. It also illustrates why it is not easy to make the right decision.

In itself, the act of outsourcing is neither 'good' nor 'bad', clear or obscure, something to seek or to protect oneself against. It becomes a profitable or a dangerous enterprise depending on the degree of *our* preparation and on the homework done by the insourcer; the level of control over the functions to be outsourced; the contractual clauses embedded in the service level agreement (SLA) regarding the deliverables; the existence or absence of design reviews, as well as the costs associated to outsourced activities and the results being obtained.

A basic reason behind the often critical comments that are made in this book is to stimulate and guide, to encourage senior management in being in charge and in investigating with diligence the different alternatives prior to signing up an outsourcing contract. Both the results of my research and personal experience suggest the need for developing informed responses, understanding the opportunities and the risks. The text presents the facts and it also offers a critical commentary on individual aspects of the outsourcing process.

The text divides into 14 chapters, which fall in four parts. Part I looks at risk and reward in the economy of the twenty-first century. The focus of Chapter 1 is enterprise management. Chapter 2 defines outsourcing, insourcing and their relationship to leveraging business activities. Because it is inescapable that outsourcing and insourcing involve operational risks, this subject is treated in fair extent in Chapter 3. Chapter 4 looks into supply chain integration, and the contribution the internet provides to the management of time.

Is there value differentiation through outsourcing and insourcing? This is the theme of Part II. Chapter 5 explains what it takes to be in charge of insourcing and outsourcing agreements. This job is do-able, but it is not easy. Following this, by means of practical examples from engineering (Chapter 6), manufacturing (Chapter 7) and information technology (IT) (Chapter 8) the text explains:

- the benefits the newest advances in technology can provide when they are well managed, and
- the types of business partnerships which stand a better chance to leverage one's own resources through outsourcing.

Emphasis is placed on why companies must examine IT for enterprise management within the perspective of their particular business challenges, and more precisely their strategic plans. Through practical examples, the text shows that there is synergy between the new economy, electronic commerce and dynamic business partnerships which involve plenty of outsourcing.

The focal point of Part III is the advantages to be gained from better organisation; also by employing the best available skills. Chapter 9 outlines the prerequisites to rigorous organisational studies, and it explains why are these fundamental to successful outsourcing agreements. Because there are so many demands on available human resources, Chapter 10 brings into perspective the personal characteristics and cognitive complexity required by the new technologies. Chapter 11 explains why globalisation needs a better educational system and lifelong learning.

Part IV concentrates on cost control, and the way the notions of profit centres and of internal billing help the bottom line of outsourcing agreements. One of the reasons why companies outsource is to save money, capitalise on economies of scale and improve efficiency. Not all these objectives are, however, reached as it can be seen by examining results being obtained by most companies which venture into outsourcing without the necessary system of checks and balances.

One of the major deceptions is that of unrealised cost savings. For this reason, Chapter 12 advises to extend *our* company's system of cost control to the insourcer. Chapter 13 explains how to bring innovation and cost control in IT through re-engineering. Chapter 14 emphasises the importance of return on investment (ROI) studies, how these should be conducted and what can be expected from them.

The aim of some of the critical comments made throughout the text regarding outsourcing and insourcing is to send the reader back to the outsourcing contract he or she is studying, or has signed in the past and is likely to repeat. Not until we effectively use constructive criticism can we make headway in contractual agreements with counterparties. The basic issue is not one of being for or against outsourcing, but rather of clearly establishing under which terms this should be done.

Anyone attempting to produce a general synthesis of the significance and extent of outsourcing incurs manifold debt. Mine is apparent in the Acknowledgements. Let me take this opportunity to thank Stephen Rutt and Caitlin Cornish, for suggesting this project and seeing it all the way to publication, and Lindx Auld for the editing work. To Eva-Maria Binder goes the credit for compiling the research results, typing the text and making the camera-ready artwork and index.

Valmer and Vitznau   Dimitris N. Chorafas
June 2002

List of Abbreviations

BSP   Business Service Provider
BPO   Business Process Operations
ASP   Application Service Provider
SLA   Service Level Agreement
SEP   Somebody Else's Problem
MECE   Mutually Exclusive and Comprehensively Exhaustive

Part I

Risk and Reward in the Economy of the Twenty-first Century

1

Enterprise Management in the Economy of the Twenty-first Century

1. Introduction

During the second half of the twentieth century, several business sectors, such as merchandising, financing and technology experienced far-reaching changes, with a great impact on the way we live and work. Scientists describe the rapid technological evolution through the thirty-year-old *Moore's Law*, which says that at equal cost microchip power would double every 18 months, and *the law of the photon* which suggests that communications bandwidth triples every year at steady cost.

Significant developments have also taken place in finance. One of them is derivative financial instruments, the leverage they make possible, and the huge risks these involve in terms of leverage and exposure.[1] Another is globalisation, which has enlarged not only markets but also sourcing opportunities – including outsourcing – making feasible a wider than ever optimisation of costs.

Since business and industry are directly affected by globalisation, deregulation, innovation and a fast-moving technology, it comes as no surprise that at the dawn of the twenty-first century people and companies are trying to identify products, processes and solutions which act as drivers of change in an organisation. One of these drivers is thought to be the 'virtual company' (see below) that came along with the expansion of outsourcing (see Chapter 2).

Whether or not it is a fad of recent years, outsourcing should be never seen as a 'me too' attitude. This is the worst possible strategy, as suggested by the omega curve in Figure 1.1, which, incidentally, has also characterised other trends and novelties. Industrial leadership requires that decisions are always based on careful study, including the analysis of alternatives, their opportunities and risks. There is plenty of them with outsourcing and 'insourcing', including a horde of 'operational risks' (see Chapter 3).[2]

As companies try to position themselves against the forces of the future, new technology and novel business opportunities are seen as drivers of change. An example are the opportunities provided by the Internet (see section 4 and

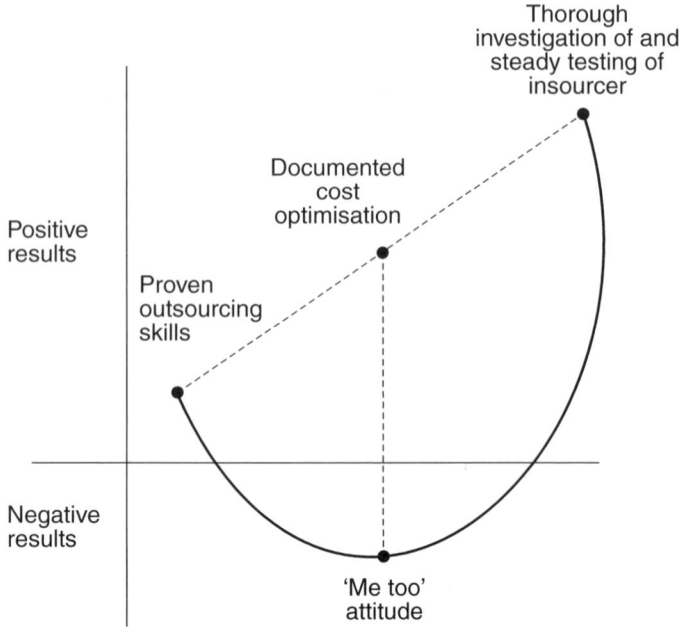

Figure 1.1   Good and bad strategies for choosing an outsourcing solution

Chapter 4) which makes feasible the acquisition and delivery of products and services in a more competitive way than otherwise possible; improved access to online solutions; and the use of high-tech as a strategic weapon.

- Hardly a day goes by without some company announcing it is gearing up to service its customers online.
- It is becoming increasingly difficult to find an industrial sector that does not have a website; while many websites become transactions oriented.

The expanding horizon of online business is the best documentation of the new economy's reach and vitality in spite of temporary setbacks,[3] but like old soldiers, sound management principles don't fade away. The best ways to look at business opportunity is to evaluate critically whether our company is solving a problem or making someone else's life easier.

- Do we have a product or service that people and companies need?
- Are we gaining an advantage by turning to the computer to do a given job classically done manually?

Precisely under this light should be examined outsourcing and its twin concept of insourcing (for a definition see section 2) which are the main themes of this book. 'The worth of a State, in the long run, is the worth of the individuals composing it,' said John Stuart Mill, the economist. In precisely the same manner, the worth of any concept is the substance of its deliverables. The key question then is whether or not outsourcing is able to deliver.

2. Definition of outsourcing and insourcing

Outsourcing is the delegation to another party – the *insourcer* – of the authority for the provision of services. This is done under a contract that incorporates service level agreements (SLA – a list of abbreviations will be found in the appendix to this chapter). While no two SLAs are exactly the same in scope and content, the way to bet is that in their core will be included issues such as:

- functionality
- cost
- quality
- timeliness of deliverables.

Typically the definition of risks is not a part of SLAs because not every outsourcer or insourcer appreciates that risks and responsibilities are integral part of any agreement even if they cannot be delegated by the outsourcer to the insourcer. Yet, personal accountability is a basic principle in enterprise management, and it should be fully respected in every contract. The insourcer assumes risks which *de facto* also remain at the outsourcer's side.

Accountability encompasses all four factors expressed in a nutshell by the above four bullets: Functionality, quality, timeliness and cost. Innovative, high-quality products and services at cost lower than that of our competitors is a fundamental pillar of enterprise. Entrepreneurship is not a status to enjoy, it is an attitude to have; an attitude necessary to everyone who aspires to be market leader. Therefore, solutions connected to outsourcing and to technology-centred services discussed in this book should not be seen as a way to discharge responsibility, but rather as a different means of doing a job, provided we are ready for it and we know-how to manage it. Being ready and having the appropriate skills is centre point to enterprise management.

Much can be learned about the validity of often optimistic hypotheses currently made about outsourcing by studying what has happened in the recent past to companies which have gone through a boom and bust cycle. As with every other enterprise, the course of the current drive to outsourcing and insourcing will not be alien to boom and bust. We should always learn from the past to avoid repeating the same mistakes and to protect in the best possible *our* core capital.

Down to basics: outsourcing and insourcing define the different aspects of a two-way business. Until quite recently, the term 'outsourcing' was used to identify a process which involves, under contractual terms, both parties in an agreement: The one farming out a service and the other providing that service for a certain fee. This narrow sort of definition has not been satisfactory because it led to confusion. As a result, a new term has come into being: 'insourcing', to identify the party which accepts rendering a specific service or services under certain conditions and responsibilities. The insourcer is faced with:

- the challenge of getting it right
- the cost of getting it wrong.

Outsourcing and insourcing is a bilateral agreement and it is not monolithic. Neither is it necessarily the best policy for very entity. Figure 1.2 outlines the five most popular strategies available today with outsourcing and insourcing. It is always good to have several options for what we are doing. It is also wise not to forget that each option has its advantages and disadvantages – operational risk being among the most important among the latter, as Chapter 3 explains.

The 'internal utility' option in Figure 1.2 is a lone wolf strategy. For instance, the board may decide to set up an independent business unit which acts as the insourcer of procurement services of the company's other operating units located anywhere in the world. Many companies have done so, because the mass effect strengthens their negotiating power. The same is true of an independent business unit which provides information technology services to all other divisions and affiliates.

Contrasted to the internal utility is the option of the 'external utility'. It may be an independent service bureau or a peer-level common infrastructure or alliance (more on this in section 3). In the late 1980s four major Wall Street investment banks joined forces to develop a common, time-shared global network because of the costs involved in doing so alone. (This venture did not last long.)

The third option presented in Figure 1.2 is that of a business service provider. We will see an example with custody. The insourcer providing this facility is usually a competitor institution which has the technology and know-how to support a specific service at lower cost than other institutions do through internal sourcing.

There may also be a negotiated take-over of an internal service department, for instance IT, by a third party which operates it at a fee. The premise (which is not always kept) is that because of greater efficiency and less nepotism, this fee will be lower than what IT used to cost the company as a fully integrated cost centre or internal utility.

The fifth option in Figure 1.2 is that of an application service provider (ASP). Classically, this has been as independent service bureau with its own data centre(s), programming and maintenance people. These are the black-and-white

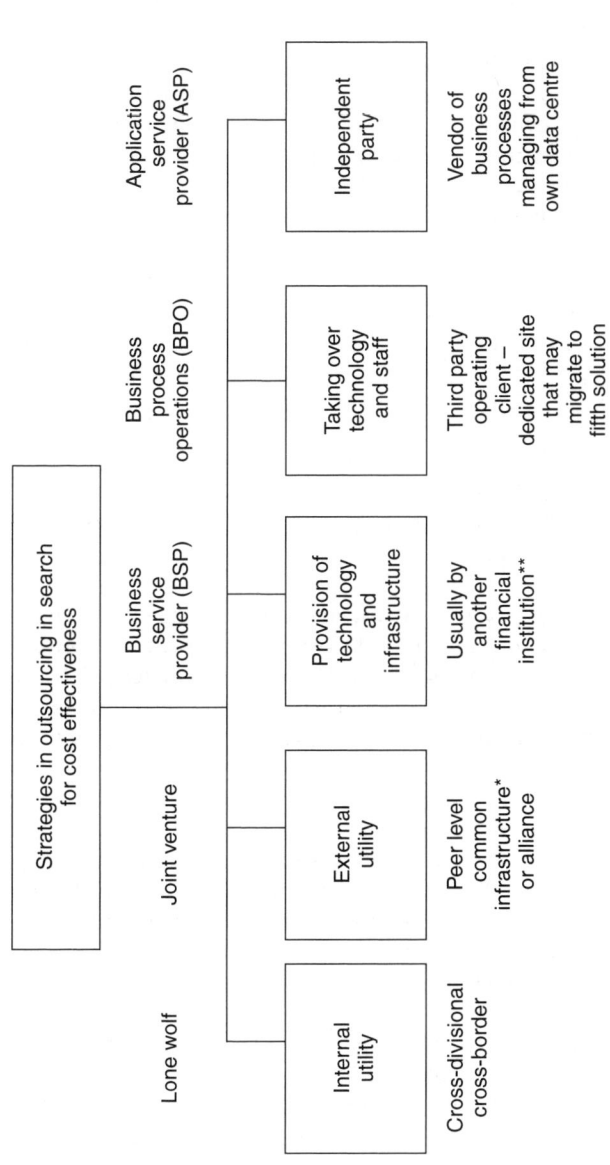

*Competitors at frontdesk but partners at back office
**Example: custodian

Figure 1.2   Alternative paths to an outsourcing solution

five options, but there exist also tonalities of grey. For instance, an ASP which acts as business process operations (BPO) manager over a given time-frame. Many companies steer away from hybrids because they often lead to ineffi-ciencies and confusion. Insourcers are in this business for profits, but what is driving the outsourcers? The main reasons stated by outsourcers are: possible cost savings, capitalisation on a mass effect, and lack of internal skills (more about this in Chapter 2). Procurement is a classical outsourcing activity. Lack of raw materials and the need for specialised components has been an age-old reason for outsourcing agreements.

While in all likelihood materials have been at the origin of outsourcing, today many types of what is considered as traditional type contracts involve services. Small companies hire a lawyer, rather than employing internally a legal counsel. They also hire an accounting bureau to do their general accounting job, or a certified public accountant (CPA) for their internal auditing. The 'virtual company' in the new economy greatly expanded the outsourcing of services. But:

- problems of internal controls and security exist when companies out-source and outskill some of their core functions
- while at the same time the benefits in terms of lower costs and knowledge acquisition are not always evident.

There may be plenty of reasons for using outside suppliers of services. Aside capitalising on skill, outsourcing may help to extend the reach of a certain process, reduce fixed cost or (in fewer cases) improve efficiency. These reasons, however, have to be factual and documented, and this is not always the case. The pros say that outsourcing has emerged as a key technique with the new economy (see below), because too many demands are posed on available human resources. It is wise to challenge this notion.

Contrarians to the growing wave of outsourcing suggest that few of the experiences so far available with outsourcing different business activities justify the originally prevailing assumptions, which anyway tend to be too optimistic. There are, however, ways to be in charge of outsourcing agree-ments. We will see several examples on this in Part II. The basic problem are not of being for or against outsourcing, but rather of:

- thoroughly researching the pros and cons
- refocusing attention on competitiveness
- forcing management to reconsider the best way to perform the work to be outsourced, prior to doing so.

Part and parcel of the equation of prudent handling of outsourcing and insourcing agreement should be the fact that it may prove most difficult and costly to reverse outsourcing. Therefore, managers considering the wisdom

of outsourcing some business functions will be well advised to ask themselves some basic questions.

- Why are we outsourcing?
- What are we outsourcing?
- Which are the core activities we do *not* wish to outsource?
- Can we be in charge of the outsourcing process?
- What's the projected cost/benefit? How sure are we of that projection?
- How can we get the most from an outsourcing arrangement?

There are some services like fleet vehicle management, healthcare processing, business office rental and others, for which companies have tended to
rely more on outsourcing solutions than on internal ones. Custody is a classical example of outsourcing in banking. It is outsourced because of lower
cost made available through mass handling. 'We don't have the critical mass
of customers to do the proper software for custody and depreciate it. Not
even to cover the running cost,' said a senior European banker during our
meeting. International banks which have the critical mass, outsource custody for time window reasons. Prior to its merger with JP Morgan, Chase
Manhattan worked out of a DP Centre in England because its time window
is practically half-way between Tokyo and New York. This attracted several
American banks with correspondent institutions in Europe and Asia which
decided to use Chase as custodian.

3. The search for higher return in the new economy

As we saw in section 2, the example of custodians as insourcers brings up
some interesting characteristics of the outsourcing business, because
custodians are rather special insourcers who compete with their clients (the
other credit institutions) at front desk, but collaborate at the back office.
They are, in this sense, business service providers (BPOs) who team up with
their competitors because of a strategic alliance, joint venture or for bottom
line reasons.

To better appreciate the role shared by external utilities and BPOs, which
have been the second and third options in Figure 1.2, it is advisable to keep
in mind the changing structure of multinationals and the way outsourcing
impacts on the business which they do. Multinationals used to be domestic
firms with subsidiaries abroad. Now they organise globally along product or
service lines, outsourcing some function and executing inhouse some
others. This, too, however is changing.

Current projections suggest that in the future multinationals will be held
together and controlled by strategy rather than capital. This means that they
will operate within the framework shown in Figure 1.3 which, at the same
time, helps in defining the domain where outsourcing and insourcing can

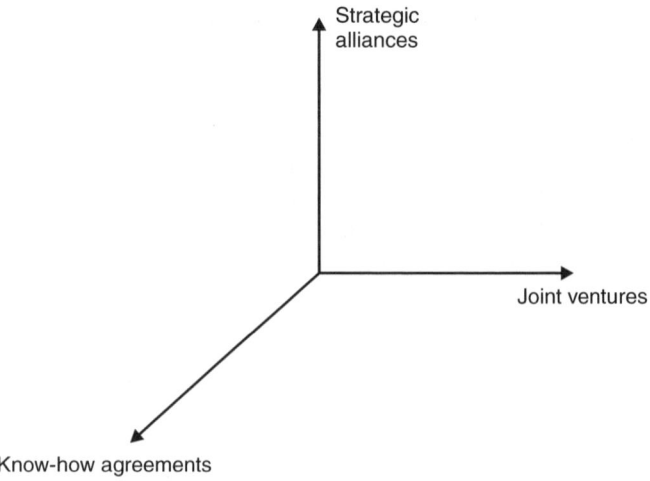

Figure 1.3   Frame of reference of the new enterprise architecture that may result from projects such as oxygen

play a most critical role. Sprawling multinational organisations need a new kind of top management which stands for global strategy:

- balancing conflicting demands on business being made
- looking after short-term and long-term results
- caring for stakeholders: investors, customers, suppliers, employees and regulators.

Global strategy poses its own demands and challenges in selecting a business partner for outsourcing, including the criteria for choices. With custody services, for instance, the fact is that there are not many global custodians left anymore. This puts under stress the list of criteria an outsourcer can apply in choosing an insourcer, but at least two critical issues should be retained:

1 *scalability*, a problem which exists in all bilateral business ventures, and including custodians
2 Tier-1 *information technology* solutions, which differentiate the more successful insourcers from the less successful ones.

An example on the second bullet is 'fund accounting', a value-added service. This is not a natural activity for all custodians, though some are tooling up to it. I do stress the need for top-tier information technology because, as the reader will see in the subsequent chapters, it is cornerstone to the success of practically all outsourcing solutions. Because first-class IT is key to good performance,

- The better-known custodians put more than 50 per cent of their IT investment into discretionary projects.
- By contrast, small firms cannot even put a quarter of their IT budget into discretionary solutions.

This argument on leadership in one sector of the new economy, IT, should be extended to all others. The search for higher returns in the globalised business environments involves human resources, products and services, markets, and financial staying power. In each one of these domains companies must come up with more cost-effective solutions than ever before.

It is therefore appropriate to look into the new economy as a whole, including both the goodies and the pitfalls it brings along with it. A long, hard look is necessary to give perspective to our discussion and help position outsourcing into the right context. (The rest of this chapter addresses itself to the new economy, technology and the Internet. We will return to outsourcing in Chapter 2.)

Outsourcing or not-outsourcing, sound enterprise management is at a premium in the new economy. As an *MIT Report* aptly underlines, a true entrepreneur is someone for whom creating new markets and products is much stronger than protecting the status quo.[4] As Robert Metcalfe noted in that same issue 'One sign of who won't succeed are people who think a sudden flash of brilliance will have the world beating a path to their door.'

The search for increased efficiency in the new economy, which first established itself in the United States, sees to it that at the end of 1999 technology stocks accounted for about 24.5 per cent of the value of the S&P 500, up from less than 10 per cent a decade earlier. More to the point, in 1999 *all* the S&P 500s gains have been represented by technology companies, while the rest of the market was down slightly.

The new economy moved forward with the upswing of equity invested in technology, but this was followed by a financial earthquake in the 2000–2001 time-frame which, according to some opinions, has been a blessing rather than a curse. The economic ups and downs keep us constantly on our toes, forever bringing up challenges to:

- open new market perspectives
- lower the cost of products or service
- develop a new generation of products
- just make our deliverables more attractive in a tough market.

Over the past three decades, the electronics industry has gone through a number of ups and downs cycles, some of which were the industry's own

fault. Take component shortages as an example. They led system manufacturers to double and quadruple-book orders for key parts. Overbooking
caused component suppliers to add more manufacturing capacity, and this
led to overproducing the desired goods. When supply came close to the
leveraged demand, many of the overbookings were cancelled and suppliers
were left with huge stocks and manufacturing capacity that they did not
need. As a result, component prices tumbled. In the late 1990s, as the new
economy tried to find its way, high leveraging has also been particularly
pronounced in financing companies because of their accumulation of
liabilities.

Under the banner of delivering shareholder value, companies contracted
as many debts as they could get. Market economies are areas where, when
times are good, too many people can become too complacent. Companies
overestimated the number of customers

- who would be interested in buying their products and services
- who could afford doing so at high rate.

One of the leverage ratios that should be steadily watched, particularly
in periods of market ascendancy, is that of debt service coverage. It is
computed as earnings before interest and taxes (EBIT) over interest due
(EBIT/interest) and is considered to be highly predicted. Therefore it is an
important tool in discriminating between lower and higher credit risk
entities. Many investors lost their money by forgetting that one day debts
have to be paid together with interest.

Bubbles created through leveraged business activity can best be appreciated
from their aftermath after they burst. In my books, I have generally painted
a bright picture of the new economy while making the reader aware of its
risks.[5] This positive approach has been based on the majority view of financial analysts, even if since late 1999 the opinions by economists have been
divided:

- some spousing the hypothesis of the new economy's bright future
- others thinking that projected new economy developments and more
  general structural changes highlight the limitations of our views and our
  estimates.

The pessimistic view of the new economy looked for historical precedence
to boom and bust, such as the railroad euphoria of the late 1800s, the
mining stocks of the early 1900s; and the 1930s Depression. These past
references were thought to be important because they brought into
perspective dangers which lied ahead. They are references worth keeping
in mind when we will talk about a coming boom in outsourcing and
insourcing prognosticated by many experts.

4. The modern company is the network

Within the context of the new economy, a real-life example, which can provide valuable input to enterprise management, is the rise and fall of the Internet's glamour – not necessarily of the Internet itself (more on this later). The glamour of Internet companies faded because shareholders came to realise that the return on their investment was on shaky grounds. They wanted rapid action over these companies' debt, while expecting their equity to continue appreciating.

The Internet's glamour faded away, but the network stayed. This is most relevant to what might be happening to companies which take bets with outsourcing and insourcing. Now, as in the late 1990s, the US market contains unique global technology companies which act as insourcers of expertise. The motors behind them have been young inventors creating the elusive 'next company wonder'. As investors capitalised by taking exposure to high-tech companies:

- globalisation saw to it that technology became a bigger part of life in many countries
- in key development areas the big question has been who dominates the market.

The rush towards value differentiation in online business became a battle between arithmetic – which is predictable – and momentum, which is not. Not doubt the relative standing in Internet-based online business shown in Figure 1.4 will be revised as the coming years will see the emergence of lots

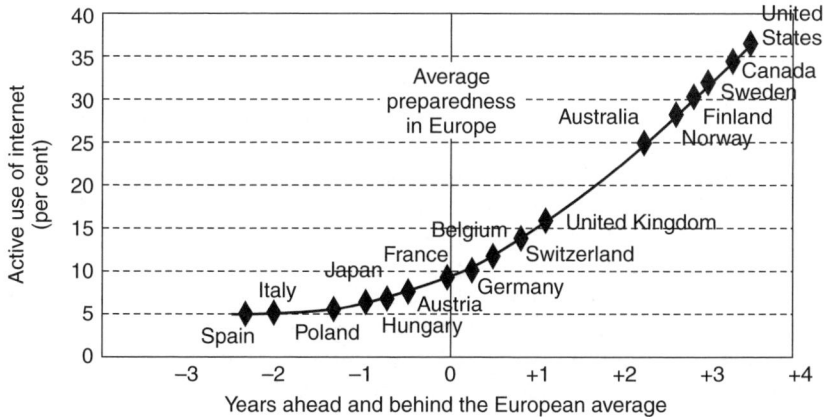

Figure 1.4 Countries ahead of the lot are best positioned to benefit from broadband Internet

of information appliances, devices simpler and less expensive than PCs intended to bring networking to the mass market.

At the bolts and nuts of new technology, wireless communications, cable modems and a high-speed phone service (digital subscriber line, DSL) will be displacing slow and error-prone dial-up lines as the path to seamless online access. By all likelihood, however, it will take a few more years before broadband Internet access becomes pervasive.

A good deal of the importance attached to network-based transactions business comes from the fact that gross domestic product (GDP) and information technology correlate. In the Group of Ten (G-10) countries today, information technology represents about 12 per cent of GDP. In a couple of decades, right after 2020, this share is expected to be closer to 50 per cent. No bank, industrial organisation, or merchandising firm can stay out of global networking, therefore out of the broadband Internet, and survive.

- Globally seamless networking is the number 1 force behind the early twenty-first century business.

In terms of promoting business activity and personal productivity, web access is today what the telephone used to be in the post Second World War years.

- But to be a player, a company must fulfil a number of prerequisites.

One of these prerequisites is to capitalise on networked information technology both for product innovation as for creation of jobs. According to the European Commission, 80 per cent of new jobs generated in the European Union (EU) over the last five years have been in information-related industries. Without a global information infrastructure, it would be impossible to realise new social solutions which respond to the aspirations of our age.

Another one of the prerequisites for leadership in global networking is the investments made in sophisticated software, like knowledge-enriched solutions. Software–hardware ratios based on software investment as a per centage of hardware investment at current prices is a good way to measure the evolution of a nation's information infrastructure. A comparison between Germany and the US is shown in Figure 1.5, based on 1991–1999 statistics from the Monthly Report of Deutsche Bundesbank, May 2001.

In parallel to breakthroughs in knowledge-enriched software solutions, comes the hardware technology which is shaping the new economy through the law of the photon. We have yet to appreciate the impact this rapid change in the carrying capacity of a communications line will have on our daily lives. One estimate is that high-speed Internet access and video interconnecting all homes and all offices will be a reality in the not-too-distant future. But there is more to this story of the photon – and that's *convergence*.

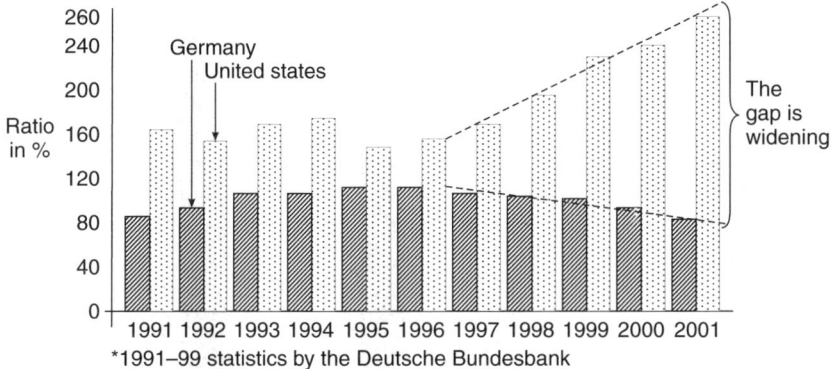

Figure 1.5 A dozen years of software–hardware ratios in IT expenditures: United States and Germany*

- Convergence refers to transformation of computing and communications technologies, capitalising on speed and interconnectivity.
- The network combines processing power and bandwidth to create platforms for a huge range of business and consumer products and services.

Among producers, clear-eyed traditional quality firms such as General Electric (GE), have been constantly remaking their businesses from within, cannibalising existing product lines before competitors do it for them. A negative example is Lucent Technologies which failed to instil entrepreneurial management spirit in its famed Bell Telephone Labs and its other divisions.

A special feature of the year 2000 World Economic Forum in Davos, Switzerland, was a panel of Internet tycoons asked to give advice to old, tired companies on how to survive. One of the panellists, Masayoshi Son of Softbank, responded to a query in a way worth recording: 'Do a new go-go Internet business unit under young, dynamic management; not under the management of the parent company. Also assign it a short timetable to stand on its feet. When it does, give it the mission to cannibalise the parent company.' Mannesmann, the German mechanical equipment company, is an example that fits this description. Its networking division became wealthier than the parent firm and its take-over by Vodafone led to a snowfall of profits for its shareholders.

If old companies don't take upon themselves the venture capitalist's role, then a vast pool of small tech companies will. The relative lack of regulations and restrictions on new businesses helps to turn into gold new ideas and products the market wants, with the result old, immobile companies would be cannibalised anyway. In Figure 1.6, statistics and estimates on Internet users per 1000 people suggests North American markets are best positioned to benefit the most from the wave of networking.

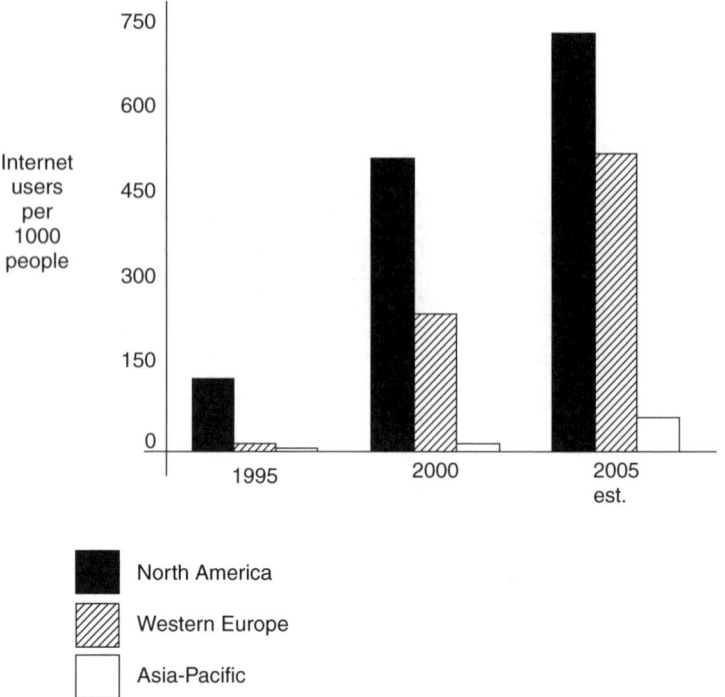

Figure 1.6   1995 and 2000 statistics, 2005 estimates of Internet users per 1000 people in North America, Europe and Asia

It is not that the Internet is the Year 2003+ penicillin, but every good manager should ask himself or herself the basic question: 'What are *my* alternatives?' The search for alternatives is needed not only to find a better mousetrap but also to stimulate the imagination and pave the way for well-documented decisions. In all matters involving uncertainty, therefore, in all pioneering projects, we need imagination and creative thinking that lead to new situations.

One of a successful manager's topmost skills is not technical in the rather limited sense of the word, but rather the will (and the guts) to challenge the obvious. This should not be a once-in-a-lifetime approach but a consistent strategy aimed at furthering one's investigative skills and goals. In this short sentence the reader will find 90 per cent of the reason why I stress so much the need to:

- recast our way of thinking
- steadily reinvent our business.

In the last analysis, this is what has made winning companies. Forward-looking plans have to be made, because of Darwinian reasons: the survival of the fittest. In several meetings with financial analysts at Wall Street I heard the opinion that since the late 1990s a company's 'wing to wing' strategy and its virtuosity in using networking to further goals have been a critical element in evaluating its growth potential, survivability and quality of its earning. One of these discussions focused on GE Capital and its four themes:

1 globalisation
2 financial services
3 six Sigma
4 Internet business.

A growing number of examples document that globalisation and innovation not only refer to acquisitions and the development of new products or services, but also the strategic relocation of *intellectual assets* to build and equip a global platform. In the example just presented, one of the goals of GE's financial services initiative is to strengthen the links it has with its customer base in multiple channels, which by many accounts is a winning strategy.

5. Knowledge companies and supply chains

Used in novel and imaginative ways, new technology and online business-to-business (B2B) solutions (see section 6) can transform old companies into more efficient and profitable ones, extending their life-cycle. Critical to this transformation is a big stride in productivity. As shown in Figure 1.7, this is characteristic of high-tech companies, while old companies usually are productivity laggards. Yet they have to match the tech companies' performance in order to survive.

The strategic question underpinning a company's growth and survival is: 'What is the business model of a successful entity in the twenty-first century?' Analysts with whom I discussed this question stressed the theme that companies that took their future in their own hands became a repository of information and expertise; in short, *knowledge companies*. (A knowledge company is one which depends more on the brains of its people than on bricks, mortar, machinery, and other real assets.) As a result of this strategic advantage, their management is able to:

• leverage a huge installed base, itself the product of years of industry leadership
• tie customers to the firm's product line(s) and marketing channel(s) for decades
• help to increase asset values making itself more immune to economic vagaries than it has ever been.

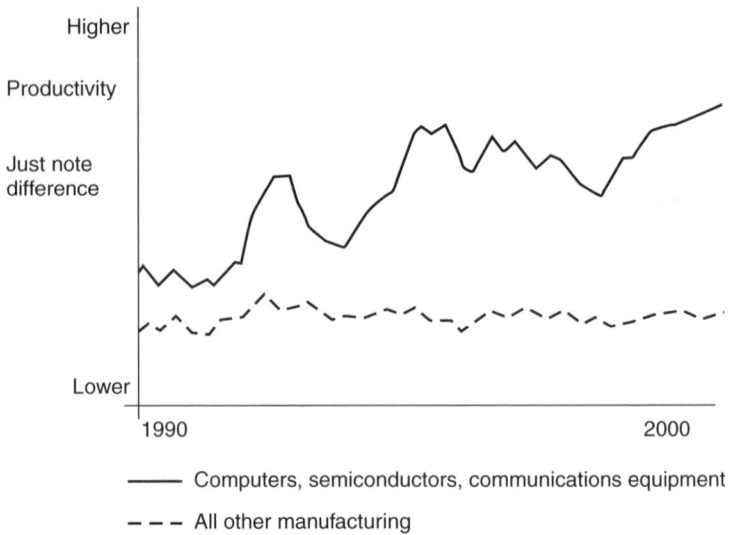

Figure 1.7   During the last decade higher productvity has been solidly at the side of new industries

These three bullets are a bible to all self-respecting boards and CEOs. They can be easily turned into critical questions asked of one's own company, helping to guide the chief executive's hand. For instance, the classic GE which was a model of consistency combined with the new, high-growth and more aggressive GE to form an enterprise valued as high as growth stocks, many of which retained their valuation despite having failed investors at one time or another.

The wing-to-wing strategy suggested in section 4 can also be used to promote transparency. The need for improving transparency through management policy and high technology is highlighted by the fact that the current accounting treatment of complex financial products, like derivatives, can only be made transparent by means of intraday evaluation and reporting – done in a way able to flash out existing problems.

- All companies should be interested in this reference because derivative instruments are at the foundation of the new economy.
- Derivative financial instruments are as well a prime example on outsourcing, as we will see in Chapter 2 with Sainsbury.

Companies should *not* use derivatives to beautify and redress through creative accounting their balance sheet but to product their bottom line. They should also seek to capitalise on their high-tech oriented divisions and gain through technology transfer. In all likelihood, more and more of the old companies will be doing what General Motors tried to do using its Hughes subsidiary. This is the internal utility outsourcing solution we saw in Figure 1.2. GM's plan has been through Hughes to:

- buy all its goods and services from its business partners through the Web
- offer new technology services with products like direct satellite TV
- enter into a variety of satellite/Internet locator services and other domains.

The man who engineered this metamorphosis at GM has been rewarded for his initiative. On 3 February 2000, G. Richard Wagoner, Jr, became the new General Motors chief executive. Wagoner is also considered, to be a production efficiency expert, and a CEO willing to let the company's auto designers spread their wings to erase the carmaker's image as a 'me-too' company.

The GM example is interesting because it demonstrates that even old economy firms start to realise if one is not a leader in new technology, one does not have a franchise over the long haul. Supply chain is a good place to enter the outsourcing cycle, because it is integral part of the B2B business (see section 6). Another good entry point into interest-engineered solutions is in research, development and engineering, as will be discussed in Chapter 6.

Several old economy companies now incorporate modular approaches to building their products that use Internet commerce to connect with suppliers practically in real-time. The sought-out result is the ability to provide the consumer with *on demand* access. An acceleration in supply chain timescales permits fast-flow replenishment of inventories. For instance, cars and trucks are made to order in a time-frame as short as a week, or even three days.

The aim of a switch to online business is not only trimming the costs. It is also forging strong, reliable partnerships with the best suppliers anywhere in the world.[6] History books will probably write down 1999 as the first year a number of old economy companies began exploring the possibilities of employing the concept of the Internet supply chain and of online retailing. The early starters, such as Cisco in supply chain and Dell Computer in retailing, did so some years earlier.

Companies able to exploit their knowledge base are the best positioned to benefit from a networked supply chain. Most interesting is the speed with which this is done. At Cisco, within months a team designed and implemented an electronic procurement system able to accommodate real-time, online bidding from anywhere around the globe.

- Suppliers access the bidding site via a standard Web browser and a password.

Unlike target pricing, where a customer typically sets a target price for a commodity, bidding suppliers set a real market price for technologies and commodities being sourced. Once they are online, they are able to view the prices being bid for a particular commodity; but they do not see the names of the other organisations involved. This is important in as much as:

- for business reasons it is important to assure that submission of bids throughout the event is in strict confidence.

It is only reasonable to expect that other old technology industries, even without direct consumer products like steel, aluminium, chemicals and machinery, will also try to become new technology users – to improve their efficiency and productivity, and therefore the likelihood of their survival.

- Supply chain is an outsourcing and insourcing activity by excellence, the oldest one on record.

Modernising the supply chain by means of networking, and making it more efficient, is a necessary supplement to current policies whereby old technology industries are consolidating and restructuring to establish their place in the new global economy – on account of the fact the latter is merciless to people, companies and nations that stay behind.

Neither is electronic commerce the only feat characterising a company's new supply chain initiatives. Cross-industry partnerships have also seen the light. Visteon, the French automotive parts supplier, teamed up with Bang & Olufsen, a Danish electronics specialist, to develop a range of car music systems able to ensure motorists enjoy the same sound quality on the move as they do at home. These joint products have been aimed at the upper end of the market for cars in the Jaguar, Mercedes-Benz and BMW class.

Is the Internet supposed to do away with middlemen since producers and customers can now connect directly? There is no evidence to substantiate a 'yes' answer. As it turns out, buyers seem to need middlemen on the Net to sort through the vast new choices of suppliers. And suppliers need to be where many buyers gather, which usually is not on individual company sites.

These Internet middlemen are known as 'infomediaries', vertical portals, or i-markets. They are using the Web to instantly connect buyers and sellers anywhere. According to some estimates, because of their central position the infomediaries might end up by controlling a quarter of the world's transactions business to business.

6. Business markets, consumer markets and the new economy

The dynamics of global growth are changing as profoundly as they did with the advent of railroads, electricity, auto transport and telephones – all nineteenth-century developments. We have seen plenty of reasons why the new economy is taking hold, while the Internet is proving to be a revolutionary technology driving the global business transformation and seeing to it that outsourcing spreads more widely than ever. The change under way is being propelled by a series of self-reinforcing applications as the Web:

- enlarges the marketplace
- helps to lower costs
- provides a pool of capital
- opens up new opportunities.

People and companies gain a direct line into markets with innovative, affordable products and services. Traditional factors of production and distribution like capital and skilled labour, while always important, are no longer the sole determinants of an economy's power. Economic potential is increasingly likened to the ability to use information in an effective way, employ any-to-any networks, and tap into databases in real time.

Technology-wise, what we have available today is only a forerunner of things to come. Computation will become freely available, accessible from something like power sockets and enter the everyday human world at home and in business. By all likelihood, at long last, the input/output to computer devices will be revolutionised through the ability to communicate naturally:

- using speech, vision and phrases to express intent
- leaving it up to the computer to locate resources and carry out *our* intent.[7]

Most interesting as well is MIT's Virtual Customer Initiative (VC), a multidisciplinary approach targeting significant improvements in speed, accuracy and usability of customer input to a supplier's product design process. These developments will create enormous opportunities for insourcing and outsourcing. We are still not there, but this is the direction in which high technology currently moves (see also Chapter 4).

So far, at current state of the art, gaining most from the new economy are North America, business-to-business (B2B), business-to-consumer (B2C), consumer-to-business (C2B), consumer-to-consumer (C2C) solutions. Figure 1.8 gives a bird's eye view of what is involved in each of these four major transaction classes. Users of B2B for large scale procurement, such as Cisco Systems and IBM, suggest they are saving 20 per cent or more of their purchasing costs.

The implications are evident if we note that competitiveness is more and more conditioned by the able use of information and knowledge. While there are still enormous impediments to the free flow of information, especially across national borders, those people and companies who overcome current hurdles gain significant competitive advantages.

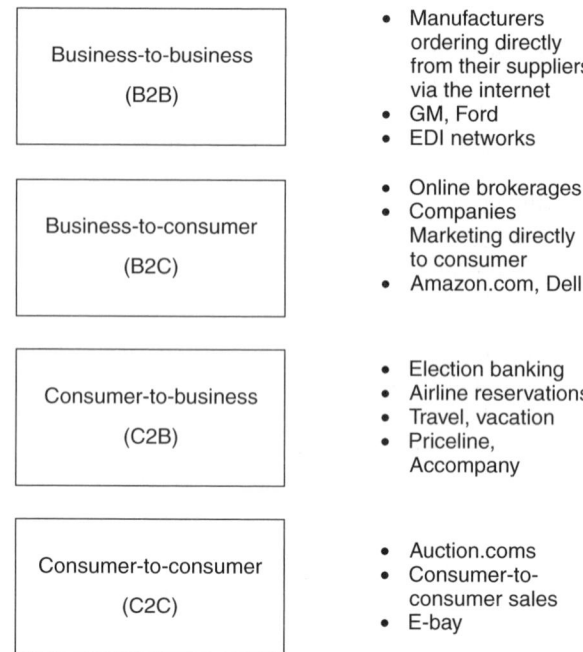

Figure 1.8 Applications domains in the Internet economy

This does not mean there will be no reversals, as the 2000–02 business low put the brakes on B2B. A short while after the GM, Ford, Daimler-Chrysler and Renault-Nissan accord, Covisint (their joint procurement subsidiary) hit the skids. Before the news of Covisint's uncertain results became general knowledge, however, six of the largest automotive parts suppliers Delphi, Dana, Eaton, TRW, Motorola and Valeo, joined forces to examine potential i-commerce initiatives in an effort to:

- face the challenge set forth by their corporate clients, and
- accelerate cost savings in the supply side to preserve their major clients' outsourcing.

In a way, what is now happening with the new economy at global scale through networks is the nearest thing to the work done at large laboratories which flourished in the early to late twentieth century at some companies (AT&T, GE, GM and IBM being examples), propelling them to new levels of competitiveness because of the aftermath of R&D. In at least some of these companies, the top advantage was not only based on basic research and innovation but also on the fact that:

- new products could cycle through experiments quickly
- while researchers made mistakes, corrected them and moved on.

The message conveyed by these two bullets fits well with the definition of i-commerce (see also Chapter 4). Down to its fundamentals, the term refers to trades that actually take place over the Internet, enabling the client to experiment (for instance on prices) while using what will eventually become a fairly standard procedure.

- Whether for B2B or B2C, buyers are visiting a seller's website.
- Either they search for information or make a transaction there and then.

Projections that have been heard for some time are now coming together faster than generally expected, but not quite the way they were originally made. In a nutshell, as waves of small businesses and consumers will operate on the Internet using next-generation information services, the Internet economy will enter a new phase, and this will be fully interactive.

Looking for information is a prelude to a transaction just like testing a model is a prelude to a design decision, even if some estimates suggest that while only 3.3 per cent of new-car sales in America, in 2001, took place over the Internet. The statistic the careful reader should remember is that as many as 40 per cent of car sales involved the Web at some point. For instance, consumers used it to compare prices or to look at the latest models.

One of the prognostications is that, within a few years, the Internet will be institutionalised in America's retail market, while other first world countries will follow. A recently developed model assumes essentially all US households being online, at least half on high-bandwidth connections. The hypotheses behind this model imply radically different patterns of consumer behaviour than those we already know. Analysts predict that mobile commerce will boom after the 2000–2002 business low is over.

According to several experts, together with cellular phones, the two-way TV set will be the popular Internet access device of the future for B2C and C2C trades. Both cellular and TV sets represent lowest common denominator points of access to a high speed, media-intensive network that defines the new consumer space. Ease of use and accessibility will be at a premium in more than one sense:

- creating a system which will be easy to approach and enter
- making information obtainable without great difficulty
- opening the online market to the influence of novel decision factors.

Notice that all three bullets concern events in the future. Experts think that some of the online facilities will be *enablers* put in place by competitive firms providing objects, processes and tools through which their clients can do something specific. These enablers will help in making transactions feasible as well as effective, and they may also give a new push to outsourcing.

Take interactive television access as an example. While the two-way TV idea was around since Orwell's *1984*, the concept that finds itself near fulfilment is novel and (no matter what sort of social problems it may engender) it promises to expand the Internet audience. A look at US statistics shows that:

- the percentage of households with PCs and the percentage with online access are both converging rapidly on the 60 per cent mark
- but the percentage of households with telephones and TVs now stands at nearly 90 per cent; it would not take much to make it 100.

What motivates many companies is that there is a vast consumer market in the 100 million US households owning TVs, and consumers are great outsourcers. However, not everything is linear. Experts increasingly believe that online shoppers started experiencing heightened privacy concerns, with the result that online consumer data is being subjected to stringent, self-imposed privacy rules. A big question is how to regulate online privacy with laws that do not disrupt common direct-marketing practices. A first step is Title V of the Gramm-Leach-Bliley Act, which concerns all financial institutions.

Still another crucial question that interests both businesses and consumers is taxation. The US Congress has established the E-Commerce Advisory Commission through the Internet Tax Freedom Act of 1998 and charged it with studying the many barriers to Internet commerce posed by conflicting international, federal, state and local tax and regulatory jurisdictions. There are signs that this commission may turn out to be more than the Internet tax commission, as some call it, by moving into explicitly defined i-commerce related tax liabilities. These will go a long way in shaping online insourcing and outsourcing in the years to come.

2
Outsourcing, Insourcing and Leveraging Business Operations

1. Introduction

Outsourcing and insourcing have been defined in Chapter 1, within the context of the new economy. The Internet was taken as an example of the fast-moving business world where new technology replaces the old at a furious pace, leading to the development of virtual companies (see section 2) where outsourcing becomes the policy of whole sectors of the economy. As we will see in this chapter, however, indiscriminate outsourcing can be fatal to enterprise management.

The concept of wholesale outsourcing of services is closely linked to that of a virtual business organisation. It is characterised by the usage of complementary resources existing in a number of co-operating firms as if these resources were under the same management. This, of course, is not the case. Third-party assets used in insourcing are left in the company to which they currently belong but are integrated 'on the fly', so to speak, to support a particular product and/or market effort for as long as this is viable.

The process described in the preceding paragraph gives to outsourcing and insourcing a totally different functional definition from that of the old economy. The underlying concept can also lead to financial and operational leveraging of business activities.

- Instead of being a stop-gap, outsourcing sometimes transforms itself into a long-term policy.
- Insourcing and outsourcing are no more the exception; they become mainstream issues subject to strategic review.

Insourcing has evolved into a lucrative business because outsourcing does not come cheap. In early 2002, AT&T signed a $2.6 billion five-year agreement with Accenture, the consulting company. The goal has been to improve at AT&T's consumer unit:

- productivity
- sales
- customer service.[1]

Just prior to that, in the fourth quarter of 2001, AT&T recorded a $1 billion restructuring charge. This was primarily for cutting 5000 jobs in 2001, and 5000 jobs in 2002. Between outsourcing and restructuring, a money-losing AT&T put on the table $3.6 billion.

Timing is another important factor misinterpreted by many firms. Few of the old economy companies appreciate that it takes 12 to 24 months to make an outsourcing agreement work, neither is there always an understanding of the intricacies which it may involve. A significant number of preparatory steps and prudential policy decisions are necessary to:

- field potentially negative effects of outsourcing, and
- support in an able manner an insourcing policy.

Take a cardinal principle in banking as an example: Front desk and back office should be separated by a thick wall, in terms of responsibility. This may be violated if the connecting links between outsourcer and insourcer are not clearly defined. Alternatively, the agreement might overlook the streamlining of the outsourcer's back office facilities leading to duplications and added costs, as we will see section 2.

2. Virtual companies and the sense of strategic outsourcing

A 'virtual company' is a temporary consortium of independent firms connected in a revocable way for a specific purpose. Typically, real companies are coming together to quickly exploit fast-changing national or worldwide business opportunities insourcing and outsourcing to one another. By so doing, virtual enterprises share costs, skills and core competencies that collectively enable them to:

- enlarge the bandwidth of their services
- access regional and/or global markets
- provide world-class solutions their members could not deliver individually.

Notice, however, that the concept of a virtual organisation is in flux and therefore it lacks a universally accepted definition. The common ground characterising virtual companies is a set of principles for 'metamanaging' industrial and financial activities. Metamanaging means at a higher-up level which depends on peer-to-peer co-ordination – not on the classical line of control.

This co-ordination targets insourcing and outsourcing work undertaken by virtual teams or groups of individuals that collectively possesses certain necessary skills. The principle is that a conceptual definition of outsourcing and insourcing requirements and deliverables makes it possible to switch from one group to another as conditions demand. To be properly executed, this approach requires that:

- each entity's management makes explicit goals and the way they should be fulfilled.
- thereafter, it is left to metamanagement to substitute itself to the central role usually played by a company's hierarchy.

Well-run virtual companies and real companies have several things in common. One of them is that their products and services, along with their other assets, are bright stars in the market's constellation, along a cause-and-effect relationship shown in Figure 2.1. Where virtual companies differ quite substantially from more classical companies is in their:

- overall strategy
- management culture
- organisational structure.

Within the globalised environment of the new economy (see Chapter 1), all three should be characterised by steady evolution. Virtual companies must

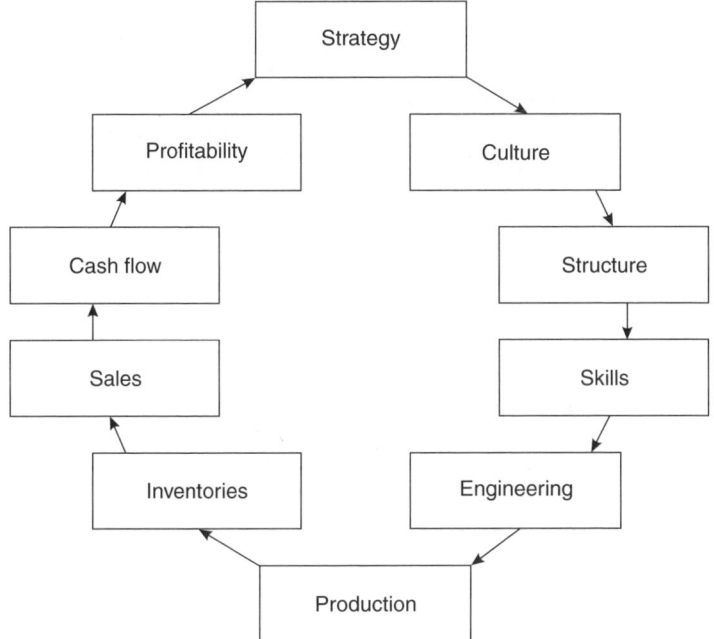

Figure 2.1 Business thresholds in a market's activity

be working in a real-time networked environment, like B2B, and be supported by virtual office systems based on knowledge artefacts (agents). Sophisticated software is vital in expanding the boundaries defined by organisational lines. Agents can speed business processes and facilitate commerce, through interaction with a broader range of business factors than is possible under traditional approaches.[2]

Virtual companies can be both outsourcers and insourcers. An example is Broadcom. Metamanagement should take notice that, because in a dynamic market intra- and intercompany resource availability can change minute to minute, advantages are accruing to parties able to rapidly perceive changing market patterns and arbitrage the disposability of their resources.

- Virtual organisations use advanced information technology to supplement the cognitive capabilities of their managers.
- Given the tight time constraints and the fact resources are always finite, they strive to provide themselves with an advantage over their competitors.

Virtual companies are practicable because telecommunications provide the infrastructure, while computer-based solutions swamp the cost of switching between different arrangements and alliances, permitting the creation of a new virtual company at reasonable cost. This means that flexibility should be at a premium in modern insourcing and outsourcing. Because, however, many insourcers and outsourcers – particularly the older companies – still use unsophisticated technology, flexibility often takes a leave, and with it profitability.

The careful reader will appreciate that these references to flexible and polyvalent insourcing/outsourcing are a world apart from old sense of outsourcing the procurement of raw materials, parts and subsystems. Chapter 1 has stated that procurement has been a classical source of outsourcing. The German industrial *Konzern*, with its vertically integrated structure and its emulation through value added tax (VAT), are based on the concept of 'vertical integration':

- from raw materials
- to final products.

Not everything that enters the switch from the old concept of insourcing/outsourcing to the new, is for the better. Most questionable are leveraging practices said to promote outsourcing, which are (incorrectly) put under the headline of 'shareholder value'. These include the process of reducing non-productive assets in the balance sheet. As we will see in section 5, this is an excuse for:

- speculating with derivative financial instruments
- using creative accounting to embellish end-of-year results.

Leaving aside the question of whether creative accounting is a legitimate practice (personally, I don't think so), these are short-term tactical approaches taken without the proverbial long, hard look. Yet, experience with outsourcing demonstrates that the better-managed projects are based on strategic decisions – which constitute the foundation of longer-term partnerships (more about this later). Figure 2.2 provides a birdseye view of the difference between strategic and tactical approaches.

Other reasons given for outsourcing are operations oriented, though in the majority of cases the associated operational risk (Chapter 3) is not brought under perspective. Still other reasons are the breaking down of traditional product and provider barriers, changing nature of distribution channels, the fact that clients are becoming increasingly more demanding, the implications of the Internet and, of course, the virtual company of which we already spoke.

That's the general coverage. In specific cases, however, not all of these reasons make sense and this is aggravated by the fact that, often, outsourcing

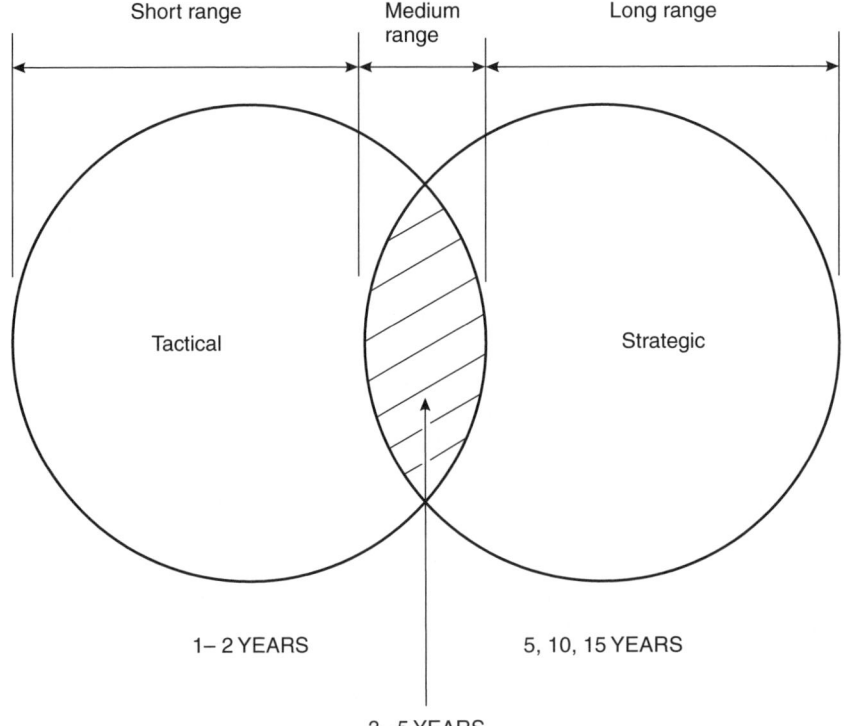

Figure 2.2   Strategic and tactical goals tend to overlap at medium-range planning

decisions are taken in a rush. Such is the case of preserving capital and getting better investment returns, the alleged drive to avoid increases in operational and infrastructural costs, the push by greater complexity of investment instruments, and the often-stated (but vague) goal to raise profitability. It would be more honest to admit that:

- the increasing business competitiveness and the often fruitless search for experienced global employees complicates the task of locating them and hiring them, increasing the appeal of outsourcing
- while integrated 24/7[3], real-time dealing systems and multicurrency, multilingual, scaleable accounting solutions are beyond the capabilities of the employees of many companies and their mainframes.

Added to the message of the second bullet is the fact that new systems solutions become even more complex because of the global universe of market and client data requirement for immediate update. More challenges are brought up by online seamless datamining, exploding communications infrastructures and the need for increasingly more flexible and cost-effective delivery mechanisms – as well as the required interoperability of trading platforms.

One has, however, also to accept that outsourcing does not solve these problems as a matter of course. It requires as much research, senior management attention, IT expertise and organisational wizardry as inhouse solutions, plus well-documented answers to functional queries and cost perspectives, including:

- the functional impact of market changes which call for an increased degree of re-engineering (see Chapter 13)
- overlapping costs of maintaining an information technology liaison and fallback, inhouse back office staff and the associated supporting infrastructure.

Indeed, many outsourcing agreements today concern back office and supporting services but, to my knowledge, few pay due attention to the cost, time and effort required to close the front desk/back office gap. Yet, failure to do so in a rigorous way leads to many surprises. The Bank of New York, which is active as an insourcer, says: 'We will work 9 to 12 months to develop a common understanding.' A serious outsourcing effort would never take this 'common understanding' for granted. Whether with virtual or with real companies, in outsourcing Murphy's Law is king: '*If* something can go wrong, it will!'

3. Learning how to apply the practice of outsourcing

Like any other skill outsourcing must be learned. What we learn about and the manner in which we apply it should answer the prerequisites of enterprise management. A good point to start is a critical investigation of what other companies are doing in insourcing and outsourcing, as well as the guidelines established by regulators. In banking, for instance, new directives from the Basle Committee on Banking Supervision bring attention to six basic requirements.

The first is that a credit institution should be very careful when entering into an outsourcing arrangement because it increases its operational risk. The second, that the outsourcing vendor must be competent, financially sound, and endowed with appropriate knowledge and expertise. Third, senior management of the outsourcing entity must assure that it concludes a contract that can remain valid over a long time period. That's the strategic aspect which I have been discussing.

The fourth requirement by the Basle Committee is that the outsourcing contract should clearly define the insourcer's assignments and responsibilities. In terms of responsibilities, risk analysis is included both at the insourcer's and the outsourcer's side. Take product pricing as an example. In option pricing,

- using brokers as consultants presents problems of conflicts of interest
- brokers have business incentives to lean towards volatility estimates which assist in deals – the so-called 'volatility smile'.

The price paid by Natwest Markets, the investment banking arm of National Westminster Bank, for mispricing its options is that it ceased to exist. Yet, in its heyday, NatWest was the second largest credit institution in the UK. After the announcement of huge losses, the bank's top management admitted that:

- risk management did not have good enough computer models
- the bank had accepted outsourced brokers' estimates of volatility that turned out to be overgenerous to the pricing of options.

This example helps in documenting the wisdom of the fifth directive by the Basle Committee: that a credit institution must analyse the impact outsourcing will have on its risk profile and on the way its internal control system works. The sixth is that the overall accountability for outsourced services remains with the board and senior management of the bank which has called in an insourcer.

The careful reader will take notice that problems relating to internal controls and of security always exist when companies outsource and outskill their core functions. And though the directives by the Basle Committee address credit institutions, their applicability is far more general, covering all companies outsourcing some of their products and processes.

American regulators have issued similar guidelines. An example is the rules let down by the Federal Deposit Insurance Corporation (FDIC) in connection to the year 2000 (Y2K) problem. These rules focused on the dependability of the insourcers in terms of solving Y2K problems, outlining basic guidelines for choosing a software house or service bureau operation for IT outsourcing. I am bringing into perspective the three most important of these guidelines.

1 Information technology is core business in banking (more on core business later on in this section).

If it were not, the Federal Reserve, FDIC, Office of the Controller of the Currency (OCC) and Office of Thrift Supervision (OTS) would not have examined 350 software houses and service bureaux in the United States in connection to Y2K.

2 Failure in outsourcing can be as fatal to a financial institution as the failure of its own, inhouse IT resources.

For this reason the regulators rounded up, and phased out as outsourcer of banking IT services, a weak service bureau. At the same time other insourcers found themselves obliged to beef up the quality of their services (see section 4).

3 The action of regulators needs to extend beyond banking not only because of Y2K compliance but also because the outsourcing of all mission critical systems must be most dependable.

In the background of these guideline lies the fact that banking and IT are indivisible. Technology provides an institution's infrastructure, and no bank can function with defective IT, even if several try to do so. Invariably, they pay a heavy penalty for this failure.

Sometime, companies with a weak or obsolete IT functionality are lured into outsourcing because the insourcer verbally assures their management that they will customise the services. To my book, verbal assurances are worth 'zero.zero'. Everything agreed upon must be contractually guaranteed – and in detail.

The customisation of the insourcers system solution to meet the outsourcer's requirements is an example of breeding trouble. Answering the question 'How much do you go for customisation?' in a conference on outsourcing I was co-chairing in London, in December 2001,[4] the representative of the insourcer said: 'Early customers have much better chance of getting customisation. As business piles up, people and time become limited resources.'

Customisation may be necessary because no two operations are the same. In customising, a great deal depends both on the technology and on the skills of the insourcer. Palaeolithic IT has trouble tooling for insourcing and outsourcing operations. Besides this, external software faces serious interoperability issues because the rest of the outsourcer's information system may be more than thirty years old. The IT executive of a major British bank was saying in one of our meetings that his institution is obliged to use college graduates to maintain Cobol programs written before these kids were born.

Never lose from sight the first of FDIC's three directives, which says that in the banking industry information technology is the core function. This is a general rule, and regulators are fully justified in keeping it in perspective. Basically, what a company perceives as 'core' has a lot to do with its:

- choice of strategies
- edge in the market
- value differentiation from competitors.

By definition, core functions are those essential to engaging in the provision of services. They include the development, management, sales, delivery and control of products. For instance, in commercial banking core functions are accepting customer deposits, making loans to customers, credit and actuarial assessments, trading in securities, managing the institution's own investments, advising the client and managing his or her portfolio.

Other core businesses for a financial institution are developing and managing new products and services, underwriting financial issues, assuring trustee functions, and a variety of fee producing services; also, managing risks by instrument, desk, trader, counterparty, and globally. The bigger banks include in their core functions:

- engaging in derivative financial instruments for trading and hedging
- capitalising on the globalisation of financial markets by establishing own subsidiaries or correspondent banking.

Correspondent banking is a sort of outsourcing, with assumed risk present at both the insourcer's and outsourcer's side. Issues like top-notch information technology and effective risk management are core for *all* companies, not only banks. One of the reasons for not outsourcing core functions is confidentiality. Another lies in the fact insourcers are not well positioned to serve the outsourcer's core functions as far as the latter's duties and responsibilities are concerned, neither can they be a substitute to the outsourcer's management. Precisely for these reasons, the board and chief executive officer (CEO) will be well advised never in life to externalise:

- internal controls
- compliance.

If a company has limitations in the domains of internal control and of compliance, *then* the thing to do is to correct them by itself – not through relegation of its responsibilities. The process of identifying and correcting functions and services which are wanting should never be substandard; it should follow a well led-out strategic plan (see also section 6).

Figure 2.3 makes reference to the policy Jean Monnet, the investment banker and father of the European Union, established to guide his hand in master planning. Monnet's policy fits hand in glove the requirements connected to both outsourcing and insourcing. In a nutshell it can be expressed as follows:

- Planning should start not at the beginning, but at the end, with the results we wish to achieve.
- By contrast, execution should start at the beginning capitalising on the resources put into place by the plan, for every specific time period.

Whether we are talking of internal execution of core functions and subsidiary services or of one involving outsourcing, this is the best possible way for leveraging our human and financial resources. It is important to take notice that always the outsourcer organisation should be the party truly responsible the planning and control, though it may call on the expertise of its business partners (one or more insourcers, see section 4). The execution will be done by the insourcer, but this should take place under the steady supervision and quality control of the outsourcing organisation (Chapter 5).

4. Outsourcing can focus on quality of service only when the deal is thoroughly planned

A steady, unrelenting focus on the quality of service can radically change an old economy company. Innovation, cost control, low overhead but high

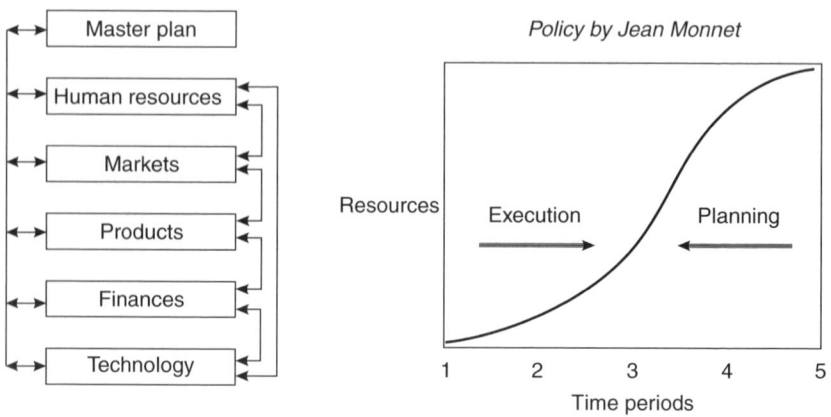

Figure 2.3 Business thresholds in a market's activity

quality help to significantly extend market potential and ability to bring value to a firm's customers. Prerequisite to this is that over the years quality-oriented culture is slipping down the organisation, all the way to lower management and employee level.[5]

One of the problems with outsourcing today is that not all insourcers have this sort of quality ethics, let alone a system which can support low cost and high quality over an extended time-frame. Both are very important, and the same is true about timeliness of deliverables. As such, they should weight heavily on outsourcing decisions.

Because planning and control is a responsibility which stays with the outsourcer all the way, the Monnet method (discussed in section 3) should address all *our* sourcing options. Another sign of good management is to develop alternatives. One of the things I learned in my graduate studies at UCLA, in the early 1950s, is that a crucial question every manager should ask himself is: 'Which are *my* alternatives?'

Figure 2.4 presents four *sourcing* options, and emphasises the basic decision steps they have in common. Practically all companies are faced with these choices all the time, and only a thorough study can tell which might be best. The problem I am refering to becomes more complex when the advantages and disadvantages of one versus many insourcers are considered.

- The outsourcer takes a major risk in he choosing one insourcer: this firm may fails.
- Therefore, some companies believe it is better to get two suppliers for the same outsourced function.

Double sourcing, however, poses compatibility and co-ordination problems which are tough enough with one insourcer but can increase exponentially with two or three. Greater complexity comes not only from having to deal with a couple or more suppliers who are also competitors, but as well from the fact the more successful projects in outsourcing are those where outsourcer and insourcer have:

- jointly developed the plan, and
- jointly implemented the solution.

As I had the opportunity to underline, outsourcing is *not* an off-the-shelf delivery of services such as back office functions – even if some outsourcers think so or insources tend to give this impression to their clients. In fact, this ready-made idea borrowed from merchandising packaged foods or home appliances is one of several misconceptions regarding what outsourcing is and is not.

People and companies contemplating outsourcing should be aware of the fact that one of the obstacles in this business has traditionally been the

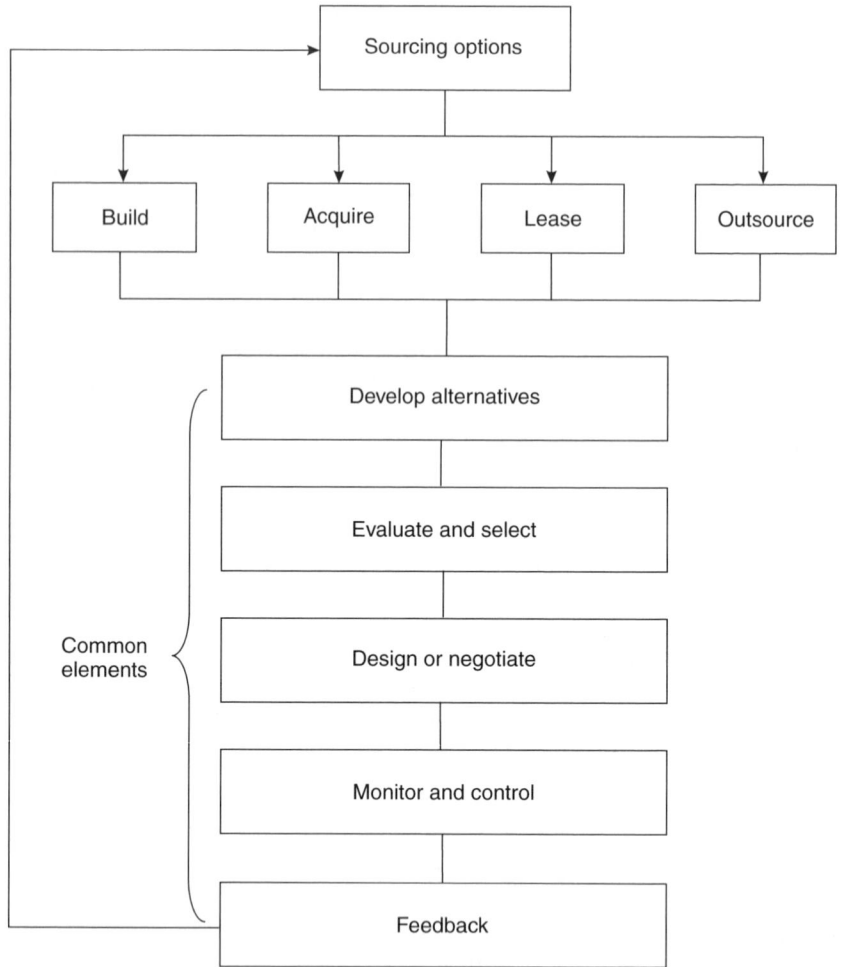

Figure 2.4   For all sourcing options we must have a system for planning and evaluation

miscommunication of goals and approaches regarding co-productions. Insourcers simply don't have the fantastic solution the outsourcer might be looking for which can handle everybody's problem at large and the outsourcer's problem in particular. As far as end results are concerned, much depends on what each party brings to the table. This further underlines the depth of the preparatory work to be done:

• Is the service to be outsourced core or non-core activity?

If core, think twice and make your solution only a stop-gap one. Target technology transfer, not a long-term approach. If non-core, then look for a long-term partnership which fits well into your strategic plan.

- Does the outsourcing consume substantial management time?

If yes, compute precisely the time it takes and it will take to manage the outsourcing relationship. It may be more than the management time you hope to save, and it may also involve more headaches than you expected.

- Is the service to be outsourced self-contained?

If not, a more or less complex interaction with other internal services can easily lead to failure of the outsourcing agreement and to a downgrading of its deliverables. In these cases, and they are many, the reason is the inefficiencies which it presents.

- Do you have evidence that outsourcing will provide a competitive advantage?

If yes, which one? The answer must be precise. The same is true of another question: Is your company ready to exploit that advantage? If not, what else must be done to gain from it? Which are the costs associated with the contemplated solution? Are the advantages covering them with a margin? Are the risks you will be taking well understood? Are these risks acceptable?

What these queries essentially mean is the need for exercising control over outsourcing arrangements, within the perspective of a documented policy which is subservient to a strategic plan. The same queries also point to the wisdom of working out points of reference which will permit factual assessment of risks and benefits. By and large, there are *no* standardised business cases in outsourcing. Each one has its own characteristics.

The nature of an insourcing/outsourcing deal, and its characteristics to which I am making reference, impacts a great deal on supplier selection and on the procedure which should be followed. For an outsourcing project of a certain size, it is appropriate to prepare fairly detailed specifications which will constitute the basis for a:

- *Request for information*, which is an exploratory first step.

Such request should be addressed to seven or eight competing but reputable insourcers, if there are that many in the market. Based on their replies a pre-selection should be done retaining about one out of two, but also tuning the specifications document by using the replies being received as the instrument for tuning. This second version will become the basis of a:

- *Request for offers*, including quality references, timing of deliverables and financial conditions.

All proposals submitted by insourcers should respond to the same set of functional and quality specifications, representing well-qualified and quantified requirements. In principle, few degrees of freedom must be left to the insourcer in order to permit a meaningful comparison of costs. Based on a real-life case, Figure 2.5 shows the surprises this can produce.

In the general case, the request for offers should be leading to a tender document which permits the factual evaluation of responses – taking the emotion out of this mission. The second round of pre-selection should be followed by on-site evaluation, visits to clients of the insourcer(s) and – if the responses are positive – to contractual negotiation(s). One of the soul-searching queries in these negotiations is 'How much responsibility will each party assume if the contract goes wrong?'

My research has documented that most outsourcing agreements overlook this crucial question of bottom line responsibilities. While functionality, technology, dependability and costs may take the highlights, it is important

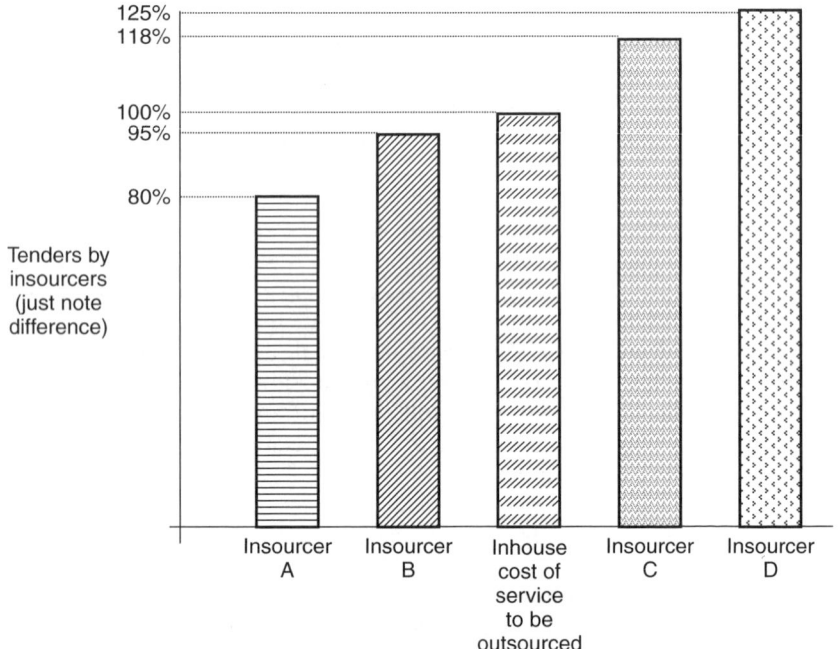

Figure 2.5 Costing of the same information technology outsourcing project by four different insourcers

not to forget the need for negotiating an *exit policy*. In this connection, relevant questions to be answered by the outsourcer are:

- Can the work be taken back inhouse?
- Is there an alternative supplier?
- What other remedies are available?

It is most vital that *exit* is considered up front, before the outsourcing contract reaches its final stage – and surely before it is signed. If not, our company will be moving to a long-term partnership which is like a tunnel, and the light ahead may signal not an exit at the end of the tunnel but an oncoming train. After the crash, lawyers (from both parties) would have a ball.

The negotiation of requirements for ongoing monitoring is another 'must', including:

- audit rights
- intellectual property rights
- formal reviews of supplier performance
- disaster recovery and contingency plans.

In short, it is most essential to manage proactively the outsourcer/insourcer relationship, and this can help both parties. The concepts brought to the reader's attention through the preceding paragraphs converge towards the need for establishing and upholding minimum criteria for authorisation of an outsourcing agreement.

Confidentiality and security are part of these criteria. Outsourcers often have given the insourcers access to their IT. No security breaches should be involved at any time, for any reason. The need for a corporate-wide policy on outsourcing has led some of the larger companies to establish a clearing house. For instance, Lloyds TSB has an outsourcing centre. Every business unit planning to outsource must get approval from that centre which looks into many issues: legal, compliance, uniqueness of service, cost, quality, reliability, brand name, money laundering, data protection, competition, and so on.

5. Outsourcing done for uplifting the balance sheet

A new sort of outsourcing practice has been recently developed, and I strongly advise against it. It is done not for skills, costs or operational reasons, but for financial engineering: uplifting the balance sheet through creative accounting (see also section 6). This is euphemistically known among bankers as 'balance sheet management for corporates', or 'a new way of financing an outsourcing transaction'. In reality it is:

- outsourcing brought a threshold too far
- a deceptive practice depriving companies of their physical assets.

The reason why I bring this type of outsourcing to the reader's attention at the beginning of the book is that some industry experts think it may become a booming business in the coming years. That's too bad. Outsourcing for balance sheet uplifting takes place both in manufacturing and in distribution. One of the early adopters, in the early to mid 1990s, has been Olivetti, which did away with its production, facilities and subcontracted to Asian firms.

Olivetti's foray into physical assets deleveraging did not help the company a great deal. If anything, the opposite is true. Because of it, the Olivetti that used to be a power in office automation is no more around; all there remains is a holding. This, however, did not discourage other companies from taking the same road. By the early twenty-first century Enron paid dearly this kind of wild outsourcing, and Alcatel is another recent example of a wounded enterprise which goes the Olivetti way.

Other manufacturing firms, too, are outsourcing the core production of their business, with doubtful results, at best. In distribution, Sainsbury, the British food retailer, released the ownership of its real estate, including that of its stores and their land. Officially, the company said it did so because it realised that 'it is not a real estate enterprise'. Such an argument did not convince the financial analysts, particularly in the aftermath of a wave of creative accounting practices which went to the rocks.

The motor power behind the outsourcing policy discussed in this section is *derivatives*. The classical definition of a derivative financial instrument is that it is a future, forward, swap or option contract. But Statement of Financial Accounting Standards (SFAS) 133, by the Financial Accounting Standards Board (FASB) redefines derivatives as financial instruments with the following characteristics.

- They have one or more underlying, and one or more notional, amounts, payment provisions or both.
- Usually, they call for no initial net investment and, if needed, this is rather small.
- They require or permit net settlements, or provide for delivery of an asset that puts the buyer at net settlement position.

Derivatives have been a risky business for banks, though if financial institutions go aggressively after these products. This happens even if some of them went bankrupt because they overplayed their hand with leveraging and derivatives. Three examples of failures are Long-Term Capital Management (LTCM), Bankers Trust and Enron.

Today, some investment banks are pushing companies to go the derivatives way in outsourcing through what they call 'an adaptation of securitisation'.

The justification they give for this push is a dubious one, at best. They say that they try to solve a typical corporate structured issue which involves:

- a substantial real estate element to be disposed of
- cash flows that can be generated by physical assets
- an active use of corporate covenants and other gimmicks.

Along these lines of reference, apart of doing away with its real estate, Sainsbury also outsourced its information technology. This included the re-platforming and redevelopment of its entire IT infrastructure. The insourcer has been Accenture (formerly Andersen Consulting). The financing is done through a new company, Store Finance, whose cashflows are generated by contract, shifting credit support from corporate covenants. Figure 2.6 shows the pattern of this deal which, financially speaking, consists of three parts:

1 A £200 million ($286 million) term facility by Barclays Capital
2 A £40 million ($57.5 million) revolving credit from the same source
3 A £300 million ($430 million) bond issue (more on this later).

As far as financing is concerned, the term 'facility' is a quarterly obligation. The bonds sold to the capital market, an issue which has been oversubscribed given Sainsbury's name on it, is a semi-annual obligation. The food retailer, of course, could have issued commercial paper without this 'innovative transaction' which put its IT on the block.

This triangular relation, the main objective of which is to embellish the balance sheet at the expense of the company's IT, does not make much sense to me. The outsourcing prerequisites which we discussed in the preceding sections are not being observed. Sainsbury can go to court because

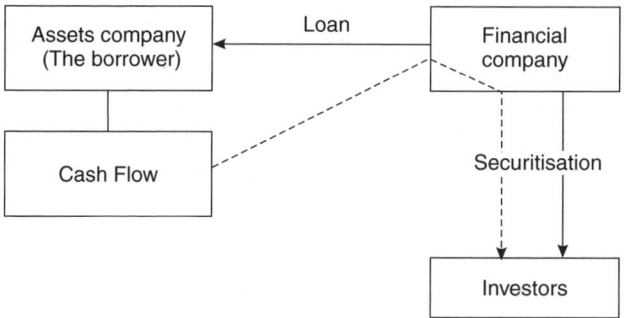

Figure 2.6 The triangular structure of the deal between Sainsbury, Accenture and Store Finance

deliverables are substandard, but it must always pay the bank and the bond-holders. This is a firm commitment and there is no appeal.

Evidently, Sainsbury, its bankers and Accenture are of a different opinion as far as the wisdom of this deal is concerned. The reasons they have brought forward to justify the transaction are both technological and financial, and, in their judgement, they make sense. After a statement that 'everybody wins', the party which presented some of the details of this case study (at a London conference) stressed those factors relating to the fate of IT. They were:

- use of latest technology
- annual savings of £35 million ($50 million)
- best global market practices
- reduced headcount
- focus on core business.

To the question: 'What is meant by latest technology?' the illuminating answer has been: 'Who knows what technology is going to be in five years'. What about the savings? How are they justified? 'Savings means £35 million less than current cost', was the reply. It's a response that left me thirsty because it is lopsided, while in principle, cutting down the budget is a welcome exercise.

- This has to be judged not in absolute terms but in connection to the deliverables.
- The fact the outsourcer is left with no way to turn off the cashflow if the insourcer does not perform, is a very bad omen indeed.

I had a professor at UCLA who taught his students that in accounting you can prove anything provided you are able to choose your system and your variables. Aside from this, cost savings from this triangular outsourcing deal seem to be the further-out plan, and one with a very uncertain future. By contrast, during the first year the IT cost will increase because of the changeover. The pattern of IT budget and spread are shown in Figure 2.7.

Time will tell if any financial and technological benefits will be realised at the end of this seven-year period; if any cost savings really will materialise, and if the 'latest technology' promises will be kept and in which way. It is too early for a verdict. By contrast, there is plenty of scope in discussing the financial side of this leveraged outsourcing deal, particularly:

- the pass-through of Sainsbury's senior credit risk
- the off-balance sheet treatment of Sainsbury and Accenture.

The way the investment bankers looked at it, this triangular contract represents a gem of strategic, financial, and operational flexibility. I look at

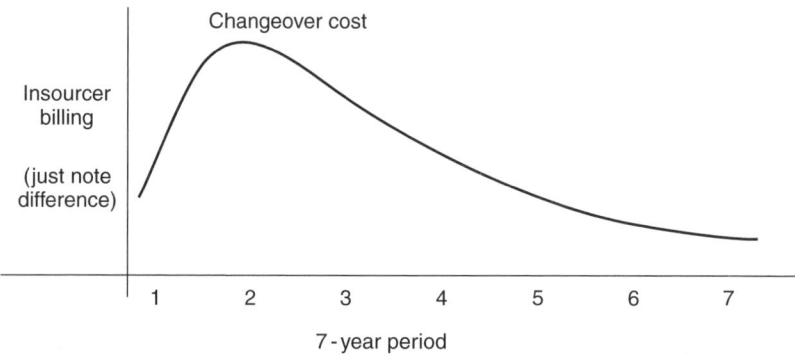

Figure 2.7 Projected budget for IT outsourcing over the seven-year period

it quite differently. The strategy is the cosmetics of the company's balance sheet; the financial centres on minimising some types of accounting inefficiencies, particularly the negative carry; the operational is (supposedly) the covenant package and accounting treatment. More precisely, however, the latter looks to me like a major operational risk (see Chapter 3).

The pros said 'Don't forget the advantage of investor diversification', but failed to explain for which purpose. All we are talking about with this derivatives/outsourcing deal is going to the capital market for financing outsourcing costs. The only sure winner is the bank which acts as financial consultant and underwriter. Down to basics, this operation has a non-transparent no. 1 goal: uplifting the stock price, which is one way to interpret the stated aim of shareholder value. In terms of financial format, the deal is fairly complex.

- It involves potential arbitrage using the sponsor's credit rating.
- It neither increases transparency for the investor nor does it reduces costs, as it is claimed.

To get money for outsourcing, the investment bankers capitalise on the securitization of corporates which is currently underway in the capital market. They see this operation as a derivatives deal based on assets and funded independently of the retailer's merchandising business. The bankers argument is that while the sponsor continues to manage its securitized assets, bondholders take comfort from:

- security over the pledged assets
- appropriate covenants attached to the overall package.

The assets are supposed to be the IT hardware and software, provided they are properly upkept. Information technology is a highly perishable asset.

Therefore, the financial guarantees by the parent company, Sainsbury, are more important than the assets reference, since they rest on the company's credit rating and the assurance Sainsbury will continue to pay the interest whether it is happy or unhappy with the quality of outsourced IT services. In this triangular structure:

- Investors take no performance risk connected to Accenture.
- Debt service and associated management charges are payable under all circumstances.

Sainsbury seems also to be confronted with other costs like Accenture fees, Swan management costs, and so on. Essentially, it is the outsourcer who takes all the risks and carries all the obligations. For the insourcer and the bankers it is 'heads I win, tails you lose'. Alternative investments, another derivative wonder with huge risks associated to it, are cut from the same cloth.[6]

6. Establishing the reasons for outsourcing and sorting out priorities

The practical examples the reader will find in this and other chapters document that companies adopt modern outsourcing practices for several reasons. Table 2.1 outlines those I most frequently found in my research. Some of them are more smoke and mirrors than reality, an example being a significant cost reduction. Singularly absent as a reason, from this table, is that outsourcing truly serves the *strategic* plan and its objectives. Yet, well-managed companies should definitely:

- tie the outsourcing strategy to their business strategy
- have a policy of knowing exceedingly well what they outsource
- Analyse the risks associated with outsourcing before committing themselves to it.

Table 2.1 Reasons given by different companies for outsourcing

	%
Reduce costs	35
Focus on core business	30
Improve functional performance or quality	16
Faster time to market	10
Foster innovation	3
Reduce non-productive assets on balance sheet	2
Conserve capital	1
Other	3

Take cost savings claimed with outsourcing as an example of misinformation. Insourcers usually promise their prospects cost savings between 10 per cent and 40 per cent. These and similar figures are typically advanced without assessing spending needs associated to outsourcing services, neither do they account for costs associated to supervision of deliverables, including:

- front-end costs which can be significant, amounting to *pay now, save later* (see section 5)
- a steady quality control program leading to corrective action
- backup contingency planning, including fire-brigade costs and other expenditures.

If lower cost is the main reason for outsourcing, *then* senior management should appreciate that the cost attached to outsourcing can be significant. In its US operations, a major European bank outsourced certain of its IT projects. A post-mortem study found that, all counted, the cost tended to be 400 per cent of those inhouse. Subsequently, the bank experimented with an IT project given to four different outsourcers at the planning stage. The analysis of the obtained results documented that every shop had a different profile in regard to:

- outsourcing costs
- operational risks (see Chapter 3).

Other outsourcing experiences converge to the example I just gave. Clear-eyed organisations which participated in this research made the point that they never accept outsourcing proposals which have substandard arguments. One of the cognisant executives pointed out three common failures with outsourcing proposals:

1 The homework done for estimating cost savings from outsourcing often leaves much to be wanted.

A 10 per cent savings, this executive said, 'would not get the approval of the board.' Even a 40 per cent reduction in operating costs may be a fake, if it fails to account for:

- study and analysis costs
- adaptation costs
- supervision costs associated to switching
- direct, life-cycle supervision costs
- value added tax (VAT), and other costs.

The point several companies made that cost savings from outsourcing might come from a long-term business partnership, not from a quick in-and-out-of outsourcing approach was well received. It should be added, however, that outsourcing deals can harbour risks, be expensive in hidden costs, and involve lots of administrative duties and extra technological expertise.

2 Lack of documented evidence that basic functions needing upgrade (or lacking internal skill) can be boosted by outsourcing.

Sometimes re-engineering and outsourcing are *not* complementary but conflicting projects (see Chapter 13). Another failure with outsourcing proposals is lack of answers to critical questions such as:

- What happens if the deal does not deliver the promised benefits?
- What if the insourcer will not have the right service ethos?
- Which are the ways and means that will make feasible an exit strategy, if the project does not deliver as expected?

Outsourcers should never expect the insourcer(s) to share ideas and strategies, or map the outsourcer's own future direction. Neither should they believe all insourcers have commitment, track record, special skills and financial strength.

Quite similarly, outsourcers should never expect the insourcer(s) to perform for them all relevant cost-benefit analyses. Neither should they rely on hype, like the often-heard argument that the insourcer(s) will achieve for them a seamless transition. Insourcers are, as well, not known for providing regulatory assistance or for waiving the need to focus on operational risk.

3 A tendency to outsource to get rid of problems. The golden rule is never outsource what you don't really know and understand.

Many of the participants to this research project were to comment that to their knowledge this golden rule is not always observed. Quite frequently, outsourcing is seen as a way to discharge responsibilities, which is a false assumption given the fact that while authority can be delegated responsibility always stays at the side of the outsourcer's senior management who remain accountable for performance. Therefore, it is wise to observe the rule:

- *If* you understand what you give away and
- *if* you consider this fair because of returns
- *then* look for the best business partner in outsourcing.

Otherwise, never outsource what you don't understand. To follow this advice, senior management must train itself in outsourcing, looking across the board and considering:

- overall advantages and limitations
- the clauses of the agreement
- resulting profitability
- effects on customer handling.

Finally, senior management should avoid like hell the use of outsourcing for creative accounting reasons. With this I make reference not only to the example in section 5 but also, more generally, to accounting systems which were not designed to handle virtual company operations but are used for this purpose. Accounting is one of the most important business services affected by outsourcing. In my experience, setting up and operating an accounting system for a virtual company is almost of an order of magnitude more difficult than the corresponding accounting solution for an old economy company which handles all its functions inhouse. Legacy software with Cobol-type programs, and the obsolete concepts underpinning them, will not do. The accounting system must use knowledge engineering in order to:

- be very flexible and adaptable as business partners change and new business partners are added with different accounting standards from our own
- be able to retain a great deal of detail about old partnerships, reintegrating past accounting data with new when past partners co-operate together once again.

In other terms, being prepared for the requirements and sensitivities of a successful insourcer and outsourcer environment is synonymous to planning for success. This, however, is not the everyday policy in insourcing and outsourcing. Instead of pragmatism, I have frequently found in my research an ideological type of debate on whether outsourcing is 'good' or 'bad'. Like apple pie and the Internet, outsourcing is neither good nor bad because of theoretical reasons, but in function of what we make out of it.

When we talk of accounting, and of financial statements and of compliance, the board, CEO and senior management must appreciate the *reputational risk* associated to outsourcing. This leads to other challenges, like the question: should the audit committee be involved?

The crucial message behind these references to reasons, priorities and procedures regarding outsourcing is that this solution is in no way a relegation of responsibility. It is not a substitute to internal problem resolution. Hence the advice: 'Don't outsource a problem that you have. If you got a problem, you fix it yourself.' Senior management should always remember that it cannot outsource its responsibility. The one-off discharge of management responsibility has not been invented.

- Painful decisions have to be made, in outsourcing basic services.
- Nobody can sign an outsourcing contract and walk away from it.

Experience teaches that outsourcing is a situation where neither the supplier not the customer is always right. Because such contracts can be tricky, both outsourcers and insourcers should always check with their lawyers. Every outsourcer and every insourcer must be prepared for the eventuality of legal risk – and this is a tall call.

3
Operational Risk with Outsourcing and Insourcing

1. Introduction

Every business involves operational risk, though some are exposed to it much more than others. This is an issue that has been known for a long time but only recently was structured as a distinct class, joining risk and market risk as a separate area of major exposure. The Basle Committee on Banking Supervision has defined seven classes of operational risk:

1 internal fraud
2 external fraud
3 employment practices and workplace safety
4 clients, products and business practices
5 damage to physical assets
6 business disruption and systems failures
7 execution, delivery, procurement, management.

Each of these can affect outsourcing and insourcing agreements, as well as the use of the Internet for commerce and banking (see Chapter 4); and each can be broken down to further detail. There are as well operational risks in business concentration, interruption of business continuity, repeated litigation, legislative changes, wanting compliance methods, information technology, development and use of models, and of course taxation.

I personally tend to classify operational risk into three main groups, the way it is shown in Figure 3.1. Those identified as more classical are the better known, but the group which I call 'modern' is gaining momentum. It is also the one which will interest us the most in this chapter, because it connects to outsourcing and insourcing. Most vital for the future is the identification and control of IT-oriented operational risks, which have a significant potential for loss due to deficiencies in control processes and the reliability of systems.

Companies attempt to mitigate operational risk by maintaining a comprehensive internal control; employing experienced, dedicated personnel;

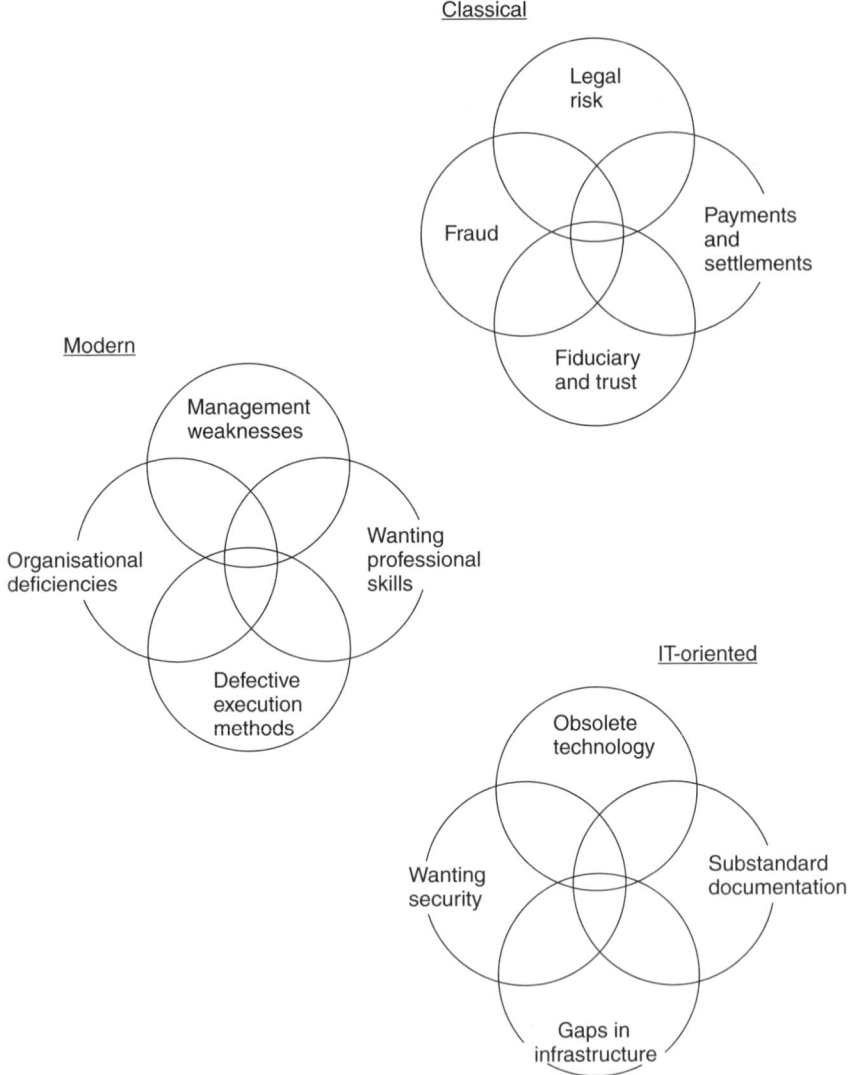

Figure 3.1 Three different groups of operational risk

and setting up an operational risk control unit. For each functional area deemed to be potentially of medium to high risk, senior management should perform a risk self-assessment. Its goal must be to:

- evaluate the appropriateness of internal controls, policies and systems
- perform operational risk tests by business line and outsourcing agreement

- provide for operational risk control through appropriate procedures and recovery plans.

Outsourcing agreements should identify and explicitly state the operational risks that may be involved. They should not allow the counterparty to hide them. The definition of each operational risk should be objective, not subjective. To get an objective definition it is advisable to start with analytics and fence reactions such as:

- 'This operational risk event will never happen.'
- 'We do not have to pay attention to this type of risk.'
- 'It's probability is a small fraction of what it takes to control it.'

The crucial issue is that what we do must be reasonable in respect to assumed operational risk. This is true of identification, control procedures, and capital allocation to each of operational risk type. Money acts as common denominator in terms of exposure taken with:

- outsourcing strategies
- Internet strategies
- products and processes
- quality and accuracy of internal control.

The calibration of operational risk management is a 'must', and so are risk mitigation policies. A great deal in terms of continued effectiveness of operational risk controls depends on management intent, contractual terms, the accurate definition of deliverables and clauses targeting quality and timeliness, as well as reputational risk provisions.

2. Operational risk control in a service economy

Outsourcing, insourcing and online execution of business transactions are characteristic of a service economy where all types if markets and of business partners (clients and suppliers) are linked in real-time. One of the causes behind the growing likelihood of operational risk is the bifurcation existing in a modern economy.

- Some parts of the economy work at a relatively slow pace, largely conditioned by age-old practices designed for physical goods.
- Other parts rush forward, propelled by the technology-driven world of Wall Street and of the City, which today operate on a global scale.

During our meeting in New York, an investment banker suggested that facing the challenges of a fast-moving service economy calls for rethinking regulatory policies, the legal system, economic theories, regulation and deregulation, trading, the design of new instruments, and technological infrastructure. Operational risk, he said, is attached to most of these factors but at an uneven level of exposure, largely conditioned by prevailing management practices.

Therefore a critical aspect of control of operational risk is properly to define the quantitative and qualitative drivers, including risk management framework and causation clauses in operational procedures. Companies will be well advised to reclassify operational risks along homogeneous lines appropriate to their operations, track them, database them and analyse them. This requires:

- great consistency in operational risk monitoring and measurement
- communication of findings and explanation of their impact on the organisation
- the definition of expected and unexpected losses with associated capital provisions.

The right methodology would focus on op risk awareness, involve training and self-assessment, include incentives (merits) and disincentives (demerits) associated to operational risks, and assure the independence of operational risk management and control functions. It will also look for ways and means for mitigation of operational risk, providing a balance between centralised and decentralised supervisory duties.

Based on a project on operational risk control, Figure 3.2 presents a framework for organisation and action. The 11 building blocks which are shown have been put in place with the objective of leading to an integrative op risk structure which can serve both inhouse activities and for outsourcing functions.

The careful reader will notice that some of the component parts characterising this integrative operational risk evaluation model are novel. An

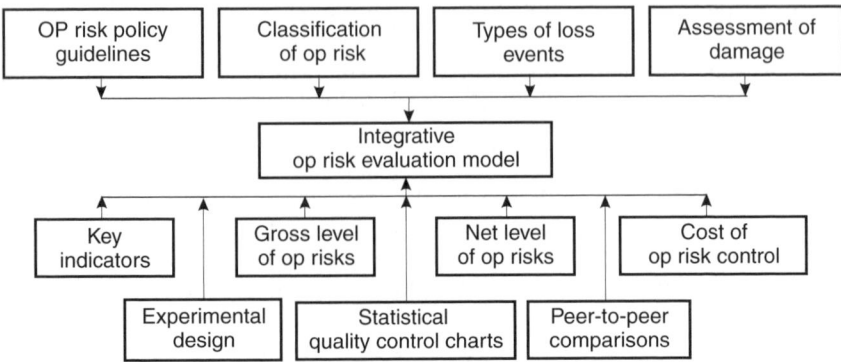

Figure 3.2   A framework for the evaluation and reporting of global operational risk

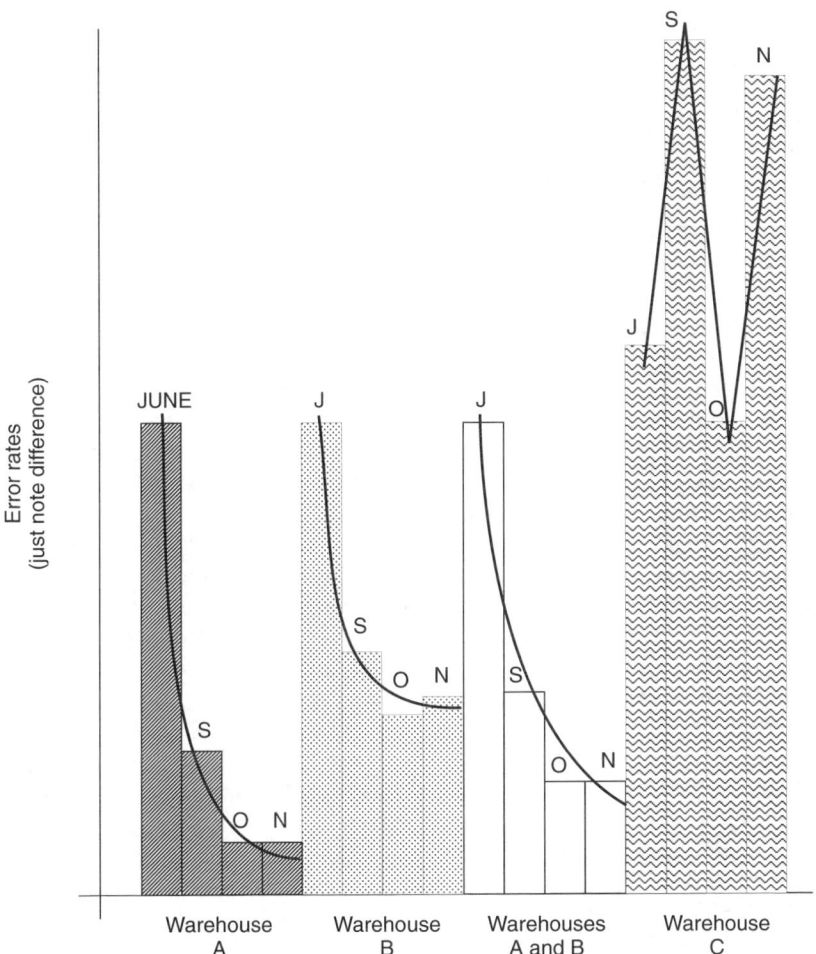

Figure 3.3   Experimental design done to evaluate operational risk control at warehouses A and B using a new method, versus the old method at warehouse C

example is experimental design which permits to evaluate the results of a new control methodology against the approach which has been classically followed in regard to operational risk management.

Figure 3.3 presents an example on the results of experimental design done to evaluate a new method for operational risk control. The object has been the reduction of error rates in shipments. At Warehouses A and B was implemented a new method which, over a three-month period (September to November), succeeded in significantly reducing the error rate. The worst performer was that of Warehouse C (used as control group) which continued to utilise the old method.[1]

Unearthed through experimental design, key indicators should be presented by a means of a scoreboard, statistical quality control charts, or peer-to-peer comparisons. These methods of presentation are very important with outsourcing agreements. In the general case, however, a clear view of what is exactly involved is vital because significant losses usually stem from uncertainty regarding the:

* type of prevailing operational risks
* unavailability of appropriate control procedures.

When faced with uncertainty, managers, professionals and other employees cannot perform their duties as instructed, nor can they exercise their authority in a manner consistent with enterprise value. This is detrimental to a service economy, because it depends on timely and accurate performance. (See also in Chapter 8, requirements connected to the control of op risk in information technology.) Everything amplifying operational risk increases overall costs, including agency costs.

'Agency costs' are defined as the costs of reducing internal organisational conflicts. Experience shows that outsourcing may bring along plenty of them. Part of agency costs is the value of output lost because of different conflicts. A sound solution to measurement and monitoring of agency risk must be based on steady internal loss reporting practices, interactively retrieving accurate loss data which extend over a period of at least five years. Other requirements include:

* operational risk calculations validated through results of experiments and tests
* an analytical op risk study process, including scenarios, simulation and stress testing[2]
* action-oriented approaches allowing execution risk, agency risk, legal risk, IT risk and other operational risks to be brought under control.

A most valuable method is learning lessons from past failures regarding operational risks and the way they should have been controlled. For instance, the 1980s and 1990s have witnessed several spectacular manifestations of operational risk in the financial services industry, including events that led to the demise of Drysdale, Barings, Kidder Peabody and NatWest Markets. In several cases agency costs contributed to mergers and acquisitions, downsizing or outright bankruptcy.

The results of monitoring and testing must be presented in a way people can easily understand. This means that many solutions will have to be studied, negotiated and implemented case by case, in relation to outsourcing and insourcing projects. General principles regarding planning, identification and control may form the wider infrastructure, but focused approaches backed up by experimentation should provide the detail.

We should use our experience with the control of operational risk connected to internal processes to improve outsourcing deliverables and reduce agency risk. In engineering, for example, rapid prototyping is instrumental in keeping friction between different speciality teams under check. Prototyping:

- provides better visibility of the end product
- helps in shrinking time to market
- assists in gaining greater effectiveness.

The aftermath of operational risk is most distressing to the entity suffering from it, but it may be an opportunity for others in the industry to gain a competitive advantage or learn what needs to be done to improve their own internal control and management practices. Those institutions which have capitalised on the failure of others suggest that a wise policy is to:

- rethink the whole issue of services in a knowledge society, as well as the reasons for their vulnerability to operational risks
- define how each type of operational risk is influenced by, as well as it influences, the evolution of the service economy as a whole
- examine every outsourcing and insourcing project or network operations not from the viewpoint of whether op risk could happen – but from that of *when* and *how*.

Materiality is important. We should always be accounting for the cost of operational risk control. Enterprise management must keep in perspective that the control of operational risk has a price, it does not come for free. We must therefore decide between hiring people for operational risk events, or absorbing the losses. If we decide to go after operational risks, among our priorities regarding the insourcer should be to answer the queries:

- What's his track record with op risks?
- How late have its deliverables been?
- Were there deficiencies in quality of deliverables?

Also critical is the answer to the query about when and how a particular outsourced service exposed our organisation to operational risks. Whether we talk of internal operations, outsourcing, or dealing with business partners on the Internet, our goal should be to turn operational risk control into a senior management tool, for instance, finding peaks in the distribution of op risk, like those due to monthly and quarterly reconciliations.

Making operational risk control a management tool means challenging the obvious. For instance, considering commissions not as an extra compensation but as revenues resulting from taking operational risk. The failure of NatWest Markets and its subsequent disappearance (see Chapter 2) provides the evidence.

3. How to play safe with operational risks from outsourcing

After having defined, researched and selected the service *we* want to out-source, *we* must thoroughly examine those factors which are time and again at the origin of operational risks though they be morphing themselves from one type to the next. As a matter of principle, it is necessary to start by iden-tifying the risks that could hit *our* company and our business partner. Then we must:

• arrange these operational risks in line of importance
• decide the level of complexity they represent.

   Based on my professional practice, Figure 3.4 presents a frame of reference which can help in this work. Identifying the operational risks is integral part of the preparatory work for outsourcing projects. Another vital part is the ability to examine *if* our op risk management unit is able to handle them. If not, we have to upgrade this unit, measure the cost of the upgrade and add it to the contractual cost for outsourcing.

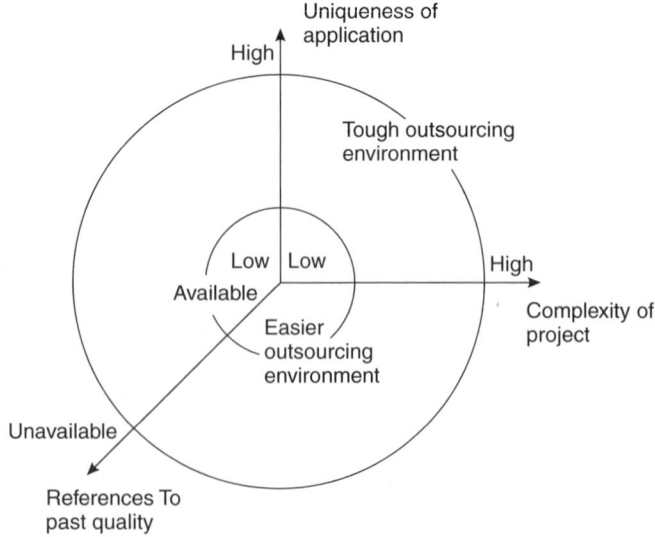

Figure 3.4   A frame of reference to help in evaluating the preparatory work for outsourcing projects

'To play safe' with operational risks from outsourcing in no way means totally avoiding these risks. This is not do-able. What is impossible is building up our defences, albeit at a certain cost. This is precisely what the preceding paragraph has suggested.

In principle, the greater the complexity of the outsourced (or insourced) project and its contractual characteristics, the more carefully we have to monitor operational risks that could hit the outsourcing agreement. Everything has to be costed, including counterparty risk. We should:

- assess spending needs associated to outsourcing
- include backup contingency planning and fire-brigade costs
- establish a quality control program which (preferably) uses statistical quality control (SQC) charts.[3]

SQC is a methodology well established since the second World War and, should be definitely used in conjunction with operational risk control, capitalising on the fact that in many cases exposure to op risk is quantifiable. It also varies over time, which permits establishing a distribution of values then associating to it control limits. There are also operational risks which are not quantifiable; intellectual property is an example.

Regarding intellectual property, and the likelihood it may be challenged by an outsourcing project, it is wise to check if the contractor is fully exploiting his intellectual property, find out whether he owns the intellectual property rights for what he does, and control whether *our* company will need to do intellectual property transfer.

These are conservatory measures. It will be redundant to add that some intellectual property, like software, is very difficult to protect because there are no laws enabling an adequate protection. But there are policies which can be profitably followed in addressing operational risk connected to qualifiable-only factors and intangibles:

- strengthening the management
- training all personnel in detecting deviations
- studying emerging best practices in control procedures.

Other policies call for doing op risk mitigation through insurance, developing contingency plans, providing consistency in operational risk tracking methods, repositioning operational risk along global business lines, and assuring there are incentives to invest in advanced solutions for the measurement, evaluation and control of operational risk events.

Some of the better approaches account for the fact that, because operational risk is, to a large extent, human risk there must be *sunset clauses* with job descriptions. For instance, approval to handle transactions is valid for one year; and/or if a person does not do any of the authorised operations in time X, then this authorisation ends. No authority should be given that lasts forever.

Life-long learning is another basic requirement in curbing aspects of operational risk related to the learning curve (see Chapter 11). As an example, in banking some traders do a rare type of transaction but are not really being updated on new rules as these develop. When the rules or the policy change(s), they still execute in the old way which leads to operational risk. A similar case exists with outsources who follow a standard procedure rarely or never updated to the client's changing requirements.

Because organisations are made of people, and many errors are man made, some companies have hired applied psychologists to look at human factors affecting op risk. Applied psychology attacks operational risk from a triple perspective: antecedents, behaviour and consequences. The most powerful classes of antecedents are those:

- describing expectations and linking to results
- occurring just before a desired performance
- being associated over time with specific consequences.

Hence the wisdom of having in place a system which clearly defines the most likely man-made operational errors, with demerits penalising their reappearance. A merits systems should reward control over these risks. For any practical purpose, this is the proverbial carrot and stick.

Some people advise measuring operational risk through 'near misses'. I am not comfortable with this approach because there is no clarity on how to identify and calculate a 'near-miss'. Among the outstanding queries are: What really constitutes a near miss? How can we quantify a near miss in practical terms? Do we really wish to establish a three-value control system: Go/May be/No go? Other questions include:

- How are we calculating what a near miss might have cost?
- How can we motivate people to identify and report near misses?
- How do we integrate near-misses into an organisation-wide op risk management framework?

There are many other challenges with the measurement and management of operational risk in outsourcing and insourcing. For instance, the operational risk control culture is very important. The proper culture sees to it that operational risk management is everybody's responsibility, and most particularly every manager's who should be able to:

- identify op risk event types and their consequences
- develop and apply a discipline for operational risk control

- gather data through a rigorous collection process, and
- involve the board and senior management in correcting the causes of op risks.

Based on these bullets, it is appropriate to add that a prerequisite to successful outsourcing is putting in place a truly independent risk control and audit function, tracking operational data by business line, monitoring loss events and gathering loss information. Another critical step is that of allocating losses between op risk classes and implementing back-charges all the way to the insourcer.

These actions should be *contractually* guaranteed. They should be established at the negotiating table because they cannot be effectively done post-mortem. Other preconditions are understanding the inherent frequency of operational risk events and likelihood of failure of preventive controls; integrating different standards and procedures in the organisation to permit pass-through of op risk information; and effectively using reporting practices to swamp operational risk at its roots.

In the background of all these challenges lies the fact it is not possible to avoid operation risk unless we go out of business. What we can do is comprehend it, reduce it, transform it and accept a minimal amount. At the risk of being redundant let me repeat that in outsourcing and insourcing this minimal amount must be contractually guaranteed and, here again, SQC charts, like statistical control by attributes, can play a vital role.

4. Measurement of operational risk through use of operating characteristics curves

As the Introduction has explained, operational risk is a polyvalent exposure in terms of its origins and the ways in which it expresses itself. It is also notoriously difficult to measure in all of its manifestations. Yet, without appropriate metrics and measurements we can do very little in terms of improving operational procedures, and controlling the risks associated to them and to the transactions which we make.

Down to the fundamentals: the measurement of operational risk requires (1) proper identification and description, and (2) a system able of aggregating and consolidating data collection across business lines, and the way in which these are supported – whether through inhouse or outsourced facilities. Another prerequisite for performance in op risks measurements is to analyse how to track progress towards uniform, comprehensive and accurate standards.

Management by exception helps, but it also poses the challenge of capturing and interpreting outliers. This is an imaginative task inasmuch as the effort to properly measure and manage operational risk is just starting.

A valid model for operational risk control will address at least five basic issues arising in measuring the accuracy of the system we are using (in fact, of any system):

1 explaining how a given op risk must be measured, including the framework necessary to assure reliable data collection
2 defining what is measured, including the issue, the data and the model which will use this data
3 specifying how data will be used to map observed performance against standards
4 assuring continuity in the representation of the operational process over a longer time-frame
5 targeting corrective action aimed to guarantee that we are in charge of the operational risk(s) which we target.

While accuracy of systems and procedures we employ is only one dimension of overall performance, it is also a most crucial one to operational risk control, and a pivot reference to whether or not we are likely to obtain end results. For this reason, special attention should be paid to the accuracy of tracking operational risks associated to each outsourcing project.

One of the elements which are critical to the accuracy of error tracking is the method we are using for the representation of the distribution of the errors we are after. Usually (but by no means always) the errors being encountered, and their likelihood, are expressed through a normal distribution, like the one in the top half of Figure 3.5. This is an approximation which sometimes is acceptable.

A distribution has central tendency, expressed through the *mean*, and spread whose statistic is the *variance*. It may also have skewness and kyrtosis.[4] We will not be concerned with them in this text. What the reader should retain is that in their work they will be always confronted by a distribution because:

- nothing moves on a straight line; all events are distributed within a certain range
- errors are indicated by those measurements beyond a given threshold, like the grey area in the right of the normal distribution in Figure 3.5.

Let's consider as outlier this small diagrammed section. We may be willing to accept all the values corresponding to the area under the curve as being conforming to norms, except those in the extreme right. However, because 100 per cent inspection is (usually) not feasible, we establish a statistical quality control plan. In this and in many other statistical sampling projects, where measurements play a most critical role in terms of accuracy of results, we are typically faced by two types of errors.

1 Type I, or α, which is the producer's risk. It gives the level of confidence.

Type I error essentially tells the risk the producer, for instance, the insourcer takes that a lot will be rejected because of sampling reasons even if the specified outgoing quality level is met. Usually we take $\alpha = 0.01$, which means it is set at the 99 per cent level of confidence.

2 Type II, or β,[5] known as consumer's risk. It corresponds to the tolerance per cent defective.

What is shown in the second half of Figure 3.5 is an operating characteristics (OC) curve – a powerful means in analytical studies. It is not possible to set α and β at the same time. Usually, we agree on α and on the sampling plan which includes the definition of the population (in this case of operational risks in an outsourced contract, by risk type) and on the size of the sample. The shape of the OC curve depends on these two variables, and this shape helps to establish β.

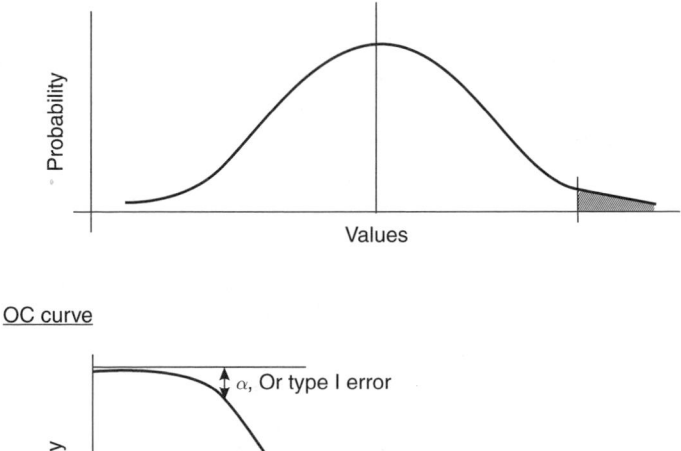

Figure 3.5 The recording and plotting of most events assumes a normal distribution of exposure, which is an approximation. An OC curve gives better perspective

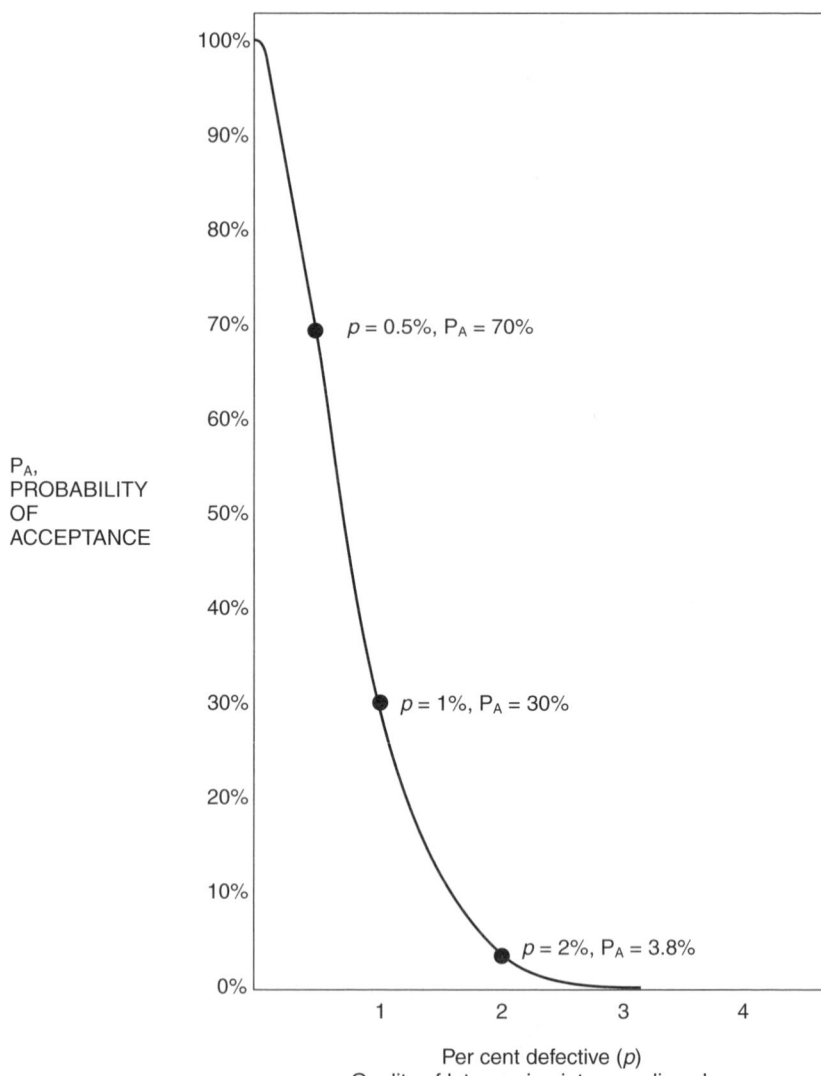

Figure 3.6   Operating characteristics curve for job lot per cent defective

This is shown in Figure 3.6, which takes as an example the lot tolerance per cent defective of an outsourced job lot. This particular plot is instrumental in indicating the per cent defective and the likelihood of acceptance of the lot. For instance P_A the probability of acceptance of a lot with $p = 0.5$ per cent is 70 per cent; while for $p = 2.0$ per cent (four tomes higher in terms of defects) the likelihood of acceptance under this plan is only 3 per cent.

Larger sample sizes, both in absolute terms and as per cent of the population under study, help in keeping β in check. The concept I just outlined is very important in outsourcing because not only third party insourcers but also strategic alliances and mergers have the nasty habit of increasing operational risk. They do so because they make information less controllable as they:

- bring together incompatible systems
- compound layers of bureaucracy
- blur the responsibility and accountability lines.

The use of operating characteristics curves helps to assure that solutions provided to the problem of measuring and controlling operational risk are pragmatic and proactive, enabling to better understand the types of operational risks, their limits and practical implications. In turn, this makes feasible more rigorous risk-based controls. The statistical tools are available. The challenge is to:

- establish the tolerances
- elaborate the statistical quality control plan.

Take, as an example, software which adjusts engine performance. AVL, an Austrian company, has developed a programming product that can alter an engine's characteristics in function of the driver's style. Known as 'DriveAdapt' this software enables a vehicle to continuously respond to the driver's style and mood by constantly modifying the engine's torque characteristics. An $\alpha = 0.01$ is acceptable as level of significance, and the job lot defective curve we saw in Figure 3.6 can nicely fit the characteristics of β.

Adaptation to driver's style is the example of a case of no catastrophic failures. Still, the control of quality of output should be constant. In the DriveAdapt case, the software analyses inputs from up to 10 sensors, depending on the vehicle and the OEM's specification. The most important ones provide data on:

- pedal position
- vehicle speed
- revolutions per minute (rpm)
- longitudinal acceleration
- clutch
- steering position.

This information is calculated in a 10ms cycle; the algorithm is dependent on the circumstances under which the car is being driven.[6] An output analysis combining the above variable can track the DriveAdapt's performance and, based on the number of misses, certify whether or not the car meets specifications.

Another piece of intelligent software comes from Cambridge Neurotechnology, in the UK. It supports a detection system that uses the body's natural Circadian sleep rhythms to sense if a driver is getting drowsy. Known as Advisory System for Tired Drivers this is based on an algorithm that analyses the driver's state of alertness by taking inputs from the steering, speed and length of time driving. Another input is up to the driver who has the option of entering comments on the previous night's sleep: Good, Bad, Poor or None.

Learning from these and other experiences involving knowledge engineering it is not difficult to project intelligent advisory systems (based on OC curves) for operational risks. Their value differentiation should be based on prognostication alerting on process drift rather than reporting after the failure. Such solutions can prove quite valuable in measuring and visualising the operational risk profile.

5. Operational risks which require steady qualitative evaluation

The executive vice president of Pechiney, the chemicals and aluminium company, to whom I was consultant in the early 1960s, had the policy that prior to outsource any project he would meet the CEO of the insourcer. For consultancy assignments, he wanted to know personally not only the CEO but also the consulting engineers who would be put on the project, particularly the team leader.

One of my fellow graduate students at UCLA, when he became director of investments of a major bank in New York, followed a similar policy. First, he put his analysts at work to tear apart the financial statements of the company he targeted for investment reasons. Then, if they came up with a positive recommendation for investment, he took it on his own to meet the president of that company before making any commitment – because the control of *management risk* was at the top of his list of priorities.

One of the rules this director of investments applied, to make up his mind, was simple and effective: If the president of the firm was oversized, he would not make an investment because 'If he could not control himself he could not control his firm either'. Think of these two examples when confronted with the choice of an insourcer, and don't believe that analysing the management's ability to be in charge is a once in a lifetime proposition. It is a highly repetitive, steady task: people change and so do their policies.

Contrary to other op risks, management risk cannot be tracked through OC curves, because it is a fundamentally qualitative issue. TIAA/CREF, America's largest pension fund, and the owner of more than 1 per cent of equity value at the New York Stock Exchange, provides another example on how to keep management risk under control. To help itself in administering its assets, TIAA/CREF steadily monitors 25 governance issues, which range:

- from board independence and diversity
- to the age of directors and their potential conflicts of interest.

Some 1,500 companies are making up TIAA's more than $100 billion equity investment and they all undergo this test. Those falling short under a point system devised by the fund get inspection visits regardless of market value, advertised performance, or quantitative factor revealed by their financial statements. The budget behind this effort is most reasonable: about $1 million a year. The benefits are:

- good-governance principles
- monitoring and encouragement of the management of companies in which TIAA invests.

For assets of $100 billion, $1 million a year is peanuts in comparison to the benefits from a close look at operational risk, but not many funds or other major investors have taken that road, for want either of will or of skill in executing a steady focused inspection. Personal meetings are indeed the only effective method I have found for estimating qualitative factors affecting a company's growth and survival.

No words can fully describe the fact that management risk counts a great deal. Organisations are made of people and managements change. There is absolutely no assurance a new CEO and his team will be better than the one outgoing. In fact, there is plenty of evidence to the contrary. Managements make blunders, and when this happens stakeholders pay the price. The senior brass itself usually opens its golden parachute.

Take the bankruptcy of Swissair, of 2001, as an example. Its AOM, Air Liberté, Sabena and other similar silly investments with minor airlines aghast with labour problems – as well as its badly judged and poorly executed forays into insourcing (particularly catering), were the worst of a series of false steps that finally dragged down a once proud airline. Until the late 1990s Swissair was one of the most admired carriers, famous for punctuality and superior in-flight service.

- It was financially stable, a microcosm of the country whose flag flied on its airliners' tails.
- It was also solid, reliable, orderly and successful – an emblem of dependability.

Mismanagement, however, saw to it that the downturn was around the corner. By mid 2001, as Swissair struggled to avoid going bust all that glory was past. In 2000 its losses were CHF 2.9 billion ($1.7 billion). The forecast for 2001, before the final crash, was even bleaker. Its debts of CHF 7.8 billion ($4.6 billion) were more than six times the value of its equity. A leverage of 600 per cent is unheard off for a mature industry like the airlines.

Neither was the future of Swissair looking so much better, as the company was loosing altitude. One of its major problems has been that it was based in a high-cost country and, with Switzerland not being a member of the European Union, Swissair did not have the freedom to expand alone in Europe. Hence, the different ill-conceived and poorly timed alliances – a sort of outsourcing to other ailing carriers – its ill-fated expansion plans.

Theoretically, as with so many other outsourcing and insourcing agreements, global alliances might have been an option, but in practice they did not fly. The deals with SAS, KLM and Austrian Airlines fell through; Singapore Airlines deserted the Global Excellence alliance; and Delta Air Lines abandoned the Atlantic Excellence. Neither did Swissair top management show an excellence of its own in steering the company in difficult times.

Under the banner of the Qualiflyer Group, a poorly conceived strategy, Swissair sought links with other small European airlines: Sabena, Air Littoral, AOM, Air Liberté, LOT Polish Airlines, LTU in Germany (a nearly bankrupt airline kept alive through political pressures on state-run banks)[7] and TAP, Portugal's flag carrier. It also hooked up with South African Airways. The result of those outsourcing licenses FOR air routes was a torrent of red ink.

- Money turned to dust in airlines where Swissair acquired equity.
- Some of the other 'partners' became customers for Swissair's catering and other aviation-service subsidiaries, this was small fry.

Altogether Swissair spent more than $1 billion on different equity stakes, on top of a similar amount building up its catering operation to make it appealing to its partners. In effect, Swissair was buying customers for the aviation-service businesses it also had to acquire. This was done without taking due account of the fact that nearly all the airlines Swissair was buying into were in deep difficulties, including killer labour troubles.

- They had hopelessly big losses and little freedom to cut costs to eliminate them.
- After the commitments were made, red ink ran all over the place and Swissair's stock tanked, as shown in Figure 3.7.

Swissair's downfall is a very relevant case study on outsourcing and the false policy followed by some companies, by having good money running after bad money and trying to save an insourcer going under. Neither is Swissair a rare example. One of the banks where I was consultant to the board had contemplated buying equity in Unisys, its insourcer and provider

Figure 3.7 The trend line in Swissair equity 1996–2001

of mainframes, when the latter was going under, to stop the haemorrhage. Finally, cooler heads prevailed, the bad investment was averted and Unisys was eventually able to stabilise itself.

Corporate insider activity is another subject which should be brought to the reader's attention because of the implications which it has in outsourcing–insourcing agreements. Because such are often concluded at senior management level, they give the outsourcer a unique view of the insourcers business health, and vice versa. This is a modern twist to age-old insider trading, and it is one of the indicators of rotten deals which have recently attracted considerable attention in the financial press.

Corporate insider activity essentially gauges buying versus selling in the shares of the actors, own companies, or those of business partners in which they are able to taken a close view. What's more, this sort of trades is increasing in a way pointing to a downfall. In July 2001, for example, insider sales have exceeded purchases by a four-to-one ratio.

This preponderance of selling is presumed to have negative implications for the performance of the companies and, by extension, for the performance of their stock. Contrarians, however, suggest that while insider buying is typically done because the executives have an optimistic outlook for the targeted company and its stock, insider selling can be done for reasons other than a negative outlook. The reasons, for instance, may be diversification, purchase of non-financial assets, end of a lock-up period on an IPO, and so on. All this is possible, but an impeding downfall is a more likely reason for selling.

6. Understanding the evolution of operational risk control policies and practices

This chapter provided evidence that operational risk is present in all types of outsourcing agreements and at all levels of the organisation, including senior management. It has also documented that policies and measures to control operation risk must account for the fact that it is lurking in practically all operations. This has to be taken into full account in developing enterprise-wide solutions.

Not only we must clearly define the nature and existence of (strategically speaking) expected, unexpected and outlier operational risks, but also track them, database them, analyse them and project their appearance in future operations, so that we can plan in advance the aftermath of exposure to them. Policies must be in place to assure that each op risk, whether due to error, failure, intent or a simple delay becomes:

- visible to enterprise management
- a subject of corrective action
- a ground for deselecting service providers.

Visibility increases with real-time data capture, standards and models becoming integral part of the operational risk control framework. Tools must be in place to permit steady self-assessment. Standards should exist for keeping under lock and key every type of op risk faced by *our* organisation anywhere in its operations, including all its outsourcing agreements. These standards should be regularly updated.

If the appropriate background work has been done, providing solutions to operational risk problems is, to a large measure, something subject to a learning curve. Because the range and breadth of operational risks is so large, enterprise management are advised not to try to address all operational risk problems at first time. The solutions which we provide must be:

- pragmatic
- at the right level of strength
- implementable and manageable
- scalable and changeable
- cost/effective.

Valid solutions adopted with outsourcing, as well as with Internet operations, must take account of different perspectives and definitions of operational risk – and they should be adaptable to the problems we are confronting. The way we manage operational risk is affected by the manner in which we are viewing IT and the tools at our disposal. Experience teaches that operational risks are better managed when they are mapped to:

- a risk indicator
- a cause-and-effect- relationship
- losses related to their appearance
- a control system which follows them step-by-step.

These four bullets speak volumes about the systems and procedures we should be after, emphasising the fact the solutions themselves must be both focused and flexible. We should not wait for the ultimate in operational risk control. Today nobody has the 'best' solution. Everybody is learning about operational risk and how to keep it in check.

As a matter of policy, we should not be afraid to develop solutions for operational risk events even if these are imperfect. The way to bet is that in ten years' time nobody would have the same sort of solution he or she develops today. Even the opinions concerning operational risk will continue to evolve – and to be different. Several opinions exist today, though we do have a consensus on the need for corrective measures.

Materiality, and by extension the answer to the question: 'What constitutes acceptable cost', is one of the issues for which universal standards don't exist. For instance, at what point is the cost of operational risk immaterial relative to the cost of managing? My response to this query is experimentation. An experimental approach is not just the best way when we are faced with unknown factors; it is the only way. Many types of operational risk are indeed issues involving both:

- experimental design, and
- thorough testing.

Experimentation is an indivisible part of any sound methodology aimed at controlling the risks confronting us. As I never tire of repeating, the tools are available. All we need to do is to apply them. Experimentation provides documentation. We always have to be comfortable with the solution we adopt, and its output – and we have to balance results versus costs.

Also important is a professional appreciation by an expert in the field we are examining for instance; the domain where operational risks are under investigation. How reasonable look the numbers? The method which we are using? Can these numbers stand comparison to real-life results? Which sort of stress test is meaningful?[8]

Table 3.1　A reporting format for operational risk

	Business unit A		
	Internal controls	**Exposure**	**IT service**
Product X	Excellent	High	Very Good
Product Y	Poor	Average	Average
Product Z	Excellent	Average	Not Material

It needs no particular reminder that the results of experiments as well as op risk statistics must be widely reported within the organisation. Recently, supervisory authorities, too, want to receive such reports. There is no formal standard reporting format on operational risk. The principle, however, is that operational risks must be integrated in a homogeneous framework like the reporting scheme by Barclays shown in Table 3.1. This is qualitative; other reporting formats may be quantitative. Both types are necessary.

Real-time reporting offers a good solution to the dual problem of speed of response, and flexibility in adaptation and upkeep. Effective reporting requires the use of filters so that specifics are reported in a way that is action-oriented. Operational risks that are not corrected quickly tend to grow multiple heads like the hydra, lead to agency risk, and end by tearing down the outsourcing agreement.

4

Supply Chain Integration and the Management of Time; What Outsourcing Should Learn from the Internet

1. Introduction

The advantages provided by global communications technology forced companies to redefine their policies and their business models with the aim of improving enterprise performance. First the focus was on web sites as information and messaging centres, but within no time this extended to transactions including the handling of intra-organisational chores, with a significant aftermath on product design, marketing, accounting and logistics.

This internet-based evolution in corporate focus allowed a number of well-managed companies to employ an integrated supply chain paradigm. They developed a framework that allows them to capitalise on new business opportunities while at the same time swamping procurement costs and giving a new push to insourcing and outsourcing strategies. These are the themes of the present chapter.

To give perspective, let me start with a historical reference. In 1996 Boeing began selling spare parts on the Internet. One year later, in 1997, Boeing processed 20 per cent more shipments with the same amount of data entry employees. Since customers can access online information about pricing, availability and order status, a large number of calls to telephone service personnel were avoided. This service has significantly improved over the years (see section 4).

In its dual insourcing and outsourcing activity over the Net, as one of the largest purchasers of non-physical goods and services, Boeing has been able to cut spending and transaction costs by 30 per cent in one year. It also instituted a program to file travel and expense accounts online. When this application went live costs plummeted from $36 per expense account report to $4.

GE Lighting implemented online procurement which resulted in a 60 per cent staff redeployment in this activity alone, a 30 per cent labour cost reduction, significant materials cost decrease (between 5 per cent and 20 per cent), and 50 per cent reduction in the time taken to award a contract to a supplier. In one year alone, 2000, General Electric:

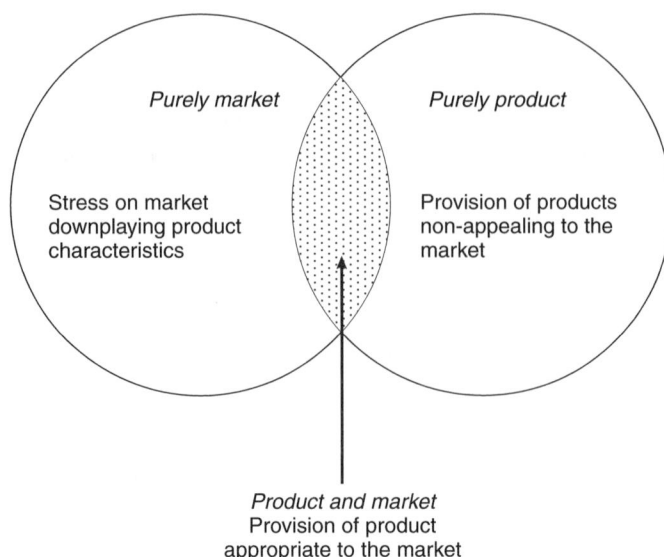

Figure 4.1   The best approach is one exploiting the synergy of product and market orientation

- bought online goods worth $6 billion
- sold online goods worth $11 billion.

The guestimated benefit in savings this online strategy gave to GE is at the level of $1.6 billion. The financial services-oriented GE Capital suggests that the core of an i-commerce strategy is to intensify relationships with business partners, using technology to leverage the company's capabilities to an ever-larger client base. GE Capital implemented its parent company's e-Buy, e-Make, e-Sell, adding to them online investment banking activities, for wealthy individuals, corporate and institutional clients (see section 2), and eliminating the *middle* of every operation:

- middlemen
- data handling
- paperwork.

Such solutions are appealing and effective because they are engineered to provide in one offer both product and market orientation. A greater efficiency is made possible through digitisation and real-time access. As Figure 4.1 demonstrates, this approach lies at the junction of old economy offering which tended to excel in product design *or* in market orientation characteristics, but not in both at the same time. Internet supply chain management aims to capitalise on the synergy of product design and market appeal, doing so at an affordable cost.[1]

2. The shift in paradigm with online supply chain

Business-to-business solutions have been introduced in Chapter 1. Their goal has been that of providing self-service capabilities. e-Buy, for example, aggregates purchasing across GE Capital with é-Auctions. The initial result has been a 25 per cent decrease in the cost of US office supplies, and a sig-nificant reduction in telecommunications costs. e-Make is expediting deal-making for GE and for its commercial customers, helping to manage business reporting processes (and assets) in paperless form.

- The overall cycle time is down by 20 per cent.
- Customers see savings in several deal-related items, including legal costs.

e-Make also cuts operating costs. The savings in just one business segment, private-label credit cards, are impressive when one realises that an application written on paper from a new customer costs $4, while an internet-based application costs $2.79. As another example, using the Web and digitised information to handle service calls means a $2.82 savings on every one of tens of millions of enquiries.

The potential of e-Sell is illustrated by one of GE Capital's high-profile initiatives, GESmallBusiness.com, which began in 2000. In just a few months, visitors to the site have been up 150 per cent, and over a billion dollars of leads have been generated – a vivid example of what e-Sell and similar online applications represent to the firm and to its customers. Neither should the swamping of operational risks be forgotten.

At General Electric, e-Business and Six Sigma Quality go hand in glove, driving greater speed, efficiency and profitability across its business lines.[2] GE Capital Aviation Services reduced Polar Air's fulfilment time from 225 hours to 84, while UK retailer Arcadia Group, a global consumer finance client, saw:

- an 8 per cent increase in recruited private-label credit card accounts
- a full-minute reduction of cycle time for in-store card applications.

Along a similar frame of reference, Charles Schwab became a foremost broker by exploiting internet's ability to reach its customers and prospective customers online. Web trading saved 20 per cent of commissions on top of discounts the client already received on manned trades. This is double the extra 10 per cent discount on Schwab's active trading online through TeleBroker and StreetSmart.

For its part, since 2000 the New York Stock Exchange (NYSE) uses extranets to communicate with about 3500 listed companies, 600 member firms and 1600 employees. NYSE adopted this solution because it wanted to improve the quality, timeliness, and cost/effectiveness of communications with its community, while at the same time providing content.

- The users are based in multiple locations, and many are working remotely.
- The extranets handle hundreds of simple and complex applications.

Digitisation, innovation and online processing see to it that the worlds of advertising and electronic commerce are converging while their dividing lines are blurring. Therefore many companies position themselves to benefit from the opportunity to leverage their business and become a leader in i-commerce, exploiting their brand name and acquiring a potent distribution channel (see section 4).

In spite of the fact internet equities have suffered from the market events of 2000 to 2001, many financial analysts believe internet commerce will be an enormous opportunity going forward, and that players like AOL Time Warner are well positioning to take advantage of its growth potential. AOL is a leader for advertisers' media buys in interactive services, with an approximately 70 per cent combined reach.

- Added value comes from the fact that, unlike television, which has a fixed amount of inventory, the internet has an unlimited amount of shelf space.
- This allows a great amount of pricing flexibility to be offered to advertisers, in order to garner a significant share of aggregate advertising spending.

In AOL's case, analysts think that some of its cost centres, such as content creation, e-mail and chat, can be converted into profit centres through selling advertising space when the advertising market booms again. Statistics show that internet-centred households watch 15 per cent less television than other households, or about seven fewer hours of TV per week. In fact, internet's prime usage hours are approximately 8:00 p.m. to midnight, directly competing with prime TV hours.

- Value differentiation is demonstrated by the fact that growth in retail PC sales correlates with the Net's ability to promote i-commerce.
- Sales statistics indicate there has been a strong trend in the purchases of low-cost PCs, now amounting to between 40 per cent and 60 per cent of retail unit volume.

Some experts look at sales of low-cost machines as a prognosticator of the emergence of true mass-market computer purchasers which is becoming the core target audience of i-commerce. At the same time that they go for hand-held devices and portables, consumers are upgrading older machines to handle multimedia online access.

An example on end-user trends in internet commerce comes from eBay. In 2001, registered users past 30 million, about the same level as Amazon.com; Gross Merchandise Sales (GMS) were up 23 per cent year-to-year; but auctions per user were slightly down, with the result online revenue per user and 'take rate' (or online revenue as per cent of GMS) somewhat degraded. eBay takes heart from the fact it did not crash.

In fact, in 2001 gross margin at e-Bay was strong while customer acquisition cost (CAC) remained flat (at $14). General and administrative expenses were also flat as per cent of revenue at about 14 per cent. Operating margin, excluding non-cash charges and payroll option taxes, stood at 23 per cent, driven by better than expected gross margin and increased operating leverage. eBay said that its cash and equivalents position remained strong:

- improving the company's financial staying power
- allowing it to take advantage of acquisition opportunities.

These results must be interpreted in light of prevailing economic conditions. In 2000–01, the US was in the midst of a recession deeper than many people have actually acknowledged. Companies like eBay and Amazon survived because they were a great consumer concept with agile user interfaces: easy, friendly, with good customer support. They set the standard in many ways for buying and dealing on the Net. This is the standard to be targeted by insourcing and outsourcing.

Post mortem it can be stated that while the 2000–2002 low was an earthquake to the dot-coms, successful i-commerce merchandisers survived the slam. Their difficulty has been the back end: inventory, warehouses, fulfilment, returns, obsolescence. Successful companies handled this challenge because they had a smart group of managers and a first-class consumer franchise.

The examples I have taken in this section have been chosen from the best capable of offering comprehensive, well-enabled integrated services in the new economy. Let's face it, i-commerce or no i-commerce, the biggest assets of a company are its customers, its people and its technology. These should be the guiding lights of enterprise management and focal points of interest in insourcing and outsourcing.

3. Living and working in Internet time

'I wasted time, and now doth time waste me,' Shakespeare wrote in *Richard II*. 'I can give you anything but time,' Napoleon once said to his lieutenants. One way to appreciate Internet time is to think that the half-life of technology keeps on getting shorter. For many firms today, time is a prime source of competitive advantage. But let's not make any mistake about it.

It is people who have momentum, know-how and imagination – in short, who are working hard to make time tick to their competitive advantage.

'We work at internet speed,' said Nina Brink, former CEO of Rotterdam-based World Online International. Comparing her company to some of its competitors she added: 'They work at monopoly speed.'[3] The able use of time is so critical because *time is a unique resource*

- It cannot be accumulated like wealth.
- Yet without time we can accomplish nothing.[4]

We are forced to spend time whether we choose to or not. And we should appreciate what Shakespeare said about three things that don't return in life:

- an opportunity that has been lost
- a word that was spoken
- time that has passed by.

In spite of its vital importance to our daily life and to our business, of all our resources time appears to be the least understood and the most misman-aged. Time can be neither outsourced nor insourced. The argument 'We buy time' is just a way of talking; but productivity helps. 'In finding its own question of time-poverty, our culture is actually confronting the eternal question of the meaning of human life,' suggests Jacob Needleman.[5]

- From a macroscopic viewpoint, time is a period that elapses between birth and death. What one accomplishes during this time is one's legacy.
- Day to day is a different matter. For every single person time remains a largely esoteric concept, whose meaning is not thoroughly appreciated.

If the steam engine was the prime mover of the industrial age, and the clock is central to the industrial society, the computer is the information extension of the clock. Networks bring the clock into the broader and deeper environment of any-to-any communications. This is one of the basic concepts underpinning internet time and its metrics.

Can we measure Internet time? There are two answers to this query at different conceptual levels. The higher-level answer is that we need a notion of the management of time. An example is what Toyota has said – that it is looking to produce a custom-made car in two-and-a-half days (more on this later). The other answer, at a lower level, relates to the need to have metrics which allow us to plan and control what we do – and whatever else happens – per unit of time.

Take as an example the difference between daily and intraday reporting of financial transactions. Until the mid 1990s stock exchanges and financial institutions considered that up to three daily values were enough to represent the beat of the market: high, low and closing price. Today, this is absolutely inadequate. Traders and investors need intraday prices and many analytical studies require data recorded tick by tick.

Something else missing from the traditional approach to time recording is the conceptual phase shift which should accompany the introduction of internet time. This rests on historical and philosophical grounds. In ancient mythology, Chronos (the Greek word for time) was the God of mankind who ate his own children. This is the best metaphor in defining our current conception of time and its far-reaching effects.

- The paradox of time is that nobody seems to have enough of it, yet everyone has all the time that is available.
- The empire of Chronos is rich beyond belief, mismanaged as no other place, and moving fast.

One of the reasons behind the mismanagement of time is the lag we allow to exist between the collection of facts, decision and action. Compressing this lag is important because in the execution of a decision, or of a plan, delays are usually fatal. Also, in the digital age in which we live, time becomes increasingly non-linear. Times past, present and future can coexist.

Stephen Jay Gould was to suggest that 'The idea that time continues to accelerate in a maddening manner – making yesterday's products obsolete before we can reap the benefits of their use – becomes compelling as a defining metaphor for the inception of the new millennium', and Michael S. Dell gave a practical example on the business sense of time compression: 'In the late '80s and early '90s, Dell measured component inventory in weeks. Today, we measure inventory in days – and soon we will be clocking it in hours.'[6]

'What about exploring time as we explore space?' asks Arthur C. Clarke. According to Albert Einstein, there is no real distinction between time and space but, Clarke suggests, we are still faced with the uncomfortable fact that whereas it is easy to move in the three dimensions of space, we seem capable of moving in the fourth only at a constant rate of 60 minutes per hour – and always in the same direction.

Clarke also advises that H.G. Well's *Accelerator* is an extremely useful concept to our age. Even if the rate of perception could be speeded up only two- or threefold, there are times when that might be invaluable. For its part, the 'Decelerator' would certainly be an effective way of killing time for those people who like it better dead. With the business concept of time and the notion of an accelerator/decelerator, we have the four-layer structure of internet time, shown in Figure 4.2, where each higher level is a metalayer of the lower one.

A small but practical example of the 'decelerator' is the weekend. (An even better example is the socialist 35-hour week in France.) From the nineteenth century all the way to the Second World War there has been a clear

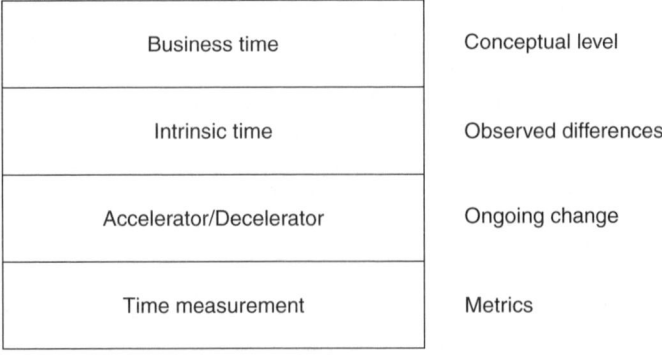

Business time	Conceptual level
Intrinsic time	Observed differences
Accelerator/Decelerator	Ongoing change
Time measurement	Metrics

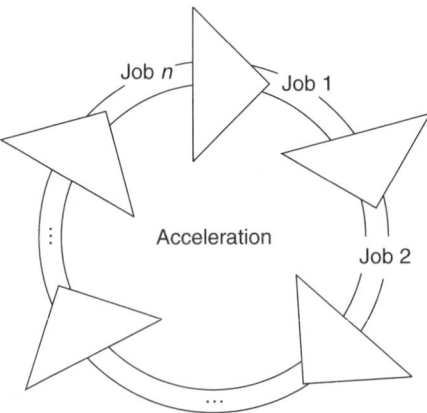

Figure 4.2   Internet time can be seen in two ways: a structure with metalayers and a spinning wheel

distinction between the work week and the weekend. But already after the Second World War international consultants dropped this 'obvious' difference. For them, a 'Sunday' may be on a Wednesday and Christmas may be celebrated forty days down the line or never come. Making professional people work harder is the *accelerator*.

- Today, with the internet, for a number of professional people days and nights are fused into a kind of timelessness.
- Networks extend the office to the home, and people steal cycles to work around the clock. By so doing they accelerate time's pace.

With acceleration, people bring into their lives *intrinsic time*. The underlying concept is presented in Figure 4.3. In two words, activity time and clock (or physical) time don't necessarily march with the same pace. Within

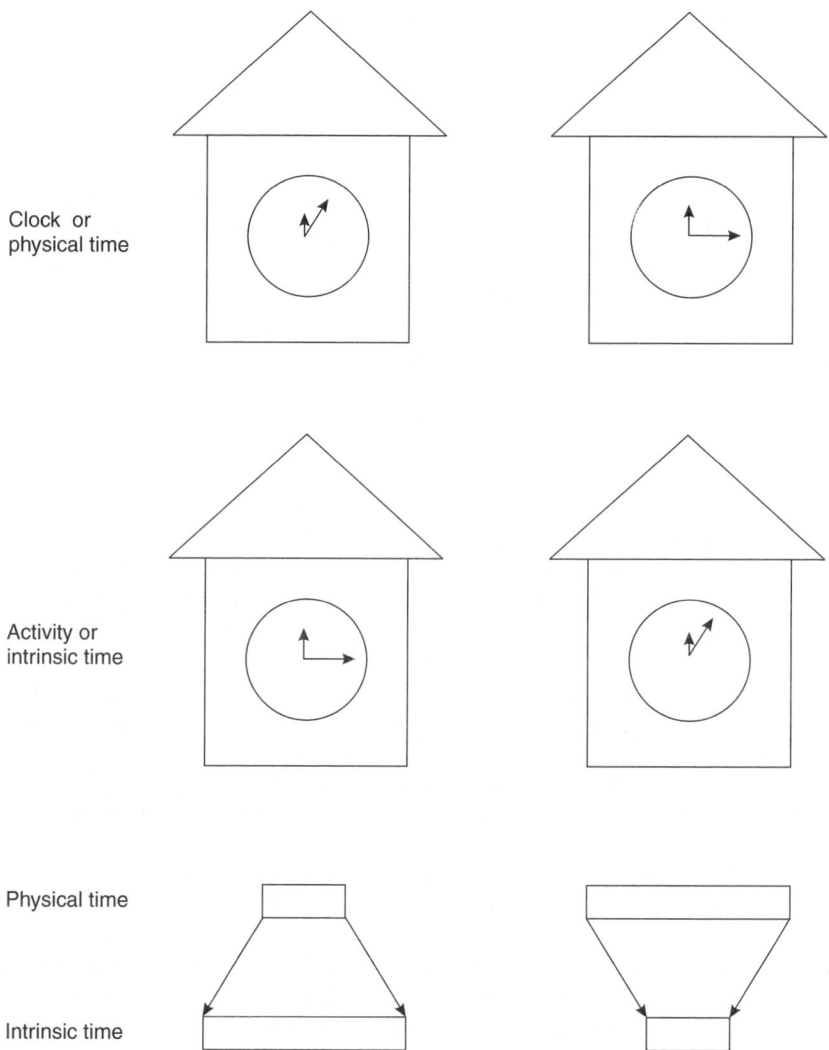

Clock or
physical time

Activity or
intrinsic time

Physical time

Intrinsic time

Figure 4.3 Time deformation results from the fact that physical time and intrinsic time are not in phase

certain limits, clock time is standard while activity time changes radically from one marketplace to another.[7] Trading over lunch hours for example is fast in New York because the American dealers take their lunch along; while their Japanese colleagues go for a long lunch at a sushi bar. Internet time moves fast for people who are busy working online, *as if* being online is accelerating clock time.

The other side of Internet time is an increasingly punctual life. This concept is not new but only recently did it start becoming part of a more generalised practice. An orderly life which made its first appearance in Byzantine monasteries is not natural to mankind. By now, however, a big chunk of humanity has become so regimented by the clock as to approve the aphorism 'Time is Money'.

By increasing the accessibility of professionals and insourcers of services Internet time makes this felt. Because 'time is money' is a concept which filtered down to our subconscious, people and companies are interested in the apparent compression of time, defined as the ability to do in a moment what in earlier days required weeks, months or years. A busy person can do in less than an hour what somebody else needs a whole day to do.

4. Fast flow mechanisms and dynamic pricing help in changing our culture

Being online does not help much unless we know-how to exploit the advantages which it offers. A good way to look at goods traded on the internet is as a flow of products and services representing *usage rights* over time. This is the concept behind fast flow replenishment (FFR), manufacturing and inventories which are just in time (JIT), and internet commerce at large.

The more competitive is the environment in which we work, the faster should be the turnaround, because this is key to profits. Since 2000, at Compaq the final configuration was fixed only days before production, and that design would typically sell for only a couple of weeks before being changed again. Fast turnaround saw to it that a standard Compaq model sold for less than three months. Speedy turnaround allowed the company to:

- take better advantage of changes in price and technology
- serve in an able manner both its own bottom line and the market's needs.

The strategy which capitalised on this concept saw to it that PCs arrived in stores a few hours after completion, and good were always kept up to date. They acquired a new dimension in the stretch of time usually seen as assembly line operations and inventorying. The concept behind JIT (just in time) is that if a product is produced without being ordered, it begins to lose value. Therefore, in a highly competitive market:

- every producer tries to maximise the use of his facilities, and
- at the same time, uses technology to minimise inventories.

A key component of internet time along the definition given in section is the culture underpinning it. Phil Condit, Boeing's chairman, has said that his company tried to accelerate its production too fast, without changing a production-engineering system that had barely altered since the Second World War. That Second World War culture was fine for bashing out hundreds of identical B-52 bombers, but modern airlines have four million parts and are customised for individual airlines.[8]

Boeing learned that lesson the hard way. A new system to control the supply and stock of all these parts, cutting inventory costs, was introduced in March 1998. Re-engineering targeted the trimming of the number of special features the company had to produce for different airliners, without making the customers feel they are getting a pure off-the-peg product. This has been achieved through a computer-based production management system designed to:

- deliver new efficiencies
- keep operational risk under control.

The efficiency concepts I am outlining are cornerstone to insourcing and outsourcing. They are transferable into sales, thanks, to a large extent, to the internet. An example is last-minute auctions whether for airline seats or for vacations. Cruise companies start offering on the internet bargains to people with flexible schedules who may take their vacation in the Bahamas, the Caribbean islands, the Virgin islands, a Panama Canal crossing or elsewhere – at reduced cost wherever there are free cabins.

For hotel rooms, too, pricing is no longer fixed but actively shifted up and down over time, depending on demand and resource availability. In Las Vegas, is the same hotel and at the same floor rooms have no more a single value. A double room may cost $300 per night during Comdex; $60 on Thursday that same week when the hotel empties; and $110 during the following weekend as demand picks up.

Dynamic pricing is of great interest to outsourcing and insourcing, because it is a forerunner of things to come. Goods and other services are like rooms and airline seats. They are most valuable when they are wanted. Therefore, clear-eyed enterprise management sees to it that they are priced cheaper when there is a slack in demand or they fail to sell. Consumers who watch their budget become conditioned to wait for sales.

- Prices change with demand.
- Demand changes over time.
- Time makes the difference in prices.

An issue connected to differential pricing is the so-called *predatory pricing*, selling goods below cost. The courts tend to regard predatory pricing as legal fiction. The caveat is that while predatory pricing is theoretically against the law, in practice it is nearly impossible to prove it, unless a company makes it its steady policy.

In the new economy, the pricing of goods and services requires a *dynamic financial analysis* (DFA) methodology which in a way similar to the fast-flow method. For enterprise management reasons, with DFA a model is developed of the entire entity's operations according to:

- current plan
- alternative plans.

The complexity of the model depends on the accuracy we wish to obtain, market parameters, and complexity of operations. In a financial institution, for example, DFA will simultaneously involve: interest rates, sales, claims, expenses, profit margins, cashflow, and the likelihood of catastrophic events. DFA models are used with a set of scenarios of the future, to project operating results. Challenges include the:

- consistency of these scenarios
- fact projected results are assumption-driven
- inclusion of future correlation between financial risks, and other factors.

Analytics are at the core of the DFA methodology, just like they are cornerstone to FFR and JIT. The message the reader should retain from this reference is that the whole pricing algorithm changes radically – and this is not a job that can be, or should be, outsourced, though consultants may be used for technology transfer purposes. Depending on demand and time:

- prices will be below cost at certain moments and well above in others
- the accurate and punctual sensitivity to customer drives will make the difference.

Current projections indicate that a time-dependent distinction will be increasingly made between *friction* pricing and *friction-free* – Bill Gates's term for profitless. This distinction practically means that pricing mechanisms permitting dynamic adjustments become increasingly efficient and finely tuned to demand.

Even overhead costs should be seen from a time-driven, not unit-driven perspective (see Chapters 12 to 14). Efficient pricing meditates against what von Mises said about socialism and bureaucracy being: 'fascinated by the plan to transform the whole world into a bureau'. The paradigm shift in dynamic pricing of services, as well as manufactured goods, requires a very significant acceleration of response time.

- With networks, response time has become the secret weapon of business, because it underpins competitive advantage.
- While providing the most value for the lowest cost remains relevant, the added requirement is doing so in the least amount of time.

Added value will always be important but down to basics the real value differentiation is speed in deliverables – from goods to prices. Aldous Huxley once observed that the greatest invention of the twentieth century was *speed*. The greatest invention of the twenty-first century may be *velocity* – the acceleration of speed which is made possible through advanced technology.

Nobody should skip lightly over the impact of speed and velocity. Internet-based solutions are only as fast as their slowest link. In a channel sense, in the coming years we will see dramatic improvements in broadband access technology that will provide higher average access speeds from the internet backbones right down to terminal backplanes. But is our internal organisation and culture (see Chapter 9) able to turn access technology into a competitive advantage?

Let me conclude with this thought which integrates DFA, FFR, JIT and intrinsic time. Technology has isolated us from the natural cycles of day, month and year that once governed the pace of our work. Now Internet time opens a window to man-made cycles and with it heralds the collapse of old cultures which are unable to adapt. That is what the new economy is all about.

5. Client base, brand loyalty, and the security challenge

One of the lessons insourcers should learn from recent industrial history is that since the late 1980s matter-of-course client loyalty to a single provider of goods and services is in decline. Both for manufactured goods and for financial and other services, customers increasingly compare and evaluate quality, and price(s) as:

- products and services wanted by the most profitable clients become more complex
- the most important clients look not only at individual items but also for an integrated range of solutions.

Because of this, the dynamic maintenance of account relationships becomes cornerstone to the policies of both clients and providers of products and services – hence to both outsourcers and insourcers. Among financial institutions, for example, investment counsellors able to handle high net worth individuals have become one of the bank's most critical resources.

In banking, to a very substantial extent marketing means relationship management. Able solutions require giving full profit and loss responsibility to the investment officer or the trader doing the sales job. Senior executives and board members should look at the deliverables through the frame of reference shown in Figure 4.4. Organising for relationship management requires:

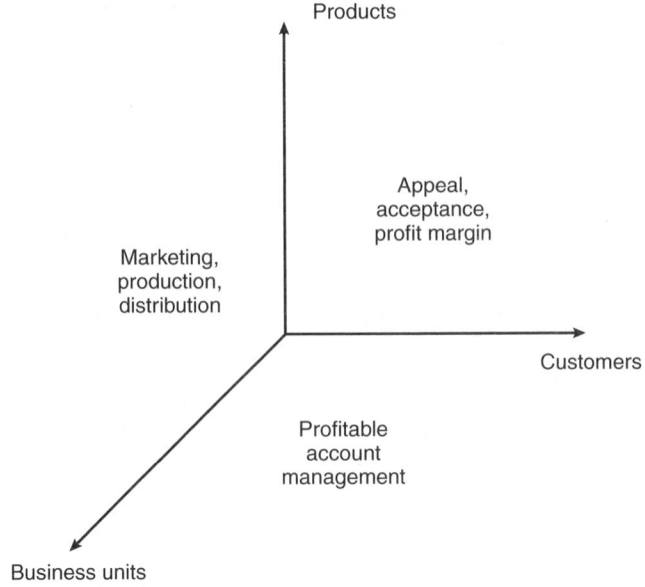

Figure 4.4   Cash flow and profitability evaluation must be seen among three axes of reference

- skills and know-how to handle an increasingly sophisticated customer base
- system solutions capable of mapping all business products and their profitability in real-time
- customer mirror services which assist in evaluating what a customer relationship costs and what the bank gains from it.

Theoretically the Internet provides the online link to the client base, practically it is of limited service to the bank without databases which are fully updated and self-sufficient, able to provide interactively information by profit centre, product, service, and customer relationship. This is rarely understood by old economy companies which have joined the Internet revolution for 'me too' reasons.

Is not brand loyalty enough to keep the customer relationship alive? One of the prevailing concepts at the beginning of internet commerce has been that brand loyalty would be weak. Subsequently, experience gained during the late 1990s has shown that brands are quire important to i-commerce, most likely because they underpin some critical functions in any trade

- building trust among clients
- communicating quality assurance
- helping in lowering search costs.

Against some of the predictions made by experts, internet users continue to turn to recognised brands. Amazon.com and Yahoo, for instance, owe much of their dominance to the strength of their brand name which has proved to have a snowball effect – while, as we saw at the beginning of this section, with brick and mortar outlets brand loyalty has diminished during the last decade. Brand name is important, but it is far from being the whole story.

Headway in Internet commerce comes at a certain cost. Sales promotion is not the only expense associated with it, particularly for those companies which are growing fast. To face an increasing demand for its expanding range of products, Amazon.com has build warehouses coast to coast, so it can buy direct from publishers and eliminate reliance on book wholesalers. The groundwork goes well beyond Internet brands.

Brand loyalty helps as a defence mechanism to bring up the entry price. Early branding turned Amazon.com into a leading firm while newcomers face an uphill struggle. A basic lesson from the experience of the late 1990s, when i-commerce boomed, is that second-stage brand building has become very expensive. Something similar has happened in the early 1980s with PCs, as the entry price of new personal computer firms escalated.

Still another interesting lesson from i-commerce is the amount of advertising and sales promotion needed to maintain the brand in front of the public's eyes. At the same time there is evidence that branding is not that crucial for every product and for every company. After having tried hard to establish a brand on the internet, by early 1999 Ford Motor seems to have a staged a retreat. Jacques A. Nasser, then the company's CEO, dismissed the Procter & Gamble-style approach as inappropriate for Detroit. 'That formula won't work,' said Nasser. 'Cars and trucks are very different from consumer products like toothpaste.'[9]

Enterprise management must appreciate that, like any other market place, online business opportunities require investment decisions which are thoroughly weighted. Board members and senior executives must understand that such investment decisions are no one-tantum affairs but a continuous process subject to steady re-evaluation along the decision cycle shown in Figure 4.5.

A different way of looking at this reference is that i-commerce is by no means a sure way to win leadership in the market. Statistics can be deceiving. While the volume of consumer-based electronic commerce has grown rapidly in some markets, the value of transactions is often low. In fact, i-commerce watchers suggest that for many companies it is too low to justify the heavy costs of establishing and maintaining web sites for transactions.

• The volume of transactions and their value are two quite different things.

Companies which have gained experience in electronic commerce are searching for reasons behind this statement. An evident one is lack of

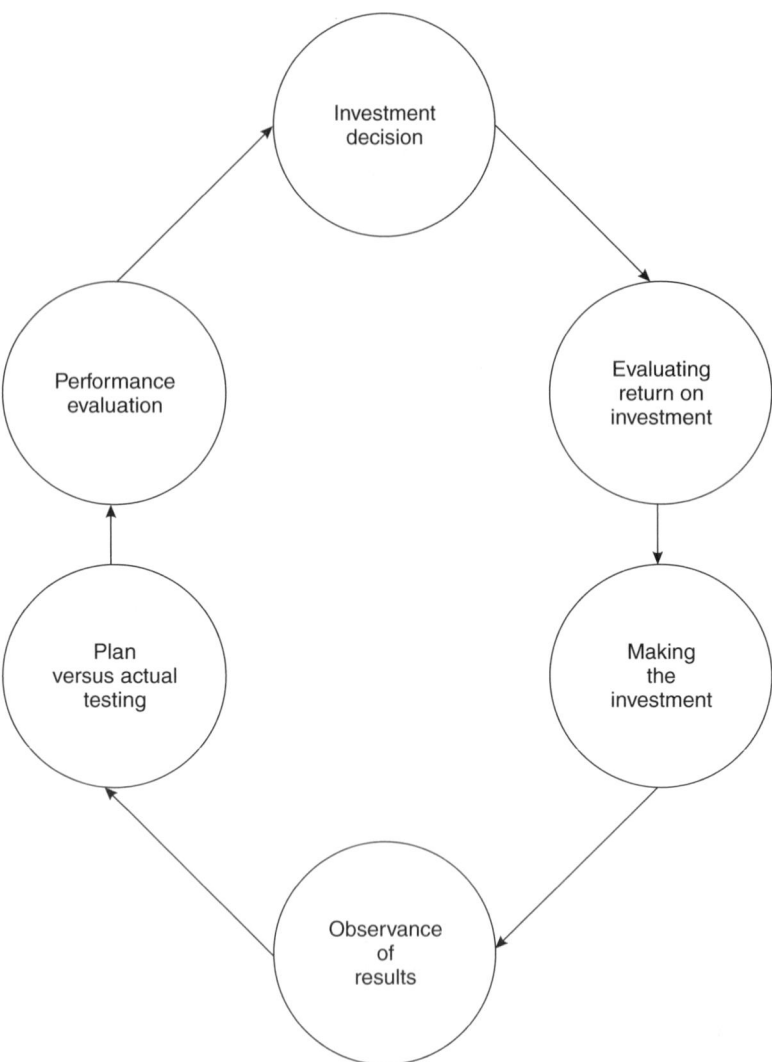

Figure 4.5 Investment decisions are no one tantum event but a continuous process requiring re-evaluation

security, which has been a problem from the beginning and so far it has not been solved in a satisfactory way. Practically every day, events document that without adequate safety mechanisms different malicious schemes can easily mislead even the most cautious reader of information. On 7 April 2000, an anonymous internet site published a bogus story intimating that

PairGain Technologies was about to be acquired for approximately twice its market value.

- that site employed the look and feel of the Bloomberg news service, and
- this artifice made it appear authentic to unsuspecting users.[10]

A message containing a link to the story was simultaneously posted to the Yahoo message board dedicated to PairGain. The link referred to the phoney site by its numerical IP address rather than by name, and thus obscured its true identity. As a result, many readers were convinced by the Bloomberg look and feel, and accepted the story at face value despite its suspicious address.

The result has been a hole in the pocket book of investors. PairGain stock first jumped 31 per cent, and then fell dramatically, incurring severe losses to people who thought they discovered a great opportunity. This hoax has been controlled rather promptly, but others linger on. The use of the Internet technologies may make such attacks to public confidence elusive, with the result being a severe financial aftermath.

Neither are technologies heralded as the solution to online security risks the 'sure thing'. Take the chip-in-card as an example. In March 2002, Canal + , the French pay-TV network, charged that its key rival NDS Group hired hackers to break the supposedly uncrackable code on its smart card and then put the secret on the Web. NDS denied that claim, but Canal + said that it suffered a $1 billion loss in a $4.1 annual business.[11]

6. The management of technology requires clear objectives and lots of know-how

What outsourcing may offer a company is the know-how, but as the title of this section states though necessary this is not enough. When building a strategic information system, or an internet commerce solution, we must address both the needs of our people and those of customers in the market we are after. Logically this requires an improved system for party-to-party communications and time management (see section 3).

Many companies adopt the internet out of a 'me too' attitude, but only the best see to it that for their own people, their clients and other business partners administrative chores and trivia are weeded out of their jobs thanks to their online interaction. Outsourcers and insourcers should appreciate that the changeover from current paper-based practices to a new interactive system is never easy. Sometimes this job is like trying to change the tires on a moving car.

- Winners do not put on the internet their old paper-based systems and procedures, or their legacy data processing.

- Losers do precisely that, and they end by repeat the same mistakes faster and at a much higher cost, in spite of all the money they spend on technology and on outsourcing.

In 2001, the MIT Sloan School of Management and Arthur Andersen launched a five-year, $10-million research program to advance understanding of the sources of economic and social value in the new economy. Known as the New Economy Value Research Lab, this program addressed globalisation, electronic commerce and Internet technology, aiming to perform rigorous corporate and academic research to determine the new rules in business and industry. The project concentrated in four domains:

1 how businesses are investing in different assets to create economic value
2 how financial markets evaluate the prospects of companies in the new economy
3 what constitutes prudent risk management in today's changing business environment
4 what's the best performance measurement and financial reporting of assets and liabilities.

The common background of these four bullets is the management of change. This matters greatly in forward-looking insourcing and outsourcing contracts, as well as in the implementation of technology. All four bullets are a direct responsibility of a company's board and CEO, because they are at the heart of both the rise of technological entrepreneurism and the changing relationship between the provider of services and his clients.

The chief executive officer and his immediate assistants must appreciate that companies which read the future are keen to capitalise on the relationship between technology strategy and performance in insourcing/outsourcing agreements. To do so successfully, they define the new skill their managers need to acquire within the framework of the strategic aspects of technology, learning from industry leaders about changing patterns of innovation. These include a wide array of issues:

- from the way we understand the process of innovation and its market impact in a market-wide sense
- to internal organisation, structure, and staffing strategy, as well as the means for planning and control.

Tier-1 companies are always keen to link their technology strategy to their overall corporate strategy, relate technology to markets and customers, and place emphasis on agile implementation. For return on investment reasons (see Chapter 4), they evaluate their technological effectiveness but also move products and services to market at fast pace.

Regulated environment

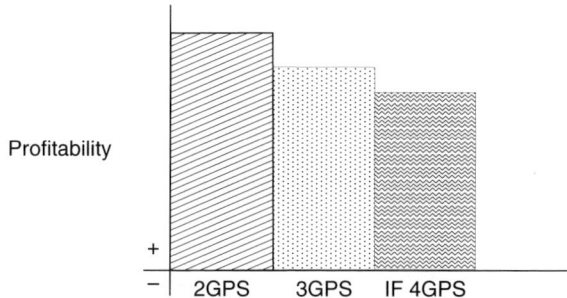

Non-regulated environment: if we are first in market

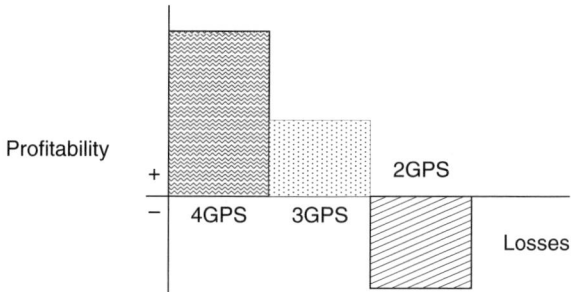

Non-regulated environment: if competition is first in market

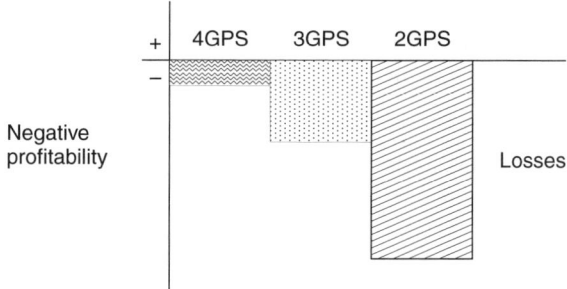

Figure 4.6   Product profitability and sophistication of information system solution

In the late 1980s Bank of America did a fundamental study on cost and return with financial products related to the level and sophistication of technology used by a credit institutions uses. The results of this study are still valid and they are shown in Figure 4.6. Three generations of products and services (GPS) were considered.

1   The first generation (1GPS) was largely manual and therefore they are no more of relevance.
2   The second (2GPS) have been mainframe-based, batch-oriented legacy approaches.
3   3GPS was client-server oriented, operating in real-enough time, but void of knowledge engineering artefacts.
4   By contrast, 4GPS have been characterised by an integrative system solution, with agents and sophisticated software – the best available at the time this study was made.[12]

The pattern in Figure 6 is self-explanatory, therefore it does not need much discussion. The Bank of America analysts differentiated between a regulated and a deregulated environment. In a regulated environment 2GPS solutions were a little more profitable, because 3GPS cost more money. But this turns on its head *if* the bank operates in a deregulated environment, where:

• profitability is significant with 4GPS solutions. It is acceptable with 3GPS, while 2GPS is a loser.

Notice however that this is valid *if* the bank is first in the market with new products and services. If not:

• with 4GPS it might still break even or lose only a little money; losses are bigger with 3GP, and they become a torrent with 2GPS.

I bring this study and the facts behind it to the reader's attention because, as I found in my research, many companies go for outsourcing without appropriate analysis of what they want to attain and without examining the level of technology used by the insourcer(s). This way, they move backwards rather than forwards, while they pay lots of money. A specific case comes to my mind where:

• the outsourcer had 3GPS technology, and
• the 'chosen' insourcer had medieval 2GS technology.

Besides the level of technology, it is absolutely important to assure that the solution we choose fits *our* company's strategic plan. Take as an example how Schwab targeted Swiss investors. Charles Schwab is the biggest Internet stockbroker and has no physical presence in Switzerland. Its strategic solution has been a big media campaign to persuade Swiss retail investors of the advantages of its online services, particularly in fees.[13]

• The fee for a US equity deal is $29.95.
• The fee on UK equities is still cheaper, $23.

If a client buys 1,000 shares of Microsoft at approximately $90 a share, Schwab charges a flat $29.95 for online and $39.95 for telephone dealing compared to a $1,500 per transaction charged by the typical Swiss financial institution. Schwab can afford to do this because it is organised in a way that it can survive:

- its costs are low
- its technology is high.

With such discrepancy in terms of fees, Swiss brokers must fight to keep control of their clients. In April 1999 Credit Suisse launched 'Youtrade', an internet trading service for Swiss securities, making the forecast that by 2005 a quarter of all private securities transactions on the Swiss exchange would be executed online.

The problem the typical broker faces is that he does not have the culture and expertise Schwab has with internet investing (see section 7 on the hype about websites). Schwab capitalises on its experience with 2.5 million customers with online accounts in America. The company executes an average of 100,000 to 110,000 trades a day, which is more than the total number of trades on the London and Frankfurt stock exchanges.

7. Understanding and avoiding the common hype about websites

Whether the internet connection is designed by our people or the work connected to it is outsourced, it is wrong to think that developing an website is something done once in a lifetime. Or, that what we have accomplished would remain invariant over a long stretch of time. Indeed, this idea of permanence, which is widespread, is the first among a dozen of popular hypes about websites.

The second hype is that websites are inexpensive and operating costs are trivial. Nothing more untrue. As practically all companies which set up shop for i-commerce have found out, there are both start-up costs and operational costs – so much internal as external – and many of these costs are not to be recovered. The third most common hype is that websites can be set up and dismantled quickly. This might be the case only when the company has plenty of direct experience, which is not the typical.

Don't ever believe software vendors who advertise their wares as 'so easy' to install on the Web that one practically needs no prior experience. Don't go for the fourth hype, either: 'If you set up a website you are *always* ahead of your competitors'. 'Always' is the overstatement of the internet age. If you are not very careful with what you do, you can lose big money with websites. And because technology moves fast, you have to steadily watch what your competitors are doing, otherwise you fall behind.

The reasons why these first four items came up as internet commerce hype can be found at the origins of online transactions. Computer products has been the number 1 item in purchasing on the Web. By exploiting this business opportunity Dell Computer has turned itself into one of the top five personal computer companies in the world. But it has not been that easy, and the fact is that Dell concentrated on a dual channel:

1 sales over the net, and
2 sales by telephone.

The success of Dell attracted many imitators, not only among PC firms. April 1998 was a milestone as Dell passed the cap of generating more than $4 million a day from its website. This was important to the company because it represented a 400 per cent increase over the amount it sold on the Internet in April 1997. It also caught the eye of many other manufacturing and merchandising firms.

Few companies have really bothered to investigate cost and return with i-commerce, evaluate the kind of products which move faster, or analyse what it takes to establish a first class website. This has been a management failure rather than one due to lack of documentation. For instance, while computer products have been number 1, the number 2 most popular item in internet sales is books. Amazon.com is the first online book seller, but it has still to turn a profit. For a couple of years its stock price was propelled by the fact that millions of internet users visited its online book store, and thousands of investors hope to make a quick buck. When these hopes were found to be unfounded, the stock tanked.

The fifth hype is that once you set up a website you don't need to tackle it again. Nobody can accuse Amazon or Schwab for not knowing how to manage their websites, because they appreciate that if an early mover gets everything right: website, order fulfilment, distribution, payments – *and* cares about steady upkeep – newcomers would find it much harder to knock it off. But *if*, by contrast, the website is poorly designed, choice is minimal and delivery uncertain, then the downturn would be faster than in the physical world. The sixth hype about websites is that most customers needs are served from a single outlet. This is not true for at least two basic reasons.

1 The way to bet is that (other things equal), the most appealing websites are specialised.
2 Business units care for their bottom line, hence they are reluctant to share costs they don't control.

The seventh hype is that websites are located easily and you don't need to do a business-specific versus portal choice. Easy locating is a myth, particularly when one uses different search engines by business unit. For example, Yahoo!, AltaVista, Lycos. Bridging the gap of different engines is important because there is synergy in using the Web for sales. The marketing of autos provides a good example. Two companies, Microsoft's Carpoint and Auto-by-tel, dominate car sales. And both are important in providing customers with fairly detailed information about vehicles they might want to purchase.

- Evidence shows online research is the first step towards becoming an online shopper.
- The influence of information provision on internet retailing increases in importance.

The careful reader would want to keep in mind that rewards will not come just as a matter of course, and this brings up the need to be aware about the eight common hype: 'You don't need an architecture for website(s).' Exactly the inverse is true. Architecturing is a 'must'. As an example, Figure 4.7 provides the processing cycle from internet to private network and payment chores. The ninth hype in connection to the cyberspace goes like this: 'Websites can be scaled and changed fast.' Scaling is of course possible but its flexibility diminishes with greater security, complexity, and design parameters beyond the initial small set.

The tenth frequently heard hype with websites is that one can depend on customers to provide feedback leading to a new design. Companies which have believed this have been deceived. Those best managed now appreciate that they must have an R&D budget for i-commerce, and they should do

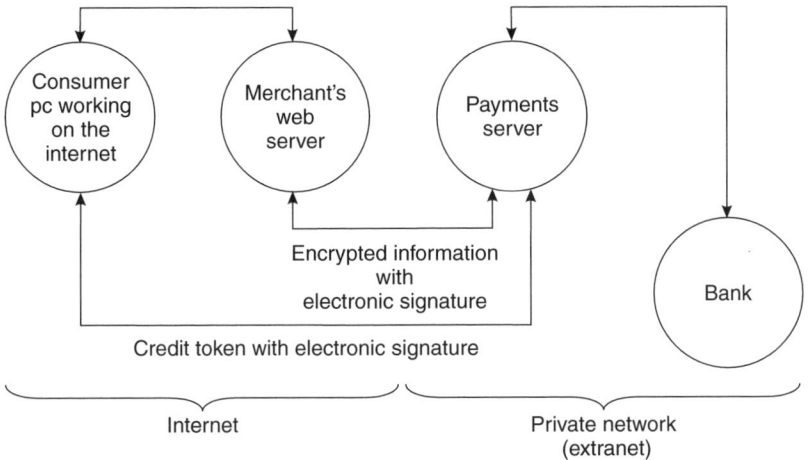

Figure 4.7   Payments processing cycle involving Internet and private network

their own development work. This being said, market feedback is important and it can also be thought-provoking. The point I am making is that after pursuing the customers comments, we should be doing some original research and development which permits us to:

- better respond to market drives
- optimise the way we use of technology.

Another widely held misconception is that i-commerce is somehow immune to the need for management control. Many people, including some experts say, 'There is no reason to audit websites'. That's plain nonsense. There is plenty of reason for doing so; every business must be audited. Most evidently, this is true of all outsourcing projects.

Finally, the twelfth hype I have encountered with internet commerce has a great deal to do with a large number of failures in outsourcing. It is based on the wrong premise that there is no need to back-up websites. This is too near-sighted for my taste. Reliable back-up should always be provided; it is part of the responsibility of managing websites – and outsourcing agreements.

Part II

What's the Value Differentiation with Outsourcing and Insourcing?

5
Being in Charge of Outsourcing Agreements

1. Introduction

The problem is not one of being for or against outsourcing or insourcing. This is a pseudoproblem. The real issue is how to establish the proper conditions which will permit one to be successful with outsourcing and insourcing projects, if it is decided to follow that strategy. The study of these conditions and subsequent implementation has a great deal to do with:

- technical planning
- management control.

It will be a false assumption to believe that problems connected to deficiencies in human skill at the outsourcer's side will be solved through farming out projects. Human resources are vital to every company and the resolution of personnel problems cannot be handled by farming out the responsibility for them.

- *If* an enterprise does not get the best people at the bottom of its management pyramid
- *then* some years down the line it is not going to find them at the top, no matter how much outsourcing it might be doing.

The acquisition and development of human resources is a very serious business and it must be handled in a careful manner. A study at MIT came to the conclusion that the difference between hiring the best person and hiring an average person can be a factor of 50-to-1. The best person will:

- have a polyvalent background
- be innovative and imaginative
- challenge the obvious

- be flexible and adjustable
- have a deep sense of planning and control.

What is true of human resources is also valid in connection to outsourcing agreements. Effective plans must be done and these require perspective and experience. Harry Truman once said: 'You can always amend a big plan, you can never expand a little one', and Dwight Eisenhower was to add: 'The plan is nothing. *Planning* is everything.'

Both outsourcing and insourcing need a considerable amount of planning. The evidence provided through my research is that the aftermath of failing to do proper analysis for outsourcing can range from significant difficulties to disaster. I press this point because very frequently companies going for outsourcing have not done the study and analysis they need to:

- get a fair amount of dissent
- develop alternatives
- examine the possible pitfalls.

Without criticizing anybody, here is a list of what can happen with the insourcer: Laws and regulations are not properly observed, there is conflict of interest, a cultural clash develops between outsourcer and insourcer, while inflexible contracts limit business strategy and handicap changes in objectives which may become necessary. The four top problems with outsourcing that I have identified are:

1 cultural

leading to agency costs and subutilisation of resources provided by the insourcer;

2 technical update

– technology moves fast, and so does obsolescence in skills, software, hardware and systems solutions;

3 wanting methodology

and its alter ego, conflicting methodologies, because of heterogeneity in systems, methods, tools and languages between outsourcer and insourcer;

4 lack of quality control criteria

– these should be both quantitative and qualitative – and they should be contractually defined between the counterparties.

Added to these pitfalls is the fact that loss of control of key resources leads to ineffective management at the outsourcer's side. Also, benefits, like tax advantages can be miscalculated and this increases the original estimate of outsourcing costs.

2. Satisfaction and dissatisfaction with outsourcing agreements

Let's start with the premise that projections made without a factual and documented study to substantiate them, are nothing more than theories destined to bite the dust. When the appropriate planning and control functions are not in place, promised improvements in service and performance are not delivered, speed to market and shorter development cycles become an illusion, and personnel problems increase rather than being eliminated.

Without focused project planning a windfall of contract termination problems hits both firms – outsourcer and insourcer – and there may be legal action due to reputation damage. Particularly in connection to human resources, there is loss of inhouse expertise that took a significant time to build. These are some of the problems companies need to appreciate *before* entering into an outsourcing agreement.

Quite often senior management does not pay proper attention to the importance of understanding what it is getting into with some of its business partners. This particularly happens in a rush to find 'any solution' without taking the time to examine its aftermath. Yet, a basic management principle is never to delegate something you don't understand *and* control. Outsourcing is a form of delegation. Because the proper preparatory work is lacking, it is not surprising that

- on average, statistics indicate that about 40 per cent of companies outsourcing IT are dissatisfied with the service
- the peak of dissatisfaction can be as high as 70 per cent, according to the opinion of cognisant executives who contributed to my research.

These same executives pointed out that it is particularly difficult is to fine-tune the work done by partnerships and 50–50 joint ventures. A partnership can be successful only when the partners are perfectly clear about the goals to be met, who drives the common entity, and who is responsible for:

- deliverables
- timetables
- expected quality
- outsourcing/insourcing costs.

Deliverables should not be outlined just in general terms. Operational risk (see Chapter 3) is the result of failing to properly analyse and description of deliverables expected from outsourcing. It is not always recognized that if management does not get a fair amount of dissent, the result is in inability to examine the possible pitfalls and therefore to describe what should truly characterise the quality of deliverables.

As these paragraphs document, planning for an outsourcing agreement is not too different from planning for any other project. The principle is: what is worth doing should be done well. As with any project, there is plenty of need for preparatory work, as well as for critical questions to be asked and answered.

- What do we expect to gain from this contract?
- Where are we *now* in terms of services to be outsourced?
- Where we want to be through outsourcing?
- Which conditions will bring us from 'here' to 'there'?

Going from 'here' to 'there' means that we must keep the transition taking place in control. We should also develop contingency plans and exit strategies. Contracts are not forever. One day they end; sometimes they end abruptly creating legal risk but even if they end smoothly this means still another transition.

To answer the queries outlined in the four bullets in factual and documented manner, as I have already mentioned, we must establish clear goals and objectives, evaluate risks and benefits from outsourcing, as well as review and analyse strengths and weaknesses of existing operations. Also, our expectations must be realistic, and we should never outsource for the wrong reasons.

It is self-evident that we should choose the right business partner. This is the more important as the best way to look at outsourcing is as a long term partnership. Relationships have to be worked out, including shared vision and goals. An open and honest attitude is most essential, including sharing the rewards. Optimism about the outcome must be tempered with the reality of deliverables. Other things equal, these will be more satisfactory:

- *if* there is an end-to-end evaluation of objectives and contractual clauses
- *if* functionality, quality, cost and timeliness are contractually guaranteed.

Long-term partnerships should have a long-term governance structure, including the possibility of evolving the terms of the agreement as the market evolves and adaptation becomes necessary. Chances are a dynamic market will make the original outsourcing terms obsolete. The management of change is an indispensable ingredient of modern business, as underlined in Chapter 4.

A sound strategy for both the outsourcer and the insourcer is to make sure that they base their relationship on the four pillars for growth and survival in an environment of high competition, visualized in Figure 5.1. Insourcers

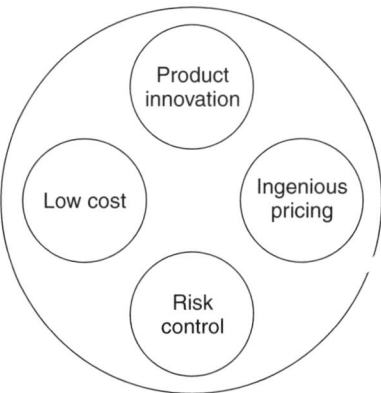

Figure 5.1 Pillars of a strategy for growth and survival in an environment of high competition

should appreciate that, unless they have a truly unique product, the market for their services will be steadily under pressure by competitors.

The best policy for outsourcers is to never let go their stride for greater efficiency. A good part of what they gain through productivity they should offer it to their clients through lower cost, better quality or both. Both parties must make a clear effort to avoid the wrong premises which are sometimes wishful thinking. Here are three examples of wrong premises.

- Fundamental to any outsourcing project is the *transfer of control* because the outsourcer/insourcer relationship is like a blank cheque.
- The outsourcing organization transfers the *ownership* of a business process to external supplier(s).
- The outsourcer does not instruct the insourcer on *how to perform*; he or she only communicate what they wants to buy.

Outsourcing often fails to deliver because of a number of reasons which have their origin in what was stated by these bullets. Neither is it true that the outsourcer can abdicate his responsibilities even if he wanted to do so. An example is to believe that IT outsourcing takes care not only of technology but also of re-engineering the internal systems and procedures or other of the outsourcer.

One of the often encountered pitfalls is the failure of assessing the potential impact of outsourcing and, along with it the baseline measures; the latter may not even be understood. Another reason is that all aspects pertaining to confidentiality and feasibility have not been outlined, let alone confirmed. In short, the outsourcer is not clear about what they are really seeking in terms of service. Instead, they let the insourcer's interests decide for him.

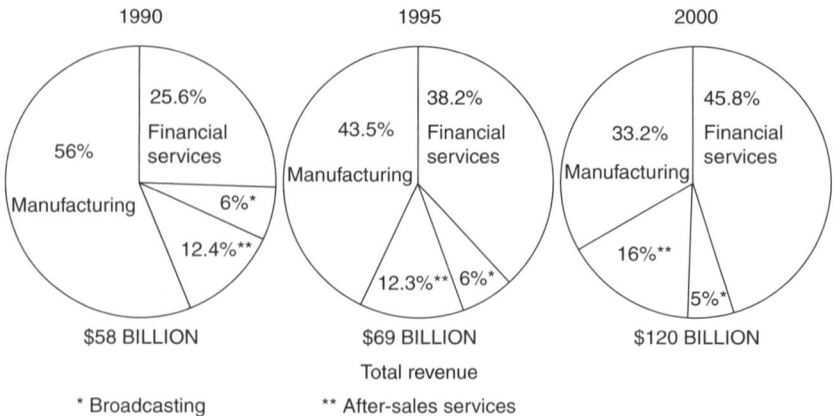

Figure 5.2   General Electric's transformation in ten years

One of the most frequent failures cognizant people in the industry brought to my attention is the tendency by outsourcers to believe that lack of a clear definition of what is 'success' and what is 'failure' is all right for some or all of the contracted projects. Or that insourcer(s) will take care of all security issues connected to outsourced services.

Ill-defined deliverables, mismatch of expectations between insourcer and outsourcer, inadequate service level agreements (see section 5) are characteristic of companies which fail to adapt their business. How dramatic can be the change required for adaptation, particularly among well-managed companies is seen in Figure 5.2. Within ten years General Electric has reinvented itself twice. Static business plans and static outsourcing deals crumble.

3. Evaluating benefits and selecting contractual norms

An English recipe about cooking rabbits advises, 'First, catch the rabbit.' In outsourcing terms, this translates into identify credible suppliers who can be reliable, long-term insourcers. Several critical references characterize this evaluation, not the least among them being the survivability of the insourcer. Other key criteria directly concern *our* organization and the preparatory work we have done.

- Have we tied our outsourcing strategy to our business strategy before considering farming out work?
- Is there commitment to outsourcing in our board and senior management?
- Do the suppliers we are examining know the business *we* are in?
- Do these insourcers have a suitable operating model and first-class support?
- Are the cultures of these insourcers compatible with our own culture?

Another basic query is whether a contemplated outsourcing agreement can exploit open architectural perspectives as well as the benefits of standardization which prevail in the industry, and our internal norms. Theoretically standardization and customization of the outsourced application may seem to contradict each other. In reality, if the project is well structured, they are more complementary than might seem at first glance.

This duality of standardization and customization bring up some other basic queries. Do the insourcers have the capacity and skills for a re-engineering programme? (see Chapter 13). Are they willing and able to help our people in re-engineering? Do the insourcers have a cost control culture? What has been their past experience with the governance of outsourcing programs for their other clients? Do they really care about:

- sharing responsibility
- maintaining focus on objective(s)
- steadily monitoring timeliness and quality of deliverables?

The results of my research document that, in a properly run outsourcer/insourcer relationship, the governance structure is not an afterthought but a very important upfront issue. It is most critical to identify project dependencies, even to discuss them with regulators if their nature touches existing rules and compliance requirements.

- Roles and responsibilities must be analysed from the start.
- Financial and operational matters must be detailed and approved by the board.

Another crucial issue is a plan outlining the migration strategy connected to outsourcing, human resources agreements, as well as precise functional roles and responsibilities. Successful outsourcing projects typically establish upfront the risks and liabilities, connecting them to project dependencies and obligations assumed by the counterparties. I would definitely include in this reference quality inspection, arrangements for auditing, and a change management mechanism.

The nature of the two companies (outsourcer, insourcer) and the type of agreement may dictate further conditions. One of the reasons senior management involvement in outsourcing is vital, is that industry-type joint ventures need to manage unit costs. The problem with outsourcing among credit institutions is that many banks are not tooled for unit costs.

- They are not even in a position to appropriately measure start-up costs.
- This ensures that many outsourcing projects are not supported through analytical accounting.

At the same time, the competitive nature of peer-to-peer outsourcing agreements and joint ventures makes people defensive, and lack of first class management running the common effort aggravates this problem. The fact is that most entities tend to assign second level people to the partnership. Another problem is that the partners don't always agree on choice of priorities, even if they have the same list of goals.

For all these reasons, outsourcing should be part of an end-to-end operating model – not a one-off discharge of responsibilities. This makes so much more important the case of regular business contingency testing, and it underlines the importance of change management which should be brought as a early as possible to everybody's attention in both the outsourcer and the insourcer organization, not way down in the cycle.

The above problems are not eased by the fact that there are no standard formats for outsourcing agreements currently available. Indeed, given the large diversity of these contracts I doubt they will be contractual norms in the near future. Outsourcers, however, have every advantage to develop an inhouse format to be observed by every department, in every area of operations. An example is given in Figure 5.3 (see also section 5 on service level agreements).

Even if the insourcer subcontracts to many firms and has his own sort of contract, the outsourcer should require that *his* clauses prevail. These clauses should be both introvert and extrovert, paying attention to the fact that the practice of subcontracting can lead to wanting quality, delays, and other failures. Half-baked outsourcing agreements are at the origin of many pitfalls because they make control by the outsourcer both complex and remote.

Therefore, it is necessary to clearly establish responsibilities and put in place a robust control structure. Both an operational discipline and performance metrics must be in place. The outsourcer occurs greater risks if this discipline is weak or deficient. Keep in mind also that:

- no two outsourcers have the same time pressure or act according to the same requirements in terms of servicers they are after
- no reputable outsourcer would buy an insourcer's technology services that are at the end of their life-cycle (see Chapter 8).

Price negotiations are another major issue. They trim the insourcer's baseline, but they are important to the outsourcer because in a highly competitive market his own profit margins tend to drop. In brokerage, for example,

- clients want volume discount and execution guarantees
- brokers are forced to rationalize and use lower-cost execution channels.

Brokerage houses, and other financial institutions, which are in control of their market and of their costs, only deal with the most sophisticated

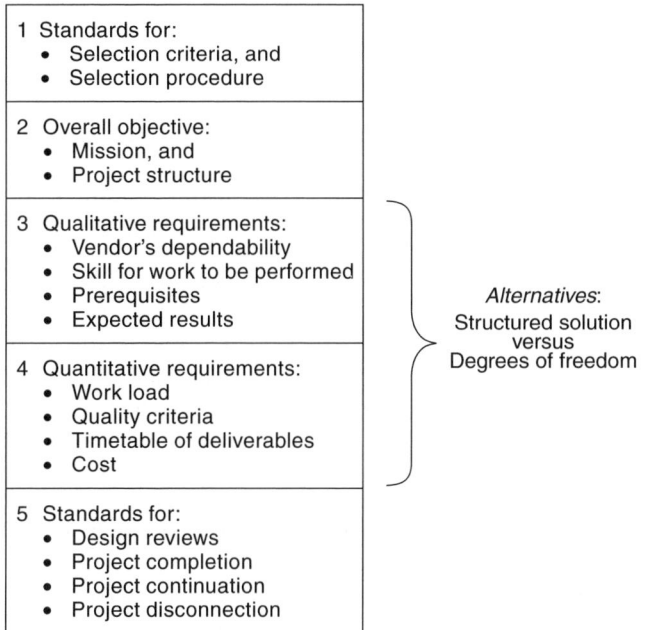

1 Standards for:
  • Selection criteria, and
  • Selection procedure

2 Overall objective:
  • Mission, and
  • Project structure

3 Qualitative requirements:
  • Vendor's dependability
  • Skill for work to be performed
  • Prerequisites
  • Expected results

4 Quantitative requirements:
  • Work load
  • Quality criteria
  • Timetable of deliverables
  • Cost

5 Standards for:
  • Design reviews
  • Project completion
  • Project continuation
  • Project disconnection

Alternatives:
Structured solution
versus
Degrees of freedom

Figure 5.3 A methodology to guide the outsourcer's hand in developing norms for agreements with insourcers

suppliers and they want solutions not just a bare-bone service. If they don't obtain these advantages they don't outsource. An one broker put it: 'We might pursue an outsourcing policy for supply chain integration but there really aren't currently any suppliers who know the business as well as we.'

Finally, in a number of outsourcing deals projected savings have nothing to do with reality. A specific case which comes to my mind from the early 1990s is that of a plan made for a seven-year outsourcing project. It suggested savings of $300 million over that time-frame, and an outsourcing agreement was signed based on that premise. Post-mortem it was found that the failure to account for migration costs saved $150 million from that initial estimate, and budget overruns ended by producing a $200 million loss rather than leaving $300 million in profits.

All of the issues discussed in this section outline the need for a systematic partner selection: They also explain why some peer-to-peer agreements don't succeed. Two or three entities an insourcer found as clients may have differing priorities as well as design characteristics with respect to the solution they are after. They may feature contrasting operating styles and culture, involve a number of miscalculation, and also lack explicit commitment by the people involved in the deal.

4. Potential efficiencies and inefficiencies with outsourcing

As a general rule, outsourcing projects are relatively complex transactions which can lead to potential efficiencies but also inefficiencies. To appreciate what these efficiencies and inefficiencies might be, it is proper to remember the reason(s) behind interest in outsourcing. One of them is new business initiatives which have put pressure on a company and altered its environment. Another is uncertainty on whether or not outsourcing is a good idea to start with. Take as an example an article in *BusinessWeek* about the Japanese Matsushita Group. At first it says that Matsushita's advantage is that it makes itself many of the key components which it needs for its end products: optical pickups, system chips, and displays. It does *not* outsource them. The implication is that full inhouse production is a competitive advantage. Then, as the article goes on, the tone changes. Reference is made to financial analysts who 'want (Kunio) Nakamura [Matsushita's president] to fold money-losing JVC into the parent. They (the analysts) say he also should boost outsourcing and shift more work to low-cost China.'[1] Here, the implication is that doing almost everything inhouse is not really a brilliant strategy.

Flexible strategic partnerships, particularly if they guarantee rapid implementation, fall somewhere in-between doing everything inhouse and old-style outsourcing. Strategic partnerships, however, can have a downside. An example is IBM's outsourcing of the operating system for its personal computer (PC). Getting the disk operating system (DOS) from Microsoft – which was then a start-up – made the mainframer's PC immediately available to the market. It would have taken IBM one to two years just to do the kernel of a DOS. Outsourcing saw to it that:

- IBM brought out the PC in a timely manner and, by so doing, it created a new era in computing
- but the outsourcing contract did not seem to have been thoroughly studied, with the result to make Microsoft IBM's number 1 competitor in IT.

Eventually Microsoft overtook IBM in capitalization and every other software company in market share. The lesson to be learned from this case is that *if* strategic services have to be outsourced, *then* this should be done after a very careful analysis and only on a temporary basis to gain time, with technology transfer attached to it. Responsibility should never be relegated.

I particularly underline these issues because under the heading Business Process Operations (BPO) come now processes which remind me quite a bit of the IBM/Microsoft example. For instance, some insourcers advise their clients to wholesale transfer their business processes as well as the control over them to their supplier. This is *too irresponsible* and has to be avoided at all cost. A company must be in charge of its outsourcing agreement(s), as we will see in Chapter 7 with reference to Toyota.

Being in charge of the outsourcing agreement(s) does not necessarily mean that one does not trust the insourcing partner. Otherwise the out-source should not have selected him as a supplier of products or services. What it means is the need to stay in control, exercise responsibility and account for the fact that some key variables affecting the agreement steadily change. For example:

- track record and commitment
- experience and special skills
- financial strength and survivability.

In the last analysis, the board and senior management of the outsourcer organization are directly accountable for results. These include the out-sourcer's product quality infrastructure; and personnel; rigorousness of pro-posed implementation plan; flexibility in accommodating the outsourcer's specific needs; and the availability of security guarantees. Other require-ments for which the responsibility of board members and of the outsourcer's CEO cannot be delegated are:

- evaluating the staying power of the insourcer(s)
- examining their technology and skills
- comparing inhouse versus outsourcing costs
- establishing metrics, measures and monitoring activities necessary to control the outsourcing relationship(s)
- providing for continuity in the outsourced project(s).

Management does not always appreciate that there is nothing worse than stop/go with outsourcing projects. An example is given in Figure 5.4. The IT project in the background of this figure started at time A and it was supposed to be completed at C. After a significant amount of work was done, it was interrupted at time B because some of the issues which should have been originally settled at the negotiating table, and were not, led to friction and to wanting deliverables.

This project never reached point C of total transfer of the outsourcer's IT functions to the insourcer. Both the insourcer and the outsourcer were, however, committed to go ahead. After renewed negotiations, this project was restarted at time D – at a higher cost. The second plan called for completion at time E at a cost shown in Figure 5.4 and was completed at E but at a significantly higher cost (E´, just note difference).

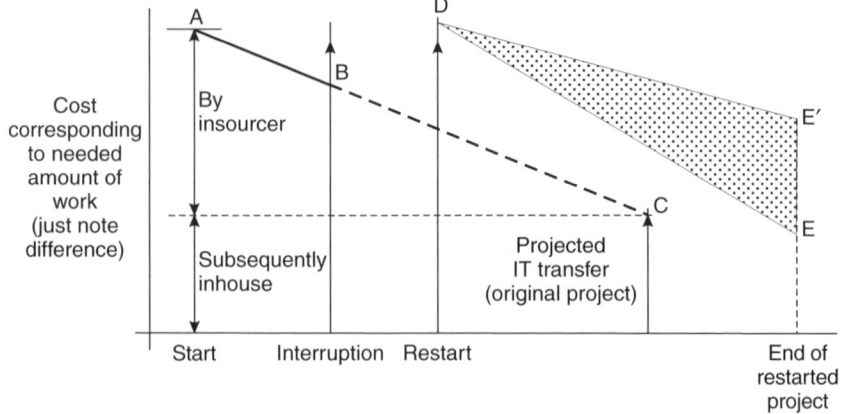

Figure 5.4   There is nothing worse than stop/go with outsourcing projects

In this example there has been a single insourcer of all the IT functions of the outsourcer firm. In other cases outsourcing needs are not met by a single provider. Dealing with a group of insourcers for services which correlate with only another and/or are using the same information elements, can be a tricky business which ends up in lots of headaches and a complex pattern of relationships. My experience with triangular arrangements is not positive. They often open the road to legal risk, particularly when:

• there are service failures
• it is difficult to identify the responsible party.

Legal risk is an important consideration. When we look at basic principles regarding outsourcing we see that in the longer term there is a clear distinction between good and bad contracts, just as there is a distinction between valid and invalid management. Good outsourcing contracts are typically connected to:

• sound strategic plans
• well-defined analytical processes
• evaluation decisions which consider risk, cost and return.

The risk assumed with outsourcing, including legal risk, should never be taken lightly. Not long ago, Michael Foot of the Financial Services Authority (FSA) expressed some concerns about the financial industry's drive to outsourcing and its possible aftermath. Because of these concerns, FSA's most recent proposals for regulation of outsourcing activities embrace:

- each company's general obligations
- requirements for entities entering into outsourcing
- the contract with the service provider (see section 5 on Service Level Agreements).

There are plenty of activities which should be taken care through a prerequisite study and settled at the negotiation table. However, many are left on the backburner like contingency, confidentiality and subcontracting. Others are core to the management of every financial institution. However tempting may be to outsource them, a bank can never outsource its internal audit and compliance functions.

FSA aptly says that credit institutions and other entities under its authority must be concerned with every aspect of outsourcing, and make sure that all details which can impact arrangements with the insourcer(s) have been worked out. Senior management should always remember the entity's business objectives. One of the basic goals is to steer away from reputational risk. With outsourcing, reputational risk can arise from all sorts of reasons, a frequent one being mismanaged outsourcing practices and poor definition of the responsibilities assumed by each party.

5. Service level agreements with insourcers

Every outsourcer–insourcer business relationship must be regulated through a thoroughly studied, legally valid and functionally explicit Service Level Agreement (SLA). When starting with the practice of outsourcing, a good way to approach planning and control connected to a service level agreement, is to look at other companies in one's industry branch and see what they have done. Most particularly what kind of *problems* they had. This is a policy which has been successfully followed with the Manhattan Project selecting the companies which acted as contractors.

At the Manhattan Project, of Second World War fame, the scientists responsible for quality assurance did not start evaluating the counterparties at the president's office. They went to the back alleys of the factory, emptied the garbage bins and examined the produce that has been rejected. In a similar manner, when visiting other companies to learn about their outsourcing experience, some of the key questions the managers responsible for this mission should ask are:

- Which specific problems have presented themselves?
- How often these problems came up? How were they resolved?
- Did you lose control, at some time, of the outsourced service?
- Which factors see to it that the insourcer relation degenerates?
- Which corrective measures were taken? What has been the result?

These questions, and the answers to them, are important no matter the exact nature of the outsourcer, whether this company is a business process outsourcing (BPO) entity, business service provider (BSP), or application service provider (ASP), the way they have been identified in Chapter 1.

Typically, a business process outsourcing entity acts as an insurer who takes over technology and staff and operates a dedicated site that might migrate to an enterprise solution. Examples are State Street/Merrill Lynch, Northern Trust/KBC (NatWest), and JP Morgan/Schroder. Schroder, for example, uses several insourcers. In late 2001, Schroder Investment Management has adopted the Global Fund Administration System (GFAS) from Mutual Fund Technologies (MFT), a subsidiary of Fidelity Investments. This service was developed for Fidelity itself, and it was launched as a commercial offering in 1998.

Chances are in a BSP relationship the clauses will not be precisely the same because a business service provider is a different entity than the BPO. As an insourcer, it focuses on providing technology and infrastructure, and may or may not source staff from the client. An example is the HSBC/Gartmore agreement. The object of a BSP does not need to be only information technology. Asset management is a type of BSP outsourcing.

The application service provider is the more classical third party, such a service bureau or software company that branched more aggressively into insourcing. Typically, it provides enterprise technology managed from its own computer center(s). Small companies have been farming out their IT to service bureaus since the beginning of the computer age, because mainframes were so expensive. Then in the 1970s and 1980s with minis and PCs many brought their IT back inhouse.

A thoroughly research and analysed service level agreement is absolutely necessary whether we talk of BPO, BSP or ASP outsourcing/insourcing relationships. It may well be that a BPO or BSP is our company's business partner in other activities. This does not wave the need for a well studied, legally bullet-proof service contract. Here is an example on what can go wrong. In early December 2001, Merrill Lynch and Unilever's pension fund settled out of court in a £130 million ($182 million) law suit.

- Unilever had sued Merrill Lynch for negligent management of its pension money.
- Merrill Lynch offered £70 million ($100 million) to settle the case.

To keep legal risk to a minimum, service level agreements must be factual, documented and precise. Because service failures can happen the SLA should specify – among other issues – that the outsourcer's auditors have the right to examine all documents and staff of the insourcer relating to the provision of contractually specified services. Typically, auditors want to see every bit of information. They know they should not put their signature on something that cannot be audited.

Board members, the CEO, and auditors, must be well aware that any original reasons which starts the outsourcing ball rolling can lead to mismanaged contracts and practices – whether the original reason has been a drive for business re-engineering, pressures for cost reduction, access to new skills and technology, unloading 'non-core business', or a search for handling 'difficult' problems. The latter is, incidentally, a false reason because usually difficult problems are those issues management does not fully understand.

The careful reader will recall that issues and services over which the company's management does not have full control should never be subject to outsourcing. Only when we fully understand what we are outsourcing can we plan the supplier relationship with due diligence; define all assets; properly negotiate deliverables in hardware and software; and focus on services that will be affected. This makes possible to:

- properly structure the SLA in a functional and legal sense
- associate to it licencing, maintenance and insurance responsibilities
- provide for negative service charges and penalties because of non-observance of the clauses by the insourcer.

The board must realize that with outsourcing it is too easy to overlook key management issues such as retention of overall control, upholding of the original business objectives, and the fact this is a business partnership, not a one-way delegation. Another common failing is that of not making provision for *exit*, including early termination. circumstances change and the chosen insourcer may not be able to hold on with his commitments.

An SLA should not underestimate auditing's role, either. There are several reasons behind the emphasis on auditing and corresponding explicit clauses of the SLA. One of them is that internal audit functions have become the alter ego of risk management. There is a shift of emphasis in internal audit towards including the auditing of risk as well as of the company's internal control. New regulations push in this direction.

Organizational issues, the outsourcer/insourcer integration challenge, and every present operational risks make advisable that prerequisite study must target the service level which is visible to senior management and the clients. Leadership, flexibility and cost/effectiveness require:

- a robust program structure
- clear communications strategy
- consensus and commitment by everybody affected by outsourcing.

There is no lack of issues that should be examined both *before* entering into an outsourcing contract and *after* it is in process. Here are in a nutshell the six most frequently made mistakes in outsourcing which negatively affect the service level agreement. Senior management and the auditors should be fully aware of them.

1 Failure to focus on broad, future-looking analysis, by concentrating too much on status quo comparisons.

Many outsourcing agreements are made from the near-sighted viewpoint of which solution is cheaper *today*. When this is the case, the results are bound to be substandard in the longer term.

2 Decoupling outsourcing solutions from business strategy.

Or, using the wrong business model, which leads to lost business opportunities and legal risks. I have often emphasized this pitfall.

3 Over-delegation by senior management, along with badly chosen criteria for control purposes.

Examples are failure to look at insourcer survivability, poor methodology, medieval technology, questioning human potential. Each one of these factors contributes to the project's efficiencies or, alternatively, inefficiencies.

4 Failure to test the stated advantages, beyond cost savings.

For instance, availability of latest technology, best market practices, focus on what the insourcer may be good at.

5 Going with the herd in outsourcing vital services.

Many companies now outsource manufacturing, but retain research, design, marketing and branding. The failure of Olivetti and Alcatel, among many others, should be a reminder of risks with such practices. (More about this Chapters 6 and 7.)

6 Little or no attention paid to contract termination problems.

This shortfall goes all the way from backup services, to reimporting skills, and to legal risk associated to closing down a contract. As already mentioned in this chapter, the exit strategy must be integral part of a service level agreement, with outsourcers be prepared to face a worst-case scenario. Section 6 explains why.

In conclusion, both a *macroscope* and a *microscope* are necessary to look into service level agreements, as Figure 5.5 suggests. The macroscope is top

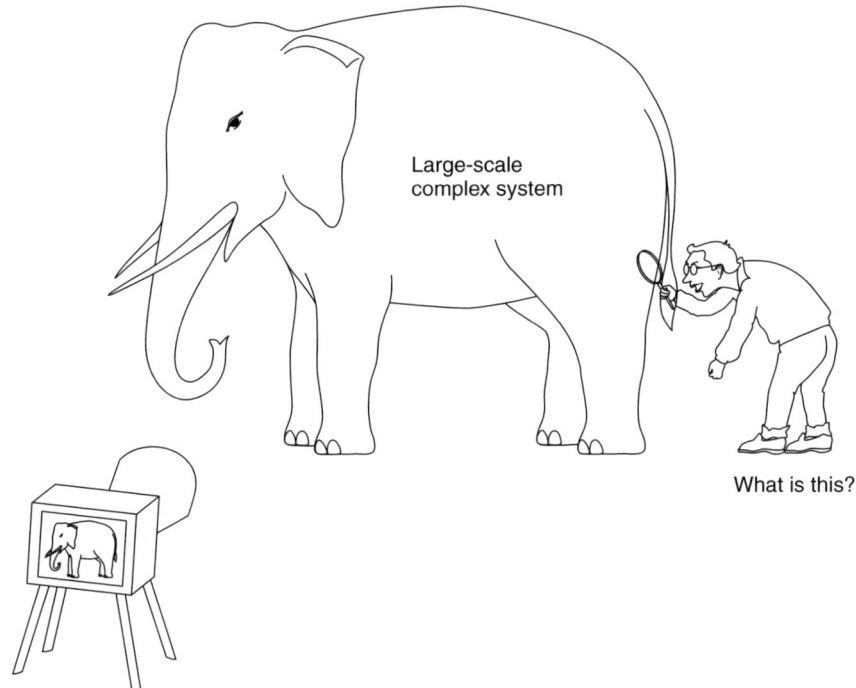

Large-scale
complex system

What is this?

You can't see anything without a *macroscope*.

Figure 5.5 Many outsourcing agreements are large scale, complex systems

management's evaluation of the strategic aspects of outsourcing, expressed through the policy decisions that must be taken. The microscope is attention to detail. The two complement one another; they are the pillars on which rest lasting outsourcing solutions.

6. Beware of outsourcing deals that turn sour

A growing number of credit institutions and other companies are outsourcing their information systems. They do so because they do not understand that information technology is core business to them and outsourcing can have negative strategic impact, particularly when it is associated with loss of skills in IT – and the difficulty of rebuilding from scratch a tip-top team.

Setting aside the fact that many companies are getting increasingly disenchanted with outsourcing, because of the experience they had with ill-conceived SLAs, senior management should keep always in perspective the message conveyed by factual reports. These indicate that roughly three out of four companies have encountered serious problems about the whole outsourcing process or at least some aspects of it. KPMG did a study on outsourcing involving 123 fairly large companies. What it found is that:

- 40 per cent of the dissatisfied firms said they became too dependant on their insourcer
- 37 per cent said a main reason of their dissatisfaction was their lack influence over service levels.

Lack of influence over service levels means that these entities had no control over their supplier.[2] As a result, many executives suggested they were determined to ensure that, second time round, they will get a better deal. This evidently starts with proper selection. Here is a list of ten criteria for evaluating outsourcing proposals, based on my experience.

1 Carefully look for consistency – and for hidden discontinuities.
2 Examine all the hypotheses being made regarding outsourcing and its deliverables.
3 Challenge the obvious and tear to pieces the offer you receive to find hidden flaws.
4 Analyse quality assurance references provided by other outsourcers.
5 Analyse supporting statistics: the statistics must be bright; the conclusions are our own.
6 Carefully examine reliability and fallback clauses.
7 Evaluate quantitative/qualitative analysis of projected deliverables.
8 Pay attention to personal responsibilities, identified at outsourcer and insourcer side.
9 Pay attention to deadlines and built-in ways for corrective action.
10 Evaluate cost-effectiveness over short, medium and longer term.

It should not come as a surprise when I say that many companies which followed this list, and cared to do a thorough analysis of 'pluses' and 'minuses', decided to keep their information technology out of an outsourcing practice. Citibank is a different example when planning to outsource its legacy programs.

- It took care to establish 'pluses' and 'minuses', taking the time needed for this study.
- Then, two days before signing up, Citibank pulled out of the projected outsourcing agreement.

There was a revolt of the bank's business managers because of the risks involved in outsourcing, and this is by no means a one-off example.

Other credit institutions found the hard way what Citibank established through appropriate study: technology, outskilling and outsourcing projects can lead to troubles.

• General Bank of Luxembourg signed a contract with Andersen Consulting for 50 systems experts to work for three years.

This time-frame elapsed, but the project still went on. The response which I got from General Bank executives, specifically in personal banking and in risk management, was fairly negative in terms of improvements in the IT tools in their disposition.

• Bankgesellschaft Berlin employed inhouse 90 expatriates to revamp its risk management system.

All attention focuses on what to do with information technology, not on internal controls. This primary interest has been misplaced because when the internal controls system is poor, no IT solutions would fill the gap. The evidence is that in 2001 Bankgesellschaft went almost bust and was saved the last moment by a handout of the City of Berlin (its main stockholder, which itself is bankrupt).

• Swiss Bank Corporation (SBC) delegated to Perot Systems the whole responsibility for its Millennium Banking solution.

This happened before the merger with UBS, in the mid 1990s, but after SBC bought a 30 per cent equity in Perot Systems. Following the merger, SBC adopted for the combined banks operations most of the information technology UBS had developed, which meant that the years spend with Perot Systems for the Millennium Banking largely went down the drain.

• With a 1997 outsourcing contract, EDS took a huge compensation equal to 2 per cent of the equity in Banca di Roma for the bargain price of 160 million lira ($91 million at that time). This is a ten-year outsourcing program.

In Rome, cognisant people said the goodies EDS took home worth between 2.5 and 3 trillion lira ($1.4 billion–$1.7 billion). This has been the largest IT outsourcing signed in Italy. Equity in a major credit institution is the best fee for an insourcer, better than the alternative of payment in hard currency.

• Banco Ambrosiano Veneto, another major Italian bank, outsourced its IT operations in a vain bid to slash administrative costs by $200 million over a few years.[3]

Ambrosiano Veneto's board made two wrong decisions: that IT lies outside the bank's 'core activity', and that outsourcing leads to 'significant savings' resulting from 'improved efficiency'. The bank also looked for disposing its two IT service companies. But the deal was not cheap.

Banco Ambrosiano had to pay out over $590 million during the decade 1997 to 2007 to Germany's Systemhaus. This is the IT services division of Daimler Benz. Systemhaus was the insourcer chosen to run the bank's divested IT operations, though Ambrosiano retained its coinvolvement in applications development evidently at a higher cost. This took care of both 'decisions': That IT is not a bank's core activity, and that IT outsourcing automatically results in significant savings.

As these and many more examples demonstrate, nothing seems to have been learned from some outstanding failures connected to IT outsourcing, like the *Confirm* project. Here, in a nutshell, is what has happened to a predecessor to current IT outsourcing drives. In the mid 1980s the *Intrico* Consortium was formed by:

- American Airlines Information Services (AMRIS)
- Hilton Hotels
- Marriott Hotels
- Budget Rent-a-Car.

The goal was to develop, use and market the most advanced reservation system technology made possible. These were the plans, but they were not led to fruition. The *Confirm* project was cancelled five years down the line after a number of lawsuits. During these years:

- it cost millions of dollars in overruns
- a torrent of bitter accusations among the senior executives involved in this disaster.

Confirm's original goals became unattainable as hundreds of people working for different companies over so many years lost sight of what was needed and wanted. One by one, *Confirm*'s objective have bitten the dust – but the red ink remained, as a reminder of the tendency of outsourcing projects to go wrong when detailed planning and rigorous control have taken a leave.

7. The JP Morgan example: an entity may be both outsourcer and insourcer

Down to basics. Outsourcing or no outsourcing, the drive to cut costs, do new advanced IT application, and employ the best available technologists has to be part of any grand design. The overriding concern of any board of directors and CEO should be that the minds of the firm's technology management have to be firmly focused on the direct link between business strategy and the information technology supporting it. The critical questions then become:

- Are *we* learning from past experience?
- How do we use other people's failures to improve *our* results?

Not much seems to have been learned from the different outsourcing failures like *Confirm*. Some years down the line, in mid 1996, JP Morgan signed a seven-year contract with a consortium known as the *Pinnacle Alliance* to handle day-to-day computer services. This contract, which was worth $2 billion, put together some of the rivals in IT: Computer Sciences Corporation (CSC), Andersen Consulting, AT&T and Bell Atlantic.

The Pinnacle Alliance had its own offices within the JP Morgan to handle four major data centers: in New York, at the bank's Delaware headquarters, in London and in Paris. Its also involved other core IT systems than those originally projected. CSC was the lead supplier and managed about 80 per cent of the Pinnacle business. In a curious switch of management principles, CSC was responsible both to Morgan and to the other Pinnacle partners.

- Critics questioned whether this outsourcing strategy with split management responsibility had any chance to work.
- They pointed out that the solution was not really cost-effective, and that it would eventually lead to duplicate effort.

The critics proved to be right. In JP Morgan's case, within a year-and-a-half from Pinnacle's start the bank added IT people – it did not slim down. According to reports, one-third of Morgan's IT-related staff, amounting to more than 900 extra people, have been added to the bank's payroll from May 1996, when Pinnacle was set up, to October 1997 – in less than 1 and-a-half years. Most of the new recruits were employed to:

- run new computer development projects, and
- support critical systems which proved necessary to build inhouse.[4]

The pros said that no matter the expense outsourcing liberated the bank from routine IT activities and enabled it to get down to its strategic goal of putting technology experts physically closer to the traders who create the bank's revenue. The critics pointed out that the split between new developments and operations, as well as between competitive systems and legacy programs, was the worst possible solution.

- It was bound to increase JP Morgan's overall IT costs.
- It was sure to take a toll on efficiency because split responsibility never gives commendable results.

While it outsourced its IT services, JP Morgan worked as an insourcer of finance-related functions. An example is its *Arcordia* project, which became the bank's derivatives processing subsidiary. The comments I heard at Wall Street were that the silver lining of JP Morgan's huge exposure in derivatives was that it had developed an expertise in models and IT services necessary to handle derivatives risk. Value at risk was given as an example.[5]

As 2000 came to a close, JP Morgan merged with Chase Manhattan. A year later, at the end of 2001, JP Morgan Chase abruptly closed down its London-based Arcordia. The official explanation has been the economic slowdown, but that move represented another blow to the outsourcing market with JP Morgan Chase until then being bullish about its major push, as an outsourcer, into the aforementioned service sector.

Arcordia was launched in May 2000 and survived the takeover of JP Morgan by Chase, with the decision then taken to move the latter's derivatives book to the Arcordia service. At the time, Arcordia also seemed to be gaining Bank One as its first customer. Bank One however decided to move all of its derivatives activity to its head office in Chicago. Analysts did not fail to notice that:

- the demise of Arcordia coincided with a winding down by Bank One of its Global Trading Operations (GTO) initiative
- a decision to outsource to Arcordia would have seen the processing transferred again, this time to London.

One of the reasons cited by JP Morgan for starting the Arcordia project in the first place was the ability to retain back office staff, by making them part of an independent commercial entity. Some analysts however said this was not cost effective. The facts proved them right; according to some sources the cost of ownership of the Arcordia system has been a key issue compound by system problems. Both seem to have contributed to the decision on close-down. Arcordia's software was originally built inhouse in the mid 1990s, starting with 300 staff.

- Like nine women don't make a baby in one month, a staff of 300 did not shorten developed time.
- The only sure result of 300 people assigned to a single project is high cost; equally likely are low quality and long delays.

Bank One's GTO initiative was not more lucky, though initially it seemed to have been relatively successful in selling its services, with seven clients recruited since its original launch in 1998. The GTO services initially covered forex, then they were broadened to money markets back office operations. The software being used was developed inhouse on Tandem back in the 1980s.

Let alone that the software was old and inflexible, Tandem was absorbed by Compaq, and it was no more in business. Therefore GTO had sought a broader and more modern system solution for its services, coming out in favor of Demica's Citadel – a choice which seems to have paid no attention to supplier's survivability. Correctly,

- the Bank One board rejected the investment
- the decision was made to cease marketing the GTO service.

According to some reports, Bank One felt that there was a conflict with its priorities, and GTO customers were informed that they would need to make alternative arrangements. Some of these customers were themselves no more around. Donaldson Lufkin & Jenrette, a large outsourcer to GTO, fell by the wayside after its acquisition by CSFB; others have gone elsewhere. The couple that remained were believed to include Leonia Bank, the first to sign up.

With Arcordia and GTO out of the way, the only other core back office insourcers which remains in the forex/money markets domain is the rather recently launched SOCX, which is based on a commercial software package. It is a joint venture between Deutsche Bank and Wall Street Systems. Ironically, at the time of its launch, SOCX cited Arcordia as having helped to define the market the new venture is after. SOCX may be feeling a little nervous with this paradigm gone under water. This is just one example among many IT fiascos.

6

Can We Leverage R&D and Engineering through Outsourcing?

1. Introduction

Contrary what many people and several companies tend to believe, innovation is primarily a matter of ingenuity and concentration, not of big, expensive and usually slow-moving laboratories. This is particularly true about product innovation, therefore applied research and development. Basic research is a different proposition, which does not mean that big numbers can produce better results than a small highly learned, motivated and well-equipped group of people.

Most often, when deliverables suffer this happens because senior management does not take care to break the vicious cycle of obstructionism characterising a good deal of research and development (R&D) efforts. As a French joke has it: the reason no results come from cancer research is that more people make a living out of cancer than die from cancer.

In terms of industrial R&D, breaking bad product development cycles requires:

- making better choices about when to commit to a certain project, and when to opt out
- dealing with the persistence of more and more 'improvements' in product development efforts
- initiating and seeing through a steady upgrading in effectiveness of product development functions, including time, cost and quality control.

As section 6 will demonstrate, in every R&D project individual and project performance must be tracked on a weekly and monthly basis – whether this project is done inhouse or it is outsourced. Many well-managed engineering companies are using a 'war room' concept to come up with results which are difficult to get out of researchers and project managers under *laissez-faire* conditions.

Down to the fundamentals: basic and applied research, as well as development, is promoted by the investment in *knowledge* made by people and by society as a whole. The way to measure investments in peoples' knowledge is to go beyond basic school training and look into other criteria which have a significant impact on R&D and innovation:

- higher education
- money spend on software (a knowledge industry)
- budgets for R&D as a per cent of gross domestic product (GDP).

Figure 6.1 dramatizes the differences existing along this frame of reference between the United States and selected countries in the European Union

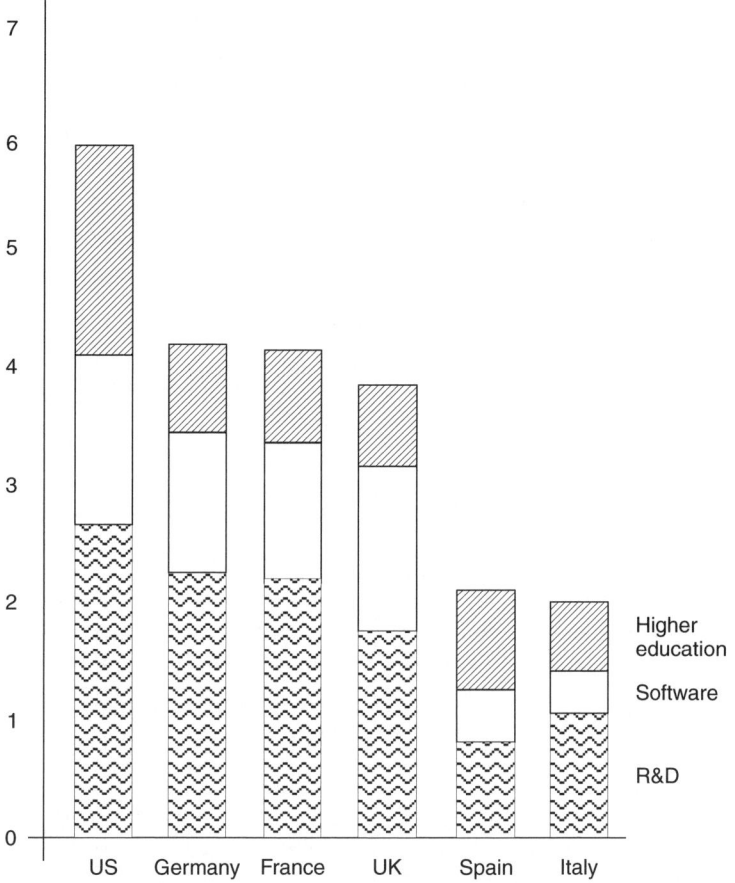

*Statistics by OECD

Figure 6.1 Investments in knowledge as per cent of GDP vary tremendously between countries*

(EU). These statistics by the Organization of Economic Cooperation and Development (OECD) are telling. As the careful reader will observe, there are still substantial differences in levels of knowledge generation between the US and Europe, though some progress has taken place during the recent years in parts of Europe.

Notice that particularly lagging in Europe is the higher education budget which in the US includes R&D money because of sponsored projects. University laboratories are indeed one of the most fertile places for outsourcing R&D because that's where some of the best scientists of today are educating some of the best scientists of tomorrow.

Last but not least, it is appropriate to keep in mind that product innovation has many aspects, because novelty comes under different guises. In the 1960s and 1970s, the Japanese decimated the Swiss watch industry after having siphoned out the business of the German photo-machine industry. They did so by emulating existing watches and photo apparatus, improving upon them and significantly lowering their costs.

Nicholas G. Hayek brought watchmaking back to Switzerland by mass producing low-cost plastic Swatch watches that are not just timepieces but fashion statements. Hayek's innovation lies in his ability to create a popular basis for a product pyramid with Swatch at low end, Pierre Balmain in the middle, and Longines at the top.

- In a way emulating Alfred Sloan's product classification in the auto industry, Swatch serves as the mass-appeal brand.
- At the same time, the mass product is also a firewall, making it more difficult for competition to get a toehold.

Both with cameras and with watches, the strategy followed by the Japanese in the post-Second World War years was to use this firewall brand strategy to take away potential buyers of the more expensive offerings in each product line. Outsourcing or no outsourcing, this should never be overlooked by businessmen – yet many companies are practically ready to cede the low-end, entry-model market to competitors who later move up the product pyramid to capture the high net worth individuals market where the profits lie.

2. Innovation is basic to every strategic plan

One of the best examples which bring under perspective the role of innovation as a strategic factor, comes from the auto industry. In the decade of 1910 Henry Ford made the auto affordable to the masses by capitalizing of the efficiency of the assembly line. With this, he conquered the American public buying affordable motor vehicles. In the late 1920s, Alfred Sloan, the CEO of General Motors, took the auto market away from Ford by capitalising on the fact that autos don't only need to be transportation engines, they can also become fashion statements – if designers and producers change yearly their styling.

It took nearly two-thirds of a century until, in the 1990s, Toyota revolutionised the auto industry once more by capitalising on innovation promoted through technology. Its two most important contributions have been just-in-time (JIT) manufacturing, and offering to the client the ability to 'design' (so to speak) his own auto, which can be delivered to him or her in three-and-a-half days.

Few people indeed appreciates the far out impact of this *virtual customer* (VC) project which is now institutionalised through the Virtual Customer Initiative at MIT. This is a multidisciplinary approach improving the speed, accuracy, and usability of customer input to the product development process. It is a kind of outsourcing fundamental design characteristics to the client himself.

The VC goals include virtual customer methods that are accurate and relevant to the product development team. By developing and testing new web-based methods, MIT researchers seek to radically reduce the time lag between customer input and product development, doing so at a fraction of current cost.

The virtual customer initiative is a talking example on how IT and new communication technologies are adding dramatic new capabilities, for rapid and inexpensive customer input, to all stages of the product development process. Industry-sponsored projects at MIT (hence outsourced initiatives) include FastPace, Web-based Conjoint Analysis, Virtual Concept Testing, Information Pump, and User Design. These methods are proving valuable for:

- identifying opportunities
- improving the design and engineering of products
- testing ideas and concepts much earlier in the process, when less time and money is at risk.

Let's now look into some of the risks of exposure associated to licensing advanced engineering products. For this we will take an example from aviation (other examples are given in section 4). Like the Japanese did with German cameras and Swiss watches, Boeing went well beyond the Caravelle design it licensed from SudAviation by:

- developing the concept of an integrated product line with interchangeable component parts
- going ahead to conquer the global civil aviation market for nearly forty years.

The case of Caravelle is a talking example of what can happen by licensing a product without having studied the further out aftermath: *What if* the

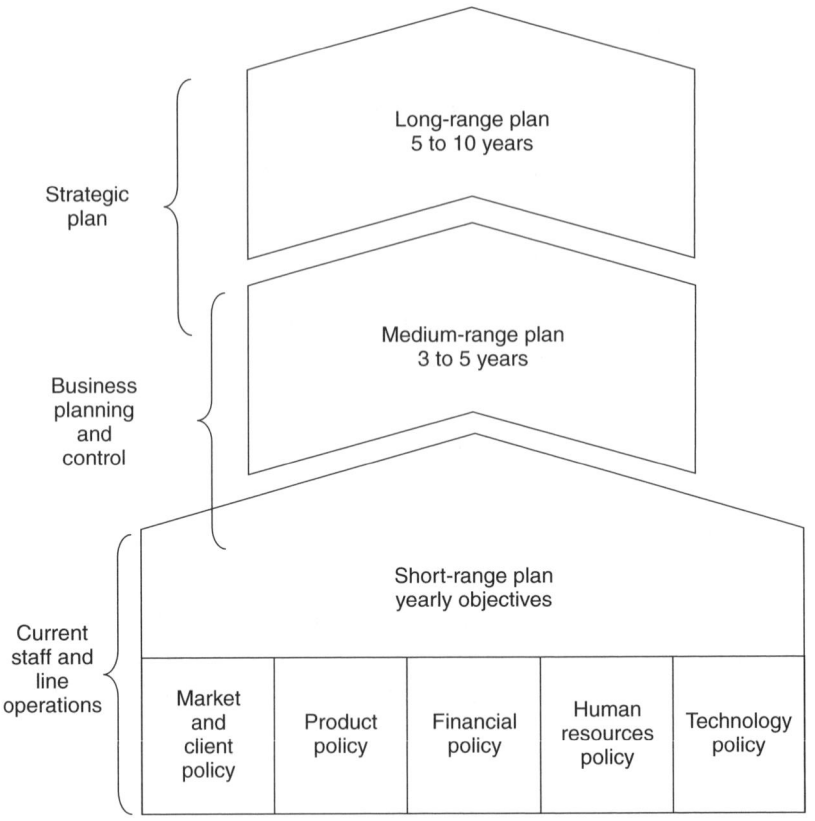

Figure 6.2 Decisions on product policy should never be made without the benefit of a strategic general direction

licensee becomes a competitor? In the 1960s SudAviation licensed to Boeing its very successful short-to-medium range Caravelle without having done its homework on risk and return. Boeing never produced a single Caravelle, but it learned from it and developed its even more successful 727 and 737 series.

The 707 airliner, which itself was a development based on a military air-cargo plane, was extended by Boeing downwards towards 727 and 737, and upwards to the 747. By contrast, SudAviation locked itself into the Caravelle (whose market eventually died out), then jumped to the development and construction of the flying white elephant known as Concorde. Eventually SudAviation learned its lesson and came out with an integrated series of air-frames which gave Boeing a run for its money.

The 'A 360' series of SudAviation is a good example of outsourcing and insourcing agreements in R&D and manufacturing, since all of these planes are the result of a co-operative effort between aeronautical firms in five different EU countries. In a fast-moving world where new technology replaces old at a furious pace, there is no alternative to taking an integrated approach and the proverbial long, hard look – including the many dangers associated to misjudging the breadth of the product line, or its expansion without a product plan which looks away into the future. This is explained in Figure 6.2 which:

- brings under perspective the five main current plans, together constituting the short term master plan
- integrates this short term plan to the further-out medium and long range plan. The latter establishes the strategic perspective.

No outsourcing plan regarding research and development, or a licensing agreement, should ever forget that there is a direct relationship between customer satisfaction market leadership, the quality of products and services, the amount of money a company's customers invest in its offerings, and the risk the licensee or outsourcer will walk away with the prize. This is as true of engineering as it is of manufacturing, sales and after sales service. In all three sectors the goal should be to:

- increase customer appreciation of *our* products
- better short-term and long-term profitability
- improve the ease of technology absorption
- assure the licensee or insourcer does not become our competitor.

One of the roles of R&D and innovation which cannot be delegated to insourcers is to answer the question: what new technologies hold the most promise for *our* company and its customers? When responding to this question, companies invariably find that new applications and business models require not only new products but also an investment in infrastructure to create the right conditions for wide-scale business and consumer use. Cisco calls these 'tornado' markets, which can be described as a rapid uptake of cutting-edge products to progressively larger client populations.

A company's ability to address these opportunities stems from its expertise with current products and services and its customers response to them. Sensitivity to market wishes and drives – down to the individual customer – is a responsibility which cannot be outsourced. If the human capital of our firm is tier-1, it should be directly responsible to transform products and their applications, and bring about new design characteristics that open the door to a number of market opportunities. Fundamentally,

- This evolutionary ability is what distinguishes a successful company from one which fades away.
- Product *and* market flexibility is a basic characteristic of innovation both at every company level – from start-ups to mature entities.

In a way fairly similar to what was said in the Introduction about the crucial role of higher education, there is a most significant difference in venture capital – and therefore in start-ups and new firm activity – between the US and the EU, as well as among the different European countries. The histogram in Figure 6.3 is based on OECD statistics from 2000. OECD defines:

- start-up statistics as 'percentage of adults engaged in the process of creating a business'
- new firm activity as 'percentage of adults owning (solely or partly) and managing an operating business less than 42 months old'.

Companies described by both bullets are fed through venture capital. One of the surprises in comparing Figure 6.1 and Figure 6.3 is that France which is in the lead in terms of investments in knowledge, lags behind in start-ups and new firms. The opposite is true of Italy and Spain. This is a subject which requires deeper research to unearth the reasons, some of which have to do (by all likelihood) with heavy social charges and the rigidity of labour markets.[1]

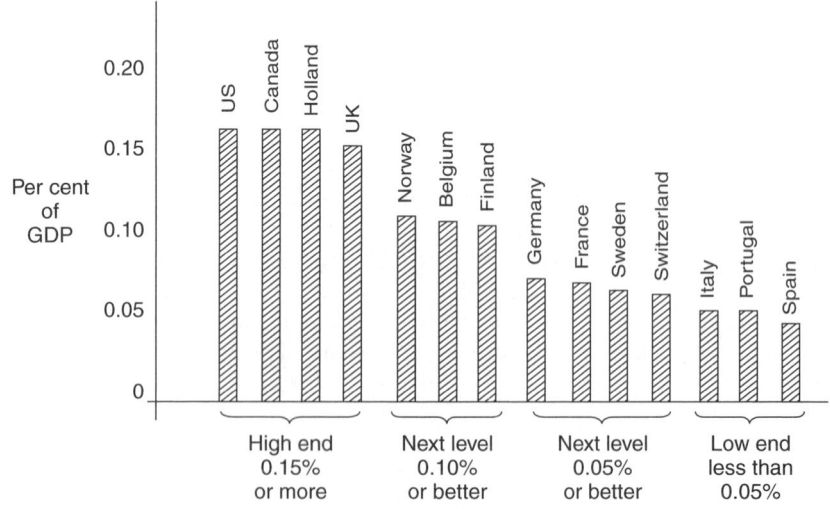

Figure 6.3 High end and low end of investments by venture capital companies as percentage of GDP

The statistics in Figure 6.3 are very important because whether we talk about a company or a country as a whole, innovation is most critical to its strategic plan. Innovation is at its best when there exists competition within R&D and its commercialisation. Both companies and countries can derive significant benefits by developing competing technologies. Knowledge-based teams should be in a race to come up with the best solution. Competition drives people towards producing their best, and it diminishes the time for deliverables.

3. How Charles Kettering characterised the process of innovation

A competition policy is particularly wise when we cannot predict which technology will eventually dominate. Hence the idea to promote a range of technologies, which helps to stimulate interest in projects competing head on. Alternatively, a great deal can come from the ingenuity of a person who has the guts and imagination to challenge the 'obvious', as we will see in this section.

In 1933, during the worst of the Depression, Charles Kettering invented the electric car-starter and with it doubled the market for automobiles. The very innovative GM's vice president of R&D strongly believed that business will come back when business and industry brings to the market products that people *want* to buy. Even in the depth of the Depression he was not worried about the future of America, but he was worried about how long it was wise to wait for business to come back instead of going and finding new opportunities. Kettering's motto has been: 'You have got to coax business back. It isn't going to come back by itself.'

These are very wise words which apply hand-in-glove to the conditions characterising the 2000–2002 deep recession. Kettering added: 'You can't sell anything to anybody if he is perfectly happy with what he has.' Charles Kettering coined a definition for research, saying that it is an organised method of keeping everybody reasonably *dissatisfied* with what he already has. This clear-eyed definition of R&D has been valid not only when it was stated in 1933 but also seventy years down the line.

- The positive aspect of outsourcing R&D is to provide extra gear to this 'organised method' of end-user dissatisfaction.
- *If*, for whatever reason, this cannot be achieved, *then* I would question the outsourcing of R&D in terms of its return on investment (ROI).

Charles Kettering also noted that need is often the mother of invention. He gave as an example innovations that came out of the First World War: radio, talking pictures, new paints, new types of gasoline. The effect of these new products on the market was leveraged by the arrival of credit as a way to buy things. 'So we unleashed all of that, and profits began to go up, and speculation went along with it,' Kettering said. 'But we forgot one thing. We forgot that markets are not indefinitely elastic for the same kind of stuff, and that is where we made the mistake.'

As a result of the late 1920s bubble, development work stopped. This, Kettering was to suggest, revealed that the great research laboratories which existed at that time were research laboratories only from the standpoint of reducing costs, substituting of materials and cutting down labour – but real innovation was wanting. Therefore, he aptly remarked that so far as research laboratories are spending a great amount of time on:

- what new products 'they were going to do'
- What the next line of services 'was going to be'.

there was no significant contribution to innovation and to business coming out of it. As Kettering had it, 'We are just beginning to realise now that it takes a long while to develop a new line of products, and that you can't do it overnight.' So he got a different way of looking at research, which might be more intelligible to non-technical people: 'Research is to find out what you are going to do when you can't keep on doing what you are doing now.'

Real research and development is the antithesis to the frequently encountered policy of using R&D money to just keep the wheels turning on old tired projects which usually lead nowhere. It takes leadership, not just money, to get results out of research.

Kettering's concepts about the importance of true and steady innovation were repeated during the July 2001 Internet Summit, in the middle of the twenty-first century's first economic turbulence and its devastating downturn in technology. Steve Ballmer, Microsoft's CEO, said: 'The best antidote for pessimism is great new products, great new services and great work. Super-interesting things get people engaged. That's the key, in my opinion, to getting out of the doldrums.'

As with the auto industry in the early 1930s, many of the companies represented at the Internet Summit were struggling. They were not sure whether they would be alive or dead by next summit. They had got on the Internet road and thought it would go forever, then found it wasn't paved all the way through. What were they going to do under these circumstances?

- The Internet boom of the 1990s had been all about new stuff, like AOL, eBay, Yahoo, and online games.
- But it became obvious during the 2001 Internet summit that there were not many amazing new products or services to tell consumers about in the new century.

No one came up with an auto-starter after adversity struck, like Kettering did in 1933, to jump-start the market. The excitement about the Net which unleashed profits and speculation, creating a boom a decade earlier, was dying out. In an environment where consistent novelty is taken for granted and people expect more of it every day, failure to produce it can be lethal.

No wonder that in the 2000–02 time-frame, the Internet begun to shrink. In 2001, the total number of websites went down as domains registered during the late 1990s Internet boom were being dropped. By November 2001, 36,458,394 sites were found, shrinking to 36,276,252 in December.[2] The number of domains not renewed exceeded the number of new registrations.

There was also a decline caused by failures at hosting companies. Signs appeared on the wall that the people who brought about the Internet revolution would not necessarily be the new innovators. Some proved to be one-track minds, and even scoffed at what seemed to them 'too different' to be true. This happen for the first time in industrial history.

Take, as an example, a brilliant inventor like Thomas Alva Edison. Among Edison's well-known contributions are the light bulb, phonograph, and motion picture. Yet, along with such successes, Edison stubbornly stuck by numerous errors in judgement – for example, calling radio a 'fad'.

There is a great lot of famous prognostications which went wrong. 'I think there is a world market for maybe five computers,' said Thomas J. Watson, Jr, IBM's chairman, in 1943. 'But what … is it good for?' asked an IBM engineer at the company's Advanced Computing Systems division in 1968, commenting on the nascent microchip. In fact, IBM engineers seem to have had an aversion even for transistors. When in the early 1960s some of them complained that transistors were unreliable, then IBM CEO Thomas J. Watson, Jr., handed them transistor radios and challenged the critics to wear them out.

Watson, Sr, was by no means the only pioneer who failed to live with his time. Ken Olson, founder and CEO of Digital Equipment Corp said in 1977: 'There is no reason anyone would want a computer in their home' – and by believing in his own words, as if they were a gospel, he missed the PC revolution and eventually sent DEC to the rocks.

What eventually became staple items of our society have often been taken for worthless fads. 'The telephone has too many shortcomings to be seriously considered as a means of communication. The device is inherently of no value to us,' read a Western Union internal memo in 1876. 'The wireless music box has no imaginable commercial value. Who would pay for a message sent to nobody in particular?' asked David Sarnoff's associates in the 1920s in response to his prompting to invest in the radio as a consumer product. In fact, voice was considered in the 1920s as a hindrance rather than added value. 'Who the hell wants to hear actors talk?' asked H.M. Warner in 1927?[3]

And there is also Bill Gates who, in 1981, made the profound statement '640K ought to be enough for everybody'. If so many people of renown who have been pioneers in their business goofed in their prognostications about the future of 'this' or 'that', there is no reason to believe that you or I will do better in projecting the course the new economy may take and the innovations which could become its motor. There is, however, one thing which looks quite certain: extrapolating from past experiences is like driving on a turnpike at 100 mph by looking through the rear-view mirror.

4. Acquisitions and development. Risks associated to outsourcing

Immobility may well be the greatest risk society has faced in its long history, but nothing is really risk free. Any business activity has associated to it a swarm of credit, market and operational risks. Take aggressive company acquisition as an example of risk associated to R&D outsourcing. A real-life example is Monterey Networks, an optical-routing startup in which Cisco Systems held a minority stake. The Monterey outfit was a quarry with:

- no customers
- no revenue
- no up and running products.

What it did have was millions in losses racked up since its founding in 1997, and some brains Cisco wanted to acquire. For this reason, it paid a half-billion dollars in stock to buy the rest of the company in 1999. But within days of closing the deal, all three of Monterey's founders, including its engineering guru and chief systems architect, walked out the door, taking with them millions of dollars in gains from the sale.

High-tech mergers and acquisitions are a modern form of outsourcing R&D, because their main objective is to *buy time*. But losing the brains one acquires, right after having paid the money, is a distinct possibility. 'I came to the realization I wasn't going to have any meaningful impact on the product by staying,' said H. Michael Zadikian, a Monterey Networks founder.[4] Eighteen months later, Cisco shut down the business altogether, sacking the rest of the management team and with it taking a $108 million write-off.

There are hundreds of Monterey Networks type acquisition deals, and all of them are talking examples on one of the most popular strategies of outsourcing R&D through aggressive buying of smaller companies. Some put a new name on this process: acquisitions and development (A&D). In essence, it is a way for a company to shortcut the usual research cycle.

The belief in the results it could obtain through an aggressive acquisitions and development outsourcing strategy has led Cisco to gobble up more than seventy companies in the 1994 to 2002 time-frame. Its management tackled that as the solution permitting rapid extension of the company's products towards new market entries along the pattern shown in Figure 6.4.

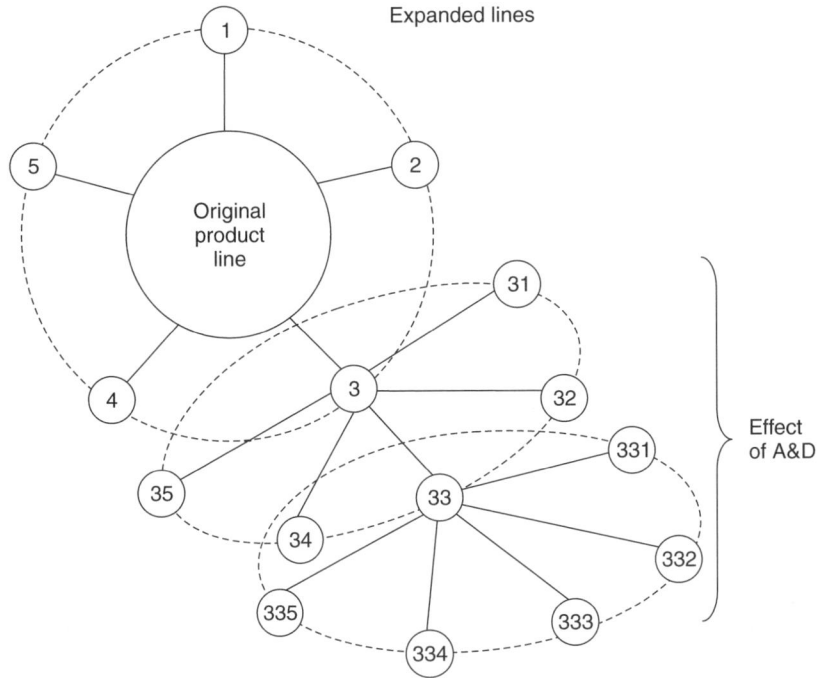

Figure 6.4 Properly executed, an acquisition and development policy amounts to buying time

- A newly acquired product line, for instance switching, can be been expanded through A&D into optical switching.
- Then, again through A&D, this new product can be endowed with gear allowing to present the client with an integrated solution.

There is really no rule about the hit rate of A&D. John Chalmers, Cisco's CEO, seems to suggest that in the case of his firm some 80 per cent of acquisitions have happy ending. Financial analysts say that something just below 50 per cent is more realistic. Even if it is so, it would not be that bad. There are companies which seem to be satisfied with a 15 per cent success rate, which is really nonsense.

The difference between 15 per cent and 80 per cent is so wide that there is no way to talk about a likelihood of success in A&D. Much depends on how well the deal has been studied, the substance the be found in the acquired engineering company, whether or not the 'acquired' brains will stay on board and, of course, leadership and the chemistry of the deal.

Too many variables are involved to allow an a priori opinion in the abstract, but there are some facts worth recording. By means of A&D, Cisco changed itself from a router company to a networking systems provider. Acquisitions of innovative product outfits have laid the foundation for some 50 per cent of Cisco's business, as it stands today. 'We bet on products 12 to 18 months out,' says John Chambers, 'We took dramatically higher risks.' He also suggests that:

• his company's acquisition strategy was aimed at acquiring brainpower more than products.

This has the risk that when the knowledge workers of the acquired company leave they take with them a good deal of the expertise and experience of the acquired firm. Nobody is immune to the brain drain, particularly so companies which depend on talent in order to grow and survive. 'The talent goes up and down the elevators every day and can go in a heartbeat. All you're buying is the furniture,' Walter Wriston, the former CEO of Citibank, once warned.[5]

No serious person should forget that there are risks associated with outsourcing, including A&D which means taking control over the insourcer. Therefore, companies looking for A&D or for outright outsourcing of processes, products and services should always identify the exposure that could hit them including the risks inherent in their insourcing partner:

• counterparty risk
• country risk
• operational risk
• intellectual property risk
• quality risk, and so on.

Each type of risk should be properly identified and the items in the assessment list arranged along two criteria: likelihood and importance. The next vital step is to examine if we have experience with the control of these risks, and whether *our* risk management unit is able to handle them. If not, it is absolutely necessary to upgrade this unit prior to following an A&D or other strategy of engineering outsourcing.

Indeed, managers with experience in A&D see to it that they not only measure the benefits from the upgrade such policy can produce but also add to the contractual cost – the monetization of the risk(s) they have identified. They also appreciate they must steadily monitor the market change and other factors that could hit the outsourcing agreement, including stress tests focusing on whether the outsourcer will need to do intellectual property transfer towards the insourcer.

Based on historical evidence, contrarians to A&D policies and other types of engineering outsourcing bring forward adverse reactions to farming out projects. Here are four quotes from companies which examined outsourcing deals and rejected them. 'We might pursue an outsourcing policy, but we currently found no suppliers who know the business we are in, as well as we do.' 'We would like to outsource some of our activities, *if* we could find a credible supplier.'; 'Why should we pay full service prices when we don't need most of what the insourcers offer?' 'Why should we pay extra money for outsourcing services on machines and software which are as obsolete as our own.'

5. Multisourcing design tools and being aware of pitfalls with linear thinking

One of the most crucial activities in any business is the management of change. Sometimes change is forced upon us due to market evolution, while in other situations we initiate change because we hope that it will improve and enhance our competitiveness. This is true with the tools we are using, and to keep their options open many companies choose multisourcing.

- Designers no longer use tools from a single vendor. Instead, they rely on best tools available from multiple vendors.
- Multisourcing enables them to take advantage of different feature strengths, at various stages in their flow of design activities.

A direct aftermath of the trend towards multisourcing is that vendors of engineering design tool kits must work hard to develop new means and methods which, at the same time, are featuring greater compatibility and integration with other products. Able solutions to engineering design tools are going beyond simple sharing of compatible file formats.

- The ease with which information can be exchanged between tools directly impacts a designer's overall productivity.
- Clear-eyed designers want to benefit from the ability to write scripts that drive tools in a flow, while also permitting easy benchmarking.

The principles outlined by these two bullets enable companies and their computer-aided design (CAD) operations to better control every aspect of their engineering process. Whether engineering design is done inhouse or is outsourced, at a premium should be the ability to support a seamless flow between the tools used by the different designers (see also section 6).

Take image analysis and display as an example. Operations connected to this process include: image registration, image analysis and statistics, double-precision data support, region-of-interest processing, spatial transformations, filtering and 2-D filter design, noise reduction, image enhancement, morphological operations, deblurring, block processing, colourmap manipulation, colourspace conversions and, experimentation with multidimensional support.

Because no single tool will cover all these activities in the best possible manner, the synergy between multisourced tools is very important. As design activities grow more sophisticated, designers face the problem of how to integrate different specializations and how to debug efficiently their work. Different research projects demonstrate that designers spend most of their time in verification, trying to simulate and debug their produce.

- In the course of mainly creative work, one major concern is time spent trying to locate a problem.
- The next challenge is that designs undergo multiple transactions as they pass through different tools in a work flow.

An error found at the finishing analysis stage might actually have originated at the design entry stage. If the tools are integrated seamlessly and are equipped with agents,[6] they could actually talk to each other, cross-probe themselves, and automatically locate the original sources of error. One way of doing so is event analysis.

Event analysis enhances the power and flexibility of engineering design. An event occurs at a particular time after a condition is met and significant insight can be obtained by analysing data as it is received from design tools (or instruments). Event analysis contributes to ongoing experiments and design activities by assisting in identifying errors and in taking timely actions, provided a consistent set of warning messages is send back to the workplace.

One of the mistakes frequently made with the choice of engineering design tools, as well as with A&D at large (see section 4) is direct result of a belief that the process characterizing the transition from basic research to after sales service is generally linear. This is absolutely untrue. Based on fifty years of hands-on experience in engineering Figure 6.5 shows the twisted road through which travels any product file from the laboratory to the end-user and field maintenance. The critical variable in this figure is dependability through time – which requires a whole battery of tools.

'Anything linear is probably wrong,' says Joel Moses, Dean of the School of Architecture and Planning, MIT. 'In complex systems you usually have feedback loops. In R&D, we've long had this notion of a linear chain from basic research to product development, and we know that that's wrong. Unfortunately, not enough people operate as if they know it's wrong.'[7] The same is true regarding all types of studies.

Another mistake frequently made with engineering design, including both inhouse projects and outsourcing, is that people and companies are not wary of pitfalls which morph themselves from one stage of product development to the next. Because they are not careful, they tend to go for pies in the sky. For instance, with outsourcing, they believe in multiple benefits available at once:

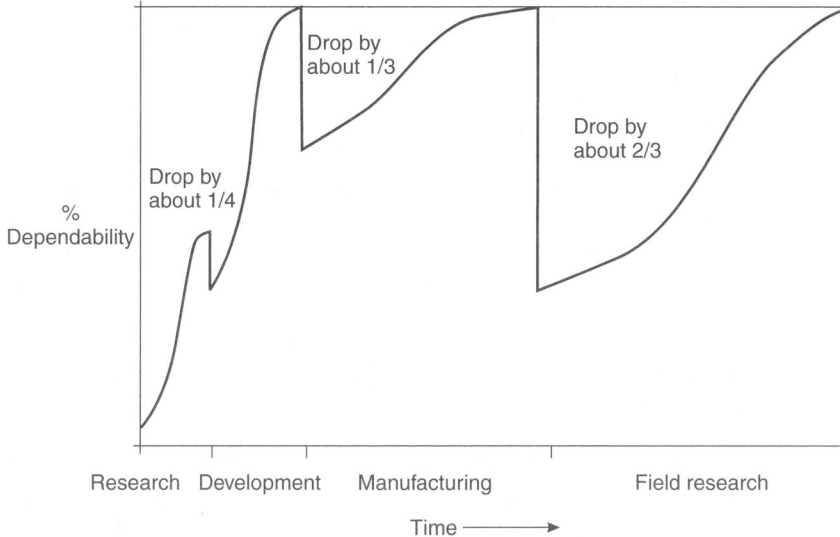

Figure 6.5 The old way of working in airtight departments of research, development, manufacturing and field service is detrimental of overall dependability

- cost savings
- economies of scale
- improved span of control
- swamping errors because of standardization.

One at a time, anyone of these five bullets might prove to be factual but it should not be taken as such a priori. Nothing is it self-evident. Therefore, a thorough study must precede outsourcing decisions and aim to enhance management's understanding of the:

- entity's exposure of outsourcing risks
- technology used by the insourcer
- counterparty's financial staying power
- nature and likelihood of deliverables.

For instance, *if* the company decides for IT outsourcing (see Chapter 8), *then* the deliverables must represent a huge leap forward in its technology, provide means to face greater complexity in business operations, and solve problems rather than creating new ones.

Finally, because R&D is so much labour intensive, it is appropriate to examine, as an extension to its challenges, the further out aftermath of outsourcing human resources skill. According to a study by McKinsey, outsourcing the management of human resources can:

- save a good chunk of the cost
- even positively impact employee satisfaction.

Many people, however, (including myself) do not agree to this argument because, outsourcing or no outsourcing, humans resources are a company's number 1 competitive advantages. But it is always wise to consider the counter-view. One of the participants to the research project on which this book is based brought up as an example *Exult*, a human resources outsourcer, founded in 1998. This company now manages employment issues for a number of Fortune 500 companies, including Bank of America, BP Amoco, Unisys, and International Paper.

The transactional and administrative processes International Paper has outsourced include payroll, benefits and systems support for 70,000 employees. This is a ten-year, $600 million contract. The Bank of America contract covers regional staffing and recruiting. A major challenge which I see with such contracts is that of retaining employee loyalty and motivation, when it becomes known somebody else looks after them. R&D is a people-intensive activity. Will outsourced personnel management make knowledge workers kick?

6. Project management. Is it wise to outsource it?

Whether the engineering project is done inhouse or it is outsourced, it has to be managed. The emphasis on quality, timing, cost and performance often leads to painful choices, including that of killing the project. This is true both at the outsourcer's side and at that of the insourcer. It serves precious little to continue a project which started poorly and/or it is going badly.

An example on action taken by the insourcer is offered by KPMG Consulting. Every Friday senior vice-president Kenneth C. Taormina grills his salesforce on every single deal, asking: 'What do we need to get it done?' 'There's a lot more emphasis on measuring things that we wouldn't have measured before,' says Managing Director Darryl B. Moody.[8]

Projects should be steadily reviewed and management must have the guts to kill even some of its pet R&D projects. When KKR bought RJR Nabisco through a leveraged buyout it unearthed and stopped the premier project sponsored by the previous management. This grandiose project represented an ill-fated $1 billion attempt to develop a smokeless cigarette nobody seems to have wanted.

Another interesting reference is that made by George Anders: 'Next to go was Cookeville, an ambitious $2 billion plan to build two high-tech bakeries using robots and optical sensors, instead of human beings, in making cookies.' It was ludicrous... 'In one instance, Cookeville planners wanted to install $10 million of robotics to eliminate three jobs held by forklift operators.'[9]

It is unimaginable what bureaucratic planners would do when projects are left to run without checks and balances. Living in an ivory tower and detached from the salt of the earth, some project managers have trouble finding their footing as the market environment paces ahead. Priorities should therefore be targeted to:

- bring everybody down to earth, or move them out of the system
- evaluate projects in a way that original goals are never lost from sight.

Whether engineering design projects are insourced or outsourced, a fundamental rule should always be that cost and functionality are addressed through a well-established process of project control. Events unearthed through design reviews (see section 7) must be used to do simulations and cross-probes, tracing errors back to:

- the tools employed earlier in the design flow
- miss-steps which went undetected
- wanting progress reports connected to any given design phase.

A data acquisition facility should support a wide range of functions. For instance, the designer working in a multisourced tool environment (see section 5) must be able to set event information, evaluate acquisition status, define triggers and callbacks, and preview data while the device is performing a data acquisition session typically consisting of four steps:

1 initialization, creating a device object
2 configuration, including manipulation and control of data
3 evaluation of the object, including sending data streams
4 termination, including visualization of configured device.

By extension, in a multisourced design environment functions must be provided for previewing and extracting data for analysis. Tools must stream data into the workspace, supporting the ability to work with such data in the designer's chosen format. Functions should also be available for logging data and events, as well as for extracting information without hindrance because of differences in format and protocols characterizing the multisourced environment.

It is self-evident that project management must be endowed with appropriate tools and methods. Project control facilities should be employed to create information about the project, such as directory structure, design files, and identification of collaborators by phase and design section. Sophisticated design flows should be on hand making timing information available to workstations collaborating in the design network.

Whether a project is fully insourced, partly outsourced or fully out-sourced, any changes that the designers make to meet their goals must be mapped on the design files and presented in the form of assignments or con-straints. This is an integral part of project management.

• Changes need to be properly identified, along which decisions which motivated them.
• They should be processed through a phase of synthesis, to permit that alterations are evaluated post-mortem regarding their wisdom.

Let me add that the themes connected to multisourcing of engineering design tools and product design perspectives presented in this section are at the very roots of the mechancs of outsourcing engineering facilities. By con-trast, the acquisition and development perspectives discussed in sections 4 and 5 were the dynamics. The two complement one another. They also bring up the need for examining the role of design reviews and their impact on the life of an engineering project – as well as the expected deliverables.

Every project has a risk factor associated to it, suggested the Royal Bank of Canada. If it is late or of low quality, the decision is to kill it. Design reviews are made every two weeks, evaluating both projects and project managers (more on this later).

Since project management is confronted with so many challenges, it should definitely benefit from proper planning. Whether an engineering design project is done inhouse or it is outsourced, the best way to plan is to start, not at the beginning, but at the end of it. Figure 6.6 presents as an example the method developed by Jean Monnet, a senior banker widely considered to be the father of Europe. The backwards simulation of an execution plan is designed to meet human factors which are dominating the successful completion of projects – with emphasis being placed on deliverables.

In the background of this walk-through simulation, which starts at the projected end of the project, lies the fact that very often project managers do not understand the end-users', needs. This is definitely a human factor with a horde of possible repercussions. Quite often this backwards walk-through will make evident that:

• the project's scope has been ill-defined
• the project lacks people with appropriate skills
• the chosen technology is substandard
• the project's progress is managed poorly
• managers ignore best practices and lessons learned
• users are resistant to change, and
• sponsorship is lost somewhere down the line.

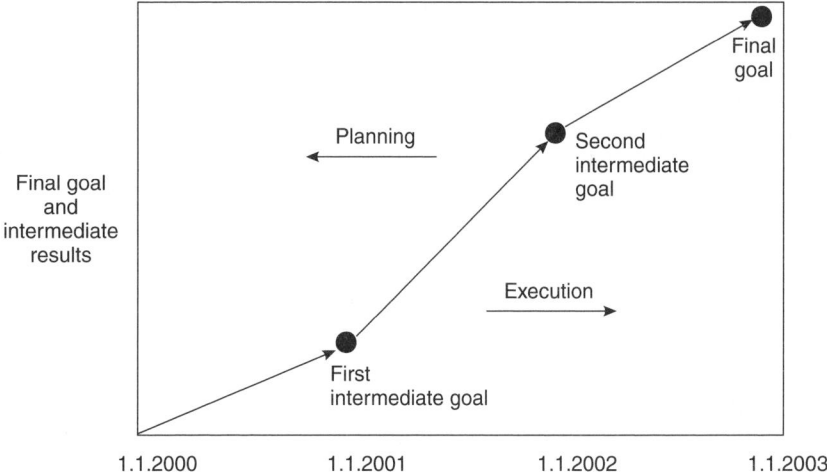

Figure 6.6 Backwards simulation of a plan designed to meet specific objectives

Experience with this method demonstrates that moving backwards corrects many of these ills because it obliges people to think in terms of intermediate goals and resources needed to meet them. It also makes it mandatory to conduct design reviews after the project starts and goes forward. This is cornerstone to successfully completing an engineering design mission, whether the project is done inhouse or it is outsourced.

7. Meeting the challenge of design reviews

Management planning and control is a fully integrated activity. Planning without control is daydreaming, and control cannot be exercised without palnning principles, yet a challenge I often encountered in my professional work is that many companies lack the *progress review* culture, and they don't appreciate what it takes to maintain a state-of-the-art verification environment. As engineering projects continue to increase in complexity,

- verification requires both engineering *and* management skills, and
- policies, ways and means to face the challenges for verification teams.

A sound policy is that of frequent design reviews. The mission of a design review is to control the project schedule, cost, functionality and quality during the development cycle. The schedule is all-important because time-to-market is a crucial factor in product design, as companies must bring their products to market faster than their competitors; but the other factors, too, are crucial.

Take as an example the observance of quality criteria. Some companies turn their wheels in a vacuum when they are verifying quality because they have not made it an explicit target. Therefore, it is not subject to complete verification. When this happens, the design review process is wanting.

In a meeting in Detroit in the 1950s I was told that American automobile manufacturers thought 'quality' was too vague a metric to measure but learned to do it in the face of Japanese competition (which, ironically, had tremendously benefit from American quality control theory and tools).

The alter ego of quality is cost. This, too, must be a major theme in design reviews, whether the project is made inhouse or it is outsourced.

- Few engineering project are able to control timetables, quality and cost at the same time.
- Nevertheless, all three factors are most crucial to all projects at all time – and they should be religiously observed.

An ongoing challenge too is the recruiting and retention of talented engineers to staff verification projects. As a result, many companies are moving to *verification outsourcing*. They are employing an outside group of engineers to do design reviews – essentially technical auditing – which allows these companies to bring their products to market faster. This approach can have several advantages.

Companies specialising in outsourcing design review know-how often retain highly skilled engineers who have a variety of project experiences and knowledge of multiple, complex verification issues. The best insourcers who are undertaking design reviews:

- devote years to developing a sound methodology and verification tools to drive their business
- bring a high level of expertise to each of their technical auditing projects because they possess the necessary wide range of domain experience.

By outsourcing verification of its inhouse and/or outsourced engineering design projects, a company can better track timetables costs, functionality and quality using the skill and knowledge of specialists devoted to verifying complex systems and designs. These design auditors work in a way similar to that of certified public accountants (CPAs) and they are at least supposed to be independent of inside pressures to produce a positive-looking report.

Conflicts of interest, of course, cannot be excluded – but they should be minimized. *If* an insourcer serves as a consultant to an engineering company, *then* he should not be qualified to do design reviews even if he has highly specialized personnel for that function. As the downfall of Enron, among so many other cases, documents the same people who do the advising cannot and should not be the controllers.

Also, whether the design reviews are done inhouse or are outsourced, the engineering firm and any other company should have a design review culture and the appropriate methodology. An example on a methodology which I learned in the early 1960s at General Electric, and I have been using since then very successfully, is given in Figure 6.7. It calls for:

- major design reviews at 25 per cent, 55 per cent, 80 per cent and 90 per cent of a project's timetable.

These are milestones which roughly correspond to 10 per cent, 25 per cent, 50 per cent and 75 per cent of the project's cost.

Between the major design reviews should be verifications, or minor design reviews, preferably done weekly. 'Every project has a risk factor associated to it,' suggested the Royal Bank of Canada. 'If it is late or of low quality, the decision is to kill it. Design reviews are made every two weeks, evaluating both projects and project managers.' Weekly is a better frequency than bi-weekly. The policy which I follow is that:

- The major design review can kill a project, if the need be.
- The object of the minor design review is to solve problems, redirect the effort, and do away with conflict – but it can also lead to an extraordinary major design review.

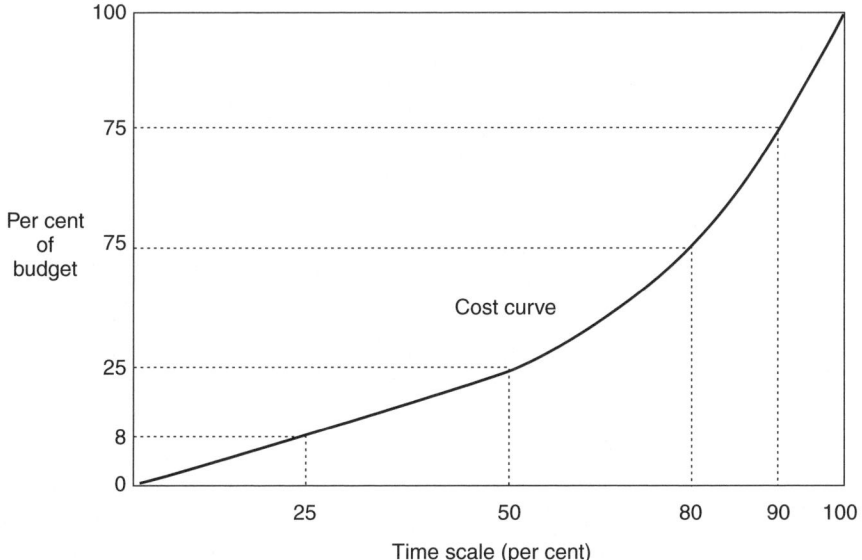

Figure 6.7   The need for design reviews is present in any project

Provided that the principles outlined in the foregoing paragraphs are observed, there are good reasons to adopt a policy of outsourcing design reviews. The value of verification outsourcing lies in the quality of engineers of the insourcer and the speed at which they can verify the project, helping customers achieve quicker time-to-market and other results. However, the outsourcer's senior management should participate to these design reviews.

Outsourcing of technical auditing could also help in solving a company's dilemma of allocating resources to recruiting top engineers, a difficulty faced throughout the industry. Hiring inexperienced designers with little domain and verification expertise may cause more problems and cost more money than outsourcing, without necessarily having access to a wealth of engineering talent at the control end of the profession.

In some cases, insourcers are able to provide verification expertise to customers located in remote areas who cannot attract a qualified staff due to geography. And cost control might be another benefit of properly negotiated technical auditing outsourcing projects. Because many insourcing staffs use their own tools and equipment dedicated to verification methodologies, customers may end by paying less for hardware, software, staffing, and retention.

- Using a group of engineers with the skills and expertise to efficiently conduct verification might lower price.
- At the same time, it could also greatly reduce the potential for errors and alterations, that end up being very costly since so often they are created by pressures internal to the company.

In conclusion, design reviews are a 'must'. In several cases their outsourcing provides focus on verification tasks and, therefore, produces quicker results. This means faster time-to-market for the company's products and a greater emphasis on product costs and quality. Outsourcing a complex project can provide an experienced team of engineering professionals committed to the verification function – but make no mistake about it: the final responsibility of the results rests with the outsourcer's own top management.

7

What It Takes to Outsource the Pattern of Production

1. Introduction

Outsourcing the pattern of production, or at least part of it, is nothing new. Lamp companies, among others, do it as a matter of course. To bring costs down, they specialise in certain types of lamps, manufacturing these types both for themselves and for some of their competitors. In the latter case, they are stamping on them the other company's name or logo.

In the motor vehicle industry, typically 50 cents to the dollar of an auto's cost represents parts bought from suppliers, which is one of the best example of massive outsourcing of production processes. The key questions, therefore, are not whether or not to outsource some of the manufacturing activities, but rather:

- Under which conditions this should take place?
- How well an outsourcing agreement can compete with inhouse solutions?

A factual and documented answer to these queries requires gaining a broader perspective from a merchandising viewpoint, not only from the narrower angle of manufacturing. For the purpose of this chapter, the manufacturing and merchandising of man-made goods will be considered from the broader viewpoint of world trade which means:

- no matter where they may be made
- no matter where they may be sold
- for any purpose these transactions take place.

A recent article outlines the strategy Toyota follows, with its global team of insourcers, in building on time and within budget the Central Japan International Airport, also known as Tokyo's Centrair.[1] The gameplan rests on three pillars:

1 cost benchmarks for suppliers
2 competitive bidding for contractors
3 orderly but plenty expert advice.

To get people who think outside the box, Toyota's Yukihisa Hirano, the man in charge of the project, invited a team of 15 independent international consultants to review blueprints. They recommended more than fifty time- and money-saving changes which helped to shave 20 per cent off the main passenger terminal's cost.

This example on outsourcing of skills is a subset of much broader activities which characterise globalisation (see section 4 on offshore outsourcing). Another, one of the visible consequences of a globalised market, is the notable increase in world trade for goods, over the last fifty years. The share of global trade in production items has risen rapidly since the end of the Second World War. Foreign direct investment has also grown significantly, especially over the 1990s. These two subjects correlate.

Statistics from the World Trade Organisation (WTO) indicate that while world trade as a proportion of global production – that is, the overall total of gross domestic products (GDP) around the world – came to around 10 per cent in 1970. This figure has more than doubled to stand at about 25 per cent today. Up to a point, such an impressive rise can be explained by the:

• behaviour of consumers
• role played by countless small and medium-sized enterprises (SME).

The SME are primarily insourcers and their demand and supply has a decisive influence on world trade. Another crucial factor is the large flows of merchandise and commercial services that occur within multinational corporations. It is estimated that this inhouse cross-border dealing accounts for one-third of all global trading in goods, and it can be seen as a sort of internal outsourcing to foreign affiliates with lower labour costs.

• Merchandising and commercial services relate to each other as complements and/or substitutes.
• This is evidently true of cross-border production factors, although the latter are also ruled by the law of minimum costs.

Purchasing managers, importers and consumers have a list of preferences regarding where they buy which guide their hand, even if they cannot satisfy all of them all of the time. Consumers go for cheaper goods because their incomes and budgets are finite. When deciding what to buy they have to assess the different ways and means available to them.

Companies, on the other hand, are competing with each other in three markets:

1 the innovation market
2 the lowest cost purchase market
3 the sales market.

These are fundamental elements of the manufacturers endgame. As shown in Figure 7.1 when considering only three factors; Agriculture, mining and manufacturing, the latter today represents about 80 per cent of global trade – nearly double the share it had in 1950 (see also in section 6 the comparison of manufacturing to services). To recapitulate, outsourcing in manufacturing should be seen within the broader perspective of a worldwide approach rather than a very limited viewpoint within a single country. Notice also that in the global landscape competition is driven by learning processes (see Chapter 11), innovation (see Chapter 6) and productivity gains (see Chapter 8).

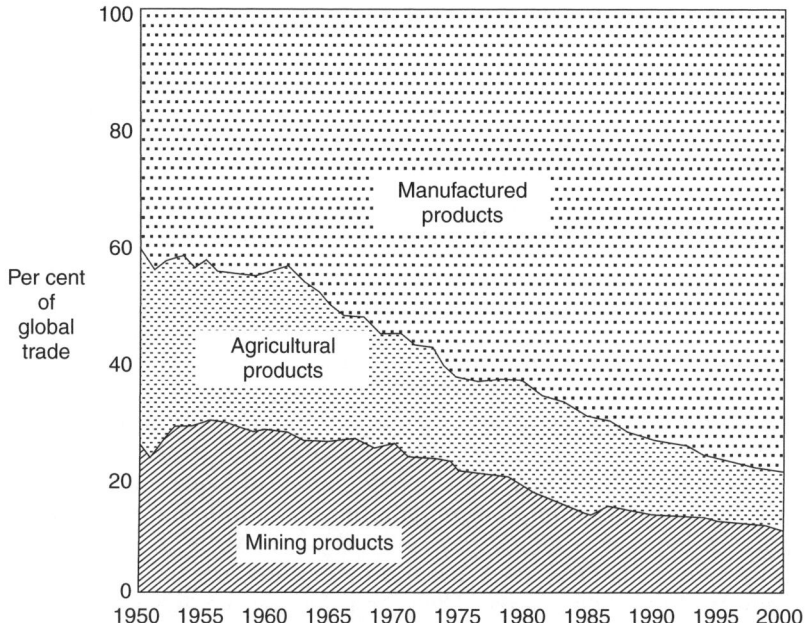

Figure 7.1   Major classes of merchandise as a per cent of global trade, 1950–2000

2. Markets, products and the manufacturing industry

Since the 1960s the United States, Western Europe and Japan have been going through a profound economic shift prompted in great part by the globalisation of manufacturing. This sea change in their economic structure and the aftermath it brings to the different regional and local markets is rendering some basic industries obsolete. With them a good number of time-honoured industrial practices also go out of the window.

Because manufacturing still has so much of a labour content in terms of direct cost, prevailing conditions in many countries, like high social charges, make transborder outsourcing necessary. Costs are always a driving force. Prior to opening up manufacturing facilities in America, BMW studied the prevailing labour costs and found that in the mid-Atlantic states (where the factory was made) they were 50 per cent lower than those in Munich, while in unionised Detroit they stood at 75 per cent the German labour costs.

The ability to compete on a cost basis in the global market has not escaped the attention of small and medium-sized enterprises which are major beneficiaries from the big companies' outsourcing. SMEs have integrated into world trade to different extents. In the United States, for example, 12 per cent of SMEs export their merchandise, while in Italy the comparable figure is 80 per cent. In both the USA and Thailand, these SMEs account for about 10 per cent of national export volumes, while the corresponding proportion in Taiwan is 56 per cent, in Italy 53 per cent and in Switzerland 40 per cent.

With regard to world trade statistics, the euroland has the highest share with a ratio of exports to total world exports at around 19.5 per cent, above that of the United States (15 per cent) and Japan (8.5 per cent). The degree of openness, measured by the average of exports and imports of goods and services as a percentage of GDP, stands at 16 per cent for the euroland. This is higher than that in the United States, where it is about 12 per cent, and of Japan's 10.5 per cent.

However, there is a catch. Most trade for individual euroland countries takes place with other European Union area countries. Therefore, from a regional perspective, this is internal trade and hence it is unaffected by exchange rate movements of the euro *vis-à-vis* other currencies. The important distinction to keep in mind is that to monetary union individual member states were considered 'small or medium-sized open economies', with significantly higher ratios for the average of exports and imports of goods to GDP.

Indeed, after 1 January 2002, the statistics we just saw have changed. For the euroland as a whole, exports of goods as a percentage of GDP is now just over 13 per cent, while imports of goods is slightly above 11 per cent. External trade in services is significant, but less than that for goods, with exports and imports of services as a percentage of GDP at around 4 per cent.

The dynamic nature of cross-country trade sees to it that as global competition intensifies and the artificial barriers which were protecting certain markets crumble – and with them a number of local industries – it becomes increasingly apparent that those companies are best positioned to survive which are:

• low-cost producers and distributors
• at the same time offer high-quality products and services.

Technology can be instrumental in achieving this sort of dual goal provided that it is used with imagination (see also Chapter 8). This is not always the case; policies which can sustain growth and survival come as a matter of course. Careful planning and evaluation are necessary, particularly because the manufacturing industry is in transition and transitions bring challenges. The ability to lead in global insourcing is one of them. At the same time, failure to undertake the necessary transition ends in:

• much higher costs
• loss of competitiveness.

A manufacturing enterprise can go out of business and die if it is not able to steadily reinvent itself. This means if it does not revamp and update its products, processes, markets – but also, if not primarily, its human capital, its culture and its structure. For reasons we have already seen, the management of change should be the number 1 goal of industrial strategy – that is, a company's master plan against its corporate opponents.

Outsourcing certain phases of our production process is integral part of the management of change, but it should not be done without an appropriate study including stress tests (see section 5). As shown in Figure 7.2, from planning to execution, the proper methodology for an outsourcing agreement includes several crucial steps. Every one of the elements in this block diagram contributes to:

• the success of outsourcing if it is properly done
• its failure if it is poorly performed or left out of the equation altogether.

The setting of goals for outsourcing part of the production pattern should assure continuity year after year, while never failing to observe cost-effectiveness also has its own targets. For instance, slashing spending, shrinking overheads, significantly improving products and service quality, achieving faster inventory turnover, and swamping inventoried goods through just-in-time (JIT) deliveries.

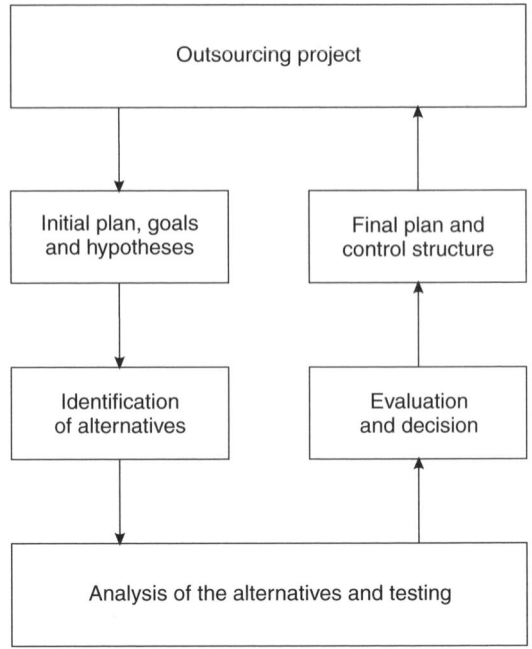

Figure 7.2 Modelling an outsourcing project involves a great deal of study and experimentation

• The common ground of these references is cutting down the creeping excesses in people and in materials.
• This requires both a policy and a culture focusing on results rather than complacency and hopeful thinking.

When a company must lower its prices by 10 per cent, 20 per cent, or more every year or improve its performance by the same amount, it does not have time for resting on past laurels. It has to implement in fast succession effective solutions; that where outsourcing comes in as one of its strategies.

Avaya makes this point in its 2001 annual report. With reference to outsourcing of certain manufacturing facilities, it says that in May 2001 it closed the first phase of a five-year strategic manufacturing agreement to outsource most of the manufacturing of its communications systems and software to Celestica. Under the agreement, Avaya received approximately $200 million in cash for the assets it transferred to Celestica. Prior to that, in September 2000, in conjunction with its restructuring plans to exit certain manufacturing operations, Avaya had sold its manufacturing facility located in San Jose, California, to Sanmina. (More about the decline in inhouse manufacturing in section 3.) However,

- not every insourcer who happens to be around is a reliable outsourcing partner
- to worth their salt, outsourcing solutions have to be properly negotiated in terms of deliverables: timetables, costs and quality of products.

To manage outsourcing in an able manner we need a system of meaningful *metrics* and steady *monitoring*. We should always be measuring the performance of the insourcer, and this we cannot do that if we are not able to measure our own performance and cost-effectiveness (see in the three chapters of Part IV how and why cost control helps the bottom line of outsourcing agreements.

It is appropriate to take note that cross-border deals increase the complexity of metrics and measurements, even if they provide a better landscape for selection and, by all likelihood, of lower production costs. This means that the outsourcer organisation must carefully study its policy regarding the controls which it would apply. It may for instance choose to limit the number of insourcers in order to supervise them better. Toyota provides an example of a major change in outsourcing policies. It is:

- moving away from having multiple suppliers of parts and accessories
- aiming for no more than two suppliers for any one part.

These suppliers will be independent companies, but Toyota will for all practical purpose run their manufacturing operations. They will get the Toyota account only if they agree to being advised and inspected by a special Toyota manufacturing consulting organisation, which will evidently put emphasis on metrics and monitoring in a way that suits best the outsourcer.

Other companies, too, are or have followed this policy. In its heydays, Marks & Spencer maintained pre-eminence by keeping an iron grip on its suppliers. Wal-Mart has done the same thing and it continues doing so. Not only does it control the costs and quality of its suppliers but it is also channelling the resources of these suppliers through its marshalling yards according to its own, not their, plans and schedules.

3. Doing away with wrong ideas about production and outsourcing

Wrong ideas abound in the manufacturing industry. For instance, many people wrongly believe that when manufacturing jobs decline or the country's production base is threatened, this production bases has to be protected through high-rising walls. People who think that way are not clear-eyed enough to understand that, for the first time in history, society and economy are no longer dominated by manual work – and the effect of 'protecting' labour-intense activities is tantamount to making a bad situation of high cost/low productivity even worse.

Because technology advances by leaps and bounds, a society can house, feed and clothe itself with only a small minority of its population engaged in agriculture, construction and manufacturing. That is why protecting ageing and crumbling sectors of the economy does not work. State policies that pay old, smoke-stack industries to hold on to redundant people can only harm a country's productive capacity and society as a whole.

What is true of society and its industrial base is valid of individual companies as well. Managers who have a good grasp of what is required for being efficient, look at the whole world as their possible production base. They challenge the 'obvious', and examine new possibilities all the time, so that they keep themselves ahead of the curve.

Because after the Second World War American industry taught itself how to keep on a dynamic track, many success stories in outsourcing come from the United States. Cisco Systems owns only two of the 34 plants that manufacture its products, and in this insourcer landscape the production process has been highly automated. Roughly 85 per cent of the orders come into and out of the company without ever being touched by human hands; and 52 per cent of them are fulfilled without a Cisco employee being involved.

'To my customers, it looks like one big virtual plant where my suppliers and inventory systems are directly tied into the ecosystem,' says Cisco's CEO. 'That will be the norm in the future. Everything will be completely connected, both within a company and between companies. The people who get that will have a huge competitive advantage.'[2]

As should be expected, technology companies are more prone to and better able in automating their outsourcing than others, but not all enterprises know-how to make the most out of this activity. Many look at it as a way to relegate responsibilities rather than to be super-efficient, the latter requiring a fair amount of ingenuity.

Poor management policies and organisational failures do not allow gain advantages from outsourcing, as inefficient inhouse practices are carried to the insourcer's shop. In one specific case I have in mind an astounding (and irrational) 68.5 per cent of all engineering work has been done on the production line, resulting in a swarm of problems. When this is the case, it makes no sense to outsource anything.

Performance statistics are greatly improved when the company takes a holistic view which integrates inhouse production facilities with those being outsourced. Detail is very important, and it should be explicitly stated by product, production facility (inhouse and outsourced), quality characteristics, due date and other crucial variables. As Figure 7.3 demonstrates, there must be in place an integrative, interactive planning and control system.

While there is no guarantee that good organisation will lead into agreements which are always problem free, but this is the way to bet. *If* we choose

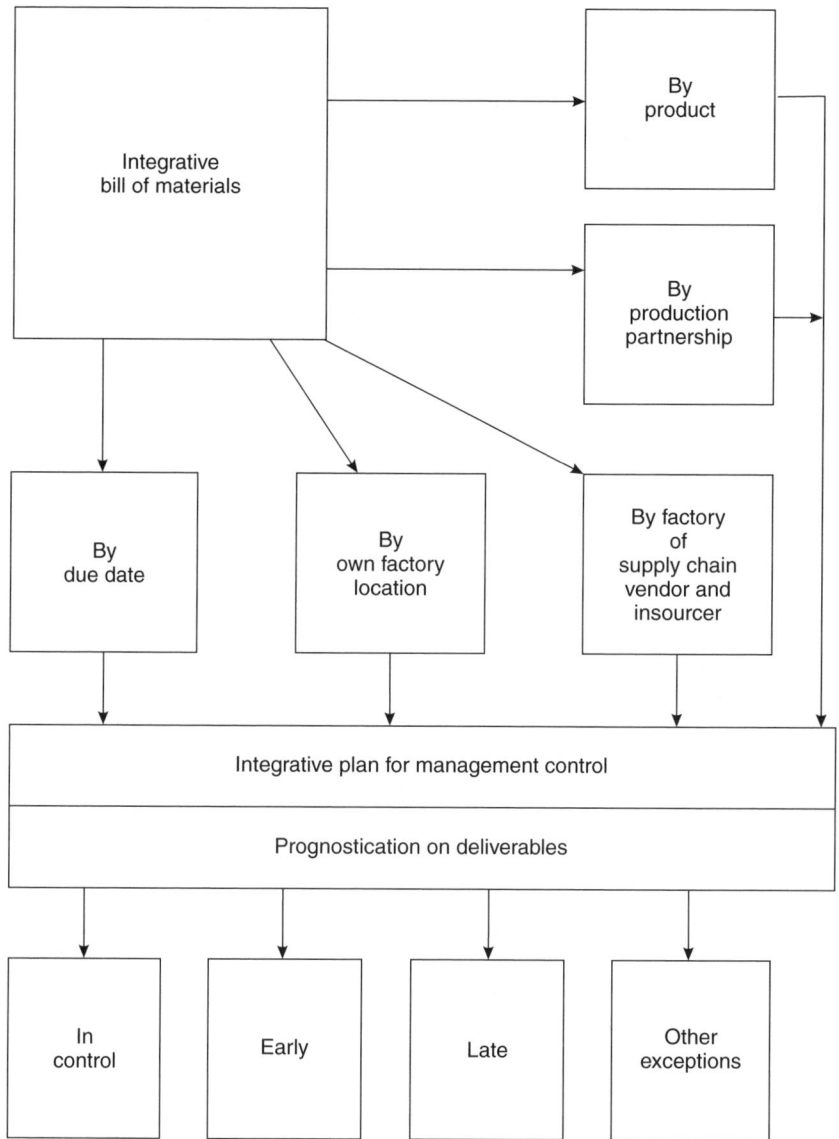

Figure 7.3 Planning and control should be company wide, include insourcers, and permit a bird's-eye view of operations

a networked manufacturing model, *then* our planning must be an order of magnitude more accurate than otherwise. In Cisco's care, for example, a network of suppliers and contract manufacturers delivers an unusually large chunk of Cisco-branded merchandise direct to customers. This business model is supposed to:

- keep fixed costs to a minimum
- eliminate the need for inventory
- give management an instantaneous, real-time fix on orders, shipments and demand.

The way a recent article had it, however, the model behind this system failed to account for the double and triple ordering by customers tired of waits for shipments. To correct this problem, Cisco began to stockpile parts and finished products. 'We made a conscious decision when our lead times were 12 to 13 weeks to build inventory, because we were having a sizeable amount of revenues on the table every quarter,' said one of Cisco's executives.[3]

Bugs can exist in any system and, usually, most of the glitches of a system show up after it starts operating. Sometimes the adopted solution has been chosen to cover up other weaknesses, or for leveraging reasons. The more the leveraging, the higher the probability of failures. An example is outsourcing at Enron, which has been a major management blunder.

Most energy companies back trading operations with hard assets, such as power plants. These allow them to guarantee a supply to the buyer. On the contrary, Enron worked furiously to shed power plants and oil- and gas-generating fields. (The French Alcatel, a telecommunications equipment company, did the same for its line of business.) Enron's management believed it could earn higher returns by:

- using its trading and technology expertise
- tapping assets owned by others in markets including steel, pulp, paper and broadband communications.

Financial scandals aside, this strategy of disinvestment was a major contributor to Enron's bankruptcy. The company's salient problem is that it suffered from a crisis of confidence, not a meltdown of its core business. Because financial assets are more easily manipulated than physical assets, Enron leveraged itself at unreasonably high levels which proved to be unsustainable. An out-of-control outsourcing was part of the leverage.

No rules are available on how much of its production base a company should keep inhouse and how much can be outsourced. Practically, every company tries to find its way, but it is always wise to avoid the extremes. This does not mean one has to put up with inhouse inefficiencies. The best is to have forward-looking policies (see section 4), using a sharp knife to cut costs and technology to improve performance.

The able use of technology is always opposed to mythology which many people in business and industry espouse. The products of industry, and the production processes themselves, are not some kind of monument around which myths are built. Neither do they have some sort of supranatural qualities; nor is there any reason they should not change over time. By contrast:

- change is the keyword not only of science but also of industry
- this is true even if there is widespread resistance to change and renovation.

Time and again outsourcing activities are being handicapped because of resistance to change. Experience teaches that resistance to change mainly comes from those who stand to lose significant advantages they have today. Because they know-how to capitalise on the inefficiencies of the current system they don't want to see that system being replaced by something else, even if it is crumbling.

Industrial history teaches that companies which depend on shopping for value for their survival, but fail to change their policies and their methods, condemn themselves to decay. A study done by National Association of Securities Dealers/Automatic Quotation System (NASDAQ) in the mid 1990s has shown that, to survive, a computer technology company must reinvent itself every two-and-a-half years. This reinvention cycle characterises today many companies, including financial institutions, whose survival rests on the able use of high technology.

Astute management is able to appreciate that a great deal of change has come not only through outsourcing certain facilities but also by putting internal production facilities in competition to the insourcer. Bankers Trust used this strategy to whip its IT people into greater productivity. The board had authorised the bank's departments to outsource their IT needs *if* the conditions they got from insourcers were more favourable than those prevailing inhouse; in other words, *if* inhouse IT could not match the insourcer's conditions.

Down to the bottom line, the endgame is productivity and some companies are much more capable at it than others. At Ryanair, the independent Ireland-based European airline, revenue per employee is 40 per cent or more higher than with the major airlines. In 2001, Ryanair carried 9 million passengers with 1500 employees, while Aer Lingus carried 6 million passengers and had a staff of 7000. In this case the difference is not 40 per cent but 700 per cent.

Ryanair did not outsource its carrier fleet. It is running it itself, but at a high level of efficiency. What is true of the fleet is also true of its sales activities. Since the launch of Ryanair.com in January 2000, 65 per cent of all tickets are sold online, with more than 250,000 bookings each week. Today, agents account for 8 per cent of sales, and their commissions have been slashed to 5 per cent from 7.5 per cent.

4. The changing face of production: cell-based manufacturing and offshore outsourcing

Alternative products and processes don't always succeed, but there is no way to decide about them until we have seen the market's reaction. Take alternatives to petroleum products as an example. Pollution from nearly 200 million vehicles utilising 67 per cent of the petroleum currently consumed in the United States has induced many engineers, labs and companies to search for alternative fuels.

If the tidal wave of vehicles and their inevitable exhaust gases are not going to ebb, why not look for alternative energy sources? John Heywood, of the Department of Mechanical Engineering, MIT, did so and he came to the conclusion there is nothing like petroleum as motor fuel in terms of the energy it produces per unit of volume. All other alternatives that now exist seem to be worse by a factor of two or more.

'Alternative fuels don't offer as much as we thought on first sight because there is a significant energy loss in comparison to petroleum-based fuel,' says Heywood. 'But it's not likely to be an either/or choice. Fuel cell technology will just take a long time to perfect before it becomes attractive to users.'[4] Something similar can be said about alternative manufacturing technologies.

In this section we will talk about two alternative production processes which have met with some greater success. One is cell-based manufacturing, an approach designed to replace long transfer lines (the old Henry Ford model, where a worker does a single repetitive task all day). The other is an organised offshore outsourcing. Contrary to the method used with assembly lines, small manufacturing cells offer workers a complete and fairly efficient environment for:

- making component parts
- assembling a variety of parts into a product
- gaining greater efficiency because of being better stimulated and more productive.

In this sense, cell manufacturing methods can be time and money savers. Companies using this approach have also found that a cell strategy helps to lower absenteeism, and may as well assist in obtaining overall reduction in investment while providing greater manufacturing flexibility. Furthermore, cells:

- lower direct labour costs
- reduce throughput time
- shrink floor space requirements.

Inhouse restructuring of production methods along the most modern and efficient solutions currently available should always be examined as an alternative to outsourcing. New technology has driven companies towards personalisation of goods and services, and this resulted in the demise of mass production. Yet many firms continue to work with obsolete production methods and tools. They have failed to take notice that there is a fundamental change for which they must account.

When company size and/or culture lead to an insensitivity to efficiency requirements, then economies of scale turn into diseconomies. Outsourcing or no outsourcing, this issue of sensitivity to both customer wishes and modern production methodologies is among the basic reasons why in many fields economic activity has moved from large firms to small, more innovative and more flexible firms:

- from IBM to Compaq and from Compaq to Dell
- from Sears Roebuck to Wal-Mart
- from AT&T/Western Electric (now Lucent) and Northern Telecom to Nokia and Cisco.

Another interesting characteristic of our time is that in an epoch where creativity is the cornerstone of business success. Product and process obsolescence comes rapidly and without warning, leading experts to suggest that the twenty-first century can best be characterised as an epoch of creative destruction. In my professional experience I have found it often difficult to convince boards of directors, to which I have been consultant, that as people and products die, factories, too, die. We should not be attached to old, crumbling structures.

Cell-based manufacturing is much better able than long assembly lines to respond to changing market requirements and to the personalisation of products and processes customers now demand. Generally, the companies that are more prone to adopt new production techniques and capitalise on technology's advances are the ones that cannot afford to do otherwise because they see that they will be out of business. A good example is that of gold producers and their mining costs.

The 1997 to 2001 time-frame has been a terrible one for gold mining companies and for most people in the gold industry. The price of the precious metal fell below $270 per ounce. That was bad enough. Even worse would have been, the potentially substantial rise in production costs had it not been for the able and steady use of technology.

Over the years, as a result of this huge price difference, once-profitable mines became unprofitable. Some were shut down and new mines were not being built, as they could not attract financing since the gold industry was out of favour with investors. Therefore, the best managed firms sought salvation in alternative mining methods.

To survive, gold mining companies saw to it that expenses were cut to the bone and the carrying values of their assets were reduced. To be able to afford to wait for better times, they took hedge positions and tried to be cash-flow neutral – no matter how low the gold price might fall on world markets. New investments went almost exclusively to the upgrade of production technology. For mining companies this is an activity they cannot outsource.

The lesson taught by this reference is that in hard times the best strategy for survival is to focus the company on what's truly important, taking the steps which are necessary not only to see through an extended period of depressed prices but also to thrive when prices improve. Alternative solutions must be tested. In some cases, as with cell-based manufacturing, they work. In others, as with alternative fuels, the results are not so exciting. Offshore outsourcing falls somewhere between these two examples.

On the surface, there is no ground why offshore outsourcing should be that much different than contracts given to inland insourcer firms. In real life, however, the differences between inland and offshore outsourcing can be significant, and this for different reasons. Among others, cultural and language barriers, see to it that many companies do not position themselves in a way to understand the:

- wider managerial requirements
- technical requirements associated to offshore outsourcing.

Understanding the managerial requirements associated to offshore outsourcing means appreciating which risks management are taking with offshore production deals–not only in the sense of quality of produce but of other factors as well, like child labour, country risks and legal risks at the offshore insourcer's site. Other considerations are financial.

- What's the project's ROI? How well is this projection documented?
- Can the projected deal be seen as a longer-term partnership? Why?

Management control often suffers with far-away offshore deals, bringing up crucial questions such as: is it possible to be in charge of functionality and quality of deliverables?; how much managerial support should be given by the outsourcer to the insourcer?; what has been learned in terms of best and worst practices from similar experiences?; can the risk(s) be mitigated?; if yes, in which way?

Many of the managerial questions to be asked should come upfront: can geographical hotspots be avoided?; how will the switch from one offshore outsourcer to another be made?; how clean is the supply of utilities in the country being chosen?; the transport means?; what's the back-up?; the output plan?; the legalities? Unless these queries have been answered in a factual manner, offshore outsourcing is not recommended.

Just as important is understanding the technical requirements for offshore outsourcing, down to the detail of how this process actually works under different country and company settings; which products or services could or should be outsourced (IT, others); and what kind and size of projects are best suited for offshore outsourcing; and how can these integrate with projects back home.

An integral part of choosing the offshore country (for instance India, East Europe or others) is to thoroughly examine which risks are taken with offshores, including company and country risk. Also, how can continuing handholding be assured – all the way from design and manufacturing to maintenance. In an age where communications solutions are all important, it is absolutely vital to analyse:

- what sort of communications links must and can be established with foreign teams
- how frequently these should be activated, and how frequent should be the person-to-person contact.

Just as important is to know upfront what kind of barriers may show up over time: cultural, political, juridical, linguistic and so on. As the careful reader will appreciate, these questions are not asked as being for or against offshore outsourcing 'in principle'. Rather, it is a matter of asking detailed queries and of getting documented answers. My experience tells me that not every company is keen to do so, and this is indeed regretful.

Let me add one last piece of advice on this subject of production outsourcing. Organisations are made of people, and any solution should pay a great deal of attention to the human factor. Jack Welch, the former General Electric CEO, once said it was 'important for the organisations to continually remove the bottom 10 per cent of their employees.'[5] That's an advice from a highly experienced and capable person which applies to outsourcing, and it should make the reader think. Removing the bottom 10 per cent of the outsourcers, say every year, is a steady task which requires thorough planning and an existing strategy.

5. Both outsourcing approaches and inhouse solutions must be foolproof

'If you can't measure it, you can't improve it', W. Edward Deming once said.[6] To 'measure' it we need *metrics*, and to choose the proper metrics and methods for measurement we need to unearth hidden factors behind the process which we study. Subsequently, we should do stress tests[7] until a product or process confesses its risk-related secrets.

In any line of business the first law regarding exposure is that the *risk you took is the risk you got*. Over time, a trade or a loan that seemed reasonable and prudent by classical criteria can turn out to be catastrophic. The risks were hidden. A credit risk should not have been taken in the first place, but it was, because of poor analysis or bad judgement. Management is not always as careful as it should have been.

With engineering products and services, and therefore with production processes, this is not excusable. Since the Second World War and the 1950s we have a huge body of knowledge in quality control and reliability engineering.[8] Products and processes often fail because of deficient quality controls and substandard specifications.

- This is what is implied by what is known as *dead on arrival*.
- A product or progress is unreliable because it does not perform at exactly the time it must execute its mission.

Reliability engineering teaches that the 'U' curve shown in Figure 7.4 characterises the life of all processes and products. Both natural and man-made

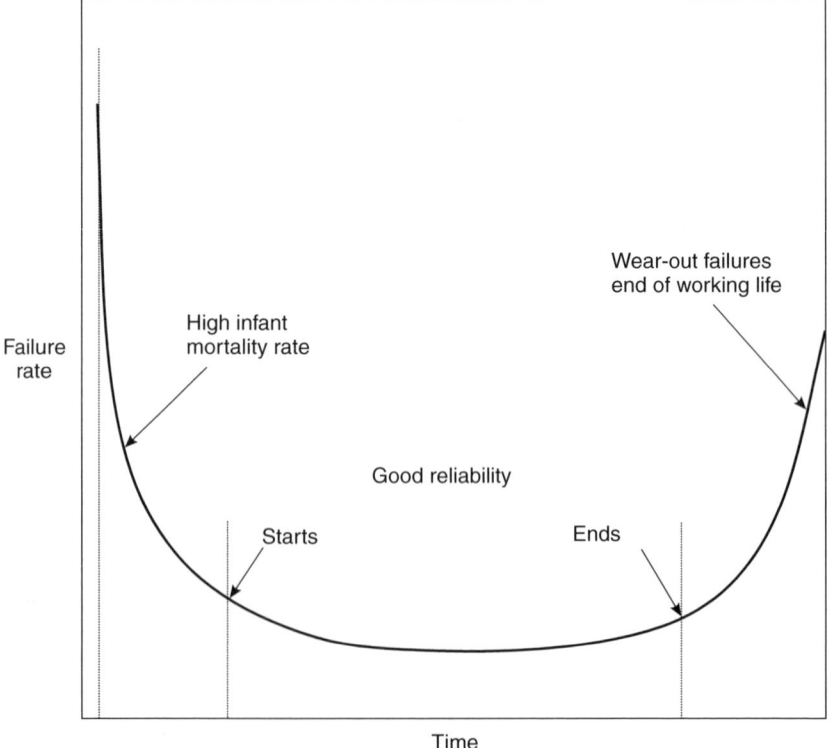

Figure 7.4 Natural and man-made systems have baby failures and wear-outs. Our goal should be high reliability

systems have baby failures at the start, and wear-outs towards the end of their life. Nothing works forever. The reliability curve in Figure 7.4 is, in essence, a life curve.

It is not only products that decay. The interaction between the process and the people running it is another failure source. Generally, this class of assumed risk is due to a factor named *asleep at the switch*. It characterises cases in which monitoring has been sloppy, with people responsible for the product or process violating the company's own basic rules.

In finance, for example, many credit institutions fall victim to an under-estimation of the severity of the down cycle in a given market. The general belief that by operating in many markets a bank achieves a portfolio effect that reduces overall risk is itself rotten, because it fails to account for the dispersion of management's attention. Having real-time data, using a daily global-risk chart that highlights worst-case scenarios, and making sure the right people are in control of the risks, are part of an effort to cope with that problem.

In manufacturing, merchandising and after-sales service the inordinate risk being assumed may be embedded in deficient control procedures – and it could hit both the outsourcer and in the insourcer. Here is a practical example. As it has been found post-mortem, the salesforce at different Enron Energy Services (EES) was routinely inflating profit estimates for long-term contracts they were negotiating. This practice:

- enriched the salesmen
- boosted the reported short-term profits by Enron.

Afterwards, however, many deals turned out to be loss makers, and they contributed to bringing the company down. Enron's top brass was showing its one-dimensional capabilities at a time the company's business demanded three dimensions. *If* Enron's management cared about riding on risk, *then* it had to get its hands dirty and be in change of risk control.

EES is a good case study in outsourcing. The company was founded in 1997, and it sought to convince businesses to outsource all of their energy needs to Enron. Its products ranged from electricity and natural gas to workers who would maintain boilers. A report in the *Financial Times* said that, according to allegations by former employees, EES racked up losses of more than $500 million despite reporting a $103 million pre-tax profit in 2000.[9] Salesmen were paid huge commissions on deals without much responsibility for how those deals later performed.

After three years of operations, EES had signed long-term contracts worth more than $30 billion. But according to some reports, the insourcer's com-pensation system had provided an incentive to the salesmen to sign a number of flawed deals. The salespeople were paid commissions based on the upfront earnings the company could book on these long-term contracts, even if:

- pricing was not transparent
- future payments were not predictable.

Every insourcer should appreciate that this is a situation open to a great amount of abuse. Before the policy was changed in 2001, the EES sales team could routinely guarantee customers generous discounts on large deals without making sure those savings were feasible. Added to the insourcer's risk was the fact that several contracts made no provision for price increases over their life-cycle.

Post mortem it has been said that Enron's senior management endorsed the salesmen's business behaviour because it contributed to the company's short-term profits at a time when other ventures, such as broadband trading, were not bringing in money. This was highly unwise from a managerial point of view. Instead of following this *laissez-faire* attitude, Enron's management should have conducted stress tests to find out:

- what current policies were profitable
- which ongoing products were worth their salt.

A great many examples of risks being assumed and their costs can be taken from engineering. For instance, the US Department of Commerce has estimated that the cost of fracture amounts to $119 billion per year, which is more than 1.1 per cent of the US gross national product. The same Department of Commerce study also predicted that half of this cost could be saved by using better design tools based on fracture mechanics technology. In engineering, cracks are caused initially by manufacturing defects and are possibly aggravated by localised damage. Both insourcers and outsourcers should appreciate that many uncontrollable risks start as fabrication defects and then get aggravated.

For example, microscopic cracks may grow through various mechanisms such as fatigue, stress-corrosion or creep. The growth of crack leads to a reduction in the strength of the component and eventually to a sudden and catastrophic failure. This defines the task of the fracture analyst as one of determining if the residual strength of the structure after a crack has developed is sufficient to sustain operational loading; also to evaluate the safe life of the structure if the crack is found to grow as a function of time or operational cycles.

A similar logic applies in finance, all the way to derivative products. Both in engineering and in finance, stress testing allows the flashing out of potential failures and the evaluation of the pattern of the product's or process's useful life. Some of this stress testing is destructive. For instance, current trade practices demand that incandescent lamps must have a useful life of 2000 hours with a standard deviation of no more than 200 hours. Two thousand hours can be simulated over a relatively short time-span by increasing the voltage. This has the effect of ageing the lamp much faster than under normal operating conditions.

Because increased emphasis is now placed on reliability, the use of damage tolerant design is spreading from its initial roots in the aerospace industry into many other industry sectors. Furthermore, as the requirements for quality, reliability, cost-effectiveness and product performance have increased, it is absolutely necessary for competitive reasons to provide risk information.

Among the existing techniques for risk prediction is experimentation through numerical models. This allows the analyst to focus on root causes embedded in the design since the computer model is conceptually simple, can be handled quickly, and automatically provides needed results when fed with proper data. Companies outsourcing part of their production facilities will be well advised to keep risk information at the top of their list of requirements from the insourcer.

6. The changing pattern of production and the role of services

The traditional economic conception of services as a tertiary sector, or set of economic activities, greatly undervalues their actual role. Today's economy is one of services and these need to be viewed as functional components of the value chain associated with all products and processes characterised by manmade activities. Therefore, the contribution of services to every sector of the economy must be properly acknowledged and measured.

- Innovation in services is proceeding rapidly, and it increasingly poses challenges to the traditional way we have looked at anything outside agriculture and manufacturing.
- In all their emerging forms, the internet and digital wireless technology are transforming the way a wide range of services are being produced, intermediated and consumed.

There is also a fast-developing concept of knowledge-based services like the design of custom-made derivative products. Knowledge-enriched instruments are helping to document that the production and consumption of many services are increasing but also their changes in sophistication. This requires an advanced base of knowledge and skills as well as new intermediaries spawned by advancing technology.[10]

Sprawling technology-based services are evidently affecting the pattern of production and, other things equal, they lead towards outsourcing. This is documented by statistics on patterns of production in the United States, Europe and Japan: In Western Europe today the services sector is the largest, accounting for about 67 per cent of total production; in percentage terms, it is behind the 72 per cent in the United States but way ahead of the 60 per cent in Japan.

The reader should be aware of the fact that the growth of services affects all layers of the manufacturing pyramid shown in Figure 7.5, though it does so much more at the higher level(s). (In this figure WS stands for workstation, LAN for local area network.) Therefore it must be supported through a fully distributed information technology, enriched with knowledge artefacts. Emphasis must be placed on mobility and real-time tracking.

Researchers at AT&T Laboratories in Cambridge, England have created a computer empowered to automatically know where its user is, where the engine itself is, and what resources it needs as it follows its user around an office. This *follow me* personal solution can deliver user-associated data to

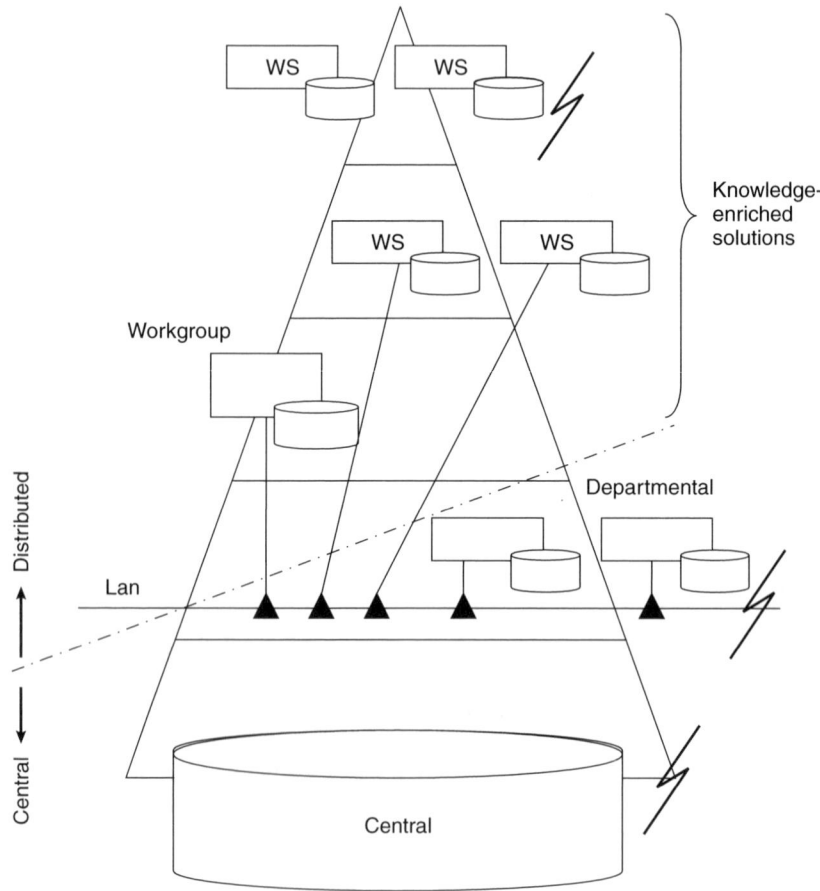

Figure 7.5   The higher a layer is in a pyramid the more it must be supported through knowledge artefacts

the nearest screen and route the enduser's calls to the nearest phone.[11] At MIT, Project Oxygen (the Intelligent Environment) foresees that computation will enter the human world nearly everywhere, handling our goals and needs. We will not have to carry personalised devices around with us. Instead:

- Anonymous devices, either hand-held or embedded in the environment, will bring computation to us no matter where we are or in what circumstances.
- These devices will personalise themselves in our presence by finding whatever information and software we require, leaving it to the computer to locate appropriate resources and carry out our wants.[12]

A group of researchers are working at the MIT Media Lab to create new sensing modalities and enabling technologies for responsive spaces, creating novel forms of interactive experience and expression. This work is highlighted in diverse application areas, ranging from interactive music systems to smart highways or wearable computers. While these projects are still in the making, others – like the able use of intelligent artefacts – have already made their mark in the service economy.

The reference to retain is that mobile agents mean mobile knowledge. In the 1950s and 1960s system solutions were centralised. In the 1970s and 1980s distributed environments were static, even expert systems had locality. This changed with interactive agents, in the 1990s. Post-year 2000 advanced system solutions:

- follow dynamic design programs
- make use of mobility mechanisms
- address networked applications.

Such solutions demand me rethink the executable parts of programs, including: flow of computation; distributed data space; and dynamic execution. The advantage of mobile code, through agents, is that it makes feasible *mobility of knowledge* over networks. Therefore, reliable broadband networks must assure any-to-any communications, and this reference evidently includes all:

- inhouse facilities
- business partners
- insourcers and outsourcers.

The knowledge artefacts running on the network must serve their masters by supporting them with every detail. They should be able to know who creates and uses which documents, and they must be looking after the time of deliverables, their quality and cost. Solutions must evidently reflect the fact that practically every business is creating an environment that:

• begins to compete every day on the internet
• uses microchip technology to substitute manual work.

Companies which continue to be labour intensive or to use mechanical and electrical components that no longer are cost effective are committing financial suicide. Microchip technology is a decisive factor in a service economy. A car now has up to 100 processors, and that's where the non-human intelligence resides.

As for the internet, practically everyone is announcing that they are using it to cut costs across industry boundaries. Nearly every company is affected, from retail trade to engineering and manufacturing – a statement fully documented the automotive, aerospace, electrical equipment and other industries.[13]

This reference to the evolution of services and their impact on outsourcing is important because, among other reasons, it brings into perspective the need for controlling the risks associated with outsourcing agreements in plain contractual terms. Let's face it, business and industry do not know well enough how to control the dependability of services.

Much can be learned in terms of ways and means of controlling the risks associated with services from the basic principles for outsourcing and outskilling led by the regulators. For instance, the German Federal Banking Supervision Office advises credit institutions that any agreement with a third party must be approved by the board of directors and senior management. Clauses in any outsourcing agreement must specify:

• standards for working with the vendor
• effective policies and means for their observance.

Not only there should be a written contract, but it should also include detail on conditions and controls. Confidentiality and security of information must be cornerstone to any outsourcing decision, and auditing rights must be spelled out to enable the outsourcer to conduct a meaningful analysis of the insourcer's performance.

Part and parcel of these guidelines is that both the bank and the supervisors must have access to all third-party working papers and databases. Most importantly, the bank's internal control system should be extended to the outsourced functions. Assets must not be commingled because of outsourcing. If they are, ownership of each asset must be fully identified.

To counteract operational risk, the outsourcer's senior management should maintain its overall responsibility for results. For instance, cost supervision is very important, because costs increase with time, subverting the original conditions. Because of all these reasons the regulators require that banks submit to their supervisory authorities their outsourcing plans, while the latter retain the right to audit the contracts and their aftermath.

Though many of these conditions are specifically applicable to banking, with minor changes they can be generalised and made pertinent to all outsourcing contracts. Particularly germane to research, development and production outsourcing are issues of confidentiality, technology transfer, timetables, costs and deliverables, as well as the extension of the outsourcer's internal control functions into the operations of the insourcer organisation.

8

Outsourcing Information Technology and Managing IT Operational Risks

1. Introduction

A great deal of the flexibility in R&D, A&D and manufacturing, as well as of the ability to control outsourcing agreements discussed in Chapters 6 and 7, is the direct result of an able usage of information technology. But like any other product or process, information technology has also its risks, most particularly operational-type risks – the theme of this chapter. Operational risk due to IT and risks related to outsourcing activities correlate with and impact upon one another. First, however, the good news.

In spite of the big strides information technology has made over the last twenty years, it is a long way from exhausting its potential. Many analysts expect to see a powerful new economic engine emerging during the next decade that uses new technological solutions, promoting better organisation and methodology to a real-time service-oriented form of enterprise architecture.[1] The solutions this will bring will be supercharged with tools from knowledge engineering focusing on the end-user – both at home and in the office.

While this transformation is in process, rapid change, uncertainty regarding the pace of emerging technologies and the market's response, as well as fierce competition, will characterise huge segments of the IT industry. This means that a company's market position will always be at risk, and its ability to maintain its current market share will depend upon its ingenuity in:

- satisfying customer requirements ahead of its competitors
- enhancing existing products with more attractive features
- developing and introducing new approaches to the use of these products
- achieving market acceptance of its technology-oriented solutions, at an acceptable cost, before its competitors do so.

This process of companies reinventing themselves through technology grows more challenging as the pace of change continues to accelerate.

Open source software, new computing devices, novel microprocessor architectures, the internet, and Web-based computing models are among the competitive challenges a company must meet. *If* senior management does not successfully identify new product opportunities, and develop and bring new solutions to market in a timely and cost-efficient manner, *then*:

- the company's business and bottom line will suffer (see Chapter 6)
- demand for its products will wane, while the market moves elsewhere.

Take telecommunications as an example. Research in active networking has demonstrated the potential for a technology which allows customised packet processing inside the network on a programmable per-packet, or per-service basis. This solution targets information caching, packet filtering and multiparty data communications, facilitating:

- rapid service deployment
- flexible flow management
- the ability to run a service on a network in a way similar to that of a program installed and executed on a computer.

This is a significant evolution of concepts originally developed in the early 1990s whereby the network plays the role of the computer shared among different parties, while owned and operated by a network provider. Such service creation, which has characterised the Intelligent Network for voice traffic, is now extended to data streams, multimedia and other service-oriented products in the making.

Active networking, however, also poses challenges that must be overcome for a solution to gain acceptance for use in communications environments. A serious challenge is that of developing a new concept for service creation and management, with proper identification of operational risks involved in exploiting customised network processing. Users must be guaranteed security and dependability in running their own services on a virtual network through a holistic approach rather than only at terminals and servers at its edge, as currently happens with the Internet.

The level of control which needs to be exercised in a network-wide sense is an issue challenging both outsourcers and insourcers. In the 1990s, as long as the market for devices to build increasingly more cost-effective networks has boomed, there has been a gross lack of focus on reliability and security associated with end-to-end system solutions. This has to change if information technology is going to play a significant role in expanding the frontiers of globalisation.

2. The role of information technology in expanding the frontiers of globalisation

Since the mid 1960s, information technology has been steadily making breakthroughs in business and industry because of its twin supports of computing and communications – in contrast with the use of IT to mainly serve accounting-centred routines which dominated the first twenty years of computer usage. The fact that technology has become a key player in commerce helps in significantly expanding its implementation horizon; and because networks know no national borders, it impacts on globalisation.

Using communications, computers and increasingly more sophisticated software to create a competitive edge in commercial activity has proved to be particularly effective to established entities able to keep ahead of the curve, not just the internet start-ups. But the preparatory stage for taking advantage of global networking is never hidden from our competitors. Therefore, tier-1 companies appreciate that:

- the time it takes to establish a commerce-related information infrastructure steadily shrinks
- other companies can catch up quickly, eroding at fast pace the competitive edge of their corporate opponents.

Internet commerce promotes this faster-and-faster business perspective with communications in the core of technological solutions, as shown in Figure 8.1. Content and database mining are providing the added value the system needs. The reference made in the Introduction to active networks which perform customised computation on a per-packet, per-flow and per-service basis strengthens this communications core.

To be able to offer our business partners added value we must decide on the proprietary infrastructure which we have to develop; one which can provide us with a visible advance over our competitors. Table 8.1 gives guidelines on how to do so, some of which are market-oriented while others address themselves to the company's own management. Notice that Table 8.1 makes no reference to networks because the supposition is that *our* i-commerce solution will be supported through the Internet (see also section 4 on using the Web for outsourcing).

Both market-oriented and management-oriented applications make extensive use of filtering and database mining. Intelligent software helps to determine what products or services people like, and to whom an advertising/marketing campaign should be addressed. Cognisant people believe that agent-based datamining technology has the potential to revolutionise

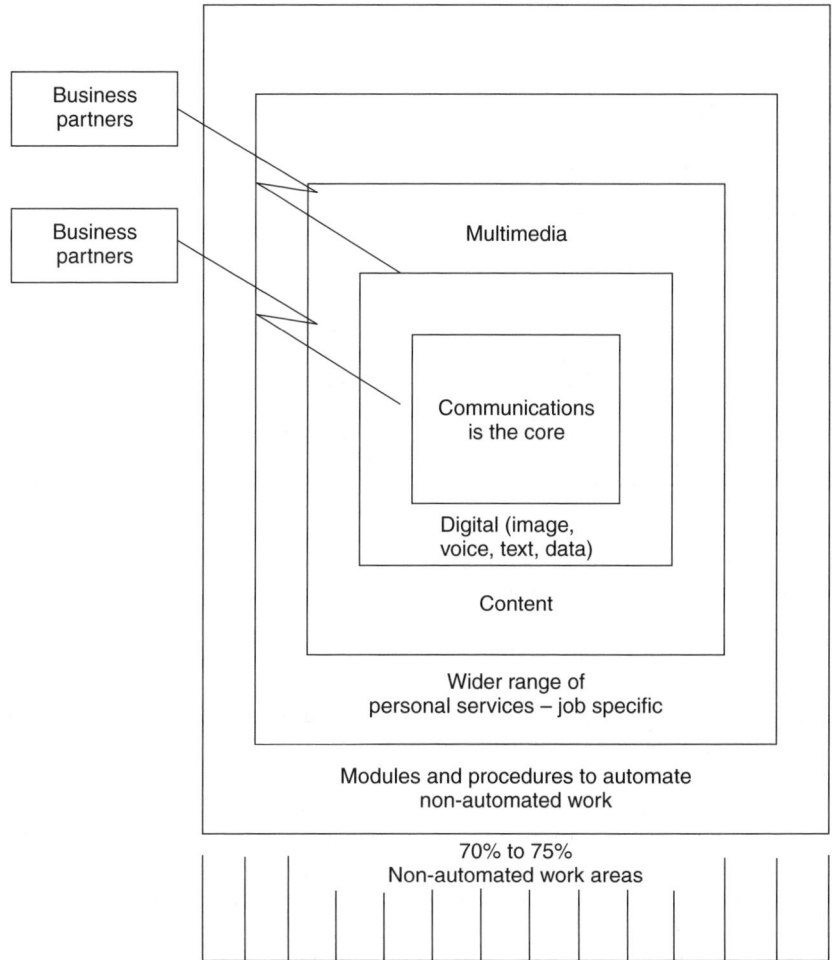

Figure 8.1 The communications core is composed of generic elements; content is added value

electronic commerce. As collaborative filtering moves out of its infancy, online shopping could challenge the trips to the mall – but we are still not there.

Strategically, with the merger of the PC and the TV, consumers will use internet commerce to satisfy many of their needs. Merchandisers and manufacturers will broadcast over the internet lifestyle images served through their products. The able use of information technology will help to display and promote the products that are on sale, as merchandisers capitalise on the fact

Table 8.1   An information technology infrastructure for electronic commerce

---

1 Market oriented

- Mining client databases
- Doing promotional campaigns
- Advancing virtual customer solutions
- Offering direct, personalised sales services
- Supporting new product launching
- Providing for fast flow replenishment

2 Management oriented

- Using intranets for management information systems (MIS)
- Making effective use of agents
- Employing heuristics and algorithms for planning and scheduling
- Providing facilities for interactive computational finance
- Developing and using virtual balance sheets in real-time
- Extending controllership to intraday operations

---

that the Web has available commodity software to involve the customer directly in selecting information about products and services on sale, by:

- presenting a wider choice than could be seen by the customer in a physical store
- giving retailers the choice of whether they want to do more of the same or whether they are prepared to explore new ways and wares.

The virtual customer concept of which we spoke in Chapter 6 is most crucial for the future of merchandising in a globalised marketplace. At the same time, it poses prerequisites for harnessing technology to produce retail profits. The new dimensions of online customer information, which merges product promotion and display with entertainment, have not yet been exploited to anything near their full extent. Even with the Internet, issues of:

- widening customer choice
- helping with selection
- reinventing the placing orders
- making payments.

are in their infancy. At the same time, ignoring the new challenge is like walking backwards into the future. There is no doubt that venturing into new areas invokes risks as well as uncertainties on whether or not one is gaining a competitive advantage or is simply incurring costs in the hope of making profits sometime in the future. Also, many people fear that, when technology moves very fast, their investments will become out of date too quickly.

The answer to this particular issue of accelerated obsolescence is that as far as a company successfully uses technology to enhance its bottom line, it will benefit from an enhanced profit stream while positioning itself to gain the next technology advance. By contrast, those companies that stand still are missing the business opportunity that might have been. It is no less true, however, that opening new paths involves risks, and there are some issues which have not had, as yet, a satisfactory answer.

The Introduction brought to the reader's attention that one of the most basic issues is *security*.[2] In spite of a horde of claims by vendors that they have solved the security challenge, there is no such thing as 100 per cent security, nor is there a technological fix to the security issue. Indeed, one of the main IT security risk challenges today is the *Internet* itself, and this in the broadest sense of the word. Security is one of the top IT risks. Others are:

- systems failures
- programming errors
- execution errors
- ill-studied access mechanisms
- incompetence and mismanagement.

Able solutions to this half-dozen major challenges (security and the five bullets) should be treated as a form of insurance which covers the worst of the weak points of IT. This insurance must be tuned in a way proportional to the impact of identified threats within the globalised business environment. What's more, IT security plans and systems must be reviewed regularly. A sound policy would:

- include a great deal of staff training
- integrate security into real-time internal control
- create an appropriate verification process for management reporting and disclosures.

Better approaches to the security challenges will demand stronger protocols, plenty of bandwidth, and a clear vision of what we target. Much will be done by way of messages which is the growth market as briefly shown in Figure 8.2. With over 70 per cent of the traffic generated by commercial applications on today's Internet, users are calling for:

- Steady, documented improvements in reliability, quality of service and security.
- A range of functional enhancements imperative for the growth of Internet commerce.

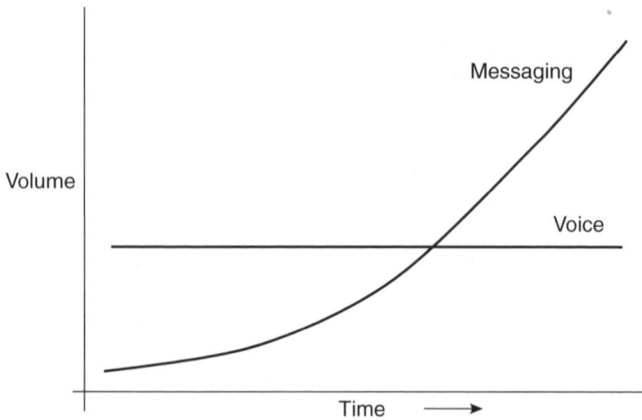

Figure 8.2   Messaging and transactions increase much faster than voice traffic

A 99.9 per cent reliability, or better, is just as important. On 10 April 2002, Heathrow's air traffic control system suffered its second computer breakdown in two weeks, causing widespread disruption and delays of up to three hours for early morning flights. National Air Traffic Services said the computer failure had occurred in the flight data processing subsystem, which collapsed for 15 minutes at 6.05 a.m. Flight capacity was not fully restored until 8.30 a.m.

It matters little whether solutions are provided inhouse or outsourced. What is important is the fact that, as on so many occasions, senior management retain full responsibility and accountability for these solutions. Short of this it will engage in self-deception, which will would become evident within the globalised business environment to which the company addresses itself.

For this reason, cross-border end-to-end internal control is a 'must'. Incident reporting must make sure the message is clear, leads to corrective action and leaves a historical trace. This is important, not only with inhouse but also with outsourced services (see sections 3 and 4). In fact, the latter need it even more than the former.

In conclusion, it is up to senior management, its personal accountability, to balance risks against gains. The decisions on technology will have to be evaluated in the same way as the more familiar investments, including the size of investment itself, needed time-scale, risk and pay-off, and impact on survival of the enterprise. These are business challenges and senior management should remember that it is no more possible to leave technology's responsibility to only the technologists. As with electronic banking, the board, the CEO and his immediate assistants have the duty to search and find those areas where technology makes wholesaling and retailing more viable and more profitable. The way to bet is that fertile areas are where technology impacts on the customer to create a distinctive virtual store identity – thereby conferring a competitive advantage to the company which uses IT as part of its strategic plan.

3. Outsourcing the services of IT professionals and their wares

Since the mid 1990s, a curious twist has seen to it that companies employing IT professionals face a major dilemma: how to establish reward systems and work environments that are both stimulating to the professionals and productive for the organisation? This challenge has always been present during the preceding four decades, but it was not always appreciated as such. Classical strategies for motivating, rewarding and leading technical employees frequently failed to work, resulting in performances which were suboptimal.

This curious twist between stimulation and effective performance rested on the fact that, while 'electronic data processing' (EDP) looked to be a new industry, in reality it was no more than morphing the old culture of 'electrical accounting machines' (EAM). As long as the EAM way of doing business prevailed, companies failed to:

- retain key technical staff
- integrate the best IT professionals into the organisation
- deal effectively with creative individual contributors.

This had evident consequences, one of the most important being the inability to build successful project management teams and keep them creative and high-performing over time. The net result has been a split personality in regard to IT policies and resources. While companies depended more and more on their advances in information technology, boards and CEOs expressed the desire to cut down on IT expenditures, hoping that IT outsourcing would prove an instrument of cost control.

- This has *not* been based on factual and documented homework.
- Rather, it came up as a result of wishful thinking, which subsequently has not been supported.

Other equally undocumented metareasons behind IT outsourcing proved to be failure of understanding and managing the role of the technology gatekeepers, and the inability to develop rewards, such as incentive systems, which are consistent with the changing motivations of IT professionals. Computer illiteracy at senior management level has been one of the major contributors to this trend to IT outsourcing, magnified by the fact that companies became less and less up to date on technologies that underlie their business. They were:

- unable to identify aspects to their organisational culture that may be responsible for poor IT results
- unlikely to utilise internal IT expertise more effectively than in the past, including their inability to move knowledge from one part of the organisation to another.

Let me take a couple of paragraphs to focus the sense of this discussion. In a way, IT outsourcing existed all the time. For instance, in terms of hardware we don't make them inhouse. In software, we buy operating systems (OR) and database management systems (DBMS); we don't reinvent the wheel. We also buy, or at least should buy, more than 50 per cent of our applications software (AS). This is not, however, the sense of 'outsourcing IT' in its present form. What this term has come to mean is outsourcing systems functions, with the excuse that they are not 'core' to our business. That's a fake, because *IT is core* to our business – no matter which it may be – in practically all its forms. This does not mean that IT should never be outsourced, but the fact that it is core involves:

- prerogatives
- constraints
- responsibilities.

Wrong policies are easily identified by the fact that, in several cases, companies outsourced together with their IT operation their top management responsibility in providing strategic direction on important IT questions; in connecting business strategy with systems and processes; and in determining risks and payoffs various technologies offer. Yet, without the least doubt, a senior management responsibility is that of making IT solutions subordinate to business strategy:

- aligning IT to business prerequisites
- avoiding *ad hoc* 'silver bullet' solutions
- understanding what can and cannot be left to the outsourcer(s).

The internet has contributed to these failures inasmuch as increasingly demanding customers are forcing organisations to adopt a cross-functional process orientation, which introduces new culture and IT requirements. Web-based commerce (see Chapter 4) is revolutionising interaction with suppliers and customers, undermining established distribution channels and changing the distribution opportunities of different products and services.

For a few years in the 1990s, outsourcing IT services was mostly an American phenomenon. Then it spread to the UK. Big service deals, such as the $2.4 billion contract IBM signed with Cable & Wireless of the UK in

September 1998, were instrumental in opening up the outsourcing market in Europe. Ambrosiano Veneto, the Italian bank, handed to a German outsourcer its IT on the grounds that it is not a credit institution's core business (a statement which is definitely *wrong*). Banco di Roma made a present some of its equity to EDS, another IT outsourcer; and Swiss Bank Corporation bought 30 per cent of the equity of Perot Systems, then let the outsourcer run its IT.

None of these projects has been particularly successful. Senior management erred in outsourcing IT, maybe blinded by what was, in the late 1990s, the glory of IT consulting and of IT research. But times change. Innovation, the historical inspiration of Silicon Valley and other tech centres, has lost it its spark in recent years because of the:

- economic nose-dives
- market saturation
- weak products.

As a result, in the broader technology landscape, venture firms and large companies alike are trimming their R&D budgets and taking on less risky projects and putting more innovative concepts on ice.[3] In different terms, the bursting of the dot-com bubble, instigated by hype and too much investment in poor ideas, has led to tighter controls over expenditures – and in a growing number of companies, including big names, the IT budget feels the pinch.

The dot-com collapse, the telecoms market downturn and corporate dissatisfaction with e-services have created a tough business case for hosting companies. In January 2002, *Communications Week International* chaired a round-table to discuss prospects with interested parties. One of the participants was Guy Willner, chief executive of IX Europe, the London-based independent collocation and hosting company. It is worth recording some of the notions which he conveyed.[4]

According to Willner, we are seeing a lot of people de-structuring their service requirements. There is in the market a load of nervous IT directors with very little budget, but with a lot of stuff in cardboard boxes (not yet unpacked) and plenty of demand for day-to-day services from their users. These people take an unreasonable amount of time to look at different services that are already being provided:

- cancelling one contract
- renewing a couple of others
- changing another one, because they have a lot of time to move the cards around.

As far as the insourcers are concerned, to be successful their business calls for a clockspeed-based analytical framework for understanding how IT activities will evolve over time, which parts of the value chain will most influence industry development, and what dominant technologies are most likely to emerge. Most evidently, able answers to these queries are the most basic of them all:

- understanding their customer's (the outsourcer's) current business
- connecting the solution they offer to the outsourcer's business plans and day-to-day operating needs.

IT insourcers have to gain credibility with the client. One of the better ways is to have some of their people work with the client prior to insourcing, so the client could see them in operation. Then, when the client's delegation visits them, its members already have a positive view about their abilities. After the outsourcing contract comes into effect, the best demonstration of the insourcer's ability is that of continuing to deliver a high-quality, timely, secure, cost-effective and dependable IT service.

A strong identification-based trust implies the parties effectively understand and appreciate the other's capabilities and requirements. This mutual understanding must be developed to the point that each can effectively act for the other. Successful outsourcing and insourcing are by every account, a business partnership – whether this concerns IT, R&D, manufacturing or any other function in the supply chain.

4. Using the Web for outsourcing

Can we effectively use the Web for outsourcing services? The current answer is 'probably no', but over time this may change as a number of products and services migrate to the Internet. While we are not going to do every type of business over the Web, present-day offerings will expand. Already some banks do their foreign exchange business through the Web. Questions of security, reliability and cost-effectiveness will, however, remain.

Cost-effectiveness should always be a worry because routine sees to it that bureaucracy takes over and even intelligent solutions become stupid. During the London conference on Outsourcing for Financial Services,[5] Piers Hemmingsen of the Canadian Imperial Bank of Commerce (CIBC) which is actively using the Internet, suggested that: 'As we put more data and services on the Web, fixed costs go up not down.' There is not much to be done about it, Hemmingsen added because:

- The growing scale of operation carries with it costs.
- Proximity to customers within an expanding geographic distribution poses new investment needs.
- An enlarged product portfolio in volume and complexity also requires investments.

- There are costs involved in an expanding regulatory framework regarding one's own Websites.

If the Internet is going to be used as *the* medium for electronic banking and electronic commerce, *then*, in terms of systems, procedures and skills, we must be ready to deal with millions of transactions per second. Given the interactive nature of Internet operations, which is also the Net's competitive advantage, most Web transactions must be handled at the front end. The drawback is that:

- big companies have massive production data in their warehouse(s)
- most companies continue to work with medieval mainframe and obsolete Cobol programs.

There are, however, exceptions. 'We have many hundreds of Web servers through the world developed over five years,' noted Hemmingsen in connection to CIBC. 'Now we try to do a more integrated system.' Integrating does not necessarily mean centralising all services since, as we will see in section 5, centralisation is counter-productive for business continuity reasons.

The reader would like to note that in terms of internal staffing for Web transactions, CIBC started with four or five developers located in one central office, but moved away from this model. The bank's experience taught management the wisdom of decentralising Web-oriented analysis and programming to each business unit. Many entities fail to appreciate the need for such policy.

One of the challenges which showed up with decentralisation of skills is that most Web developers are young and they have had no hands-on practice with legacy systems used by the bank. This is a widespread problem in business and it poses both co-ordination and integration problems, which is a steady preoccupation because in a dynamic business environment technological support should work along a three-dimensional frame of reference, as Figure 8.3 demonstrates.

In the wider context of business and industry, another challenge in assuming top-tier technological solutions has been heterogeneity in hardware and software. The problem already known from distributed information systems with minis and PCs. In an Internet environment all connected devices must work together seamlessly, and mainframes are not the only handicap in reaching this goal. This is a problem which, as documented through my research, has been widely present with IT outsourcing.

Even if companies got their first contact with insourcers by means of canvassing Websites, the companies behind these sites had not resolved, for their own practice, issues associated to seamless connectivity between sophisticated software written for internet usage and those connected legacy routines running on mainframes. Furthermore, Web strategy itself

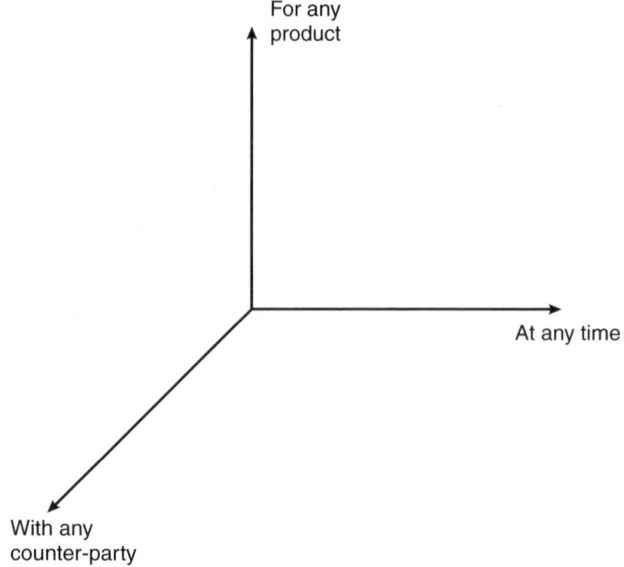

Figure 8.3 Technological support should be provided for deals in any currency, country, industry and industrial sector

is in evolution, changing over the years, and this is in no way simplifying seamless integration.

Still another challenge, said the Canadian Imperial Bank of Commerce during the London Conference, is return on investment (ROI). Many well-managed firms target spending within the customer relationship management budget. In evaluating ROI for internet-based business, CIBC asked itself *where* has it come in terms of deliverables with the organisation and implementation of its Website. Correctly, senior management decided that it would not go for a 'we too' approach. Solutions have to be focused. The bank's basic, client-oriented Web applications are:

- transaction engines
- content management
- personalisation
- customer support
- site analysis
- campaign management.

The infrastructure taken into account in return on investment studies includes carrier, hosting centre, router, Web server, application server, database server and support services such as load balancing and security. This infrastructure continues to grow as digital messages and transaction volume expands at fast pace. 'While we can do 200 to 300 phone calls a day we can handle 200,000 to 300,000 messages per day,' said Piers Hemmingsen. Between these figures is a difference of three order of magnitude. Still, at CIBC:

- about 90 per cent of sales come from the branch office network
- the Web is used for the other 10 per cent, mainly client access and lower level operations.

This figure of 90 per cent to 10 per cent should be kept in mind when planning Websites whether through inhouse resourcers or outsourcing agreements. In the case of CIBC, particularly targeted through the Web is the retail mass market. Internet banking competes with bricks and mortar as well as with telephone-based banking services, at the lower base of the client pyramid. By contrast, business lines for institutional client are:

- requiring high-grade human skill
- heavy in technology investments, including tier-1 specialised linkages.

Within the context of sophisticated client services, the Canadian bank was to note, outsourcing scenarios are rather traditional, involving networking (BT, Bell, ATT), the IT infrastructure itself (IBM, EDS), processing chores (IBM, ADP), and certain services done by third parties like payroll and printing. Advanced solutions are made inhouse. Indeed, advanced solutions can in no way be separated from the company's own strategic plan. The policy to be followed in internet commerce should be in no way something abstract or a repetition of what competitors have been doing. Basic choices have to be made and, as Figure 8.4 shows, these must capitalise on the:

- our strategic plan
- strengths of our firm
- our market targets.

A rational division of effort by major market segment and class of customers, as well as the requirements these pose, is found only among tier-1 companies. By contrast, for the majority, 'trend' rather than 'reason' have made outsourcing a rather popular choice. More than quality of service, their hypothetical justification for outsourcing is to cut costs. But as I never tire of repeating, few outsourcing project really have got positive results in terms of cost cutting – particularly so when they don't steadily examine return on investment.

Apart of ROI, security, too, is not always given the attention which it deserves (see section 2). Telecommunications outsourcing is an example where security is often wanting. There is a trend, particularly for larger organisations, to regard all communications as a separate function and to

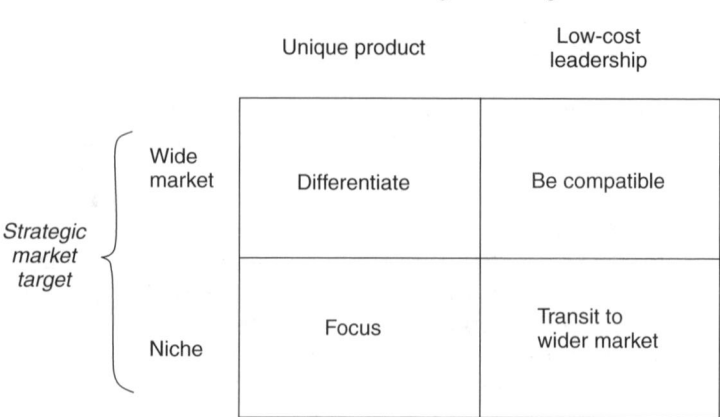

Figure 8.4 The policy to be followed in electronic commerce must reflect the company's strengths in one of these quarterspaces

outsource their network management to a third party without having done a priori the needed amount of research and, with it, an analysis involving alternative solutions.

As we will see in section 6 (and also in Chapter 9 in connection to organisation), part and parcel of this research should be the likelihood of business interruption and necessary countermeasures. For instance, in July 2001 a train accident in Baltimore ended by derailing internet traffic. This accident took place inside a Baltimore tunnel and it did more than snarl city traffic and spread toxic fumes. It also highlighted the vulnerability of the growing web of Internet connections.

- The Baltimore accident severed fibre-optic cables, affecting electronic commerce, Internet sites and e-mail up and down the East Coast.
- Many Internet service providers owned cables running through the tunnel and the train crash severed or melted those links, which hurt services in Washington, Philadelphia and New York.

Restoring business continuity was not been easy. For more than two days, dramatic slowdowns occurred for many on the East Coast who sought website access. As Internet traffic was re-routed to other cables, computer users encountered sluggish responses in cities as far away as Atlanta. Experts say that, because fibre-optic lines often run along heavily travelled right-of-way, they are vulnerable to accidents like the Baltimore fire.

Another fibre-optic outage that same week of 16 July 2001 was due to a construction crew digging a trench for a sewer line in Oregon. The workers accidentally slashed a fibre-optic cable and 50,000 people lost phone service. Previous to this, in November 2000, millions of Internet users in Australia were affected after Telstra, the country's biggest service provider, was crippled. It was believed that a fishing boat may have damaged a cable that had handled more than 60 per cent of Telstra's Internet traffic.

A few months earlier, in March 2000, Northwest Airlines was hamstrung for three hours when a construction crew accidentally cut a fibre-optic cable near its headquarters in Eagan, Minnesota. The accident crippled Northwest's communications with airports around the United States and the carrier had to cancel 120 flights while delaying hundreds of others. Let's keep these examples in mind when in Chapter 9 we focus on the role of the organisation in assuring business continuity.

5. An outsourcing–insourcing partnership must satisfy several prerequisites

I asked the executive vice-president of a major insourcing company about what characterises, from his viewpoint, the success of an insourcer. His answer has been: 'Today, in our case, in any IT project, you cannot tell who is from our company and who is from the outsourcer. Therefore, it does not really matter who leads the project because there is a common objective. This is my criterion of success.' Indirectly, the implication has been that mutual trust must be developed through:

- shared goals
- early team-building efforts.

The EVP further added that both his company and the outsourcer saw the need to yield on some issues and continue collaborating. 'We both have a purpose, and that purpose is to get the best out of the (outsourcing) agreement.' By bringing together key project players and emphasising shared goals, the project managers helped the users to analyse their requirements within the overall IT project aims.

It sounds too good to be true. In real life, sometimes, it works that way, but this is by no means the general case. In many other instances there are frictions developing between outsourcer and insourcer as, without having done their homework some companies try to offload to the insourcer everything connected to IT: from legacy mainframe-based applications to office automation, back office processes and internet commerce.

As we saw in Chapter 1, some insourcers assure these services by hosting and managing the whole lot at their own facilities, dealing with work like ongoing support, program maintenance and upgrades. This whole package is a compelling pitch, especially given the IT industry's chronic shortage of skilled professionals. Time and again I have found missing from the insourcer–outsourcer contractual obligation two crucial factors influencing end results:

- business continuity
- the longer term dependability of the service.

With relatively few exceptions, only after September 11, 2001 did people and companies started to seriously consider telecom networks, computer centres, and the broader perspective of electronic infrastructure of an enterprise as being cornerstone to the company's survival. The tragic events of the World Trade Center have heightened concerns about business continuity, and they will most probably drive a whole new set of products and services around this concept of business dependability in the longer term (see section 6).

This is a serious operational risk both in connection to IT and in regard to a number of other business factors. At stake are the concepts underpinning the current practices of distribution of nodes and servers, as well as of solutions that preserve the integrity of a firm's activities and save them from catastrophic interruptions. Single-site or even dual-site computer installation give a lot of exposure. Fully distributed servers and functions which used to be centralised, are at a premium. So are regular drills on survivability. Both are necessary strategies in the world we are getting into. Hence the questions:

- Has the outsourcer a fully distributed network and service centre structure?
- Can the outsourcer's organisation survive a vicious attack and be able to continue performing?
- Which is the fallback system in place, and how can it cope with deliverables when some of the main facilities are destroyed?

Without valid answers to these crucial queries, outsourcing projects are not up to the mark. This, as well as the fact that many IT outsourcing contracts did not deliver as originally expected in cost savings and quality of service, see to it that many experts today doubt that major corporate customers will trust insourcers with mission-critical material, though they may do so with legacy applications.

'Applications that hold sensitive information will never make it out the door,' said a major institution's executive vice-president, with outsourcing experience. Though he was not critical of the insourcing providers themselves, he was not too happy with the service which was received. He was particularly resentful of the insourcer's tendency to pay lip-service to the periodic strategic reviews required by the contract.

The advice given by another cognisant executive has been to be very careful with what is included into service-level agreements (SLAs), insisting that these spell out the details, including penalties for non-performance. 'Companies shouldn't subscribe to outsourcing services unless they get iron-clad agreements on every element of their IT service,' he suggested. As still another corporate executive had it, managing e-mail has been a particularly painful experience in outsourcing – and even more so was migrating the internal infrastructure and running multiple gateways which turned out to be a multimillion-dollar expense.

Ongoing management, which included upgrades and repairs, also got some negative comments by a number of participants to this research. Several outsourcers suggested that insourcers need to find a cost-effective way of handling changes, as well as make their services dynamic enough to sell to a broader market which might help in bringing down their costs – while keeping operational risks under control.

In my experience, there is no unique solution which can answer all of the problems all of the time. Any thought along these lines is a chimera. Insourcers and outsourcers will be well advised not only to classify and identify the operational risks they are facing in IT, and all other fields of activity, but also to establish the right methodology for tracking them and monitoring them. Figure 8.5 suggests a methodology for doing so.

Not at all surprising, when a rigorous methodology has taken a leave, is the lack of immediate response by insourcers to their request. Although, so to speak, an insourcer's help desk never sleeps, incoming calls can stack up in queue and queries may find no documented responses. Outsourcers also need to be aware that their calls for help may come at a price if the contract does not stipulate that this service is cost-free. Furthermore, changes in client or vendor personnel may cause performance problems through reduced trust and/or lost system knowledge. Added to this is the frequently ineffective handling of problems which pop up in the day-to-day relation-ship between outsourcer and insourcer. This sometimes sees to it that even if the two parties started well

- establishing structures
- exercising due caution
- achieving initial success.

they end up with frictions. The same result comes up when the business partners become complacent and kind of relaxed: structural controls are ignored and minor happenings associated with bigger issues are inade-quately attended. Because of these causes problems can rapidly escalate, significantly hurting the outsourcing project's chances for success.

There have as well been some cases where the outsourcer–insourcer agreement went through lows because it was not well studied in advance, in its initial conditions. Digiplex-Deutsche Bank provides an example. Digiplex has taken Deutsche Bank's huge data centre over. This has happened with a

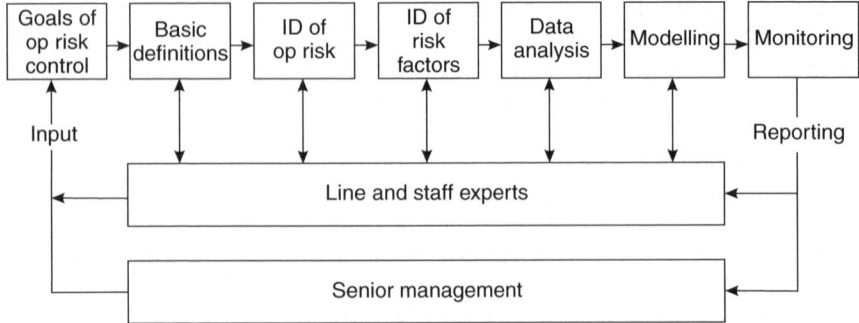

Figure 8.5   Successive steps in setting up and maintaining an operational risk control programme

couple of other banks looking for outsourcing their data centre, but Deutsche Bank's case is somewhat different because this institution was a very big investor in Digiplex.

The Deutsche Bank senior executive who made the decision to go the Digiplex way is not there any more, but the results are still around. The outsourcing project spend allegedly $25 million fitting out what was already a complete data centre to get it born again, and the deliverables did not live up to the hopes on which this project was based. This is what I heard in several meetings in Frankfurt. Deutsche Bank was not forthcoming with direct comments.

These and other problems connected to IT outsourcing–insourcing projects are not being outlined to discourage this activity, but rather to make the reader aware of the great amount of necessary preparatory work. My experience suggests the need for adding one more criterion at the top of the long list of those that should be studied to detail, till the outsourcer is satisfied with the answers. Some insourcers' superheated growth should arise the outsourcer's curiosity. Can this track be maintained? Can it lead to the longer term survival of the insourcer firm? What does it mean in terms of availability of systems skills and facilities?

6. Operational risk and the interruption of business continuity at Cantor Fitzgerald

Chapter 3 has discussed how the Basle Committee on Banking Supervision defines operational risk: a direct or indirect loss resulting from inadequate or failed internal processes, people and systems, or from external events. Notice the emphasis to *people* and *systems*. While, as I have mentioned, there are a dozen of major operational risks, three of them are particularly outstanding and they should be placed at the top of the list:

- management risk
- legal risk
- technology risk.

All three have a great influence on business continuity, but *if* it were to choose one as the most crucial in assuring the continuity of transactions, *then* without doubt my choice would be information technology. Let me add that, by all evidence, the importance of operational risk associated with IT has significantly increased as banking operations are more and more dependent on information technology.

According to several experts the trend to outsourcing, which improperly is often considered as relegation of senior management responsibility, increases the IT component of operational risk. One of the reasons is that electronic banking significantly amplifies the complexity of business operations, which is being further intensified by the ongoing process of concentration in the banking industry. Such basic reasons see to it that banks classify operational risk as the second most important category of exposure after credit risk.

At the same time, catastrophic events hit hard the computers and communications infrastructure of companies. This is true whether the IT facilities are served inhouse or are outsourced. There are, however, reasons to believe that in the former case the company can easier recover because it has direct control over its information technology. External events tend to be more perverse and sometimes of greater magnitude.

Section 5 made reference to September 11. A case study with Electronic Trading at Cantor Fitzgerald helps to explain the sense of that reference. A quick flashback will help. Looking back for three decades, in 1972 online stock brokerages were still decades off but some people had a vision. One of them was Bernie Cantor who began advertising US Treasury prices on computer screens. From then on, Cantor Fitzgerald went all the way to dominate the brokering of thirty-year Treasury bonds.

By the 1990s, Cantor Fitzgerald had about 70 per cent of the online Treasury bonds market, enabling Wall Street firms to trade bonds while remaining practically anonymous. On 11 September 2001 the brokerage (housed in the 101st and 103rd to 106th floors of the World Trade Center) was hit hard by the terrorist attack: 700 of its 1700 employees were killed and its electronics gear was shattered.

While Cantor Fitzgerald was hardest hit, other organisations too suffered a serious damage. The New York Board of Trade, America's biggest exchange for trade in cocoa, coffee and sugar, was also located in one of the World Trade Center towers. Morgan Stanley had rented more office space in the

World Trade Center than any other company, and in the aftermath of the attack many of its 3500 employees were killed.

Many other banks which had operations in the Twin Towers and the neighbouring buildings that also collapsed experienced different levels of business disruption, among them: Merrill Lynch, Lehman Brothers, American Express, Crédit Suisse Group, Crédit Suisse First Boston, Deutsche Bank, Commerzbank, Charles Schwab, Asahi Bank, Sumitomo Bank, Dai-Ichi Kangyo Bank, CAN Insurance, John Hancock, the Municipal Assistance Corp. (Big MAC), Oppenheimer Management, Northern Trust, Citigroup's Smith Barney, and Yamaichi International America.

As far as business continuity is concerned, a major threat to the global financial system has been posed by the demolition of the Clearinghouse Interbank Payment System (CHIPS), the private telecommunications system operated by the New York Clearinghouse Association for banks in the New York area. Some of its physical infrastructure was destroyed, so that the whole CHIPS system was non-functional after the terror attack.

CHIPS settles the payments of both domestic and international interbank obligations. Some of the bigger banks in the world, including Citibank, JP Morgan Chase, Bank of America, Deutsche Bank, UBS, and Bank of Tokyo Mitsubishi, own and operate CHIPS. On average, CHIPS transfers a value of $1.2 trillion daily, equal to the amount of the total daily value of payments that passes through the entire Federal Reserve System. CHIPS:

- clears and handles 242,000 transactions on an average day
- handles 95 per cent of all US dollar payments moving among countries worldwide.

Together with the disruption of business continuity in payments, one of the greatest dangers lied in derivative settlements with counterparties. If settlements are interrupted, problems will snowball and this could bring down the world's financial system. Therefore, right after the September 11 events, central banks poured in plenty of liquidity to head off a liquidity crash. Many experts believe there will be problems if the central bankers are not very careful in how they manage pumping liquidity in and out of the system. The goal is to avoid a liquidity squeeze but to do so without creating a giant overliquidity bubble afterwards.

As for Cantor Fitzgerald, with the drama fresh in its memory, it suggested that in the future Espeed, the firm's electronic-trading arm, not its brokers, will handle most of the company's business. Competition was not far behind, with a similar goal. Other electronic trading systems, a total of 75 in 2001 (up from only 11 four years earlier), were also tooling up for a significant increase in online business, among them BrokerTech, ICAP, and LibertyDirect.

The careful reader will appreciate that, in all these cases, the greatest challenge is not technology but strategic decisions made ahead of the curve. In a business where margins are so thin and volume is king *costing* and *marketing* are crucial. Electronic brokers collect commissions of as little as $5 per $1 million of securities. Their survival therefore depends on:

- doubling or tripling their volume
- steadily improving their market share.

Establishing momentum is necessary, but not enough. Brokers must maintain momentum and catastrophic events may hit that goal like a hammer. The example we have seen in this section documents that the control of operational risk is a huge management challenge because companies must strive to handle their own service delivery infrastructure *and* care for operational risks originating at their business partners. Key points of a management plan include:

- unifying the technological base
- integrating service assurance operations
- isolating and restructuring operational risk cases
- monitoring the entire network of operations
- assuring business continuity in the longer term
- rethinking customer service to upgrade quality while supporting more revenue streams.

Some companies talk about creating a self-healing infrastructure, able to automate corrective action and avoid costly duplication of monitoring work. Knowledge artefacts (agents) can be designed and implemented to enable a self-healing approach. A prerequisite for this solution is identification, classification and standardisation of operational risks to enable evaluating new services easily, as well as making changes to existing service arrangements.

Efficient provisioning for operational risk control decreases the time involved in activating new customer services, while it also permits to deploy more advanced features and services – and do so quickly. Because forward-looking provisioning decreases the manpower necessary to run the system, it ultimately reduces operational costs. Other benefits include:

- a cut-down on human errors
- improved efficiency by providing a clear and accurate view of operational risk causes.

The solution to be adopted has to be proactive. It should not simply react to a situation that already may be causing IT-oriented operational risk problems to the company, its suppliers and its customers. The right solution would meet head-on customer needs associated with ongoing services and projected functions. Moving to the concept of a self-healing infrastructure that automatically takes corrective action improves the perspective of business continuity by keeping some operational risk under control. However, it also presents many prerequisites whose satisfaction rests on skills rather than on gadgets.

Part III
Advantages To Be Gained from Better Organisation and High-grade Personnel

9
The Prerequisite of Rigorous Organisation Studies

1. Introduction

In the majority of companies management processes have been designed to support the efficient replication of what was always done. This has required a formal structure of authority and of responsibilities which came under the heading 'organisation'. By contrast, a 'reorganisation' has been something like redoing the plumbing. A reorganisation process is more successful when it is done in a rigorous manner, keeping in full view structural changes which become necessary because of:

- innovation in products and services
- the pulse of the market
- rapid evolution of technology.

The concept of organisation, as we know it today, finds its origin at about 150 years ago, when the world of business was transformed by the Industrial Revolution. Today, globalisation and sweeping technological transformations, as well as their economic aftermath, are again changing the structure of industry and of society in ways that many experts believe will be just as significant as the evolution of the original organisational notions.

To be worth its salt, any effort associated to organisation must serve the conditions of the epoch in which it takes place. A primary goal of organisation is to help in mapping the major changes taking place in the economy so that the entity can benefit from the new business opportunities being presented. In the twenty-first century, organisational responsibilities have immensely increased because products, markets and human capital are in full evolution. We need a dynamic context which enables us to think about the organisational guidelines of the future, and to consider:

- how to create value in evolving environments by capitalising on processes underlying the new economy (see Chapter 1)

- the integration of organisation and strategy, and what it takes to go from technical competence to making money
- the virtual enterprise, which bases a great deal of its design and productive capacity on outsourcing.

One of the motors behind all three bullets is advances in technology, including the real-time management of businesses, online opportunity detection; data mining for engineering, marketing and managerial purposes; and the increasing use of internet commerce. The emergence of the Web and the immediate availability of data from any area of operations has produced new organisational concepts and along with them the ability to solve online fairly complex problems. Advances in hardware, software and algorithms have resulted in a dramatic increase in our ability to experiment prior to reaching decisions.

Innovative organisations do things differently from their predecessors, but they also do things differently from one another. New organisational competencies come as a result of making careful choices after developing alternatives and understanding the interactions between structure, incentives and culture. This is leading to the integration of structure and strategy, as well as a dynamic organisational change.

What we call *organisational competence* has become polyvalent, integrating different structural concepts, such as the span of control (see section 2), with the requirement for new flexibilities which enable to take advantage of opportunities as they develop. Organisational duties, however, still include solving structural issues, delineating proper relationships, establishing positional qualifications and elaborating job descriptions. The latter should focus on three issues:

1 responsibilities, which are longer term
2 indicators, which are medium term
3 objectives, which are short term – up to one year.

In order to be able to judge if responsibilities have been answered and objectives have been reached, we must establish quantifiable measures of performance. To assure there is synergy in the organisation, we must define liaison lines which are flexible and dynamic, capitalise on new technology and its ability to facilitate co-ordination. This must be done in a way which fully accounts for market pulse and benefits from of the best that can be achieved at current state of the art.

2. Organisational studies, business objectives and span of control

Organisation is usually regarded as the establishment of co-ordinated relationships between persons assigned the performance of specialised missions.

As the Introduction has suggested, this is accomplished by outlining authority and associated responsibility along lines corresponding to missions or tasks performed by individual departments, divisions or affiliates. This definition of authority/responsibility relationships is necessary for the achievement of a company's goals.

Organisational principles change over time, because of the reasons explained in the Introduction. Structural relationships have evolved from linear to two-dimensional, three-dimensional and multidimensional structures as shown in Figure 9.1, but there is always to be found a structural relationship to hold the organisation together. This I call the 'span of management' which underpins management's ability to run the organisation. The span of management is based on four components:

1 span of control
2 span of knowledge
3 span of attention, and
4 span of support.

There is no better principle helping to define the span of control, which practically means how many managers report to a superior, than the one that

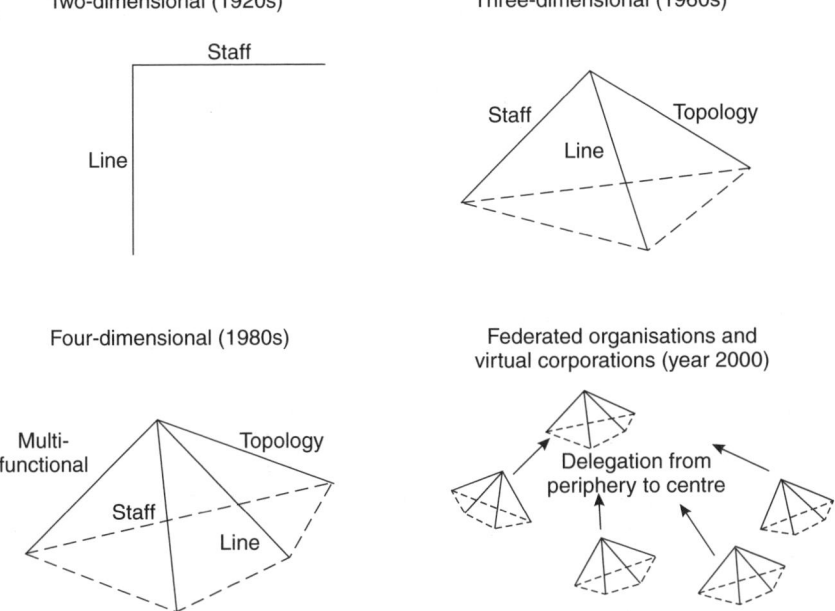

Figure 9.1   From the two-dimensional to the *n*-dimensional structure characterising modern organisations

says that it should be as broad as possible. A span of control of two or three is very bad in terms of managerial efficiency. A span of control of 12 might expose the organisation to centrifugal forces. In the modern enterprise,

- Real-time technology and agents help to increase the span of control, because they extend the manager's reach.
- With appropriate technological support, a span of control of eight is currently do-able, but few companies know how to implement it (more on this later).

The span of knowledge identifies the themes which give the company its edge in the market – from patents for its innovative products and processes to management know-how, as well as its ability to keep risks under control and to overcome adversity. The span of knowledge reinforces the span of control, and the two together lead into the span of attention. There are 24 hours per day, and management bent on the success of its enterprise is on the job anywhere between 8 and 16 hours per day.

The span of attention is enlarged by the span of support management is provided with. This means real-time systems, online data-mining, models, knowledge-enriched software, the ability to have a virtual balance sheet on request within fifteen minutes, and so on. As a matter of organisational principle which has been documented time and gain through practice:

- The better the span of support being provided, the greater will be the span of control.
- With this, enterprise will be managed in a more effective manner, with lower overheads and higher level of perception of market opportunities.

A greater span of control is tantamount to greater efficiency. As such, it has important aftermath in making the organisation more 'lean'. Fat organisations have many management layers, resulting from small span of control; therefore too many overheads and bureaucracy. Lean organisations are better able to respond to changing market conditions.

As the reader will appreciate from the preceding paragraphs, the span of control identifies the structural relationships by which an organisation is held together. Lines of authority and responsibility form a framework. Within every organisational structure individual efforts are co-ordinated by a higher-up manager to whom report individual units. Some important questions do come up because of this statement:

- How should different activities be grouped?
- How close should be their supervision?
- How can responsibility overlaps be avoided?

- How much authority should be allowed throughout this structure?
- How deeply the principle of accountability should be implemented?

The answer to each of these questions casts light on the nature of command and control, as well as its framework. Typically, in well-run organisations there are principles which can be used as guides to decision about organisation and structure. Having such principles is a wise course because most problems of management are derived from uncertainties or obsolete traditions, and they cannot be solved without guidelines.

For example, in one of the companies I was associated with a board decision was taken that the span of control should be between six and ten direct dependants, as shown in Figure 9.2. This range was chosen after a study

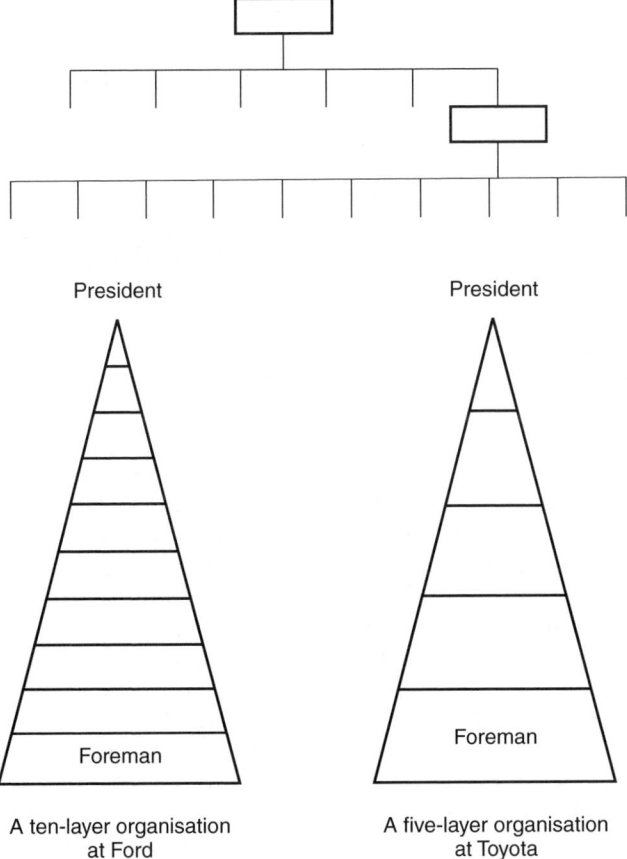

Figure 9.2 The span of control should be between six and ten direct dependants

which established the minimum and maximum number of direct dependants that can be handled effectively by a manager, within this company's type of business and at state of the art technological support.

In this same Figure 9.2 the reader will see a reference to Ford and Toyota. This comes from a meeting in Detroit where a Ford executive had said that, from the CEO to the foreman, this company has 12 management layers which a reorganisation reduced to 10. But then he added that even 10 were too many, because Toyota, Ford's No. 1 competitor, had only five management layers.

- As the span of control increases, the organisational layers diminish.
- A good way to judge the managerial efficiency of an entity over time is through a growing span of control and shrinking number of layers.

A basic principle of competition from an organisational viewpoint is that the management layers your competitor(s) does (do) not need to have, are *your organisational fat*. The more of it a company has, the less it is able to compete. If outsourcing helps to cut management fat, so much the better. This, however, is not so often the case because the board and CEO don't appreciate the destructive power of organisational fat.

There are, of course, organisational functions which should not be outsourced. An example is risk management. One of the key problems connected to overhead earmarked for the control of exposure is whether there should be one, two, or three units looking after damage prevention and repair. For instance:

- one for credit risk
- the other for market risk
- still another for operational risk.

Such departmentation is not an end in itself, but rather the consequence of historical reasons. Classically there has been a central credit risk department. More recently a different organisation has been created and assigned the market risk mission; and many credit institutions have started to have an operational risk unit. There are no God-given reasons for this split, but it is there and the challenge which it poses is not that simple.

Some institutions, like Credit Suisse First Boston, merged the two departments into one. Later, however, they reverted to two separate risk control units: one for credit risk, the other for market risk. Yet there are merits in the existence of a unified line of command, particularly now that operational risk has become a focal point of attention with part of it overlapping with credit risk and market risk.

Every institution faces this organisation problem, and those who persist in having two different risk departments cite as reasons cultural differences between the people who manage credit risk and those addressing themselves to market risk. But there are also common elements, like the analytical spirit, as well as:

- behavioural control connected to the observance of limits and other guidelines
- the rapidly increasing use of mathematical models for market risk, credit risk and operational risk.

There are as well other crucial organisational issues that need addressing, a major among them being the form that should be given to the subordinate – supervisor relationship. Solutions come in different forms. An effective recognition of this relationship takes the form of *responsibilities*, *indicators*, and *objectives*, discussed in the Introduction.

- The responsibilities should be given in headlines; they should be few and clearly stated.
- Indicators help to explain what is meant by these responsibilities, in terms of specific duties.
- Objectives should be established, reviewed and met every year. They should be no more than ten.

In conclusion, organisation and structure are integral part of the life of an enterprise. The principles underpinning them change over time because new business goals come along and the responsibilities assigned to management continue to develop, but there will always be an emphasis on span of control, span of knowledge, span of attention and span of support. Every organisational study, whether it is done internally or outsourced, should pay attention to them.

3. Business continuity and other organisational responsibilities

As section 2 has demonstrated, organisation is usually regarded as the establishment, with necessary authority and associated responsibility, of co-ordinated relationships between persons assigned the performance of well-defined missions. These tasks, like engineering, marketing or risk management, are necessary for the achievement of company objectives, indeed for survival in a highly competitive business environment.

It has also been explained why the concept of organisation is often interpreted in the sense of a form or *structure*. The structural relationships by which an entity is bound together constitute a framework. Individual efforts within this structure are co-ordinated by a higher-up manager to whom report individual units. We have spoken of the span of control and of the important queries which it brings up. One of them, among the most critical, is to assure business continuity.

In Chapter 8, business continuity has been examined from an information technology viewpoint as well as from the perspective of major catastrophes hitting our company's computers, communications and other systems. *Business continuity management* (BCM), however, also has important organisational characteristics, such as:

- anticipating incidents which will affect mission-critical functions and processes
- assuring that *our* company responds to any incident in a planned and rehearsed manner
- providing fallbacks so that business is never interrupted (or lost) no matter how serious may be the operational risk.

Business continuity must be studied and modelled. Scenario analysis is one of the tools for this type of studies. Worse-case scenarios and drills must target new risks; command and control centres and process; different types of plausible, even if unlikely, incidents; multiple invocations; proximity and the readiness of our backup sites to take over without discontinuities.

Business continuity management and its role in organisational studies are to a considerable extent new concepts. However, experience which has started accumulating indicates that BCM is more effective when examined in co-ordination with supervisory authorities and their guidelines. For instance, in the UK, the Bank of England, FSA, Treasury and Turnbull Committee have been concerned with:

- internal controls
- the financial industry's resilience.

The issues which have been brought up by the regulators, as well as through BCM studies undertaken by major companies, include outsourcing, corporate governance, internal and external auditing, liability management, interoperability, insurance (including catastrophe insurance), supply chain and internet commerce. Notice that outsourcing is at the top of the list.

Every organisational solution should reflect the fact that business continuity requires both strategic decisions and tactical moves. The eight functions which, among themselves, help in establishing an effective framework for BCM are shown in Figure 9.3. As it should be expected, operational risk identification and analysis are two of the most important points.

The impact of business continuity within the realm of organisational studies should escape no manager's attention. BCM adds its weight to the classical organisational responsibilities defined through a hierarchy – which is not necessarily the most efficient way to go about structural issues, though it is widespread. Briefly, in an organisational sense, a hierarchy is a classification according to rank or authority.

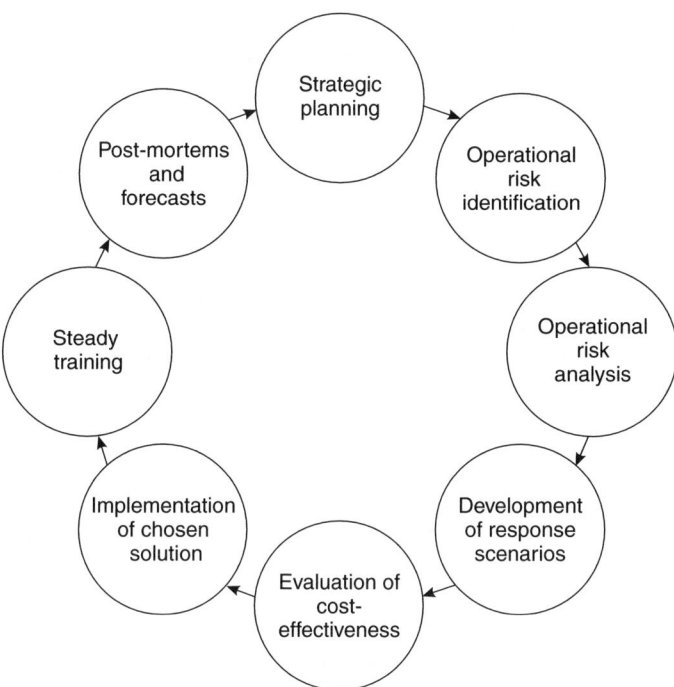

Figure 9.3 Business continuity requires both strategic decisions and tactical moves

- the greater the number of reporting levels in an organisation
- the more hierarchical it is, and therefore the more bureaucratic.

Section 5 will explain why bureaucracies tend to be very hierarchical. If the span of control is the horizontal dimension of structure, the hierarchy is the vertical one. These vertical and horizontal dimensions are inversely related. When an intermediate level of supervision is inserted in between existing organisational levels.

- the span of control shrinks
- but the hierarchy increases.

Apart the obvious high overheads, many reporting levels shield those at the top from both business annoyances and information vital to their work. This sort of *organisational illiteracy* should be avoided at all cost. The Catholic Church, for example, has a very flat structure, with only four levels: Pope, cardinals, bishops and priests. Apart from other reasons, this is the best structure to assure business continuity, but very few business corporations are as flat as the Catholic Church.

Whether the organisational study is done inhouse or outsourced to a consultancy, the wise course for people entrusted with it is, first, get its perspective; *then*, to talk to top management. Examine the alternative organisational solutions; select *one* on its merits; and put *all* effort, undivided, into making it successful. Organisational skills don't come through inspiration. One must train oneself, then train those who will be responsible to implement the chosen organisational solution as well as those who will have to work with it, always keeping in mind that:

* a critical issue in any organisational study is to understand, appreciate, explain, and enlighten
* in business, people will move in a given direction only *if* things are explained to them, and *if* there is a leader to keep them going.

In many companies not only the organisers but also senior management as a whole fail in either or both of these bullets. As a result, the entity is burdened with inefficient and obsolete structures leading to intense frustration. In addition, this problem of organisational obsolescence is frequently compounded by the lack of strategy for setting new structural guidelines and efficiency measures.

Companies who persist in having a crumbling structure cite cultural or historical reasons as an excuse. Yet these reasons can be overcome through reorganisation, which tier-1 firms have found to be the best way for behavioural control. Because organisations are made of people, there is a good deal of behavioural science in every organisational activity, just like there are overlaps between different goals put together to affect peoples behaviour.

For example, themes such as competitiveness, innovation, cost reduction and productivity overlap. As Figure 9.4 shows, however, such overlaps make it possible to focus on core activities which should be fulfilled. By capitalising on core activities, companies can do away with enormous problems they are experiencing due to the lengthy time they take to find a valid structural solution. Largely, such delays are the result of poor organisational methodology and of management's inability to deliver in a way commensurate with:

* market opportunities
* good technological support at an affordable cost (see section 4).

A great deal of know-how is necessary for exploring market opportunities. This was noted in section 2 as 'span of knowledge'. Theoretically, organisations think that a person's expertise increases as they climbs the hierarchy. Practically, these tend to be independent events. Also theoretically, expertise resides in the specialists, the staff of the organisation. The practical side is

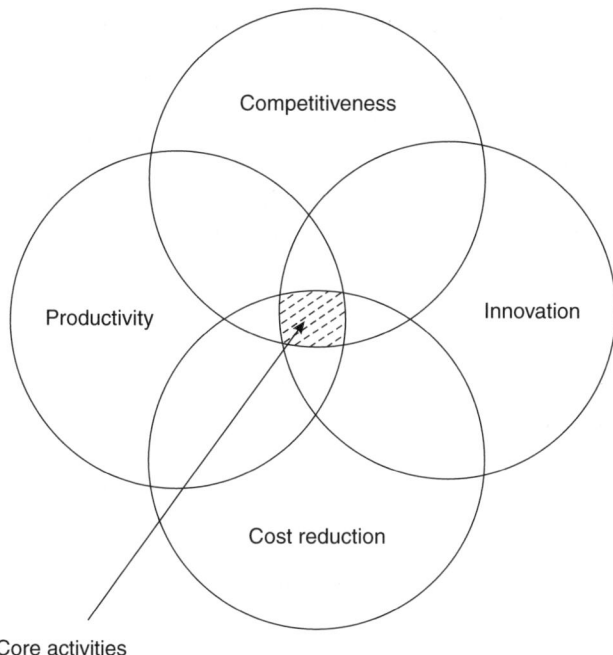

Figure 9.4 Organisational goals may be complementary but they may also overlap

best explained by the saying: 'A specialist is one who knows more and more about less and less; while a generalist is one who knows less and less about more and more.'

But there are men and women of knowledge (see also Chapters 10 and 11); and there are also knowledge artefacts, like agents and expert systems, developed by transferring human expertise on to software. Agents should reside in local and long-haul networks, and generalists must be able to access them immediately online by accessing specialised databases and related knowledge-enriched services – for instance to close on a sale during a call or to assure business continuity.

Because interactive agents and database mining can provide a significant competitive advantage, without appropriate organisation and supporting technology it is not possible to feature a closely knit trading desk which spans, say, two dozen countries in three continents. Short of an efficient integration, the people working for these desks will resemble a disjoint set of individuals who reluctantly have been brought together without any policy to work as a team. Mismanagement adds another vice. 'They are not paid to think,' said a banker. 'They are paid to sell products.'

4. Information technology investments and organisational change

Astute business executives have found out, often the hard way, that investments in information technology work best when they go hand-in-hand with organisational change. A study by MIT has looked into the effects of IT investments on the productivity and profitability of firms, and it found that return on IT investments is much bigger in companies that are also prepared to change work practices associated to their policies as well as the products and services they sell. The principle is that:

- organisational investments complement IT investments, each feeding on the returns of the other
- a valid organisation and culture further helps to promote flexibility and adaptation in IT, to capitalise on a changing market.

To be able to respond to customer wishes in real-time, is practically synonymous to company survival. It is more important to be innovative and adaptable than to be perfect. IT and organisational solutions should reflect this fact, as well as the fact that organisational change, flexibility and adaptation, have prerequisites.

- A flat structure and information sharing are two of the basic principles of efficiency.
- Information should not be jealously guarded by those who possess it, but be available to all authorised parties.

In much the same way, it is not enough for board members, chief executives, and their assistants to understand what has to be done. They have to make sure that this understanding sips down the organisation and change is forced through – even if that means getting involved in details. One of the basic understandings is the fact that technological capabilities for creating tomorrow's organisation already exist but they are not being exploited to a significant degree.

People who wish to appreciate the importance of the synergy between technology and organisation must return to the fundamentals. A prime reason why economic activity is organised is the ability to communicate while reducing the cost of communication. The costlier it is to process and transmit information, the more it makes sense to do things online. However, to execute online transactions in an efficient manner we must:

- turn the old organisation inside-out
- rethink the way in which we communicate, internally and with our business partners.

Every organisational study should appreciate that the worst return on investment (ROI) is obtained when companies are using IT purely as a way of doing 'more cheaply' the same old things in the same old ways (see also Chapter 14). The best ROI is obtained when companies are able to take things apart and find new solutions. The problem is that people resist change. Said the senior executive of a well-known financial institution: 'We tried to push technology in fund management, but people don't pay attention. We showed asset managers what they can do with expert systems, but we were somewhat disappointed to see that a question which was never asked has been: 'What can high technology do for me today that did not do five years ago.'

Somehow, in many studies connected to reorganisation, the urge to use technology is not there. Even institutions that traditionally employ technology don't make it as sharp as it should be. One of the ironies in the internet age is that quite often the people looking for the best use of high technology are those who don't really need it that much, because they deal in small amounts – $10 $30 thousand – not in hundreds of millions and billions of dollars under their management, where return on investment on high-tech can really be significant.

Consultancies acting as insourcers of organisational studies as well as of IT should keep in mind that information technology has a significant influence on how business is conducted today – and vice versa. As we have seen since Chapter 1, Internet commerce has already made it possible for manufacturers and retailers to sell in far-away parts of the globe without having a single employee there. The reader has been provided with plenty of evidence that technology is:

- tipping balances of power and profits
- changing old paradigms in nearly every corner of business.

Because of technology, there is less and less room for second raters and for inflexible organisational structures. Competitive advantages held by vertical, highly integrated industries have melted away. Many products have become both quite complex and subject to rapid change, while the market environments of former star performers are no more competitive. The surprise is that few of the old dinosaurs recognise the need to:

- forcibly slim down various aspects of their operations to achieve new efficiencies
- restructure their operations in a way makes possible state of the art response to market needs.

Both bullets call for reorganisation and high-tech. Impediments due to old, inflexible structures hamper business. They also make nearly impossible the assimilation of emerging technologies corporate innovators envision so well. In fact, stonewalling because of organisational and cultural reasons often proves to be more formidable than the piercing capability of new technology. Some experts identify a generation gap between:

- senior management, who may not view organisation and technology as a competitive weapon
- younger professionals who grew up in an environment of change and are committed to it.

This generation gap has not been created overnight. For nearly two decades the 'old chaps' and the innovators have never seemed to speak the same language. It is as if they don't work on the same planet. No lesser authority than Alfred P. Sloan, Jr, the man who in his days made General Motors the largest and most powerful corporation in the world, said so in the immediate post First World War years, albeit in somewhat different words.

In 1919, as a member of GM's Executive Committee, Sloan, along with others, performed a number of tasks concerned with organisation. In connection with them, he developed some of the ideas that he wrote up in his general Organisation Study.[1] One of the most interesting characteristics of Sloan's Organisation Study is that it was worked out on a basis of what he thought would be acceptable to all parties rather than what would form an ideal organisation, noting that:

- who says 'organisation' says the art of compromise between the ideal and the real
- this should be done in a way that the decision process is able to operate in a rational manner, not by the seat of the pants.

A sprawling company in a new and unsettled market, as the auto industry was in the 1910s and 1920s, needed a lot of organisational attention. As Sloan suggests, at the close of the 1920s the salient task before General Motors was *reorganisation*. The way things stood, by 1929 the corporation faced simultaneously:

- an economic slump on the outside
- a management crisis on the inside.

This is not unlike what happens today with technology, media and telecommunications (TMT) companies. Most of GM's plants, and those of the auto industry as a whole, were shut down or assembling a small number of cars out of semi-finished materials in the plants. The company was loaded with high-priced inventory and commitments at the old inflated price level and it was short of cash.

A thorough restructuring was needed, not only of the hierarchy and there-fore the line of command, but also of the products. One of the problems facing Alfred Sloan when be became the general manager was that GM had a confused product line, as shown in the upper half of Figure 9.5. Matters were made worse by the fact that there was a lack of a command and con-trol system, particularly management control in operations and finance, as well as a lack of adequate information about anything. The restructuring of GM's product line along the dual axes of reference, price and market appeal, was an urgent organisational study (regarding the results, see second half of Figure 9.4). Notice, however, that GM was not alone among automobile companies in facing this problem. Others were also in trouble, but that was no particular comfort because economic declines have a way of shaking out of business the weak companies.

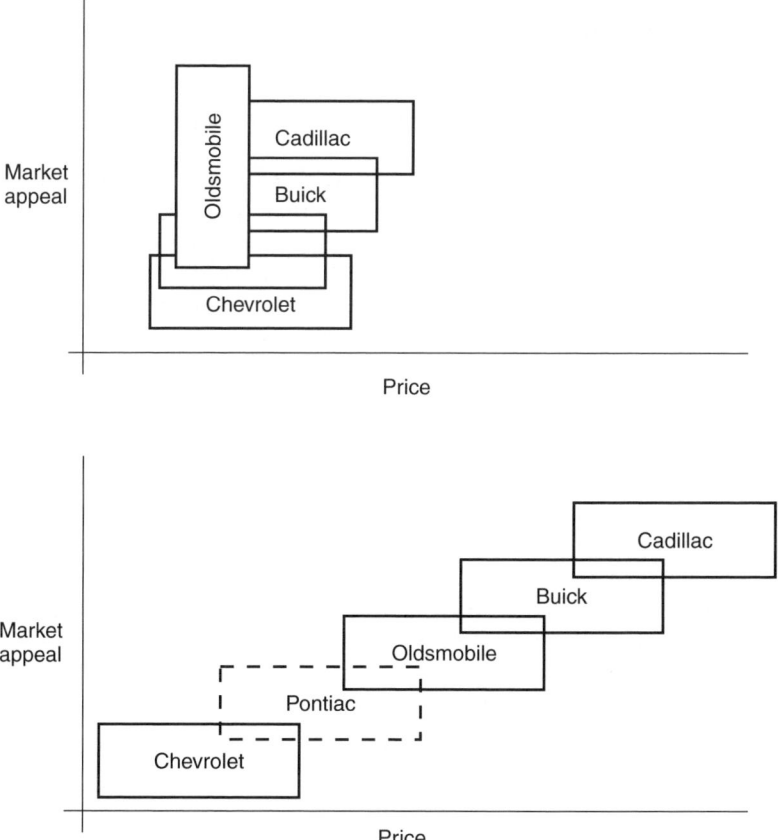

Figure 9.5   Restructuring a product line is no easy task – but it is do-able

In conclusion, part of the problem in applying rigorous organisational measures, including radically restructuring IT, optimising the product line and chopping off organisational fat, is inertia and the resistance change brings up. Some people cannot see beyond what is done today, neither can they understand the long-range dynamics of growth. However, as Sloan has shown, one may not control the environment or predict its changes precisely but, through reorganisation, should seek ways and means to survive business volatility. The hard nut to crack is that of bureaucracy.

5. Killing inertia and bureaucracy through better organisation

The vulnerability of a company because of overwhelming bureaucracy may not be immediately visible but it is there. An evidence is provided by the fact that defensive positions abound and inertia can be seen allover. Bureaucracies and hierarchies which are left unchallenged thrive with routinised tasks – and, inversely, routinised tasks identify companies which are not likely to survive. Once we replace the bureaucracy with a reformed, dynamic structure, the chain of command can be seen as radiating out, spoke-like, in all directions.

Whether the reorganisation is done inhouse or entrusted to an insourcer, the company's top management should see to it that an effective organisational style encourages innovation by short-circuiting hierarchical power through collaboration. The adopted solution should stress easy communications and a networked interaction among all business units. Three principles underpin this approach:

1 Know where to look for the information you need.
2 Have it made immediately available when you ask for it.
3 If you need help, go find it anywhere within the current structure, and pay for it.

Three principles can be achieved so much better when the organisational structure is flat. A broad span of control allows one to turn on a dime, as Sam Walton recommended.[2] It also makes possible to restructure the system fast and effectively; and it permits U-turns, therefore easy adaptation to market changes. By contrast, long hierarchies have so much inertia that it takes too much time for the system to become productive. This:

• makes impossible time savings
• deprives the company of the benefits from a reorganisation.

Bureaucratic organisations can be seen by the way their IT works. Monolithic hierarchies, like those built around mainframes, adore secrecy and the absence of information availability; because secrecy enhances the bureaucracy's status. As a result they go for legacy approaches the way shown in Figure 9.6a. Eventually thick departmental walls:

- significantly reduce communications
- end by killing the organisation and its products.

The interactive computational solution shown in Figure 9.6b works in the opposite way. The example being taken is with computational finance at front desk and back office. Information is fully shared, data-mining is interactive, and experimentation is not just a possibility – it's a policy. This is the setting which permits senior management to make efficiency the order of the day.

Fast communications and easy reach of vital data are so important because deregulation, globalisation and technology see to it that companies increasingly live and work in an unstructured information environment. People working in such an environment have little information about underlying assumptions in product and market decisions, and also find difficulty in deciphering the logic of competitors. A highly competitive dynamic market is one where only the paranoid can survive, as Andy Grove aptly stated, or those who are supported by:

- the best available tools
- the most imaginative brains.

The legacy approach

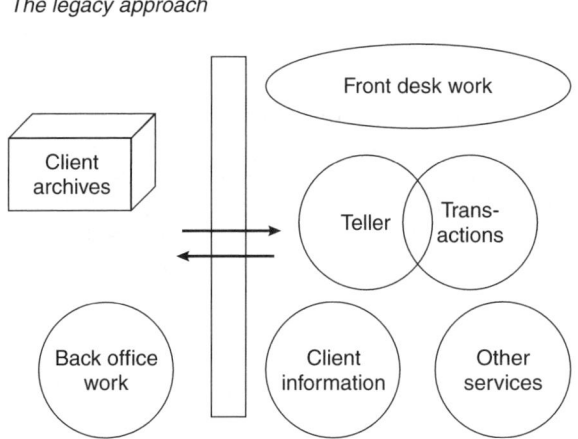

Figure 9.6a Old and new approaches to the exploitation of client information

The interactive computation finance solution

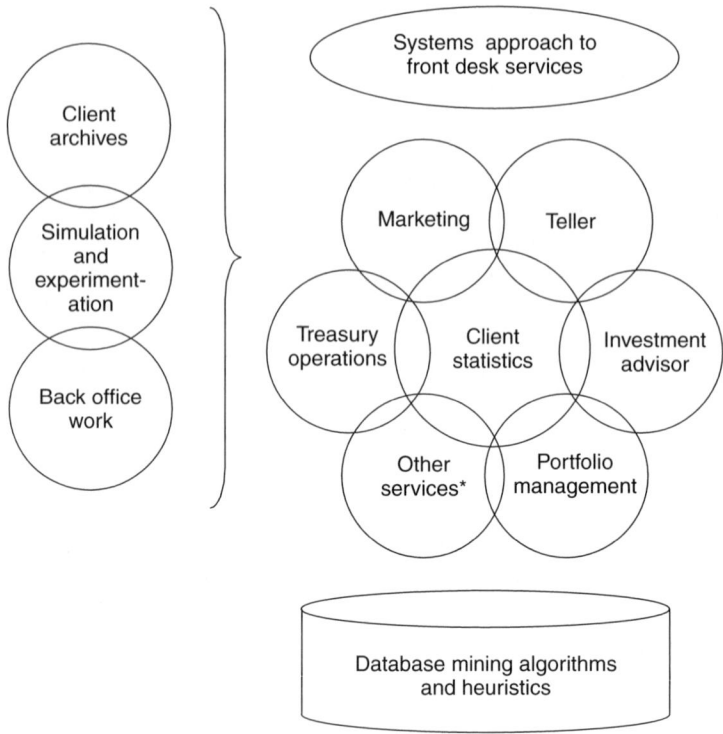

*Derivatives, currency exchange, legal advice, tax advice, ancillary services

Figure 9.6b Old and new approaches to the exploitation of client information

The search for ways and means to avoid the heavy hand of bureaucracy has been at the origin of the development of independent business units. Their concept was developed in General Electric during the 1950s in an effort to move decision making down to the smallest unit possible. An independent business unit can be defined as the smallest identifiable whole within the larger whole. The criteria used for this purpose are:

- a defined set of resources, applied to meet an identifiable set of *market* needs
- a clear cut product (or group of products) and/or service(s), in relation to a defined set of competitors
- an identifiable engineering, production and sales force able to enhance the company's cashflow.

Along the organisational principles outlined in the preceding sections, independent business units must employ high technology to deliver customised goods, instead of delivering mass-produced standard goods and services. One of the key advantages by start-ups and insourcers is precisely this ability to rapidly customise their products to meet specific requirements of outsourcers.

The structural and technical solution must be such that executives and professionals have full possibility to work together interactively independently of distance. This needs both training and timely support. No doubt the problem of effective co-ordination is not new. Talking of his experience the auto industry in the 1920s. Alfred Sloan noted that in the high tech of that time, certain areas of pressing co-ordination presented themselves; for example, the servicing of the numerous small products made by the different divisions of GM.

Separate service agencies for such small items, Sloan suggested, were uneconomic. Therefore, in October 1916 he set up a single, nationwide organisation called United Motors Service to represent the divisions with stations in twenty-odd large cities and several hundred dealers at other points. The main product divisions of GM resisted this move for a while, but he persuaded them of the need for it – and for the first time, Sloan says, he learned something about getting management to yield some of its functions for the common good.[3]

What I particularly liked in the Sloan reference is that, as far back as the beginning of the twentieth century, he established through the United Motors Service a unity of business purpose which fully observed the principle of return on investment (ROI, see Chapter 14). Sloan succeeded in his effort because he was careful to place each division on its own profit-making basis. He also elaborated a common measure of efficiency with which to judge the contribution of each unit to the whole.

It takes a leader to implement such solutions. This is a job for the CEO, rather than for the insourcer. In the general case, because of the way bureaucracy develops to protect itself and its turf, many companies don't have a system of standards of cost-effectiveness worth talking about, neither do they know how to assign personal accountability. When these fundamental stepping-stones are not in place, command and control is limping dangerously. Even the best information system would not save the day, because the entity's management is rotten in its core.

6. Why cutting organisational fat can be a rewarding exercise

One might have thought that the decades-long restructuring and consolidation in business and industry has generated unstoppable gains in profitability. This is not the case, because organisational problems and human behaviour are systematically underestimated. While several success stories can be found, the majority of companies shy from the structural challenges facing business and industry and management inefficiency continues being widespread.

Management inefficiency is a vice. The way an article in *Business Week* had it, if Toyota and Honda embody the essence of Japanese excellence, then Mitsubishi Motors represents how much damage the Japanese can do to their own top brands. The company has traditionally counted on handouts (from the Mitsubishi *keiretsu* to which it belongs) such as money from property sales and credit lines from sister companies to avoid a cash crunch. As another sign of poor management, the company has stretched itself thin by competing in too many niches, while:

- co-ordination with suppliers is ineffective[4]
- cost controls are loose or non-existent.

Whenever and wherever management inefficiencies show up, the members of the board, the chief executive and his immediate executives are personally accountable for them. As we will see in Chapters 12 to 14, personal accountability should be integrated with the concept of a profit centre. Its goal is keep at all times under perspective the results which should be obtained. Contrary to a cost centre which spends money, a profit centre makes money. Both are important, and a distinction should be made between internal and external structures.

- *Internal* profit centres and cost centres are the units into which is divided *our* organisation.
- *External* profit centres should be established reflecting the profit and loss with each client through a customer mirror.

A structural solution must permit timely and accurate evaluation across budgets, timeplans, product and service quality. A system of merits and demerits assigned in connection to personal accountability can be very helpful in this connection. Good organisation and good management are inseparable because the one supports the other. It is a sign of good organisation that management can cut organisational fat.

Tier-1 companies are effectively using both restructuring and technology to sharply reduce their expenses. Developing successful solutions to the problems confronting them is a challenge which extends far beyond the R&D lab. To appreciate how much managers have thought out their problems, it is sufficient to ask any head of manufacturing, engineering, marketing or other development:

- In which technology do you invest?
- Where do you begin the search for a better solution?
- How do you decide which project is most likely to succeed?

Also, how should the money be invested over the project's lifecycle? Errors in the allocation of resources made in the past should not be repeated. One of the most frequent of these errors has been starving managers and professionals of information they need for their work. An example on how bureaucratic organisations allocate their IT resources is shown in Figure 9.7.

- At the right side of the figure is the typical but very inefficient allocation of IT funds, the way it is practiced by most companies.
- The example at the left side of the figure comes from Teachers Insurance and Annuities Association (TIAA), and is the right way to invest in technology.

Everybody should appreciate that the search for efficient solutions is an intensive, highly interactive job. Factual and documented answers can lead to a powerful approach to linking business and technology strategy, matching products to market dynamics, and providing the basis for greater profitability. However, even the best solution would not survive the test of time unless it remained truly cost-effective in the longer run – therefore:

- flexible
- adaptable.

The problem is that flexibility, adaptation and cost-effectiveness are resisted by many people because, rightly or wrongly, they think of it as being the enemy to their embedded interests. By removing resistance to change and

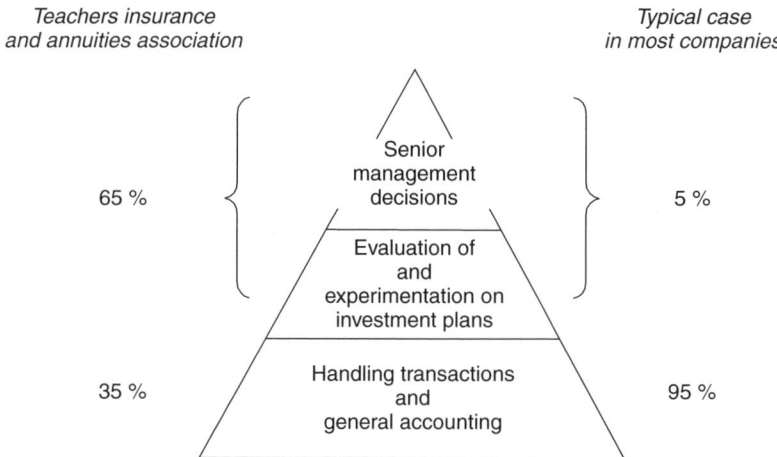

Figure 9.7 The largest part of the IT budget should be allocated to management support through technology

by creating value, cutting organisational fat helps to better communicate with, inspire and guide professionals to create a more highly motivating work environment. Killing bureaucracy and its surrogates removes some of the sources of tension that exist between organisational and professional demands. It therefore:

- enhances the relationship between innovation, motivation and change
- gets the organisation on its toes, obliging it to be more productive and to solve surfacing problems early.

The keynote in cutting organisational fat is that of creating value. No organisational solution, no innovation, no technology is worth anything if it does not create value. Therefore, the new lean and mean organisational structure which *we* adopt to grow and survive must establish a fundamental framework for:

- tracking the changing returns on business expenditures over time
- establishing the relationship between resources, performance and results.

In a poorly managed firm the middle management layers, and employment associated with them, grow and grow because there is no sharp knife to cut organisational fat and no technological support at an appreciable level of sophistication to improve peoples' productivity. By contrast, in a well-managed firm middle management shrinks, being replaced by technology. That's one of the best examples of cutting down organisational overheads.

7. Can outsourcing improve the efficiency of the organisation?

Section 6 explained why organisational fat hits the bottom line like a hammer. Take the banking industry as an example. According to the Bank for International Settlements (BIS), profit margins have declined in several countries during the last decade. The return on assets of the banking industries of 12 countries assessed by the BIS survey fell, while net interest margins (a key contributor to banking earnings), shrank in all but three countries over the late 1990s.

Improvements in net interest margins can be significantly helped through restructuring of the product lines. However, as the BIS study has found, not only among companies but also between countries, restructuring is uneven; in the latter case because of political difficulties of securing necessary cuts in employment and staff costs – that is, in terms of organisational restructuring.

For any company, a precondition to taking advantage of new business opportunities is to achieve cost-effectiveness. The dual goal is to redeploy resources towards the more profitable activities while avoiding the temptation to keep the dead horses in the product line. The best prescription for failure is to be insensitive to the developing drives in the market, and to continue with overstaffing practices.

- *If* outsourcing helps in reaching cost-effectiveness, *then* the likelihood of getting positive results improves.
- *If* outsourcing is not able to cut organisational fat, *then* it may be part of the problem rather than of the solution.

I emphasise these two *if*s because of having seen many cases where outsourcing is taken as the easy way out of a problem rather than being used to deliver a frontal attack on its fundamental reasons. An insourcer stands so much of a better chance of getting results in reorganisation and cost-effectiveness *if* the top management of the company he works with:

- gets itself involved in developing the needed guidelines
- stands squarely behind the measures being taken
- Ensures that everybody abides by the rules and fully implements the results of restructuring.

The basic decisions should be the board's and the CEO's – not the insourcer's. The task of the insourcer is largely one of putting muscles to the top management framework. This is a fairly sophisticated operation and, as with all complex organisational issues, it requires a concentrated effort to integrate tasks at various levels. Traditional easygoing approaches don't provide the kind of method needed to understand:

- structural relationships
- parameter trade-offs for greater efficiency
- information requirements necessary to make advanced projects successful.

On the other had, *if* the outsourcer of organisational design responsibilities, for instance a consultancy, cannot produce effective models from which senior management can understand the complex interactions among activities and capture the basic nature of cutting fat, *then* the service provided to the company by the insourcer is substandard.

A successful right-sizing project must be able to model sequential and parallel tasks performed in the organisation's business units, forcing people to deal with the problems as well as clearing common misperceptions about organisational issues. This is particularly important in understanding complex relationships between people and tasks, which permits the value of human capital to be promoted.

The board, the CEO and senior management should appreciate that strains could appear in any reorganisation, showing up as intense competitive pressures interacting with stubborn cost structures. Left to their own devices, these strains lead to a disparity between substance and form. Every organisation consultant should appreciate that in many right-sizing efforts there is not enough substance because of the existence of plenty of underground relationships, characterised by the grapevine, which cannot be overcome.

Quite often the board, who may have asked for the restructuring, is not giving this matter of form and substance the attention it needs – even if events point to major organisational deficiencies. For instance, the board may not be able to determine the rate of required return on investment for each unit, and this proves to be a handicap in cutting organisational fat. In these cases the board and CEO have lost managerial control over operations. When this happens, the results unavoidably are:

- organisational rust
- twisted reporting lines
- creative accounting statements
- a reduced sense of personal accountability.

Over the years of my professional life I have been impressed by the number of companies where no one knows how much is being contributed by each business unit, plus or minus, to the common good of the corporation. Nor does anyone seems to really appreciate, let alone prove, where the efficiencies and inefficiencies lie. It is natural for the different business units of a corporation to compete for investment funds, but it is irrational for senior management not to know where to place the money to best advantage. In the absence of objectivity it is not surprising that there is a lack of agreement on the best solution, with the profit resulting from the business considered abstractly, without a real measure of the merits of one solution or another. Unless this is fully recognised and corrected, plans tend to be based on a hypothetical, illogical and unsound basis.

As these examples help to demonstrate, organisational issues are not just a matter of structural studies. They are much than that. They involve cost-effectiveness, behavioural patterns, clear goals, unambiguous definitions and information which allows rational decisions to be made. Few companies, indeed only those which are best managed, place appropriate emphasis to these facts. Usually companies confine themselves to some 'material issues'. Yet, in business, as in war, material only wins hands down when the intelligence and morale of the side possessing it is at least comparable with that of its opponents. Otherwise Byzanthium, with its 'Greek fire', would have ruled the world.[5]

10

Personal Characteristics and Cognitive Complexity Required by the New Technologies

1. Introduction

One of the most fundamental issues which will characterise business and industry in the twenty-first century is that more intellectual effort will be organised around the problem to be solved than around traditional functions such as production or marketing. Because of this, a high premium is being put on skill and know-how, as well as on the personality characteristics of knowledge workers and the manner in which these match the work to be done.

Organisations are made of people, and we have finally began to realise that, other things equal, the more experienced the people we employ are, and the better they are at keeping up their knowledge (see Chapter 11), the more satisfactory will be the results of their work. This is true of all human resources whether employed in insourcing or outsourcing agreements – including *our* company's own personnel, because in the last analysis there is no greater outsourcing landscape than the personnel a firm employs, each individual being insourcer of his or her skills.

Besides know-how, loyalty and a sense of mission, another important criterion which helps to differentiate the most valuable human resources from those who are less so is that the former have an open mind and are able to *challenge the 'obvious'*. Nothing is truly obvious in daily business, neither is the past an 'obvious' prognosticator of what might happen in the future. An open mind is very important because nearly everything changes over time. Successful professionals are playing beat-the-clock quickly. A myriad examples help to document that only the intellectually young can perform in a tough, competitive environment. One of my professors at UCLA pressed the point that there is a fundamental difference between:

- chronological age of a person, measured since the time they were born
- intellectual age, describing the state of physical and mental fitness.

Intellectual age and chronological age don't correlate so well. In the modern world, particularly in Group of Ten countries, a person over 60 years of age is in a better psychological and physical condition than people in the nineteenth century were at the age of 40. At 60, or even at 80, we can be much younger intellectually than we have ever been – provided that requirements for intellectual fitness are being met.

Personal characteristics, including formal training and experience, have a great impact on the deliverables. In 2001, a study at MIT came to the conclusion that the difference between hiring the best person and hiring an average person can be a factor of 50 to 1. Typically, the best person will:

- have a polyvalent background
- be innovative and imaginative
- be flexible and adjustable
- have a deep sense of planning and control.

Effective plans require perspective and experience. Harry Truman once said: 'You can always amend a big plan, you can never expand a little one.' Dwight Eisenhower was to add: 'The Plan is nothing. *Planning* is everything.' The object of this chapter is planning for the best human resources.

2. Both an analytical mind and a doer's personality are important to success

The company of the twenty-first century will be rich in professionals and thin in managers. In a way, it will resemble an orchestra with 300 professionals and one conductor, says Peter Drucker. An orchestra does not have subconductors, the way industrial and financial organisations are currently built, with multiple layers of management. But it has a first violin – a top professional who distinguishes themself by being a virtuoso.

Today, more than ever, companies which wish to be successful require cerebral skills rather than manual skills. The knowledge-based businesses of consultancy, which implies a great deal of know-how, extends all the way from research and development (R&D) to finance, marketing, information technology and teaching. Outsourcing agreements can flourish in the whole range of these activities provided they are cost effective (see Part IV). They are helped by the fact organisations become flatter and less hierarchical.

The most accurate answer to the question of which characteristics best express the personality of successful professionals is: accuracy in analysis, ability to command a broader perspective, ability to control events and willingness to act. To appreciate why both an analytical mind and a doers personality are critical ingredients, we should start by looking at a higher level of organisational reference: that of strategic planning, and progressively move to the nuts and bolts of the way in which a person's left and right brain work.

In finance, for instance, when we talk of strategic planning, reference is made to board level, and this reference indirectly involves aspects of trading, securitisation, loans, investments and other instruments, including the opportunities and risks attached to them. Few institutions truly realise that strategic planning and risk management have in common a great deal[1] – among other things, certain qualities required by board members and by people entrusted with the control of expenditure.

Figure 10.1 presents a sort of a general statement regarding the life of an entity: person, company or nation. The hypothesis that inherited or acquired traits will continue to be consistently present as a function of time is false. The decisions made today by the board will see to it that tomorrow our company's traits will strengthen, shift, wane or decay. At a personal level, too, this process has multiple options: growth, decay and recovery.

Because organisations are made up of people, to examine our company's personality traits we must study those of its decision makers – and their styles. We employ the directors of the board, the CEO and senior managers for their brains, but in reality we do not know how the human brain works. What we know is that the brain is a multimedia and, for some people, a multiprocessing engine.

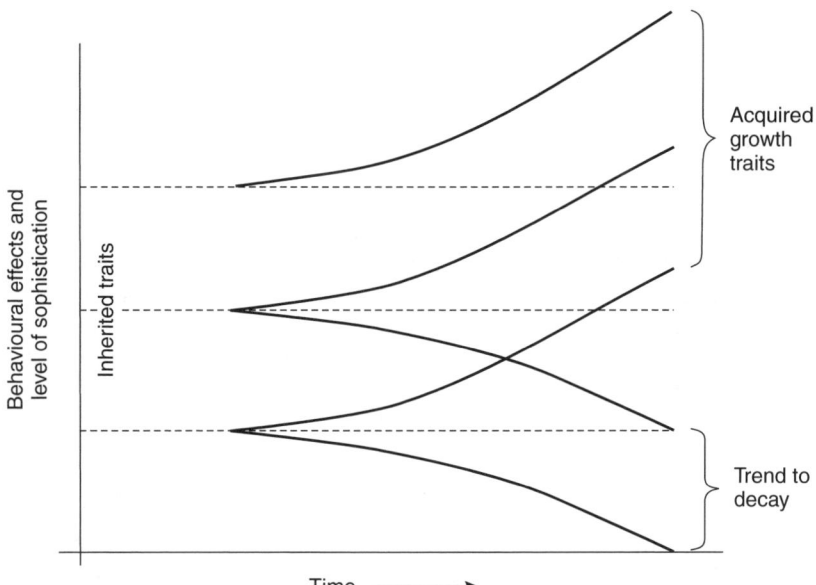

Figure 10.1 Inherited traits can be manipulated through personal effort and environmental influence

At least this is today the prevailing hypothesis, though some people have one-channel minds. President Lyndon Johnson is rumoured to have said of President Gerald Ford, whom he knew as republican senate leader: 'He is the only person I know who cannot walk and chew chewing-gum at the same time.' And Howard Hughes once stated about himself: 'I am a one-track mind.' The mechanics of thinking, at least in theory, seem to be rather simple. Low-level reflexes apart, the most likely cycle in the mechanics of the mind is:

- stimulus
- cognition
- response.

Stimulus can be observed and response can be measured. Relatively speaking, the unknown is cognition. No matter which is the managerial level of the decision maker – at board level or that of foreman – training, experience, observance, cultural values and beliefs play a key role in cognition. They influence in a significant way how we see and measure reality. They also motivate human behaviour.

While learning plays a key role in what a person will do and will be, experience also has a great impact on future thoughts and actions. The philosophy of John Locke, which dominates in America, was based upon the concept that all our knowledge derives from experience. Locke's notion was that knowledge basically comes from two experience-related sources:

1 *sensation*, which is the gateway for experience-related external world
2 *reflection*, the output of the work of the mind which recycles itself into what we do.

Locke further ascertained that, because we essentially do not perceive an object but only an idea of it, the true nature of the world around us can only be studied and ascertained by means of mathematics – or, more precisely, through analysis. More or less in an unconscious way, analytics affect our cultural values and our cultural values impact on leadership which, to be sustained, requires a significant amount of information gathering, sorting, processing, reporting and assimilating. That's the raw material of experience.

The fine-tuning of information handling for decision making is also a cultural issue, while the pivot point of the infrastructure underpinning our reasoning can be found in communications, not only with others but also with ourselves and our inner thoughts. Few people give to this inner cycle of thinking the attention which it deserves, most probably because they have not been trained to appreciate it. Yet its existence is fundamental to both

- the analytical mind
- the doer's personality.

This inner cycle builds up the ability to *know ourselves*. 'If you know yourself and know your enemies, you don't need to be afraid of the outcome of a hundred battles,' stated Sun Tzu 25 centuries ago. And he continued: 'When you engage in actual fighting, if victory is long in coming then men's weapons will grow dull and their ardour will be dampened. Cleverness has never been associated with long delays.'[2]

Knowing ourselves and our enemies (or corporate opponents) is the most fundamental ingredient of strategy. Knowing ourselves does not necessarily mean every business move and every product proposal has a completely happy ending. There can be times when an idea or a trade would not work. In those cases the board should openly discuss the unanswered question: which hypotheses about our products and/or our corporate opponent led to failure? As smart investment specialists have found out, a key reason for their success is their ability:

• to analyse the reasons for failure
• learn from them, so that they don't repeat the same mistake.

The notions embedded into these two bullets impact on everybody, and they shape the way we make decisions. Risk managers and traders, for instance, deal with the same instruments, use more or less the same type of models, employ about the same computers, share a similar type of inherited knowledge and access more or less similar information. What lies between them and differentiates successful people from the others is their:

• hypotheses
• approach
• intent
• action taken.

In finance, for instance, in more than one way, the foundations of trading and risk management overlap. In trading, people are motivated by commissions – a carrot not offered to risk managers whose mission and intent is damage control. This differentiation proves to be most vital. Traders usually prove to be more aggressive than risk managers in their daily business.

Crucial to the way we think and act are also our decision styles. Behavioural science teaches that, when it comes to decision styles, some key variables enter into play and help the course of mental processes all the way to final decision. The function entering into this process, says Dr Alan Rowe, are: cognition and perception; stimulus and response; culture, values and beliefs; choice and setting of goals; motivated behaviour; leadership qualities; information handling; interpersonal communications; ability is problem solving; and a factor of causality.

Each of these key variables can be analysed in further detail in terms of constituent parts. For example, causality is a composite of other, more basic factors, such as the environment, opportunities, challenges, prevailing circumstances and strategic plans (if any). This factor of causality is important because it plays a key role in decisions and actions, for instance, the pricing and trading of financial instruments, as well as the management of risk.

I spent time on these notions because the theoretical infrastructure in human decisions is no abstract concept or idle speculation. It correlates to the world in which we live and the course we take, deriving itself from the real world and helping to support it. At the same time, the theoretical foundations of decision styles provide ample evidence that the whole process of making decisions:

- shapes one's personality
- affects a person's behaviour
- greatly influences both thoughts and acts.

As we will see in the following section, the analytical mind does not make snap decisions, because it needs to examine a subject or a situation in depth, using logical reasoning which is largely deductive. Usually, an analytical mind does not think in *if . . . then . . . else* terms. This is the way the conceptual style is oriented, one of the reasons being that conceptual minds are creative. By contrast, the analytical mind uses inductive reasoning based, to a large measure, on judgement and beliefs.

3. Background reasons for personality traits and cognitive complexity

Organisational culture, the evaluation of processes involved in a decision and foresight about possible outcomes are, as a rule, influencing all levels of management. Many experts believe that each person has their own decision style tools, even if they operate according to a general decision framework which characterises the organisation. Underpinning this personalised approach are the quarter spaces shown in Figure 10.2.

The relative weight of each of these quarter spaces significantly impacts the personality of an individual, all the way to managerial and professional decisions and actions. The careful reader will appreciate that, apart from the reference to the left and right hemispheres of the brain (see also section 4) the framework being presented has three other axes of reference:

1 *perception and cognitive complexity* dealing with seeking, identifying, gathering and processing information
2 *observation of aftermath* of problem solving, associated with thinking and action
3 *organisational values* and *leadership style* focusing on implementing and integrating.

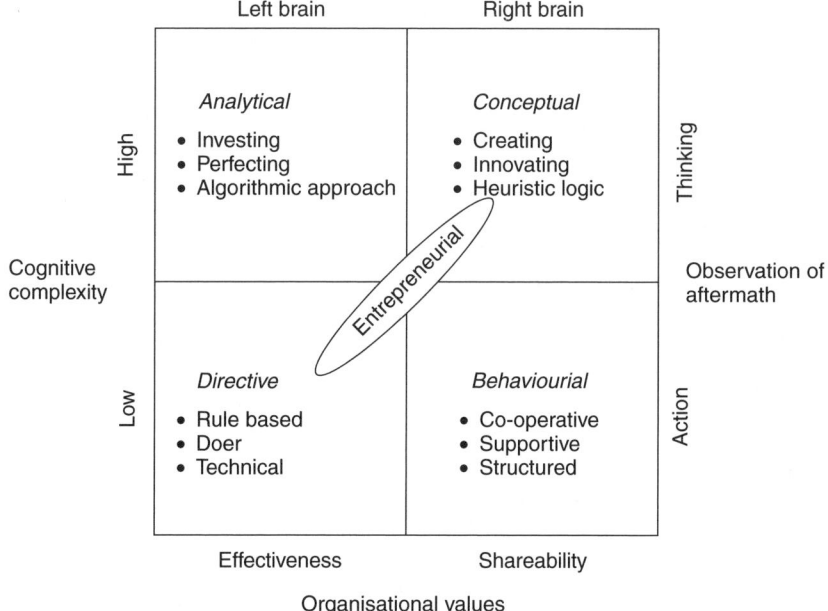

Figure 10.2   Quarter spaces in managerial decisions associated with the left and right hemispheres of the brain, leading to cognitive complexity

As an aggregate, this framework is based on existing, detectable personality traits and decision styles to which reference was made in section 2. To better to appreciate what I am saying we should, however, return to the fundamentals, namely, the relative strengths and weaknesses of the left and right brain, as well as their contribution to the way we think and act.

Researchers in medicine, biology and psychology have provided significant evidence regarding the complementary nature of personality characteristics as well as the contradictions characterising specific functions associated to the left and right brain. Medical and behavioural studies have also revealed important facts on how the brain works as well the sort of specialisation of its two hemispheres.

- The left brain is responsible for language, analysis, rationalisation, differentiation.
- The right brain supports conceptualisation, visualisation and emotions.

Researchers have been keen to find and document both basic functions and important differences in signals recorded from the left and right brain in connection to a task performed by a person. Other tests have focused on losses suffered in the aftermath of an accident affecting the left or right brain. For instance, regarding language (left brain) and emotions (right brain):

- people lost their ability to communicate if the left brain was completely cut off
- they lost their ability to make decisions if their right brain's emotional centre was destroyed.

Clinical and test insights gained about the two hemispheres led to an understanding of the way the brain works. Experiments demonstrated that rule-based approaches of the left brain keep a person at the stage of a beginner, while to become an expert it is necessary to develop facilities making it feasible to integrate:

- situational know-how
- cognitive complexity.

Both are supported by the right brain. For this and other reasons, co-operation between the left and right brain is believed to be the source of creativity, as well as a basis of harmony in one's thoughts and acts. Table 10.1 shows some of the left/right brain characteristics which substantiate this statement.

Evidence of the dichotomy between the left and right brain has been sustained by results obtained through study and analysis. Graphic and exploratory facilities constitute right-brain qualities, and it has been shown that they help to increase productivity because they enable us to assimilate complex information – which cannot be easily processed by the left brain.

- Left brain people tend to work through paradigms; right brain people through simulation.
- Left brain people are best fit to explore a specific strategy; right brain can address a cluster of strategies selecting between them through heuristics.

Right brains are conceptual by excellence, while the strength of left brains is in detail and in analytics. People characterised by cognitive complexity are able to integrate diverse sources of information, producing a meaningful representation of reality by means of modelling it in their brain. Let's also keep in mind that individuals process available information differently and, by consequence, they reach different conclusions about what has been perceived. These differences are more pronounced when we compare:

- cognitively thinking
- analytically thinking.

Table 10.1 Characteristics which differentiate left and right brain

Left brain	Right brain
Language	Visualisation
Abstraction	Pragmatics
Deduction	Induction
Quantification	Qualification
Simplification	Complexity
Objects	Relations
Details	Synthesis
Description	Meaning
Planning	Implementation
Single view	Multiple view
Crisp values	Fuzzy values
Algorithms	Patterns, heuristics
Digital approach	Analog approach
Numbers	Graphics
Static	Dynamic
Deterministic	Stochastic
Sequential	Parallel
Central control	Distributed control
Autonomous	Networked
Goal oriented	Process oriented
Synchronous	Asynchronous

As the careful reader will appreciate, the personality traits and character-istics being outlined have a significant impact on the way a person perceives their environment, assimilates information, decides and acts. What I have noted carries all the way to organisational behaviour and to the strategies adopted by a person – because it is both influenced by and impacts on personality traits and cognition.

It takes organisational and personal courage to analyse risks, pinpoint danger zones, assure there is adequate know-how and technology for managing these risks, and prompt top management to corrective action. Carrying out one's mission is not a one-off but a continuous concern whose able execution taxes personal characteristics and requires both a strong personality and significant know-how.

Colonel John Boyd has been a legendary US Air Force fighter pilot. One of his contributions to aerial warfare was the realisation that in combat a *quicker* and *flexible* response is better than faster and faster speed. This became the basis of a far-reaching theory that helped revolutionise American strategy in aerial warfare. Boyd's example is very pertinent because his personal traits don't only make a first-class fighter pilot but also a great decision maker.

Boyd applied his theory in weapons systems and came out the winner. A pilot in the Korean War who helped establish the Fighter Weapons School at Nellis Airforce Base, John Boyd never forgot the lesson he learned in the frontline while a US Air Force pilot in his mid twenties. Practically every aircraft pilot in America knows Boyd's rule: 'Take a position on the enemy's tail.'

But Colonel Boyd also appreciated the importance of analytics. At Nellis, he taught himself calculus so he could work out the complex formulas that produced a whole repertory of aerial manoeuvres. His mathematical analysis led to a report he published in 1960, 'Aerial Attack Study', which became the bible of air-to-air combat.

Similar principles hold true in business if one is observant and realises how one can get the opponent by the tail. Risk managers, for example, must be very sensitive to this argument. In terms of risk, a risk manager's opponents are, for all practical purposes, his colleagues in trading, loans and investments. For the record, here is how Boyd made his now-famous rule.

Wondering why the comparatively slow and ponderous American F-86s achieved near total domination of the technically superior MiG-15s used by North Koreans, the colonel realised that the F-86 had two crucial advantages the Russian-made plane lacked:

1 better visibility
2 a faster roll rate.

This led John Boyd to develop what he called the OODA Loop, to denote the repeated cycle of *observation, orientation, decision* and *action* that characterise every encounter. 'The key to victory,' he said, 'was not a plane that could climb faster or higher but one that could begin climbing or change course quicker.' It is difficult to find a dictum which better fits the prerequisites for a successful managerial and professional career.

• Boyd's principle is that to win, you must get inside the adversary's 'time-cycle loop'.
• The same holds true, for instance, in risk management, changing the word 'adversary' to 'trader'.

The quick-cycle combat theory expanded by Colonel Boyd in using weapons systems has since been widely applied to everything from weapons procurement and battlefield strategy to business competition. Because these ideas go against the established tunnel vision which so often blinds organisations, Boyd was not the most popular person among the top brass. Although he had allies in the Pentagon, Congress and business, Boyd's ideas often went against the grain of an entrenched military – industrial bureaucracy devoted to the procurement of the most advanced and most expensive planes – and – hence the most profitable to the contractor.

Sounds familiar? With business, too, there are many deals which are giving a hard time to the bank because of mispricing, substandard assumptions about market trends and other dubious reasons. John Boyd was always very careful about his assumptions. In one of the better-known cases, his design ideas helped give the F-15 a big, high-visibility canopy. His major triumph was the F-16.

- The F-16 is a plane lacking many of the F-15's high-tech, expensive features.
- But it is far more agile in manoeuvring, and it costs less than half as much.

In a way similar to what happens in companies with big ego but small brains in running their information technology organisation and in controlling risk, top Air Force officers were so opposed to the concept of producing a plane that did not expand on the F-15's cutting edge technology that Colonel Boyd and some civilian allies developed it in secret. Once done, F-16, whose very strategy of quick, flexible response was based largely on ideas Boyd had been promoting for years, was hailed for its performance in the Gulf War. Boyd's personality traits is precisely what professionals need the most. Star performers must have cunning, ability and inventiveness.

4. Creativity, awareness and the saturation of input–output channels

In a world characterised by turbulence, leadership includes the often-prized ability to make tough, unpopular decisions. Each quarter space, defined by the model in section 3, has basic strengths and corresponding weaknesses, some being more important than others for the specific job a person is doing. For instance, risk control and compliance agents interact with factors relevant not only to the way people make decisions but also to the actions other individuals are taking.

Fast reaction, after having done our homework, is at a premium. Alfred P. Sloan gives an excellent example on the need to be ready and react quickly when he describes how General Motors avoided the aftermath of the Depression of 1929–32 suffered by other companies: 'No more than anyone else did we see the depression coming ... We had simply learned how to react quickly. This was perhaps the greatest payoff of our system of financial and operating controls.'[3]

Skill, know-how and self-confidence developed through experience are important, but the personality traits I just described are, in my opinion, much more vital than vague notions about 'this' or 'that' characterising a candidate for a given job. Furthermore, it is wise to be very careful when choosing experts, including insistence on proof. Says Frank Partnoy: 'The best piece of advice I ever received was from one manager who suggested I could become an expert in emerging markets by telling people I was an expert in emerging markets. Over time I would fill the gaps.'[4]

'Filling the gaps' through experience requires concentration and lifelong learning (see Chapter 11); it also brings behavioural science in perspective. Behavioural studies suggest that analytical and directive processes are associated with left brain functioning, but there is a major distinction. Creative thinkers and planners are able to cope with a high cognitive complexity. By contrast, the cognitive complexity of people who are best in technical, rule-based and directive roles is relatively low.

Even if most situations are unique, these guidelines can be extremely valuable in analysing a decision process, from policy making to estimating the most likely outcomes of a risk control action. Let's recall colonel Boyd's 'observation, orientation, decision and action' loop and the importance of quicker and flexible response to events as they unfold.

For instance, given the amount of risk they assume through leveraging and derivatives trading, institutions need at the top people who can change gears fast. This is the type of person running the most aggressive companies, the pace-setters in their industry who know-how to take corporate opponents by the tail. This should be part of corporate culture, but it is no less true that corporate culture varies greatly from one institution to another.

To be quick and flexible, professionals and managers must be creative. Creativity starts with recognition of good ideas. This involves perception and sensitivity, but also demands total comprehension of the business. In a financial setting, it calls for analysis of our institution's exposure to credit risk, market risk, operational risk, legal risk and any other factor of exposure.

Key in risk management is attention to detail. As Mies van der Rohe, the architect, aptly stated: 'God is in the detail.' Attention to detail also means staying involved and following up the outstanding risks. Hands-on techniques keep the responsibility for decisions about exposure with the people managing the business day to day, not just the strategic planners. The successful risk manager:

- understands the need for risk taking but is also aware of the need for preservation of assets
- realises the importance of building checkpoints, a tracking system and firewalls to minimise losses in case of disaster.

There is more that can be said on the functionalisation of the brain's two hemispheres. Spatial perception is the business of the right side of the brain, a statement equally true of speech recognition and of conceptual qualities. By contrast, the ability to move towards decisions leading to the solution of a problem, whether analytical or directional, is predominantly the domain of the left brain.

This division of labour, to which I made reference in section 2, is known as 'brain lateralisation' and can be found in many animals, not only in man. Research results from biology and psychology have been suggesting for some time that animal life was lateralising long before living organisms were capable of verbalising. More recent studies have brought this subject forward by focusing on the reasoning abilities of human beings.

- Lateralisation is probably determined by genetics, not by the environment.
- At the same time, lateralisation is an environmental necessity which motivates us to interpret a stimulus correctly.

This realisation goes a long way from what is already known in a physical sense: that nerves are mainly contra-lateral: right receptors connect to the left side of the brain, and vice versa. Medical, behavioural and psychological research on brain functioning and personality traits is still in process. So far this research seems to have produced the tip of the iceberg in terms of intimate knowledge of the brain.

Within the perspective of this broader outline of behavioural characteristics comes the role of awareness. In Japan, the highest art is awareness of Warusa-kagen, defined as 'things that are not yet problems but are not quite right'. Both managers and workers are encouraged to report these issues to their superiors. Because this philosophy aims at constant revision and upgrading, it might be confused with innovation. Both are important, but they are also distinct.

The highest art of awareness about the unseen and the ill-defined is supported by cognitive complexity. The best way to improve cognitive complexity is to enlarge our input/output (I/O) bandwidth, particularly in connection to the very small and the very large, a process known as 'visistraction'. We don't know much about how visistraction works; neither are problems connected to the bandwidth of perception and understanding resolved. The prevailing hypothesis is that:

- simple organisms has a great capacity for I/O, but limited visistraction capabilities
- complex organisms by contrast, have a much better visistraction, but their nervous system saturates too fast.

In other words, the I/O bandwidth varies from one organism to the other, and the same is true of the characteristic level of saturation. The cell is a simple entity and, as shown in Figure 10.3, it has a high input/output quotient. Man is a relatively complex system. His input/output is much lower. The Catholic Church, the US Army and large corporations are very complex systems. Inputs/outputs can saturate them more quickly than organisms much lower in the food chain.

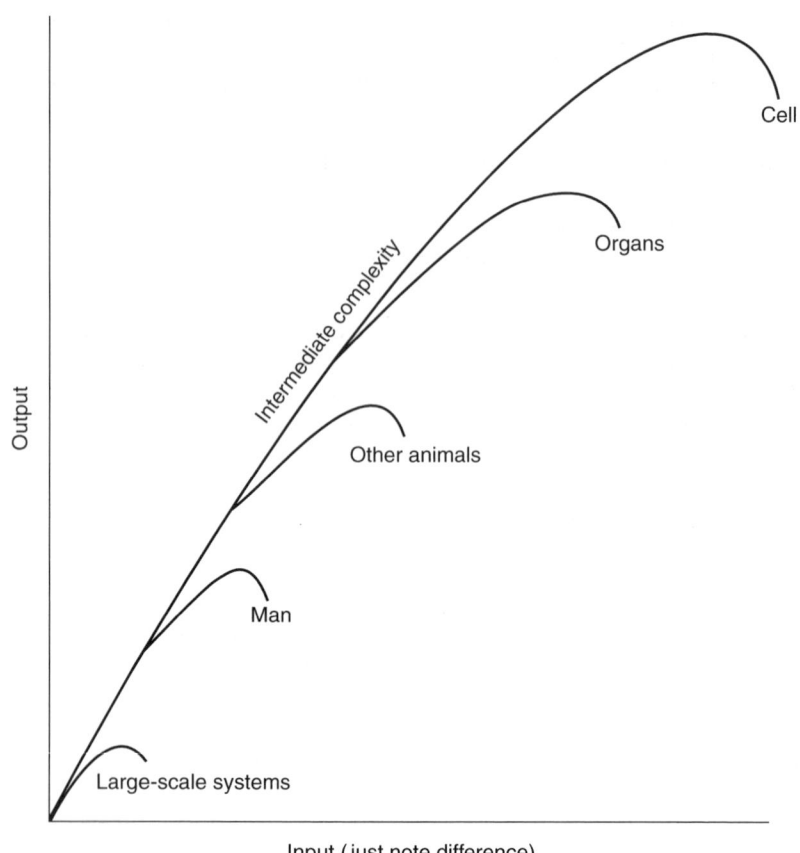

Figure 10.3 The complexity of an organism has a direct impact on its ability to absorb input and give an output

The saturation of input/output channels is not a feat reserved to large organisations. The engines embedded into the process itself may be stonewalling. This typically happens with bureaucracy. Bureaucrats tend to be in the directive, rule-based, mostly technical quarter space shown in Figure 10.2. As such, they lack perspective and are unfit for creative functions.

Important in a social as well as in a managerial sense is the fact that the left hemisphere dominates when it becomes necessary to respond to a distress call. In terms of decision making, the higher-up layer of reasoning adds substance to the qualification of analytical capabilities, but this layer is absent in bureaucrats regimented by a culture that one is promoted if one does not make mistakes – not by the successes one has.

5. A company's growth, maturity, recovery and decay depend on the personality characteristics of its people

The message conveyed by the personality characteristics examined in the preceding sections is that to reach conclusions left brain people look at inputs in a deductive logic, serial manner. By contrast, right brain individuals consider the broader aspects of inputs, including visual and spatial reasoning as well as perceived outcomes. They follow an inductive approach and therefore they generalise.

Within each major category exist of course distinctions. Right brain people, for example, are divided in terms of higher and lower cognitive complexity. The former are conceptual, innovative, entrepreneurial. The latter are behavioural, supportive and prefer to live and act within a structured environment.

These distinctions are important because to be performed in an able manner most professional and managerial activities need both right and left brain facilities, often of the high cognitive complexity class. Valuable people are good at:

- evaluating situations as they change
- keeping flexible, open to newness
- balancing business opportunity with risk control.

Qualitative rather than quantitative tools can be used to advantage in measuring analytical, conceptual, directional and other behavioural characteristics. An example of a qualitative tool is Alan Rowe's 'decision style inventory' which permits self-rating. It bases its input on a response to 20 key questions to be answered by who is taking the test. These questions and the answers are not grading intelligence. They have nothing to do with IQ. What they address is the priorities a person gives to himself in judging his own decision style. The result is a useful pattern of underlying personality traits influencing behaviour.

Examples relating to four different people will be given in the following paragraphs. Let me first explain however how the derivation of personality profiles works. Rowe's battery of tests is assisted through a computer-based inference model which bases its response on 300 points allocated to behavioural decision traits (20 questions with 15 points each allocated between 4 alternative choices).

- The more fair a person is in this self-evaluation, the more accurate would be the result.
- A person's response is compared to an inventory of 20,000 cases backing up the inference model.

The behavioural principle characterising right brain people is that they put a premium on shareability. The key characteristic of left brain individuals is effectiveness. The intellectual capabilities of men and women in the bottom two quarter spaces of Figure 10.4 are tuned to action. The trademark of individuals in the upper two quarter spaces is thinking.

Such behavioural characteristics, present in all insourcers, can be of significant importance to the life of a corporation. They are instrumental in reaching conclusions regarding the information received as well as in enabling the decision maker to make choices about alternative courses and outcomes. Cognitive complexity and brain sidedness influence the manner in which choices are made.

- The more simple people (bottom-quarter spaces) shy away from complexity and prefer direct action.
- The more cognitively complex individuals want to examine alternatives and understand the consequences before deciding.

The critical factors of any value system can be expressed in quarter spaces as in Figure 10.4. These quarter spaces both impact and are influenced by the

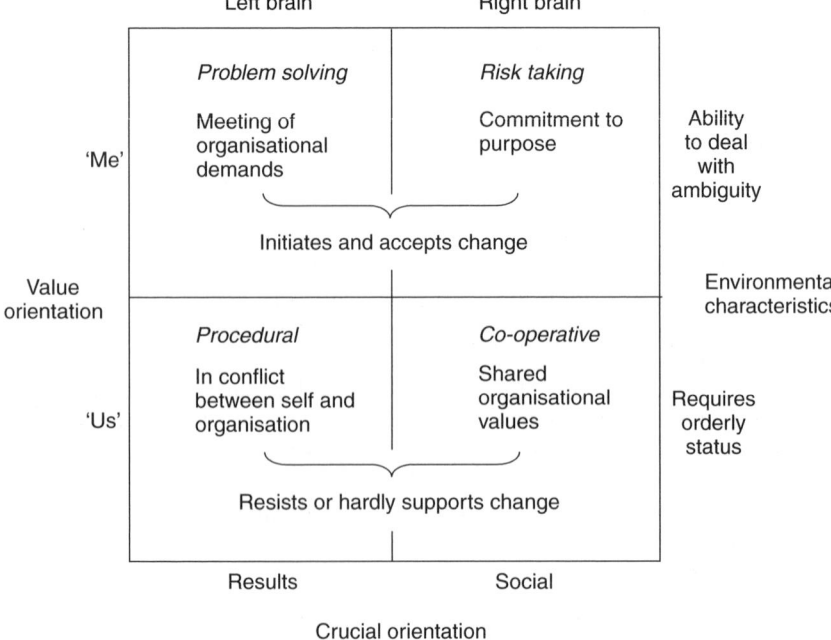

Figure 10.4 Among critical factors is whether a person initiates change, accepts change or resists change. This impacts and influences value orientation

value orientation of individuals taking the test and of the organisation as a whole. The main areas of reference are:

- 'Me' versus 'Us', in terms of value orientation
- ability to deal with ambiguity versus orderly status requirements
- focus on results versus social aspects in terms of a crucial orientation.

When they are at the beginning of their careers, and therefore unsure of themselves, most people start at the bottom two quarter spaces. As they reach maturity, the most willing and able graduate towards the upper layer (top two quarter spaces). The majority, however, do not make this move. The leaders of industry and finance are found at the top layers. That's the timber leadership is made of.

Take risk management as an example. Evaluations, decisions and results to be obtained depend not only on the information received and understood but also on thinking preferences, deliberate rigorous reviews, as well as willingness to take action. Choices made (or to be made) are often negotiated, modified, compromised, delayed, depending on cognitive complexity.

Environmental factors affect the sequence of findings and subsequent controls. Even after a decision has been made about which alternative to pursue, action has to be taken to execute that decision. This phase of the decision process is sometimes as difficult as making the choice, but it is more technical.

- It focuses on a narrower domain, defined by the broader choice of policy.
- It looks at implementation as the final test: no policy can be successful if its implementation fails.

A decision that is not implemented becomes wishful thinking. Hence the wisdom of co-involving in the decision process the layer(s) of managerial support which will be the implementers. This brings a value system into play. In any organisation, values are an integral part of strategy because they reflect the decision maker's beliefs.

In an organisational sense, the willingness to accept and support a rigorous business strategy depends on the values of the people at board level and also on the values of those who must implement the controls. When and where these values coincide, there is a natural acceptability of organisational goals and there is commitment of individuals in common objectives. In other words, while qualitative and quantitative decisions are important, behaviour within organisations, and between business units, depends on the fit between:

- individual values
- corporate culture

- professional knowledge
- management styles.

If an organisation focuses on conformity and emphasises production and control, while the individual is very self-oriented or contrary to the directives he or she gets, *then* the resultant behaviour is avoidance – all the way to avoidance of implementing the board's rules and directives. In a bank, for example, exposures, traders, loans officers, investment advisors may show up for work but:

- at best, they do as little as possible in observing the rules
- at worst, they sabotage these rules at every opportunity.

Just the same, when an organisation demands conformity and the individual is extremely focused to his or her values, the best possible result is a compromise. The person complies by putting up a limited effort to meet top management's demands, but that is all. Acceptance typically takes place when corporate values and culture are shared from the top to the bottom of the organisational pyramid.

Finally, having explained the characteristic of left and right thinkers, let me conclude this discussion with the pattern shown in Figure 10.5. In their early stages organisations are often run by thinkers. These are conceptual or both analytical and conceptual individuals (see section 6 on practical examples).

- During the growth phase, entrepreneurial people take over.
- Personalities change in the maturity phase and the thinkers move out during the saturation phase.

Whether the company will decay or survive depends on the brains of its board members and its senior management. 'General Motors is a growth company,' wrote Alfred Sloan about GM in the 1910s and 1920s. 'Thus, it seems only proper to measure the monetary return of General Motors' shareholders against the risks they assumed when investing in an enterprise with an uncertain future.'[5]

But an enterprise can also have an uncertain future when, some decades down the line, arteriosclerosis reaches the top and the entity starts to decay. *If* people in the two lower quarter spaces of the diagram we have seen in Figure 10.5 continue to dominate the organisation, *then* the downturn is unavoidable. For recovery, the company needs at the top the same sort of innovators and promoters as those who successfully brought it through its early stages and into the growth curve.

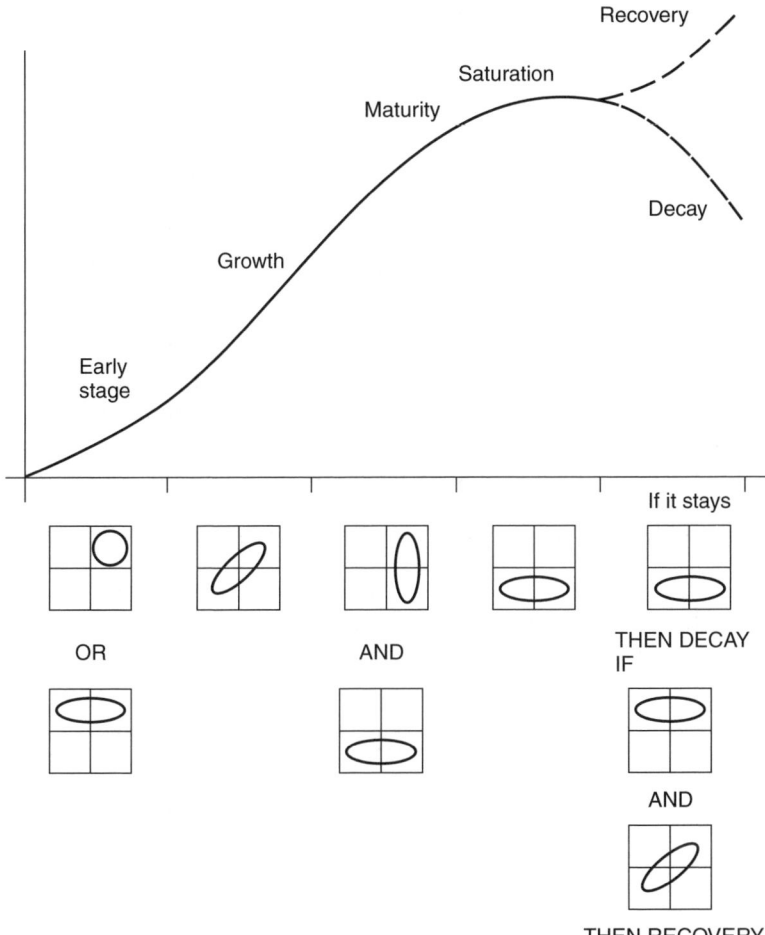

Figure 10.5 The personality characteristics of its top management decide any company's future

6. Interpreting the results of qualitative measurement of personality traits

Let me repeat in a couple of paragraphs the message carried by sections 2 to 5. No two people have the same personality characteristics. Because their behavioural styles and the way they make professional decisions depend greatly on those characteristics, it is wise to detect personality traits and cognitive complexity before assigning to them specific functions which can be executed perfectly well by certain people but much less so by others.

To conceptualise the differences between thinkers, who would rate highly in terms of requirements posed by the two top quarter spaces in Figure 10.4, Figure 10.6 presents in general terms the way a fully conceptual and a fully analytical person thinks and works. As we will see through practical examples of people who took a battery of tests, most thinkers have a mixture of the two – though one of them, analytical or conceptual, will dominate.

In this section we will consider four cases. The first two show the method; the next two demonstrate that personality traits change with time and experience. As I have mentioned, the battery consists of 20 questions, each with a four-way choice. The evaluation process is based on self-rating, the way a person perceives themselves. The choices being made are arranged in four buckets: analytical, directive, conceptual and behavioural traits.

For instance, *if* a person rates themselves, through their answers to the questions, 120 on analytical and 38 on conceptual, *then* this person is predominantly analytical. Conceptual issues are way down their priorities. This test was taken by a young graduate engineer, and as it can be seen in Figure 10.7 the higher grade next to analytical (120 points) is conceptual (79 points) followed by directive (63 points). The person who attained this score is:

- primarily a thinker (199 points out of 300)
- left brain (183 points out of 300).

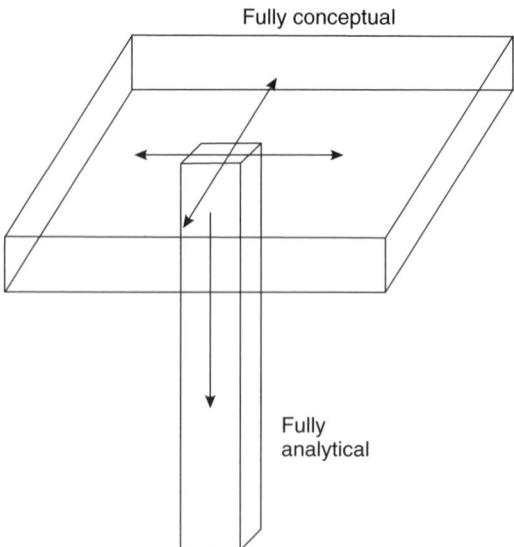

Figure 10.6   The difference in orientation and investigation between analytical and conceptual minds is significant

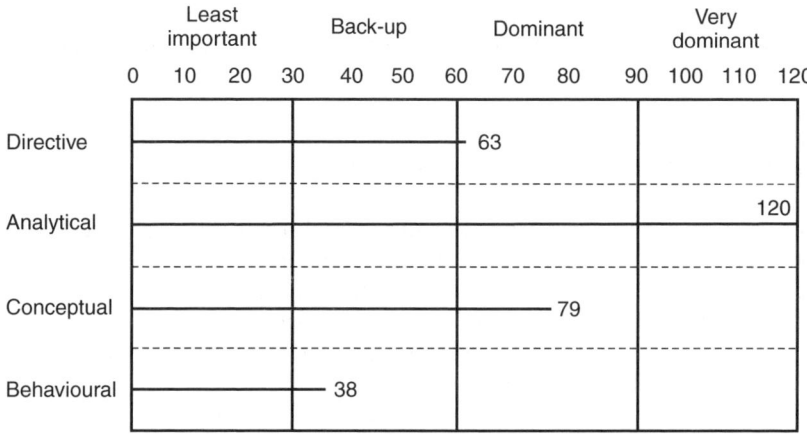

Figure 10.7　Self-rating by a young graduate engineer

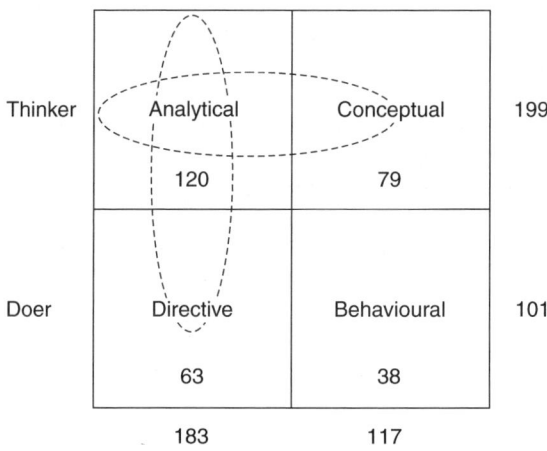

Figure 10.8　Decision style plot based on the self-rating exercise by the graduate engineer

The careful reader will remember that, as has already been underlined, this is not an IQ test. The results identify the decision style of a person, not their intelligence. These results are mapped in Figure 10.8. The analytical quarter space dominates, the conceptual comes next, followed by the directive. Behavioural traits are nearly irrelevant.

The analytical person's communications style is characterised by using carefully prepared material. Analytical personality traits show a person who is logic oriented. He or she is a problem solver, finding new ways of attacking relatively complex cases. Analytical people are also ideas oriented, and therefore innovative thinkers; they enjoys problem solving. Generally, their approach is characterised by:

- reliance on detail
- careful analysis aimed at finding solutions.

The method used in connection to the examination of results of tests on personality traits is fairly simple and is summarised in a graphic form in Figure 10.9. A person may be predominantly analytical and conceptual; or predominantly conceptual and directive – that's the stuff from which tycoons are made. He or she may be analytical and directional; or, alternatively, conceptual and behavioural.

Personality traits are not necessarily inherited. The subject whose profile was shown in Figures 10.7 and 10.8 is a female graduate engineer. Another subject who took the test is the sister of the first. A few years younger, she is an engineering student. As shown in Figure 10.10, her personality traits are primarily conceptual, but in this case analytical and directive skills compete very closely. Given the 98 conceptual and 57 behavioural points, the right brain has a slight advantage over the left. The decision styles chart is plotted in Figure 10.11.

Figure 10.12 tells a different story. The subject is again an engineer, but much older. The dominant factor is conceptual; they use heuristic logic and inductive reasoning, consider many options and can be generally considered as a creative thinker. Such a person always looks for new ideas, is very independent, and is willing to take risks – but also expects recognition. (More about the arrows in Figure 10.12 later.)

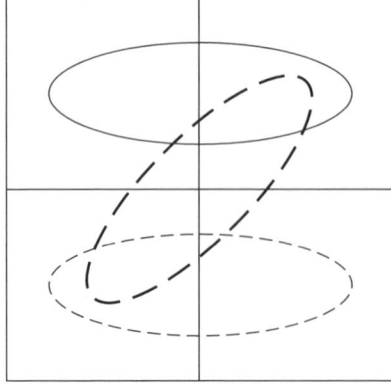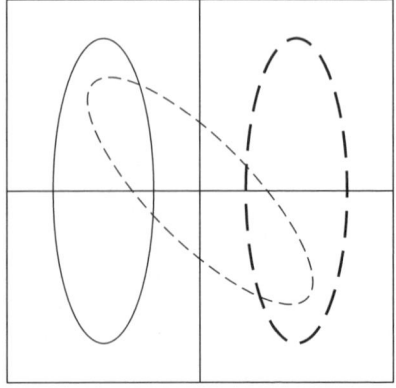

Figure 10.9   Alternative personality traits in the brain's four quarter spaces

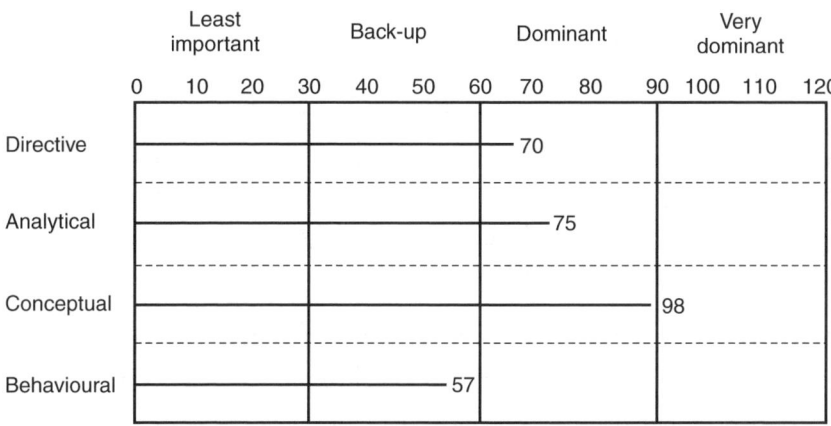

Figure 10.10 Self-rating by an engineering student

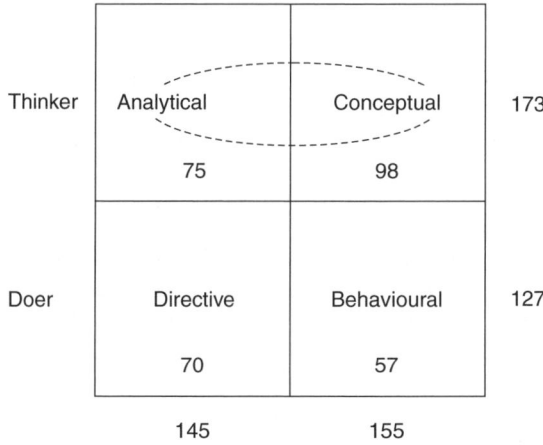

Figure 10.11 Decision style plot based on the self-rating exercise by the engineering student

Because a conceptual person is a broad thinker who sees many alternatives and is able to visualise consequences, he or she finds new approaches to problems that have not been tried before. As a rule, a conceptual person's approach to problem solving is characterised by taking diverse cues and producing a meaningful picture:

• considering many aspects and consequences of possible solutions
• looking for multiple options to enlarge the domain of choices
• finding acceptable compromise rather than a unique answer.

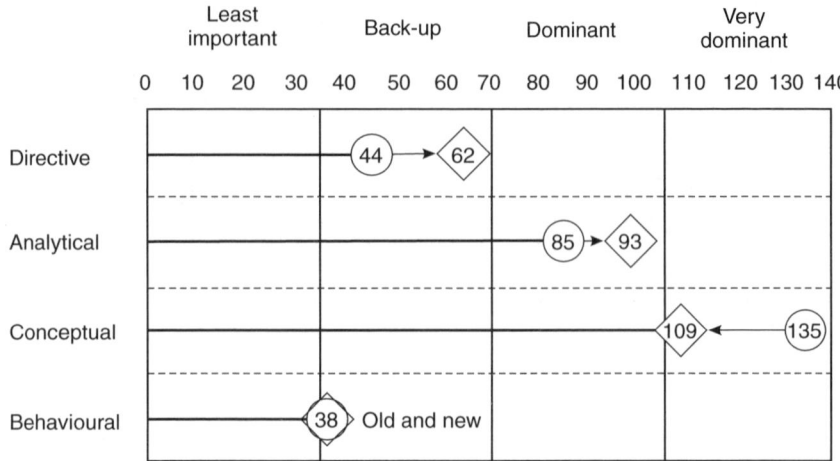

Figure 10.12   Self-rating by an experienced person after a change of career from large-scale systems design to finance (12 years interval in rating)

A conceptual person's communications style is characterised by stressing all possible alternatives, injecting new concepts, taking a broad view which considers the consequences of actions, talking things through with others, being able to negotiate, and using visual presentations or pictures. The leadership style is shown by enjoying meeting people and discussing the work to be done.

Let's now look at a fourth subject whose personality traits some years ago were predominantly behavioural. The results of a recent test are shown in Figure 10.13 (we will discuss later the change in self-grading). Like conceptual people whose right brain dominates, behavioural people, too, are relationally oriented. They want acceptance, want to be secure, delay making decisions, are receptive to ideas and could be easily swayed. They react to people and situations using natural instincts.

Behavioural people, more than those of any other style, enjoy interacting with others and are concerned about the organisation. They are good at negotiating and are sensitive to the needs of others. They are supportive. They cannot say 'no' to most requests. They are good listeners and willing helpers.

The behavioural approach to problem solving is characterised by: relying heavily on feelings and instinct, using limited information, avoiding confrontation and conflict, and looking for multiple options. The communications style of behavioural people is that of meeting other people face to face and interacting with them, making limited use of written reports, and showing concern about people's feelings. They also try to use persuasion and explanations.

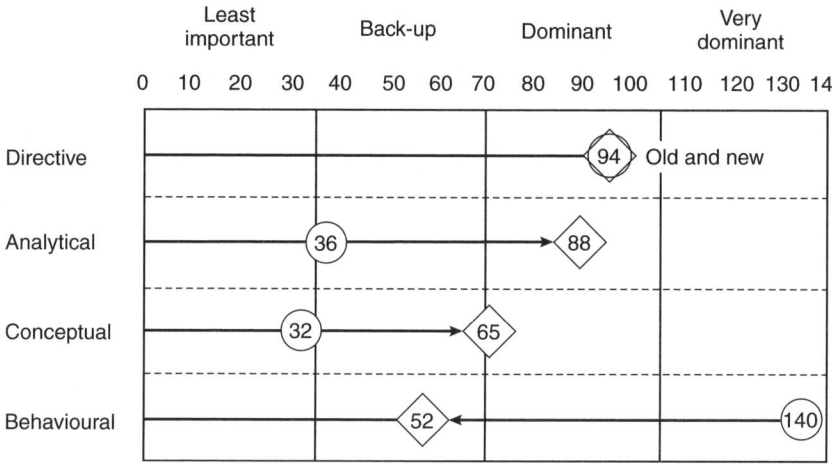

Figure 10.13 Self-rating by a person who changed careers from designer to researcher and executive secretary (12 years interval in rating)

The careful reader will remember that the second most important personality trait of this subject, which remained unaltered during the years (see Figure 10.13) is directive. People with directive decision styles are logically oriented and focused on results. Action is their primary mover, but they need structure, clear definitions and some sort of identification with the organisation for which they work.

The approach to problem solving by directive-oriented people is characterised by primarily considering current problems, then acting to find an answer. Their style is dominated by direct interaction, and they expect people under them to perform as instructed. The negative of directive people is that they are only moderately able to change their outlook.

But decision styles change, as both Figures 10.12 and 10.13 document. The self-rating in Figure 10.12 is by an experienced person who changed careers from designing large-scale computers and communications systems to financial instruments, with particular emphasis on risk management. Both jobs involved consulting members of the board of directors and chief executive officers, but the professional requirements of each specialisation were different. The distance between self-ratings is 12 years.

The aftermath of self-rating on decision styles through another change in career is shown in Figure 10.13. The distance between self-ratings is also 12 years. The scores concern a person who at the time of first self-rating was a designer and who then became a researcher, analyst and executive secretary to a foundation.

The million-dollar question now is which of all the personality profiles we have considered is the 'best'. The answer is that there is no generally 'best' profile. The challenge is to match the person to the job which has to be done – and the better method is self-rating. From Figures 10.12 and 10.13 the careful reader will also notice how much the work one does impacts on the evolution of one's decision style and overall personality. An equally important role is played by life-long learning, as we will see in Chapter 11.

11
Globalisation Needs Goals, Better Education and Life-long Learning

1. Introduction

The days may be equal for a clock but they are not for a person, Marcel Proust has written. And John Foster Dulles once said that only a very active person can be productive, and only the productive people can be free. It take both on-the-job effort and continuous learning to remain productive.

The know-how which we possess and the ability to maintain its steady upkeep have very much to do with personal productivity. That's why more and more financial and industrial companies are after superior skills. 'The ability to recruit senior guys is one of the things you expect senior people to be able to do,' says Michael C. Ruettgers, executive chairman of EMC Corporation, a leader in data storage.[1] The challenge is to find top know-how and then to keep the people possessing it steadily updated throughout their carriers.

The human resources we employ must always be first class. The more business becomes globalised, the better educated should be the people running an organisation as well as the professionals it employs. 'Better education' means the ability to perform in both ways in deep – analytical knowledge and in conceptual terms (see Chapter 10) by gaining greater perspective. This requires polyvalence in know-how and skills. The best advice I can give today to a young person is:

- to view work as an instrument of self-development, satisfaction and autonomy
- rather than to trust his or her future life in a single track through narrow-sighted work.

This turns our discussion back to basics because polyvalence requires life-long learning. One keynote fact which not everybody fully appreciates is that because of rapid innovation and globalisation the workforce has no option than to steadily upgrade its skills. Technological leadership has something to do with it because, as largely manual jobs shift to the third world, unskilled job opportunities rapidly shrink. A breakout necessitates a workforce that is:

- better educated
- more flexible.

In many countries, from mammoth China to tiny Singapore, at higher levels of education there has been a shift towards technical fields like engineering and science. With these factors in mind, experts expect that during the coming decades a better-educated workforce working with the latest technologies should continue to experience the real wage benefits accompanying productivity gains.

Estimates of projected growth in productivity vary, but for developed countries they converge to between a 2 per cent and 3 per cent annual increase in the first few years of this century. The prognostication is that higher productivity and improved human capital will provide good reasons to:

- accelerate capital spending
- lead to a faster pace of technological innovation.

Technology, however, can be a two-edge knife. A year 2000 study claims exposure to computers in early education can harm children's ability to reason, imagine and play. Some people call for legislators to refocus early education towards a programme that supports strong bonds with adults, time for spontaneous play, a curriculum rich in the arts, many courses in humanities, mathematics without the help of a computer and hands-on interaction.[2] As we will see in this chapter, the prerequisites for life-long learning are somewhat different; still the emphasis on human capital dominates.

2. Work environment and the challenge of staffing

One of the most important challenges for any firm is to create a work environment which motivates its staff; one which is conductive to outstanding performance and tangible results. A successful corporate culture is usually performance driven, and it keeps the company competitive. This calls for the proper measurement and rewarding of performance based on results. It also calls for objectives that challenge the professionals and the managers. Successful companies want to attract top talent at all levels and to provide their people with opportunities for development by:

- keeping them under steady training
- giving them rewarding jobs and responsibilities.

Internal rules regulations should foster individual responsibility and entrepreneurial initiative within teams. Senior management must assure the company's staff continues to develop and grow, both personally and professionally, increasing its long-term value on the job market. For this reason, staff must be offered exciting career opportunities with steady renewal of know-how.

The members of the board of a modern industrial and financial company must appreciate that the obsolescence of know-how accelerates over time, which means that its life-cycle is shortening. For instance, a banker who is not steadily trained loses 50 per cent of his or her knowledge in four to five years. For a systems expert, the life-cycle of know-how is two to three years. To avoid obsolescence, professionals must spend a good share of their time upgrading their skills.

• The choice is *not* whether or not to invest in learning.
• The choice is between investing or falling behind.

The personality tests discussed in Chapter 10 help in evaluating the fitness of a person for the job he or she is doing. On-the-job performance is a fundamental indicator and can be measured by the individual's contribution to financial results. As Figure 11.1 demonstrates, with statistics from patents, authors and air-to-air victories (from the Second World War), Pareto's law applies to the relation existing between per cent of total contribution and the per cent of output.

In the mid 1950s I had a professor at UCLA who taught his students that if a manager needs a job to be done in time he should delegate it to the most busy of his assistants, because that is the person who can produce results with tough timetables. Recently, one of the meetings I held in London focused on an actuarial project which was accomplished in record time. It was done fast and accurately by a very busy person.

The general manager, who was personally interested in this project and its output, found the most productive executive working for the company and delegated the project to him. Other people who worked for this project knew the general manager was watching, and that he wanted to see results. Under the right leadership they produced the deliverables ahead of schedule.

During the same meeting another quite similar project (conducted by a different firm) was reviewed which was way behind in its planning. This particular mission was rated to finish in three months, but its took two years to complete. The life-cycle of this particular project was characterised by several interruptions, a change of project leader and a restart. In this case, top management had shown no visible interest in whether or not a solution was found.

A lesson to learn from the two short case studies is that both the quality of human resources working for the enterprise and the way they are managed

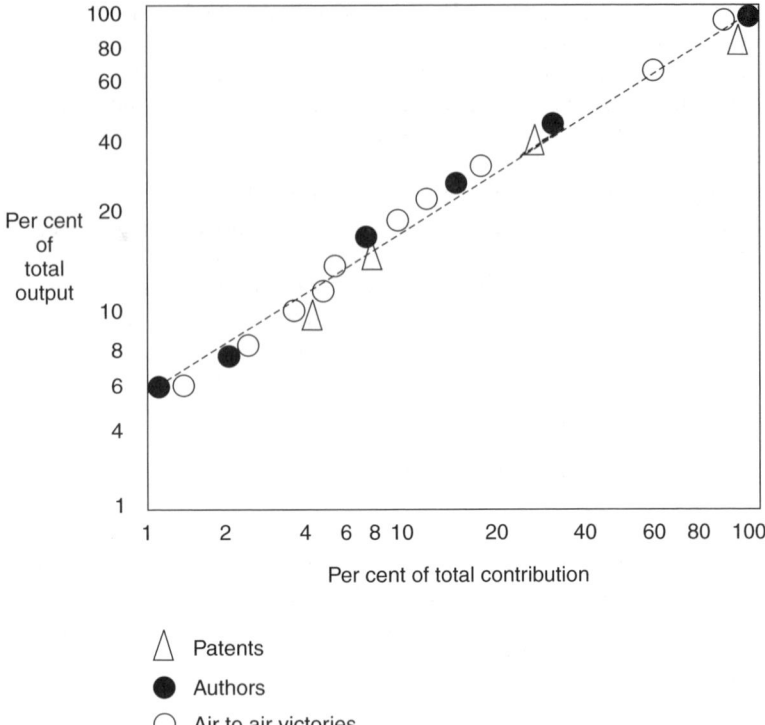

Figure 11.1 Contribution to final results

are very important. Some companies get poor results from good-quality professionals and managers because their planning and control is lousy and their organisation wanting (see Chapter 9). On the other hand, even an exceptionally good organisation (which is not easy to achieve) will not produce outstanding results with average human capital, or professionals who have allowed themselves to get obsolete.

A sound personnel development strategy should ensure that everybody in the organisation maintains and improves their employability. Not only must the company provide its staff with comprehensive training opportunities but also each person should take responsibility for their own professional development,

- recognising personal strengths and weaknesses
- assuring that they receive the necessary training in preparation for changes on the horizon.

I underline these facts because most often when an employee has been with the company for many years, personal development tends to be neglected. Senior management should also appreciate that concomitant to good training is a system of merits and demerits awarded for performance. A sound performance appraisal system is indivisible from human resources management. Personal development planning, promotion and salary must be:

- thoroughly studied
- transparent
- comprehensible.

Human resources policies must make the staff feel that they are able to influence their future through deliverables by meeting specific performance evaluation targets which are measurable. Such an approach plays a central role in the realisation of common goals and the fulfilment of corporate objectives.

When human resources get obsolete, the strength of a company – whether in manufacturing, marketing, finance or service sectors of the economy – declines. As I never tire repeating, in this age of globalised competition, human resources become obsolete very fast. How can top management keep the company's human resources on the move? 'The human donkey will not move,' Winston Churchill is reputed to have said at the end of the Second World War, 'unless it sees a carrot in the front and feels a stick in the back.'

- The carrot in the front are the *merits* or *incentives*.
- The stick in the back, the *demerits*.

Incentives can be of three types. One is company-sponsored *life-long learning*. Only leading-edge organisations are wise enough to practice this strategy. The other is setting quantitative goals (like quotas) and attaching bonuses to them. This is by far the wider-practised carrot (more on this in section 4). The third is organisational renewal by keeping the current human resources under steady competition and by bringing in new blood. In 2002 IBM instituted a personnel strategy which rests on a rigorous grading system on a scale from 1 to 4:[3]

- Employees rated 1 have obtained results beyond their set goals; they are few in number.
- Those getting a grade 2 have attained the objectives which were set for them.
- Employees rated 3 met only some of their goals, and therefore are required to improved their know-how and their performance.
- The rejects of the grading system get 4. They have not met the company's standards and would be the first to let go.

Life-long learning, merits/demerits and recruitment deserve a good deal of senior management's attention. It is a time-tested principle of staffing that if the appropriate skill and know-how does not enter at the bottom of the organisational pyramid it will not be available when needed at the top. Finding appropriate skills is a challenge which has been eased by navigating the Web. Companies are exploiting this opportunity in locating new talent. A large share of the annual intake by Cisco Systems is now over the Internet.

- Online searches can be focused and efficient.
- They are also tending to produce computer-literate people.

Six years ago, in 1997, only 3 per cent of companies bothered posting jobs on the Net. Since then, potential employers have realised that the Internet presents a wide audience that contains a vast range of qualified applicants among the young generation. Consequently, an estimated 25 per cent of US firms are now using the Web for posting job vacancies, and that number is rising.

Experts also point out that a robust job market has given professionals an advantage. The need for qualified professionals is rising and, as will see in section 5, the internet can also contribute to life-long learning. Down to basics, however. The effective acquisition of knowledge has much to do with an interplay between formal training and osmosis. Life-long learning depends on both.

3. Knowledge, paths of learning and the new economy

The knowledge society is the first human environment where rapid innovation is not only welcome but is also used as the flywheel of the economy. In addition, it is the first society where upward mobility seems to be potentially unlimited. Personal know-how makes the difference. Knowledge is distinct from other known means of production in that it cannot be inherited or delegated.

- Knowledge has to be acquired by each person practically from scratch.
- Everyone comes into the world with practically the same amount of ignorance.

Another important characteristic of knowledge is that it has to be put in a form in which it can be exploited, which means it has to become practical. Theoretical knowledge is generally available, though it takes a concentrated effort to assimilate it. By contrast, practical knowledge is one's own. One gains it by:

- training
- observation

- osmosis
- hands-on experience.

Knowledge which becomes public is almost universally accessible. People can acquire knowledge at school through a teaching process, but not all people are eager or capable of doing so (because they don't concentrate on what they are taught) – and the large majority fails to take advantage of what they learn. In a knowledge society, people who fail to learn find themselves in the statistics of core unemployment.

- Knowledge assimilation is vital because the new economy, which essentially is a knowledge economy, relies heavily on *knowledge workers*.
- Technology enterprises are an example of people and companies taking advantage of what they have learned.

High-technology industries are defined by paths of learning. As Alfred D. Chandler suggests:[4] 'In market economies the competitive strengths of industrial firms rest on learned organisational capabilities.' An entity springs out of an individual's knowledge, which evolves into organisational knowledge, consisting of three basic strengths:

- technical prowess, such as research
- functional knowledge like production and marketing
- managerial expertise in planning, organising, staffing, directing and controlling.

Innovation based on knowledge resulting from R&D creates the way to new businesses developments and gives a company the chance to succeed. It also creates a barrier to entry by would-be competitors. Once a company has built its learning base to the point where it has become a core entity in an industry, Chandler suggests, 'entrepreneurial start-ups are rarely able to enter. Instead, the core companies' competitors are either foreign core companies or domestic core companies in other industries'.

In the new economy, however, this is not necessarily a universal truth and Chandler's thesis is not carried in stone. Start-ups get their chance for two primary reasons: they offer something new, something the current industry leaders don't know or lack the vision to exploit; and they capitalise on the decaying management skills and creeping bureaucracy of existing companies who in the past have kept a hold in the industry – too long for their own good. When routine replaces personal initiative, companies fall behind in their:

- human resources strategy
- product strategy

- market strategy
- financial strategy
- technology strategy.

Taken together, these five bullets make up the master plan for growth and survival shown in Figure 11.2. Human resources is written as the first bullet because, of all a company's assets, the two most important are: *people* and *people* – its shareholders, managers, professionals, classical employees, and its clients. All these together are its stakeholders.

Quite often, the shareholders get penalised because of mismanagement at the top. Alternatively, one of the top challenges encountered by a new management when it inherits a fundamentally flawed business is that expenses are spiralling while the company is struggling to deliver the same level of service. Few boards appreciate that, next to lack of know-how, a top-most criterion of degrading management performance is spiralling costs.

Costs are brought under control by restructuring and downsizing. Restructuring internal services requires changing the line-up of executives. Often this entails breaking down the walls between product development,

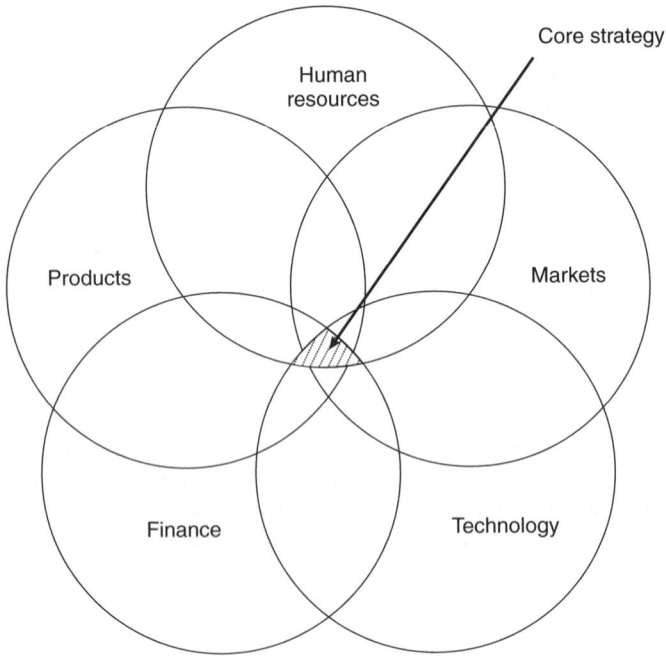

Figure 11.2 Strategy is a master plan which integrates other strategies focused by area of endeavour

sales and marketing – or between the different divisions. In the past, many intramural conflicts in an organisation were resolved by the setting of priorities. This is still done, but priorities can get out of focus and even bonuses may be paid in a counter-productive manner. Quite often:

- companies are missing their market goals as well as their internal profit targets for years running
- yet most managers are still collecting bonuses of 20, 30 or 40 per cent of yearly pay without any corresponding contribution to the bottom line.

In the new economy companies which continue this practice go down the drain. A study made by Kodak some years ago has shown that it takes six years for a firm to go to oblivion. At the same time, while it is easy to say that this practice should stop, once a bureaucratic mechanism sets in it is not that simple to dethrone it – the more so if the board and the company's top management are complacent.

Part and parcel of a process of inertia and nepotism – which can destroy even the most mighty organisation – is the fact that targets are often set in a way which is counter-productive, or was effective in the past but no more responds to requirements, which have changed. For instance, bonuses may be tied to sales growth without regard to profitability; or be associated with tiny profit improvements which should not warrant a bonus at all.

From banking to merchandising, many companies have found to their dismay that their bonus system is totally out of tune with current reality. Properly targeted bonuses should reflect priorities which must never be the same from year to year. It is most important to keep the incentives-based compensations for managers and professionals quite dynamic, conditioned by the 'To Do' list which evolves quire rapidly in the cross-border environment of the new economy.

With globalisation, not only local but also foreign competition is given a chance to take a share of our company's 'established' market. Peter Drucker makes the point that at the beginning of the twentieth century multinationals were domestic firms with subsidiaries abroad, each of them self-contained and autonomous. Multinationals now organise themselves globally along product or service lines, but this too is changing. In the future multinationals are likely to be held together and controlled by *strategy* rather than capital.[5] This means by:

- strategic alliances
- joint ventures
- know-how agreements.

This is precisely where outsourcing and insourcing can play a most critical role. Such an organisation, Drucker says, will need a new kind of top management which is not an extension of operating management. Tomorrow's top management will be a rather distinct and separate entity which stands or falls with the global company:

- balancing conflicting demands on business being made, by the need for both short-term and long-term results
- caring for the stakeholders: investors, customers, suppliers, knowledge employees, communities and regulators.

An integral part of the know-how of managers and professionals in the new economy is the attention to be paid to the growing might of stakeholders. Pension funds and other institutional investors with big stakes are becoming increasingly proactive, posing the question: what can and should managements do now to be ready for the knowledge society? What sort of lifelong learning is or will be absolutely necessary to keep one's industrial and business leadership? Is the company in which we are investing state of the art with market developments, or are its products and its structure crumbling?

4. The shortfall of trained technologists

John Doerr, a venture capitalist, suggests that some of the roots of the problems which hit technology companies in the 2000 to 2002 time-frame lay in a decline in engineers and scientists turned out by US universities. 'We ran into an incredible innovation shortfall,' says Doerr, and he argues that Congress should put up $2 billion a year in grants or scholarships to turn out 100,000 more trained technologists a year, while giving immediate US residency to graduating foreign-born engineers rather than trying to send them home.[6] Other suggestions made by cognisant business executives are that:

- the issue of personal know-how and experience cannot be viewed from a distance
- under scrutiny, pure theoretical knowledge may turn out to be illiteracy, while practical knowledge based on a solid theoretical background is the king.

Some years ago, inspectors of the labour department of the State of Massachusetts found a 15-year-old working full time in a computer shop, which was against the state's labour law. In his defence, the shop owner said that the young man in his employment was the best computer expert he could find. The judge asked for a test to be done involving some of the best computer professionals in the industry, and the 15-year-old end up in the top 5 per cent of that group.

Not only is the supply of trained technologists not able to meet the demand but also few companies honestly realise how rapidly technical skills can get obsolete and how much must be done to uphold and upgrade the knowledge base. Precisely because educational requirements are booming, in the first two decades of the twenty-first century the fastest-growing industry in any developed country may turn out to be the continuing education of already well-educated adults. As Peter Drucker puts it:

• collectively, the knowledge workers are the new capitalists, both as insourcers and as investors
• they benefit from the fact that knowledge has become the most important resource, and may be the only scarce one.

The statement that knowledge workers are the new capitalists should be interpreted in a multiple sense. Through the skills they bring to the company they contribute to its growth; and by means of options and other ways of getting a stake in the firm, they own the means of production. Then, as a group, through their pension funds and mutual funds, they have become majority shareholders and owners of many large and small businesses in the new economy.

It is wise to take notice that these knowledge workers are by no means of monolithic block. They have a variety of management styles (see Chapter 10) which, in all likelihood, would see to it that the classical uniformity in style of management would belong to the past. In the next ten to twenty years there will be not one kind of corporation but several different ones.

• This change towards a *multiversity* will be as significant as that of the nineteenth-century management style which survives today.
• Increasingly, modern companies bear no resemblance to the economic organisation behind the big impersonally run firms.

One of the major changes in the coming years is that company management, particularly with regard to knowledge workers, will be based on the assumption that the firm needs its most creative and productive people (the number 1 in IBM parlance) more than they need the firm. There is a growing challenge associated to the selection, training and retention of knowledge workers because they:

• have both mobility and self-confidence
• know they can find a new job for the asking.

Therefore, to succeed, even to survive, companies will have to turn themselves into *change agents*. They have to learn how to manage change and the most effective way to do so successfully is to create it and promote it – just like they have to organise themselves in a way they can create and promote new skills. Companies also have to learn how to turn on a dime, because experience has repeatedly shown that pushing innovation to a traditional slow-moving enterprise does not work.

The above is true not only of industrial and financial companies but of universities as well. The whole engineering education program must be restructured, merging into it a great many financial and business courses.[7] Though it may sound ironic in a globalised business environment, in order to provide valid answers to the severe shortfall of trained technologists practically every country will have to decide for itself the type of graduates it would like to have and then proceed to design a university education system, and associated curriculum, to suit those needs. This must be done within the global perspective, because no country is a remote island any more.

Without the slightest doubt, at least in the most advanced countries, the process of continuing education in the twenty-first century will be equal to, if not more important than, the basic education system. For this reason, business, industry and the universities will have to make a radical adjustment to the very notion of life-long learning and the way it is done.

- Full account must be taken of the fact that we progress to a knowledge society centred on services, and the service-provider needs to be multiskilled.

As a matter of principle, the service sector requires more innovative skills than manufacturing, and let's not forget that today's consumer is personally more aware of quality differences existing at service levels. The true service providers of the new economy are not stage hands but its motors. This is also the domain where outsourcing and insourcing has its best potential.

- Down to the fundamentals, university education has the purpose of producing the brainpower for the economic benefit of the country.

To face the technical challenges of the twenty-first century, both endowed universities, which flourish primarily in the United States, and state universities should have a strategic planning committee able to concentrate on the output of engineers, because the technically trained scientists are the agents of economic growth – if not of outright survival. In the twenty-first century, one of the top challenges for universities is how to increase the output of engineering graduates and how to re-educate those who finished their studies some years earlier.

The concept is reflected in the process of government financing of the educational system as well as of determining places in the various faculties in universities, or in promoting certain programs considered to be cornerstone to future scientific and industrial development. Lifelong learning is an integral part of this effort.

In May 1968, when the student revolution raged in Paris, I was consultant to Dr Ponte, the CEO of CSF (now Thomson-CSF). Managers had joined the students, and some of the engineers of this high-tech firm were burning the effigy of Ponte under his window. 'My problem,' said CFS's CEO as we looked at the show, 'is that I hire a graduate engineer at 25, he learns for five years, produces for another five to ten years, then he becomes obsolete – but I have to pay him til his retirement at 65.'

The whole process of lifelong learning aims to avoid this spoilage of human resources. Rather than the decay curve in Figure 11.3, continuous education can keep skills alive, helping to keep people productive with their retirement from the company and beyond. This is very important to all professionals and most particularly to technical people.

- The basis of financial and industrial competitiveness, if not of outright survival, in the next two decades is technology.
- Therefore, technology that is able to integrate into it a deep business sense will be prominent in all spheres of activities.

Graduates will have to be very comfortable not only with technical but also with financial and business knowledge. The background the university offers to them will have to be global rather in just one channel. It may sound contradictory to talk of a globally oriented background in country-specific solutions, but it is not so. The link between the two notions lies in the urgent need to constantly update knowledge as well as the fact that training must be multiskilled and very innovative.

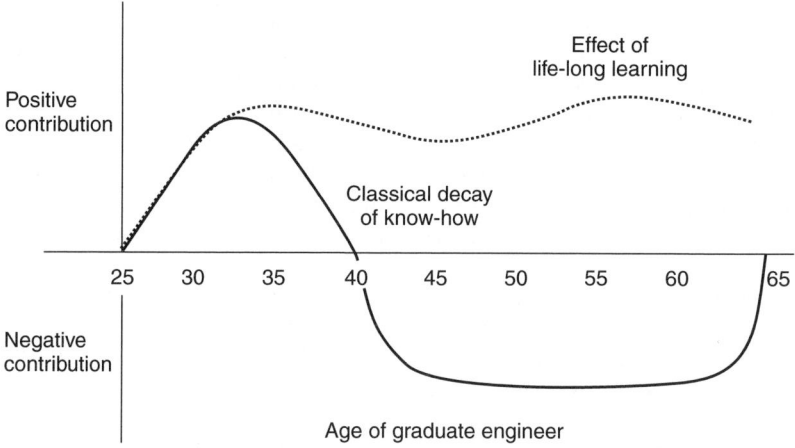

Figure 11.3 Life-long learning changes the decay pattern and keeps human capital in a productive track

The way of teaching itself will have to change. It can be significantly facilitated through networking and multimedia, as we will see in sections 5 and 6. For this reason, all students have to be comfortable with technology and able to benefit from online tools of learning, with the Internet playing a key role in this process. We will see what this means.

Globalisation and internet learning correlate. Together they lead to a borderless concept of business, further underlined by the fact that many graduates are likely to spend part of their lives in parts of the world other than their native country. Therefore, as students they should be exposed to different cultures, spending some time overseas in an exchange programme. A corollary to this requirement is that engineering and other students get training in law and business, including laws of foreign countries and global business practices. Study of languages and customs of countries should also be intensified. The problem is fairly complex and solutions to it cannot be linear.

5. The new economy and the effect of the Internet on learning

Any economy other than a very primitive one requires that people invest in the acquisition of knowledge, skills, and information throughout most of their lives. Therefore, as sections 2 to 4 brought under perspective, lifelong learning should be a basic goal in business planning. Know-how, too, becomes obsolete, particularly in times of fast developments and innovation. In the mid 1980s the Bank of Wachovia made a study that proved that a banker who does not steadily train himself loses 50 per cent of his skills in five years. Today this has become three years.

Section 4 explained that a major goal of university education is that of providing the manpower necessary for the economic benefit of society. This notion of supplying knowledge and skill to fulfil economic needs, as well as to create the infrastructure for them, is exemplified by promoting distinct faculties of science and by offering business courses. Over the ages, albeit slowly, these faculties of science, commerce and administration have been steering towards skills society needs the most, be it philosophy, mathematics, physics, medicine, law, engineering, finance or any other. Today a focal point is technology. Therefore, among the challenges for universities are:

- how to increase the output of technology graduates without starving other sectors of their brightest students
- how to reinvent themselves in order to be ahead of the curve in skills and know-how, as institutions of higher learning.

A good example is MIT's efforts to reinvent itself first through multimedia, then by means of a widespread use of new communications technologies and large-scale strategic corporate partnerships with leading firms worldwide. Those efforts also point to novel institutional alliances with governments and other educational entities. As an example, non-corporate initiatives already in progress are a:

- seven-year programme with Singapore using distance learning technology to deliver courses there
- separate multimillion-dollar collaboration with Cambridge University in the United Kingdom.

Every entity seeks to answer in its own way the needs of the future, including those posed by the Internet. For instance, the Nanyang Technological University of Singapore has a long-term target of 50 per cent of all graduates to specialise in engineering (up from the current 35 per cent). This is a tall order for many reasons, not the least of them being the availability of proper faculty and its steady upgrade. Technology is now being called into play to help in increasing the number of graduates in specific disciplines better positioned to promote society's welfare. The Internet enters into our discussion in many ways, one of them being the steering of institutions of higher education towards interdisciplinary goals.

Experts believe that another potentially more important contribution of the Internet is its use as a vector of spreading know-how. Classically, at all levels of learning, teachers and students meet face-to-face for lectures, discussions and exercises. The internet may revolutionise this concept by means of *distance learning*, where teachers and students interact while being separated:

- physically
- in time.

The underlying concept is that Web-based instruction can eliminate regular commuting to universities, colleges and other teaching facilities. The positive aspect of this concept is that it allows greater time flexibility for students to:

- work on course materials
- chat with other students
- submit written papers
- take examinations.

Let me immediately point out, however, that distance learning is not a sort of educational penicillin designed to wipe out all ills. It is a good way to reach distant students, but it is a remote way and this brings up different problems.

On the positive side, distance learning makes it possible to profit from an array of teachers and therefore a diversified knowledge base. The negative is that distance learning takes away the osmosis, the close contact of the student with his or her teacher(s). Yet osmosis is a tremendous learning ground. We are able to perfect our art by observing how the masters plan, execute and deliver.

This does not seem to be, at least for the time being, a major preoccupation as experts particularly target the ability to keep up the technical skills of a vast population, retool its members by exposing them to the knowledge necessary for the growth industries, and break the bottleneck in finding skilled labour for software, computers and communications projects. As Figure 11.4 demonstrates with data from the 1990s, since the middle of last decade there is a huge gap in employment demands between:

- the new economy industries
- the pillars of the old economy.

In that sense, lifelong learning and distance learning correlate. Thousands of Internet students can take a course, instead of the small numbers in a classroom, by using the store of knowledge of online teachers and by capitalising on broadband links. But not everything is positive, therefore it would be prudent to proceed along this path lifelong learning and distance learning through an experimental approach which permits us to test our hypothesis.

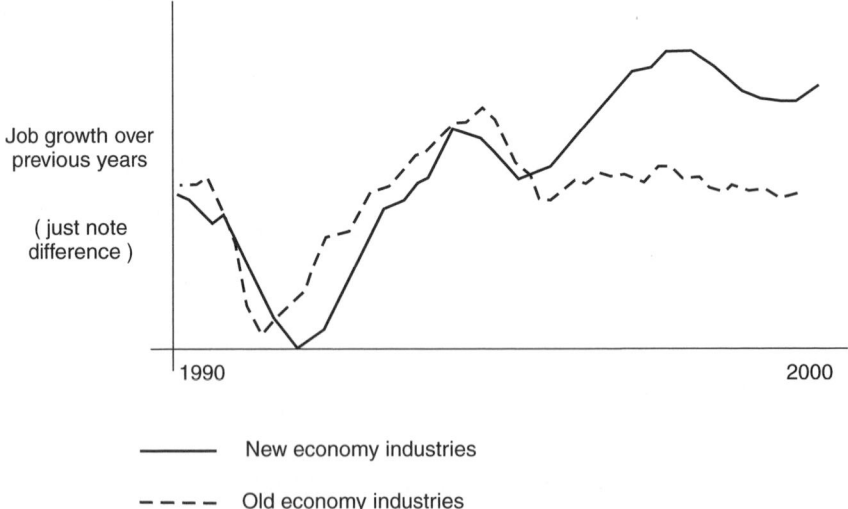

Figure 11.4   Since the mid 1990s the creation of new jobs left the old industries way behind

- Let's not forget that since the 1960s one of the technological marvels was computer-based learning; it led nowhere in particular.
- Neither was wide diffusion of learning through closed circuit TV or public television an outstanding success – though it did find its niche.

There is, of course, the natural tendency to think this time around it will be different. With the internet it might, but also it might not; we shall see. I would therefore suggest that distance learning is mainly geared to adults who want to maintain and upgrade job skills that have grown dated, or change careers altogether while capitalising on some of their present know-how and experience.

As I have stated on several occasions, this lifelong upgrade is very important because the continual introduction of new technologies makes skills obsolescence a serious prospect for all professionals, if not practically all adults. This has been a major reason why colleges and universities in America already offer over 6,000 accredited courses on the Web.

An interesting development is that some students customise their online degrees by choosing courses offered by different colleges located all over the country. On the other hand, it is just as true that in the post Second World War years in America, with the GI Bill, life-long learning (and evening learning) became of deep-seated culture – a culture that has not yet found its base in continental Europe, let alone in Asia.

In parallel with the recycling of professional skills, attention should be paid to the need for rapid development of technological expertise to close the growing gaps between supply and demand before they become crevasses. Some estimates suggest that in the next few years, in Western Europe, the demand for technologically skilled workers will exceed supply by more than 20 per cent. This growing discrepancy cannot be closed by the classical means of college-educated workers – though a lesson can be learned from Asian countries: Indian universities turn out 122,000 engineers every year, compared with 63,000 in the US.

6. Appreciating the role of Internet-based learning

Because of the reasons given in section 5, which tend to contradict one another, the last few years have seen a confusion in the minds of many people regarding the advantages of Internet-based learning, as a substitute for classical college education. Often this issue is posed the wrong way because it tends to mix the acquisition of know-how with the learning of certain skills, which is a poor practice.

In terms of knowledge acquisition, Dr Henry Kaufman is right when he says that helping young people become employable is more than a matter of schooling. Professional knowledge involves, first of all, important socioeconomic aspects which cannot be addressed through distance learning. The internet is not part of the solution as far as this particular issue is concerned.

To a substantial extent, able approaches to socioeconomic problems are a matter of being honest about obstacles to educational attainment. A major handicap, Kaufman says, is the absence of time-tested family structures – which are fundamental to the educational landscape.[8] The kid goes to school at the age of six or seven, but it lives with its family from day 1. Hence, the need to break the cycle of:

- dysfunctional families
- inadequate education
- stilted job prospects
- despair about one's own future.

Down to the fundamentals, and this in the broadest possible sense, education is not just a matter of skills. It is a process which leads to a well-rounded personality. This should be the goal of primary, secondary and university-level training as well as of lifelong learning. Seeing it through requires that we make education a 12-month per year proposition.

Figure 11.5 offers one way of appreciating the difference between the deeper, more rigorous sense of a person's inner education, and the outer aspect of skills. This is done through an x, y, z co-ordinate system. Progress

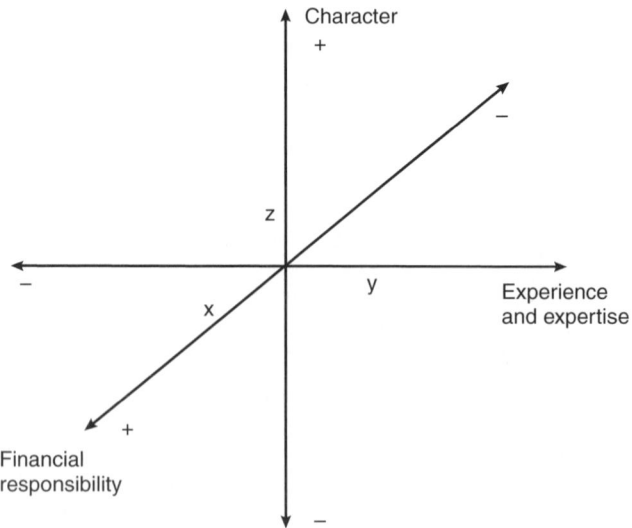

Figure 11.5 A frame of reference for the most effective self-planning and self-control

along the positive side of its axes is promoted by education, starting with the formative years in the family before the age of six.

By contrast, skills (in the more limited, technical sense of the term) could be and they should be, up to a point, taught online. This is where distance learning, including Internet-based learning, has a place. An example of what might be reached is offered by online training initiatives at CISCO and Genuity.

At CISCO, all of the sales and technical staff participate in online training. This program, senior management says, has reduced the company's educational expenses by 60 per cent, because CISCO can train up to 3000 people worldwide in a single online session for $250,000. Other companies, too, are capitalising on Internet-based services to improve their training programmes or reduce their cost.

For instance, Internet-based learning seems to have provided significant results for Genuity, a newly independent Internet service provider (ISP) which was formerly a division of GTE. In April 1998, Genuity faced a training challenge because of sweeping changes brought about by the GTE acquisition.

- In a program promoted by GTE, Genuity's salesforce was expected to grow from 200 to 1,000.
- There were new missions, including selling a novel product set and a full spectrum of Internet services.

The management of Genuity had to quickly find an efficient, scalable solution able to increase effectiveness with customers and reduce time spent in a classroom. To do so, the company leveraged Internet power by creating an electronic learning solution. Within three months after the decision was taken, in July 1998, Genuity launched Virtual University, making it possible for its salespeople to obtain on their Website real-time instruction along with the latest product information.

Genuity deployed its end-to-end network to support an application based on integrating data, voice and video. To test the effectiveness of this multimedia solution, the company trained a pilot sales group on the new Internet-based learning system. Another group (a control group) used traditional means for instruction. People trained through Internet-based learning:

- made their first sale 25 per cent faster than those who did not
- their revenue numbers were about twice the dollar amount of the control group.

In a similar manner, KPMG Consulting and DigitalThink joined forces to offer Internet-based learning services to KPMG customers. This program was integrated into the consulting firm's *change management* initiative, and it focused on the ability to get clients, employees, suppliers and other business partners up to speed on Internet technology.

Another initiative which is worth mentioning is that of British Telecom. In October 1995 it launched *CampusWorld*, providing a dedicated service for education. The goal has been to assure a platform for training in the use of modern technology as well as a testing ground for new educational applications. According to *The Manager*, some 4500 British primary and secondary schools subscribed, or were expected to subscribe, to CampusWorld.[9]

The core element underpinning the leveraging of teaching resources through information science put together by CampusWorld's consultants has been a large interactive database containing a combination of curricula and cross-references as well as other educational material. This and other experiences along the same frame of reference are interesting to watch because they bring into perspective how the school system can benefit from online training.

Indeed, since the late 1990s, colleges have joined Internet-based training efforts. At University of Pennsylvania, the Wharton School established a distance-learning programme. Launched in 1999, *Wharton Direct* delivers condensed executive programmes to more than 30 videoconferencing centres, often in shopping malls across the United States.

Also in 1999, Stanford, Columbia, Carnegie Mellon and the University of Chicago joined forces with the London School of Economics to create a Web-based management education program with UNext.com. Students access course blocks offered by the participating schools, but (as yet) they cannot earn a business degree online.

These examples by no means imply that all problems connected to Internet learning have been solved. Feedback from these and similar efforts seems to suggest that both psychological and technical issues can be sticking points. The selection of subjects for distance learning and learning style are critical, and many subjects cannot be addressed effectively by Internet-based instruction alone.

It is always helpful to remember that osmosis between teacher and student is a key issue with all education, particularly so with acquisition of knowledge and the appreciation of ethics. Many critical issues are not completely addressed by online trading, while testing done strictly through the Internet is too mechanical. Instruction and learning require interactive evaluation for certification reasons.

Distance learning experiences also point to the fact that another critical reference is the level of teaching skills required with Internet-based learning. The online instructor must not only be proficient in the subject he teaches to field questions and suggest valid approaches as problems appear but should also be a good communicator. Furthermore:

- It is not enough for the instructor to be one chapter ahead of students.
- The instructor must be able to anticipate students' questions and readily evaluate their capacities for online learning.

Another challenge is that of developing an effective syllabus for Internet-based learning. Online teaching is a different medium from the classroom; to be effective it requires appropriate tools and techniques which are often different from those we have classically employed. Better results can be obtained with Internet-based learning when students are proficient in prerequisite knowledge.

- Internet-based learning also requires students have a disciplined attitude and to be able to learn independently.
- Students lacking the background to understand and appreciate what is being taught online are likely to be adrift in a virtual environment.

All these issues, and the fact that several of the outlined prerequisites are not necessarily fulfilled in an online environment, raise concerns about the quality of education with Internet-based instruction, in spite of the positive examples that I have given. Expert opinion tends to suggest the Web is better suited to discourse than to lectures. Capitalising on the capacity for active two-way links enhances the instruction, and an equal statement is valid about learning from the Internet experience in order to improve the end results.

Part IV

Cost Control Helps the Bottom Line of Outsourcing

12
Extending Our Company's System of Cost Control to the Insourcer

1. Introduction

The new economic theory which has come with globalising and deregulation represents a significant evolution of the old theory's algorithm that profit equals short-term income minus cost. The main difference lies in a polyvalent approach to the definition of cost and of the act of costing. Down to its fundamentals, cost is not monolithic. The distortion in its definition comes from the fact of looking at profit and loss on a 'one-year' basis, the old traditional way.

The (wrong) method to which nearly everybody is accustomed is based on decisions which reflect the one-year cost of doing business, that is, forgetting there is as well the cost of staying in business, which includes research and development, innovation, technology investments for productivity gains and risks being assumed. Risk is also a cost; one which lasts longer and, in some cases, may be of greater weight than the classical cost of doing business.

Also classically, incurred costs were recovered through product pricing. But the global business environment leaves nobody a free hand in exercising pricing power. The 1990s taught us a lesson about cost pressure, whether from tight labour markets or tight supplies of almost anything. In the global economy it is virtually impossible to pass cost increases through to the end customer, unless:

- prices increase for the entire world business community
- every competitor or customer of ours, no matter where they are located, increases prices.

For example, if energy prices were to go up everywhere in the world, it's conceivable that those cost increases would have to be reflected in higher prices of products and services. But most other costs, like labour costs, are simply 'local' costs. Their principal (negative) impact would be on profits and on profit margins.

Precisely for this reason, many suppliers are put under the pressure of constantly lowering prices so that customers can keep their costs under control and remain price-competitive. Whether the supplier accomplishes this via enhancements in productivity or simply puts its own bottom line on the block by making less money, is of no concern to customers, who simply have their own interests to care about.

Not long ago, a financial newsletter gave the following advice to investors: 'Out of the total pie retain only the companies able to show profit growth of 10 per cent or more, assuming there is no ability to raise prices. Then select those firms that have enough volume growth to grow profits if prices were *actually declining* in the heat of global competition.' This is the best way those firms are able survive in the world economy as it is today. Let's face it:

- very few companies have any pricing power
- probably no industries can raise prices
- in many cases the business environment pushes towards price deflation.

Outsourcing or no outsourcing, tough cost control is a primary responsibility of senior management and this rule cannot be relaxed because 'the chosen' insourcer is inefficient. Therefore, well-managed companies must see to it that *their* cost control system is extended to the insourcer, and that the insourcer is at least as efficient as they are.

Figure 12.1 shows in a nutshell what it takes to develop and implement a strategy for rigorous cost control. The concept comes from a study I did in banking, but it is applicable throughout industry. The object of the study, in this particular credit institution, was to establish costing as a permanent well-tuned process. The basic premise has been that the measurement system which we develop and use, as well as its metrics, should be steadily maintained and dynamically modified.

Down to basics. Costs are a function of management culture, a policy of internal efficiency, and the technology we employ should steadily weed out manual operations. A full costing system includes the overall cost control structure, development of costing methods and standards, and the associated process(es) of pricing products and services. On these premises rests the proper costing and pricing of business partner relations, which go all the way from choice of products to management planning and control orientation, including budgets, profit and loss projections, and documented profitability evaluation. Insourcers and outsourcers should be very sensitive to these concepts and to the way they implement them.

2. Standard costs and the measures needed for cost control

In 1999, in an effort to become world player in an industry characterised by growing concentration, Renault, the French automaker, made a large

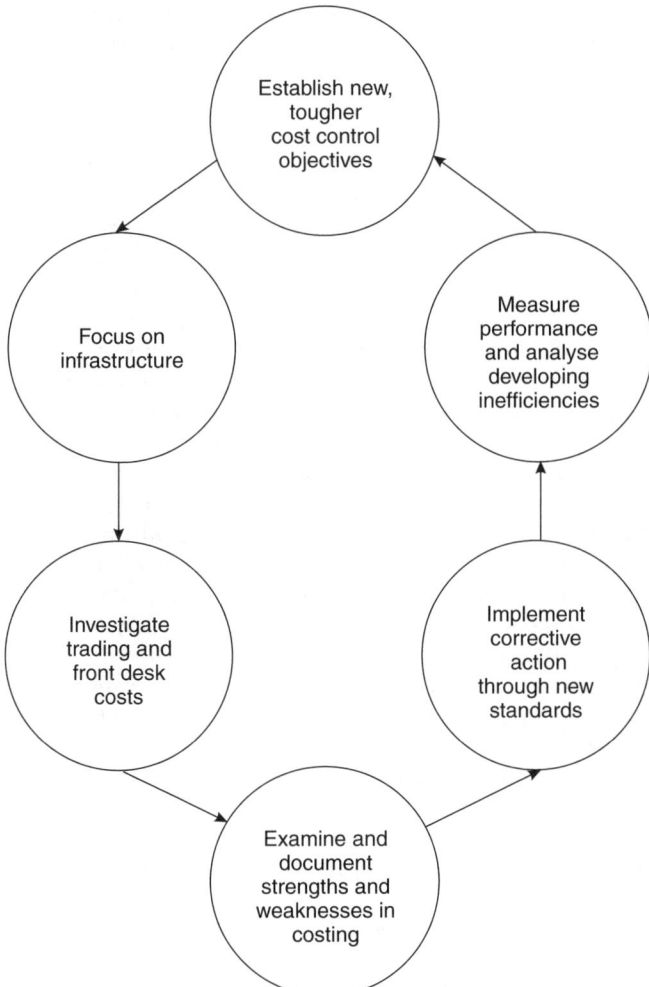

Figure 12.1 Developing and implementing a strategy for cost control

investment in Nissan Motors. Because of mismanagement during the 1990s, Nissan's fortunes were going from bad to worse prior to the Renault acquisition – from over 6.5 per cent of global market share in 1991 to barely over 4.5 per cent in 1999. Over the same time-frame, the company was in the red, even if it had a brief respite in 1996.

A falling market share and rising costs are the prescription for disaster. In a world of fierce global competition and lack of pricing power, only *low cost producers* of quality products can survive. Nissan was not the only automaker of the late twentieth century to feel the pinch. In 1979, Chrysler had to sell 2.3 million cars and trucks to break even – but the company was selling just 1 million and bankruptcy was around the corner.

- In 1982, Lee Iaccoca reduced the break-even point to 1.1 million, through tough cost control and disposal of rotten assets.
- At the same time, the new management put emphasis on styling and on marketing, bringing annual sales to 1.4 million cars within a couple of years.

Outsourcing or no outsourcing, cost control, design innovation and sales drive make the difference. The lesson from the rebirth of Chrysler and of Nissan is that catchwords don't help. It takes tough decisions supported by hard work and management ingenuity, to turn around a wounded company.

Renault assigned Carlos Ghosn to correct Nissan's vices, and he aptly started with a sharp knife to cut the fat. 'We need to reduce our costs by 20 per cent,' he told his Japanese colleagues, adding,: 'Every day they (Nissan managers) wake up, they must look in the mirror and see a reduction of 25 per cent or 30 per cent in prevailing costs',[1] to make sure the 20 per cent end result becomes a reality.

Whether inhouse or through outsourcing, it is not easy to instil a sense of urgency in surgical cost control in a company which runs down the drain for the better part of a decade. Only tough measures can do. One of the first principles Ghosn established in Nissan was that nobody in purchasing, engineering or administration would receive a pay increase until this section shows what contribution it makes to:

- cost-cutting
- the observance of the company's new cost standards.

Other problems, too, were addressed because over the company has ended up with wounded assets. For years, Nissan suffered from overcapacity, contentious relations with labour unions and feuding management. Carlos Ghosn used his experience from Renault to deal with the feuding management case. Before its restructuring, the French automaker, too, was in the hands of barons with castles, but Ghosn got them to lower their walls, by

- establishing very high standards of performance
- paying and promoting on the basis of performance, not of age or seniority.

Correctly, Ghosn wants global standards for everything: standard costs, performance targets, merits and demerits, tough cost control procedures and internal competition. The years since 1999 have shown that he was correct in his belief that Nissan could save millions and redress itself by following high-efficiency guidelines – it is most critical to cut the breakeven point to about half the current level, as Lee Iacocca showed so convincingly with Chrysler in 1979 and the early 1980s.

No company can survive just by being a nice and cosy employment outfit. Management has a responsibility to shareholders as well as to customers, suppliers and other stakeholders to assure high quality is obtained under minimal cost.

- If a company is overmanned, then it has to slim down. Otherwise, it will not survive.
- Let nobody believe that serious cost cutting can be done just by outsourcing 'this' or 'that' function. This is nothing but cosmetics.

Wishful thinking and words alone will not bring results. When deliverables are not around, goodwill will wane. A formal, holistic cost control solution is necessary and the most basic layer is that of an overall costing structure, shown in Figure 12.2. Over this comes a layer of methods including *standard costing*. The process starts with unit cost estimates which should be realistic rather than optimistic. The degree of precision and the number of activities covered by such a study depend on the accuracy required. Measurements techniques include:

- work sampling, a form of random sampling of work activities practised in offices and factories for several decades
- standard cost tables which provide *pre-established elemental times*, like method time measurement (MTM)
- the time-honoured time and motion study with stop watches, and *therblig* analysis for greater precision.[2]

Four principal factors determine the nature of the technique to be used in a standard cost study. One is the extensiveness of the job, measured through the number of man-hours per day, or per year, used in doing the work under study. The second is the anticipated life of the job, which helps determine the detail we should be after; hence the investment to do in the standard costs study.

A third major factor is man – machine considerations. An example from industrial operations is the ratio of handling time to machine time, and required special qualifications of the employee. The fourth critical factor is investments in machines, tools and equipment to be applied to this job – and the rate at which they will be renewed. Advancing technology sees to it that, with the change of equipment, productivity increases and the labour content of the job shrinks.

There are exceptions to this statement, and software is an example. We have not yet found a good way to significantly increase the output of programmers and analysts through automation of software development

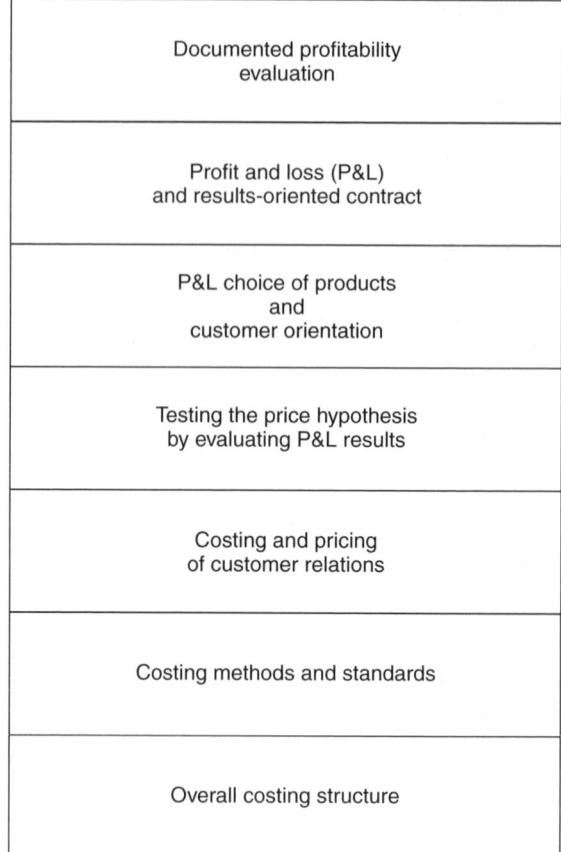

Figure 12.2   A layered costing scheme which emphasises profitability and results

functions, in spite of all the talk about fourth- and fifth-generation programming languages. Neither are all industries profiting the same way from
productivity increases. An example on diversity is given in Figure 12.3 with
reference industries pharmaceuticals and transportation.

Other things being equal, repetitive work is the easiest one to standard
cost and intellectual work is the hardest. In between comes back office work.
A leading bank coded two major classes of ongoing work at the back office,
then developed a system for databasing and for comparisons. At management level the reference activities included:

- planning and control of branch operations (client acquisition, budgeting,
  cost control)
- market planning and sales follow-up

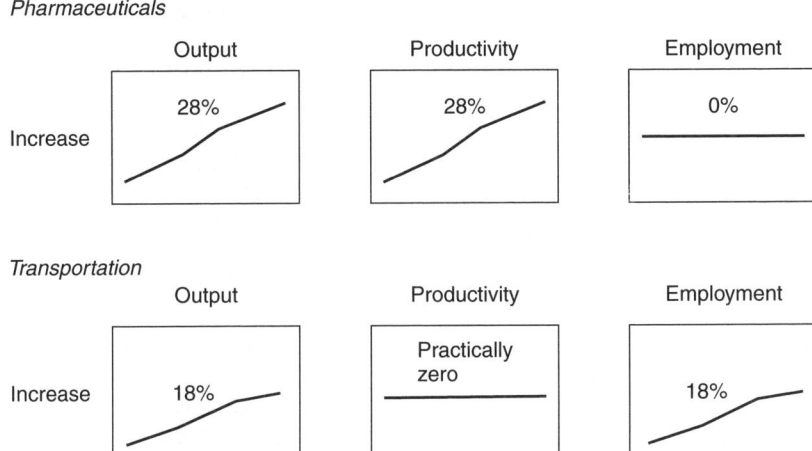

Figure 12.3 A five-year trend in output, productivity and employment

- senior level client handling
- day-to-day branch administration.

Activities identified at back office proper are: general accounting, payments of all sorts (bills, etc.), orders of payment, certified cheques (banker's cheques), letters of credit, commercial and financial paper, calculation of interest and charges, squaring of cashier operations, cheque handling, nostro (or 'ours'); loro (or 'theirs') accounts, control of registration, general management accounts (balancing deposits versus loans); also, most evidently, handling of standing instructions by headquarters, handling of customer instructions and compliance to rules and regulations. Between them, these activities provide the framework for cost control at branch office level.

A company may outsource this organisational study or it may do it inhouse. It may use the insourcer's skills to develop the standard costing system or it may do so by collaborating with another entity in the same industry, in a joint project. But whichever is the course being chosen for cost control, the final responsibility for success or failure rests with the company's own top management.

3. Profit centres, cost centres and the insourcer

All told, insourcers should be much more sensitive to cost control than outsourcers, because very often insourcing is a cut-throat proposition. Costs incurred in doing business, as well as in staying in business, are inseparable from products and processes. They should be calculated for R&D, production and distribution of all products and services, and also for overheads (more on this in section 4). They should also be recalculated when the process changes due to automation or redesign.

Section 2 brought to the reader's attention the crucial role of standard costs which, as explained, are predetermined costs computed on the specifications of a product and of a process. The object is to bring to management attention, without delay, derivatives from standard costs to help in:

- keeping the actual cost down to this standard
- avoiding future failures to reach the standard, as a matter of course.

A steady, factual cost control, however, is done not only by means of standards but also through analysis of causes of past failures. Even on the same job, standard times can vary as a function of the level and quality of management supervision which is applied, the degree of automation of the job being considered, and the training the operator underwent to efficiently use the technology we put at his disposal. Figure 12.4 shows the effect of a learning curve on labour content. The three major components of the cost of production are:

- direct labour (DL)
- direct material (DM)
- overhead.

Land, factories, branches, and equipment are other key expenses. The difference is that capital investment, once made, has to continue being depreciated whether the factory works at 100 per cent capacity or 50 per cent capacity. The amortisation does not vary with the level of production: on

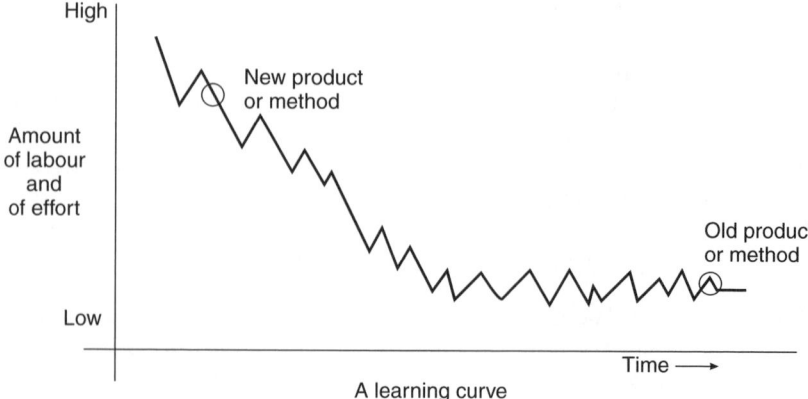

Figure 12.4 Level of user difficulty with new methods, tools, systems and instruments

the contrary, DL and DM are directly related to production and they are the primary targets of standard costs.

Typically, the cost of what is being produced is allocated to the cost centre where it belongs and profit centres. As its name implies, a *profit centre* bills for its products and services, taking care that their prices exceed their costs. The difference is a gross profit. The costing and billing procedure which I am advising is shown in a nutshell in Table 12.1. C_T represents the total cost of operations of the profit centre. B_T is its income. Evidently, B_T must be significantly greater than C_T.

Billing may be external or internal. In some organisations, the R&D and production for example sell their produce to the marketing division at a *transfer price*. Marketing establishes the price list for customers. Well-run companies see to it that DL + DM, the so-called capitalisation, is below 15 per cent of the sales price.

Classically, *cost centres* act as service units to profit centres and they are financed by the budget. They run on red ink because they don't bill their services. That's wrong. There should be no cost centres of the old model. Every service should be billed. When this policy is instituted, then each outsourcing – insourcing agreement essentially becomes a profit centre. Both the outsourcer and the insourcer have an interest in keeping their business transaction on a profit-making basis.

Insourcers must be particularly sensitive to these principles. Even if demand for their services by firms looking to outsource some of their functions may seem to be strong, competition sees to it that prices are often weak. Changes in the business psychology of outsourcing don't necessarily impact

Table 12.1   A procedure for costing and billing

Costing

$$C_T = t \bullet C_s + C_a$$

Where:

C_T = total cost of operation
C_s = standard cost/unit of time
t = time of operation
C_a = allowances, usually 10 per cent

Billing

Distributed on documented use of resources

$$B_T = \ldots \text{Bill}_1 + \ldots \text{Bill}_2 + \ldots + \text{Bill}_n$$

Where:

B_T = total billing for products and services

and:

$$B_T > C_T$$

---

on prices in a positive way, with the result that pressures on profit margins persist.

- An insourcer's cost centres would be a further drag on profits.
- Some of the expenses would tend to escape billing, adding themselves to overhead.

Profit centres should be defined along solid organisational principles. A basic rule is that profit centres should *not* overlap among themselves. Their dividing lines should be clear cut, well defined. This is not the usually case. What is most often happening in business and industry is the confusion shown in Figure 12.5. When this is the case, it becomes impossible to compute:

- profit and loss by profit centre, or
- the returns (positive or negative) obtained from outsourcing.

There exist practical difficulties with the organisation of profit centres. Foremost is the lack of top management appreciation and backing for crisp definitions of responsibilities, followed by confused ways and means for handling overheads. Also, the dividing lines between profit centres are often blurred because they do not correspond with those of operating departments.

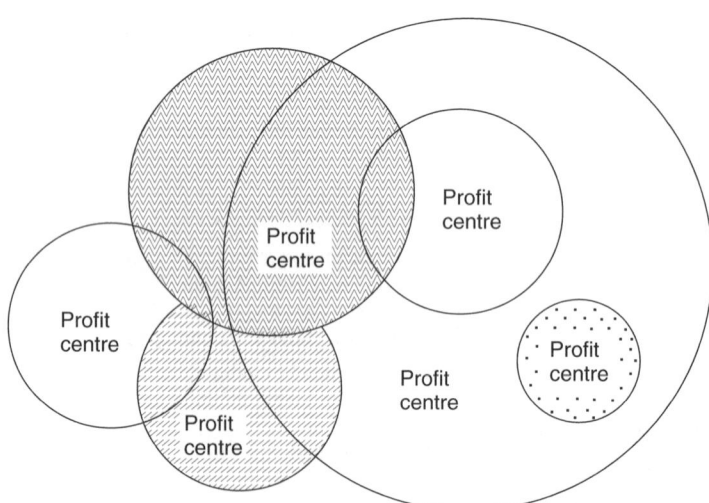

Figure 12.5   Profit centres are rarely defined in a rational manner. Most often they overlap, making impossible their manager's accountability

Another stumbling block is the choice of appropriate methodology for standard costing which fits the mission given to the profit centre. *If* we don't control the costs, *then* we can do practically nothing to ensure a centre's profitability. Still another difficulty is the lack of appropriate computer programs to process standard times and unit costs, which makes difficult timely control action by management.

There are as well cultural problems which confront a whole industry. For instance, in the majority of banks cost-cutting is still untested, even if those who practice it advise that its benefits are proven. Valid lessons can be learned from manufacturing. Gillette, an industrial company known for its efficiency, is a good example for banks. To ensure that earnings continue to outstrip revenue growth, some years ago Alfred Zeien, Gillette's CEO, established a policy of:

- gaining a huge edge in an era of low inflation by focusing on costs
- continuing cutting manufacturing costs a full 4 per cent annually.

One of the reasons for mergers and acquisitions is swamping standard costs. As America's banks consolidated over the past decade, their costs have fallen from 67 per cent to 56 per cent of income, making them among the most efficient in the world. By contrast, the average expense ratio among German banks is 65 per cent and among the French 70 per cent.

Cutting costs with a sharp knife is a business strategy. In 1996 ABN-Amro, of The Netherlands, established a policy of cutting costs at home, expanding its core business abroad, and moving only cautiously into investment banking. 'Like our competitors, we want to build on our strengths and become a global universal bank,' said P. J. Kalff, its chairman. 'But we have a different way to get there.'[3]

This different way is seen in the 17.3 per cent 1996 return on equity (ROE) nearly 7 per centage points higher than Deutsche Bank's and almost 600 per cent the meagre 2 per cent ROE by the investment banking division of the Société des Banques Suisse prior to Marcel Ospel's radical restructuring. In this example, the whole bank is taken as a profit centre. The same approach should be followed for all its divisions, departments, and business units at home and abroad.

4. The crucial role of overheads in financial results

Overheads are most difficult to handle in connection to profit centres, because no method is foolproof. Indeed, classical argument in management accounting centres around how to handle overheads. Many companies spread overheads around like water in the garden. This is a very bad policy because it leads to management irresponsibility with regard to non-productive expenses.

- *If* overheads are not visible at the level of the profit centre to which they belongs
- *Then* there is nobody responsible for them, and therefore there is no accountability.

Very few companies really know how to control their overheads. The best examples that I know are Berkshire and TIAA/CREF. Berkshire Hawthorn's overhead ratio is 1/250 of that of most mutual funds. Its after-tax cost of running the business has come down to 0.5 of a basis point of capital. By contrast, many mutual funds are at 125 basis points relative to capitalisation.

In a study I had done at the end of 1998, for example, about 40,000 people worked for Berkshire, but the group was run by only 12 people at headquarters. 'We hope to grow a lot. However, we don't hope to grow at headquarters,' Warren Buffett said in a stockholders' meeting. Berkshire's CEO is a man who knows how to run a very efficient management operation – quite distinct from the overstaffed, overpaid and overthere lot of other financial entities.

Many financial institutions, as well as plenty of other organisations, are what I call *fat cat* companies. Their awkward culture can be easily detected by their runaway overheads, a pattern shown in the top half of Figure 12.6. Cost-conscious companies have a different pattern which is shown in the lower half of that same figure. Insourcers who behave like fat cats don't survive for long. Their market will be decreamed by other companies which are more efficient.

Another excellent example on overhead efficiency is TIAA. The Carnegie Foundation for the Advancement of Teaching established the Teachers Insurance and Annuities Association (TIAA) in 1905, with an endowment of $15 million. Subsequently, TIAA created the College Retirement and Equity Fund (CREF), investing in securities. Today, TIAA-CREF owns about 1 per cent of all US stocks. It is also a very efficient organisation, with an unusually low overhead:

- 0.25 per cent for TIAA
- 0.40 per cent for CREF.

Only well-run companies appreciate that overheads means bureaucracy. 'Bureaucrats must be ridiculed and removed,' said the 2000 Annual Report by GE. The point Jack Welsh made is that bureaucrats multiply in organisational layers and behind functional walls, with the result that every day must be a battle to demolish this creeping inefficient structure and keep the organisation open, ventilated and free of waste.

To keep bureaucracy in check, and support low overheads, management has to be vigilant all the time, because the allure of bureaucracy is part of human nature. It is hard to resist, and it can return in the blink of an eye. Far from serving the profit centre, overheads (therefore bureaucracy):

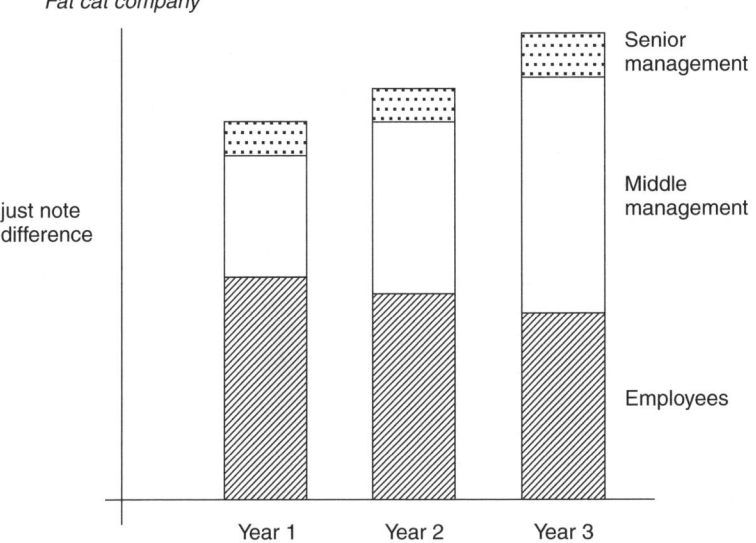

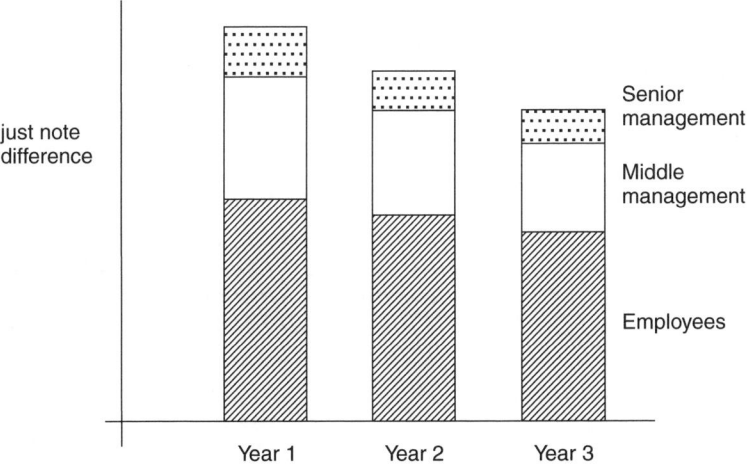

Figure 12.6   The board must use a sharp knife to cut organisational fat

- frustrates people
- distorts their functions
- limits their expectations
- turns the face of the entire enterprise inward.

Self-confidence in each manager and professional is an indispensable leadership characteristic. This contrasts to bureaucracies which are slow, self-absorbed and customer insensitive. The spirit of being anti-bureaucratic can come from early family life and school success, or it can be acquired through opportunities to lead, to take business risks, to be challenged and to win. This is the sort of spirit insourcers need in order to grow and survive in a competitive line of business.

Sometimes companies let themselves sink in a sea of self-delusion where red ink is do thick that it looks almost black. Runaway overheads are part of that delusion as the board and the CEO fail to appreciate that no company can escape the golden rule that its profitability, and its long-term survival, depend on its ability to be a low-cost producer.

Like Chrysler prior to its turnaround by Lee Iaccoca in the early 1980s (see section 2), today practically all banks are overstaffed, with personnel being their most important expense after the cost of capital (see section 5). The term which is most often (incorrectly) used in banking in connection with personnel expenditures is 'overheads' even if it also involves direct labour expenditures. There are several different ways to compare peer-to-peer staff expenditures among financial institutions.

- Table 12.2 brings under perspective overhead discrepancies in the banking industry based on cost-to-income ratio, return on equity (ROE) and capitalisation.
- Table 12.3 shows staff pay and benefits as percentage of revenues by business line.
- Table 12.4 presents earnings per employee among investment banks (from a 1987 study).

Table 12.2   Huge overhead discrepancies in the banking industry[1]

	Cost-to-income ratio (%)	After-tax ROE (%)	Capitalisation[2] (Billion $)
Abbey National	44.1	21.5	24.5
Lloyds Bank	45.6	29.1	54.5
Banco Bilbao Vizcaya Argentaria	53.3	21.1	49.9
Commerzbank	57.8	10.6	14.4
BNP Paribas	63.4	22	39.3
Deutsche Bank	73.3	23.8	53.6

Notes   Cost/income ratio of 21.5% and after-tax ROE of 29.1% are enviable
Cost/income ratio of 73.3% shows galloping mismanagement
1   *BusinessWeek*, 5 March 2001.
2   As of 16 February 2001.

Table 12.3 Net revenues, investment banking revenues, trading revenues, staff pay
as per cent of revenue and profits among investment banks (in $ billions)[1]

	Net revenues	Investment banking revenues	Asset management revenues	Trading revenues	Staff Pay and benefits as % of revenue	Pre-tax profits
Merrill Lynch	15.67	2.75	2.79	3.77	51	3.05
Morgan Stanley Dean Witter	14.83	2.69	2.48	3.65	41	4.27
Goldman Sachs	7.45	2.59	1.93	2.93	42	3.01

Note
1 *Financial Times*, 26 August 1998.

Table 12.4 Earnings per employee among investment banks[1]

	1987 Pre-tax profits (million $)	Profits per employee (thousand $)
Lazard Frères	134	183.5
Morgan Stanley	364	56.0
Salomon Brothers	225	37.5
First Boston	120	22.0
Merrill Lynch	391	9.0
PaineWebber	110	8.5

Note
1 *BusinessWeek*, 30 May 1988.

- The theme of Table 12.5 is personnel requirements versus total assets.
- Table 12.6 compares staff, revenues and profits within the same institution: Crédit Suisse.

The careful reader will observe how statistics on efficient use of personnel vary from one bank to the other, and within the different divisions of the same bank. The board and senior management should appreciate that controlling overheads is as important as the task of significantly reducing the size and concentration of positions, strengthening risk management policies

Table 12.5   Personnel requirements versus total assets

Financial institution	Assets (billion $)	No. of people	Assets managed by employee (million $)
Fuji	363	14,380	23.60
Citibank	217	57,250	3.79
Barclays	189	116,500	1.60
Bank of America	111	47,650	2.33
Tomin Bank[1]	15	2,400	6.25

Note
1   A small retail bank in Japan considered as the most efficient of credit institutions in its class.

Table 12.6   Credit Suisse Group 1999: staff, revenues and profits by business unit

	Staff	Revenue distribution (%)	Profit distribution (%)	Staff as 1% of revenues	Staff as 1% of profits
Credit Suisse	11.404	12	8	950	1.425
CS Private Banking	8.371	17	35	492	239
CS First Boston	15.185	51	34	298	446
CS Asset Management	2.000	4	4	500	500
Winterthur Insurance	25.829	16	19	1.614	1.359
Total	**62.789**				

and practices, or accelerating the development of new, more sophisticated risk management programs.

Next to the point that overheads vary widely and generally tend to be high – while in a well-managed entity it should be minimal – comes the challenge on how to handle the overhead which is there. The opening paragraph to this section made the statement that no method is fail proof or fool proof. Some approaches, however, are better than others. The best, in my judgement, is that each profit centre absorbs its own overheads at:

- corporate
- division
- department
- business unit level.

Divisions, departments, and business units should not be penalised by corporate overhead. Similarly, departments should not absorb divisional overheads, or business units departmental overheads. Each profit centre should look after minimising its own overheads, absorbing whatever remains. This increases the sense of management accountability because it makes visible to everybody the effects of high overheads on the bottom line.

5. Why cost control is a very serious business

Both outsourcers and insourcers should appreciate that nothing comes at zero cost. Everything is a commodity, and it has to be priced correctly. Oil is a commodity, so why isn't it a penny a gallon? In the difference between the price of a product or service and its cost is where the margins are. Commenting on the profitability of the American International Group (AIG), a recent article was to say: 'AIG is efficient, with operating costs a quarter below the industry average. That allows it to make what few other underwriters can: a profit before adding investment income.'[4]

Fidelity Investments is another good example. This company not only has a rich menu of fund options but also has put in place a technology which lets people do research and manipulate their accounts without an intermediary – thereby cutting labour costs. In the early 1990s, Fidelity got 97,000 calls a day, of which half were automated. By late 2000 it got 550,000 website visits a day and more than 700,000 daily calls, about three-quarters of which went to automated systems.

- The hinge is that automated responses cost the company less than a dollar each, including research and development costs.
- By contrast, the expenditure associated to responses to customer queries handled by human beings is about $13 per call.[5]

But is the automation of customer queries and answers a remedy to all problems? The fact is that it is not. Quality of customer handling plays a key role, yet it is often left out of the picture. Simple queries like an account balance might be handled interactively, but a blanket solution which automates the response to all sorts of queries can lead a company into trouble. Customers don't like to see their requests for information, or other services, handled in an impersonal way.

During the March 2000, Monte Carlo Investment Forum, Michael Bloomberg, observed that his company disconnected the 'press one, press two . . . ' silly business because it appreciates that clients and prospects want to hear the human voice of a real person. They don't like their request being handled by a registered announcement.

- Cost/effectiveness rather than just 'cost' should be the yardstick; cost optimisation takes considerable work because solutions are not linear.

- A 'full automation' approach which forgets the human factor can turn out to be a liability, particularly when this job is done by means of a technology which has past its date.

Cost-cutting is no one-way street. Companies, including formally hardware companies which recycle themselves into services, are facing enormous competition. As they get deeper into the business of giving advice, they enlarge the range of other companies with which they have to compete. Therefore they need some significant advantages, which they find through ingenious investments, not by cost-cutting.

The message the reader should retain from this reference is that cost control is a serious, multifaced business. Take, as an example, a stockbroker and his need to cut costs while at the same time continuing to focus on a growing segment of individual clients. To handle them, he must be able to provide a wide spectrum of advice and service offerings – which is a capital-intensive business.

An example of what I am saying is easily found among modern brokers who want to offer banking, asset management, trust products and other financial services to clients in a way that enhances their relationship with their firm. As their range of services expands, they are obliged to strengthen their position in capital market(s) to ensure high-quality trade executions for their clients. Simultaneously, they try to:

- reach wealthy clients at their workplace and/or home with sophisticated products
- have a low-cost channel, which provides steady service to investors with smaller portfolios, in a way that is profitable for the broker.

Brokers who can fulfil the dual role in an efficient way are those who are recognised innovators, technology leaders and the best cost-cutters in the industry – all at the same time. They are trying to assure a steady stream of products and services, without increasing overheads. These concerns about low costs and premier services are a direct reflection of the fact that in the banking industry:

- 70–75 per cent of all non-money costs are human costs
- 66 per cent of all human costs are managerial and professional
- hence, roughly 50 per cent of all non-money costs are at the managerial/professional level, and they are subject to *mental productivity*.

The need for satisfying conflicting goals practically all of the time adds up to the fact that even the best effort in cost control may not be good enough. The moment comes when costs escape top management's attention, as shown in Figure 12.7, because the board and senior executives stop critically evaluating personnel requirements, measuring performance, controlling manual costs and evaluating capital expenditures.

Insourcers should learn a lesson from those companies who, at least some of the time, have been able to control personnel costs. Technology comes to the rescue only when senior management is always on the alert in exploring its advantages. It is not enough that two-thirds of small businesses now have access to the Web and many smaller firms are engaging in internet commerce and electronic services. Even more important is their ability to ensure their customers are seeing the significant benefit of the increased productivity that comes from integrating the Web into daily business operations.

A 2001 report by the Federal Reserve Bank of New York found that industries that invested the most in information technology in the early 1990s experienced the greatest productivity gains during the late 1990s. This type of tangible benefit gives some firms confidence in the fact that the internet is still an invaluable investment; it takes much more than just 'investing' to get commendable, profit-oriented results.

Fads and trends don't help in obtaining the best possible solution. If anything, they can be misleading. Take as an example the generally spread opinion that mergers are a means of cost cutting. In early November 2001,

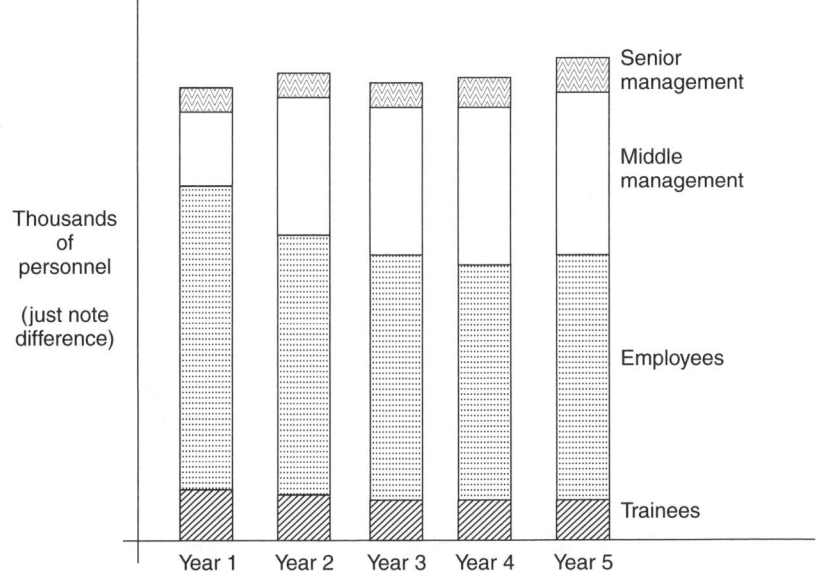

Figure 12.7 The control of personnel costs escapes attention at senior and upper middle-management level

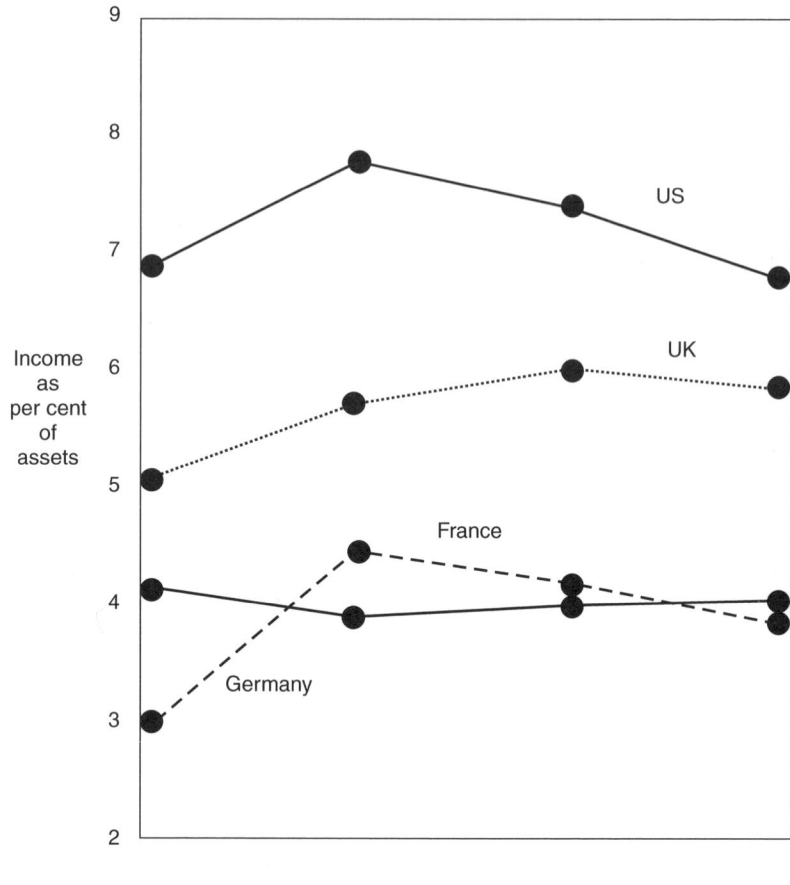

Figure 12.8 The significant difference in net banking income as per cent of productive assets

Deutsche Bank, Dresdner Bank and Commerzbank announced a merger of their mortgage banking operations which had been primarily targeting the prevailing cost structure. This move created Germany's biggest property lender, with assets of around $215 billion and an estimated 25 per cent domestic market share.

The merger of mortgage banking operations of three big banks came as Germany's major commercial banks stepped up cost-cutting efforts and shed jobs at a time of falling profits. In parallel to that was pressure for consolidation among Germany's Hypotheken (mortgage) banks which had been hit by shrinking margins and heavy loan losses after a frenzy of lending in eastern Germany in the early 1990s. But in Frankfurt the mood of analysts was not that positive.

- Many suggested that a great deal of projected savings were just a sort of management illusion.
- Others said that the cost of consolidating three divisions of different cultures would obliterate any savings, while future frictions were certain to add extra costs.

These adverse responses to the probable aftermath of a cost-cutting move did not discourage other banks from trying to do the same, perhaps because European banks are unhappy with the performance of their retail networks because of high operating costs. The problem is that most of these merger moves fail to account for the likelihood that currently projected remedies can be superficial and incapable of closing the profitability gap. Figure 12.8 gives a snapshot of the significant difference of net banking income as per cent of productive assets.

- Income as per cent of assets in France and Germany tends to cluster over time in the 3–4 per cent range.
- While it stands significantly higher in the US and the UK, the trend is negative because current cost-cutting methods and tools are running out of their steam.

In conclusion, there is really no alternative to taking a sharp knife and cutting costs, but there is no assurance the answer is outsourcing, or a linear massive reduction in head count. Neither are banks the only entities where significant cost differences exist from one company to the next. Airlines provide another example. As shown in Table 12.7, Southwest Airlines has less than 60 per cent the cost per seat mile of US Airways, the latter being chronically in the sick list. The real answer to cost control is in management vigilance, and in the policies which it adopts.

Table 12.7 Airlines which want to survive cut costs

Airline	Cost per Seat Mile (in cents)
Southwest	7.7
America West	8.8
Continental	9.7
Northwest	10.0
Alaska	10.0
Delta	10.3
American	11.1
United	11.4
US Airways (gone bankrupt)	12.5

6. Sharp and steady cost control separates the good insourcer from the rotten

Superficially, it might seem that the examples we have seen on the control of labour and other costs have little or no relevance to the insourcer's problems. In reality, these issues are at the core of senior management's preoccupations as outsourcers. They also help to condition the nature of the business relation which is established between outsourcer and insourcer.

- *If* the outsourcer has no valid system of cost control and expects the insourcer to provide one
- *then* the relationship between the two parties will move from uncertainty to chaos, with a good chance of getting beyond repair.

As section 5 underlined, cost control, and most particularly the ability to reign over labour costs, is a matter of internal culture; and culture is never acquired through outsourcing. Effective cost control requires pinpointing problem areas and consistently following up on the origins of costs: from their source(s) to their evolution over time.

Effective cost control has never been merely a matter of reports or systems that establish goals and measure progress towards them. Its implementation and upkeep demand an attitude on the part of all responsible parties which gives assurances that they will actually recognise, and take action to correct, poor performance. For this reason, important elements of a control system are:

- a steady, active effort to monitor progress in cost cutting
- the ability to break through resistance, bottlenecks and other barriers to cost control.

Specifically regarding the outsourcer/insourcer relation, a thorough check must always be made documenting progress against commitments, covering all significant cost efforts and outlining the quality of obtained results. In its simplest form this is done by a listing of projects which reflects:

- amount for labour, overheads and materials (budget) for a given level of activity
- estimated final cost of the deliverables (products or services)
- cost to date (actual) versus cost to date (plan)
- current month's expenditure (also plan versus actual)
- current month's expenditure versus last year's, same month.

Performance ratios must be calculated, such as projected and actual cost performance; per cent of planned work completed; per cent of budget spent; and per cent of schedule attained. Both quantitative and qualitative approaches must evaluate actual performance against schedules, costs and quality benchmarks.

Cost control indicators must be tracked by computer and daily updated, to tell, for instance, whether the outsourced project will wind up within budget – a performance ratio of under 100 per cent reflecting excess cost. Comparison must readily indicate whether accomplishment has been in line with the authorised expenditure. Just as important is steady follow-up on whether the outsourced work will meet expectations along the frame of reference outlined in this chapter.

Steady quality assurance is definitely a 'must'. Six Sigma, by General Electric, provides an excellent basis for judging quality.[6] *Sigma* stands for the standard deviation of a distribution. Based on a million pieces, the following can be scaled to meet any output requirements, provided we target the right quality variable and steadily measure outgoing quality level.

6 Sigma	=	3.4 defects per million
5 Sigma	=	230 defects per million
4 Sigma	=	6,210 defects per million
3 Sigma	=	66,800 defects per million
2 Sigma	=	308,000 defects per million
1 Sigma	=	690,000 defects per million

If the right metrics are in place and the protocol of observations is properly kept, *then* design reviews would help to assure management's determination to check on individual outsourcing projects. The overall progress of the outsourcer – insurer business relationship, which may comprise several separate projects that interlock as a series of interdependent steps, must be steadily controlled in terms of outgoing quality level, observance of timetables and derivatives in costs.

The use of quality controls charts is important as other company departments may be counting heavily on certain specific completion dates of the outsourced project(s) to begin testing, procurement, tooling, production or distribution connected to the deliverables. Therefore, milestones must be published and closely watched if outsourcing programmes are to be successful. An intranet serves nicely as cost-effective medium for communications.

- Costs, timetables and quality of deliverables correlate negatively with the number of people the insurer throws on a project.
- The best way to wear down an outsourcer – insurer relationship is to convey a loss of direction in fulfilling not only the written contractual clauses but also the hopes of the other party.

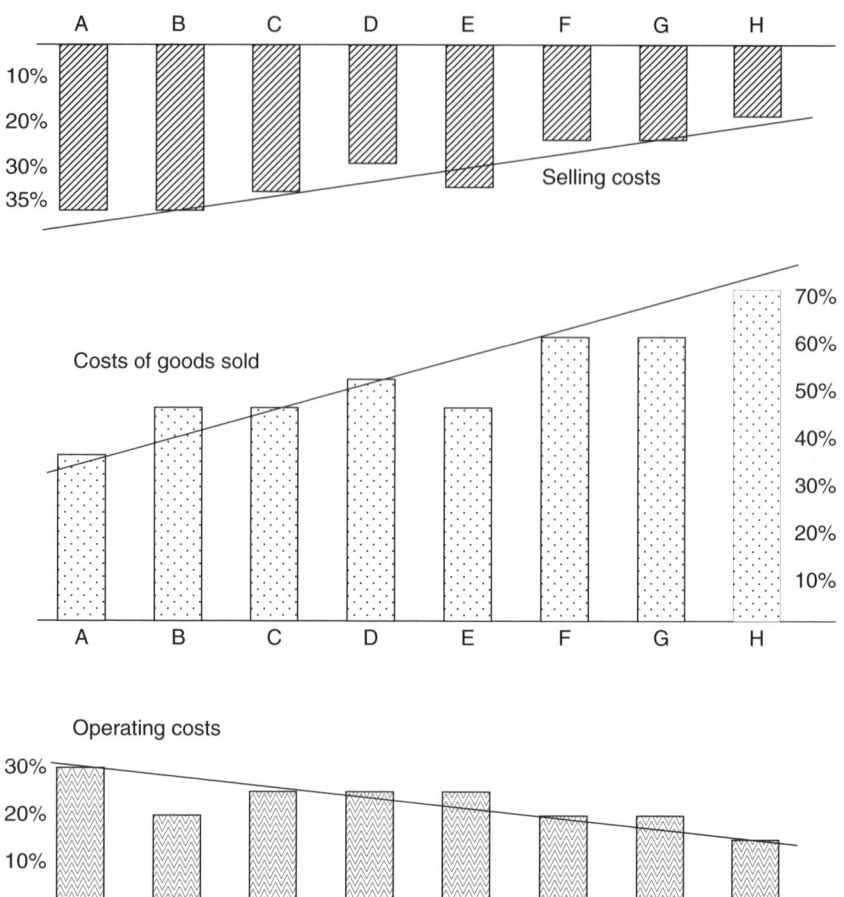

Figure 12.9   Costs of goods sold, selling costs and operating margin by eight different computer manufactures

What sort of assurance is obtained by a bank outsourcing its back office and settlements operations if the ratio I have just mentioned changed to, say, 45/25/30? Is the insourcer so much more efficient than the outsourcer as to be able to bring such change to life? Or, are the outsourced operations adding another layer of overhead over what has anyway been a poorly managed back office outfit? Similar questions may be asked for all sorts of functions that senior management contemplates outsourcing.

A good example of deception comes from inefficiencies inherent in commercial banking, which have seen to it that credit institutions lost some of their business of intermediation. One of the reasons why commercial paper and different forms of asset-backed financing replaced, to a significant extent, classical bank loans are the inefficiencies inherent in the current banking system. The total cost of intermediating a security over the life of an asset is:

- under 50 basis points in capital market operations
- but over 200 basis points in banking intermediation.[7]

Similarly, the cost of doing business in investment banking is characterised by a 65/25/10 ratio. Some years ago, a report by McKinsey/Salomon Brothers analysed the breakdown of systems expenditure for securities trading, and the statistics brought under perspective are startling.

- Back office and settlements eat up 65 per cent.
- Trade support represents another 25 per cent.
- This leaves only 10 per cent for analysis, product research and market development.

The 45/25/30 paradigm has not been taken out of a hat. It was chosen because analysis, product research and market development represent the highest potential returns to an investment bank. The regrettable results of a 65/25/10 distribution are due to the fact that, with information services, the approach being taken is still grounded to old concepts and rules in spite of huge amounts of money being spent on computers and communications.

A parallel to this biased structure can be found in the computer industry. Figure 12.9 presents the pattern characterising cost of goods sold, selling costs and operating margins by eight different computer manufacturers. As the careful reader will observe, the highest profit margin belongs to company A which keeps its costs of goods sold under lock and key while spending more on marketing.

The lesson to be retained from these examples is that *if* outsourcing agreements pay lip service to costs of goods sold, or forget about them altogether, *then* the goal of an improved profitability will never be reached. Typically, there is a very significant difference between what is hoped for and the results one gets. A great deal of this difference lies in our ability to control costs with outsourcing agreements even better than we do with operations executed inhouse.

13
Innovation and Cost Control in Information Technology through Re-engineering

1. Introduction

The use of computers in business and industry dates back to the early 1950s. However, in spite of fifty years of practice, few companies have found a good solution to controlling costs related to information technology (IT), while improving the accuracy, timeliness and quality of IT deliverables. The technology and its tools are available to everybody. What is lacking is the ability (even, sometimes, the willingness) to use technological breakthroughs and make them blossom.

Sometimes, IT audits reveal an unbelievable level of incompetence. In other cases, companies complain about two major roadblocks: costs and complexity. Both can be significant because of failures in cost control, the wrong sort of IT 'tradition', and unwillingness to challenge the obvious. Over the years, pioneers in information technology have been testing the waters.

- In the 1970s, the minis and the maxis challenged the mainframes.
- The 1980s saw the revolution of personal computers (PC) and client-servers (CS).
- Technology in the 1990s was characterised by intelligent networks and agents.
- At the beginning of the twenty-first century we have handheld devices, wireless and broadband connections at an affordable cost.

But mainframes are still around, and some people seem unable to live without them. Yet the need for greater efficiency has never been more pressing, as costs are mounting. Among financial institutions, IT-related expense now accounts for about 15 to 25 per cent of total non-interest budget – a huge amount.

Budget planners try to save money by outsourcing the company's information technology. In so doing, they often forget that IT has become the core of practically all industry sectors. By making the IT business contractual, with programming, processing and databasing being farmed out to cheaper labour, companies open the Pandora's box of risks.

- Typically, IT outsourcers fail to take into consideration security requirements, which should have been at the top of their list of priorities.
- Even if outsourcing concerned nothing other than customer billing and payment of invoices, it can give the insourcer access to routing information regarding all of the outsourcer's business partners.

This is by no means a call against IT outsourcing. Rather, it is a reminder that IT costs are not only financial. Beyond this comes the fact that money allocated to IT is often misused; it is also unevenly distributed because much depends on whether the allocation is efficient or inefficient. Table 13.1 gives some ranges under:

- the old, obsolete way of throwing money at the problem
- the new strategy guided by the nature of deliverables and by cost-effectiveness.

Outsourcing IT services under the old, inefficient approach makes no sense at all. Yet that's exactly what many companies are doing. This is self-destructive, particularly so as, in the financial industry for instance, the proportion of technology-related expenses to aggregate non-interest costs continues to increase.

With that much money in the IT budget, investment decisions on computers and communications are extremely important and the need to always keep in perspective return on investment (ROI, see Chapter 14) should not be taken lightly. Everything that has to do with IT, including outsourcing and downsizing, should be subject to management control, auditing and the evaluation of ROI.

Table 13.1　An order of magnitude distribution of IT costs

	Old inefficient allocation (%)	More rational allocation (%)
Hardware	25	$15 \rightarrow 10$
Basic software	17	$10 \rightarrow 6$
I/O, clearance, printing	$25 \rightarrow 20$	$6 \rightarrow 3$
Training	$0 \rightarrow 3$	$5 \rightarrow 10$
Architecturing	0	$2 \rightarrow 3$
Applications software:		
• New products	8	$40 \rightarrow 52$
• Maintenance	21	$12 \rightarrow 6$
Research and development	0	10

2. Re-engineering helps in promoting innovation and in improving efficiency

Re-engineering means restructuring; casting in a different form, which may be a new or an old one reinvented. Carried out by people who are open to novel ideas and ways of doing business, re-engineering assists in challenging the obvious and in getting rid of crumbling structures which, when kept around, are damaging competitiveness and reduce efficiency.

Re-engineering is necessary because technology-driven innovation requires a steady organisational change. In turn, this calls for both managerial and technical vision, as well as for building teams that balance technological and political competence. Successful entrepreneurs are able to guide their organisations through the process of innovation because they appreciate both the motivations and the barriers to innovation, including:

- how individual incentives mesh with restructuring, reframing, goal enlargement, and group performance
- the kind of characteristic structures, internal incentives and organisational processes that must be implemented to reap benefits from innovation.

It is not always easy to distinguish between redesign, restructuring and transformation, because all three tend to mesh. A similar statement is valid with regard to innovation. For instance, digital technologies for modelling and simulation offer more value for less money because they provoke fundamental challenges to organisational solutions, with restructuring a precondition in obtaining greater efficiency.

Usually, though not always, the reason for organisational re-engineering is to attain a greater efficiency through cost-cutting. In this connection we often talk of *downsizing*, which is often achieved by reducing the head count. More than this, however, the overall objective should be to create the needed conditions for cost-effective creativity, encouraging the members of the organisation to collaborate in novel, more cost-effective ways.

Based on a project I did with a major institution in the mid 1990s, Figure 13.1 presents an example or organisational re-engineering involving IT, whose primary goal has been to meet the aforementioned objectives. In this particular entity, and in many others, the re-engineering solution required an innovative style of IT which significantly assisted in improving efficiency while swamping costs.

- The effort associated with organisational re-engineering may be undertaken with inhouse human resources, or it may be outsourced.
- Usually, it is outsourced for either of two reasons: the insourcer has significant experience in re-engineering, or the outsourcer wants somebody else to take the responsibility (and the blame) in radically reducing the head count.

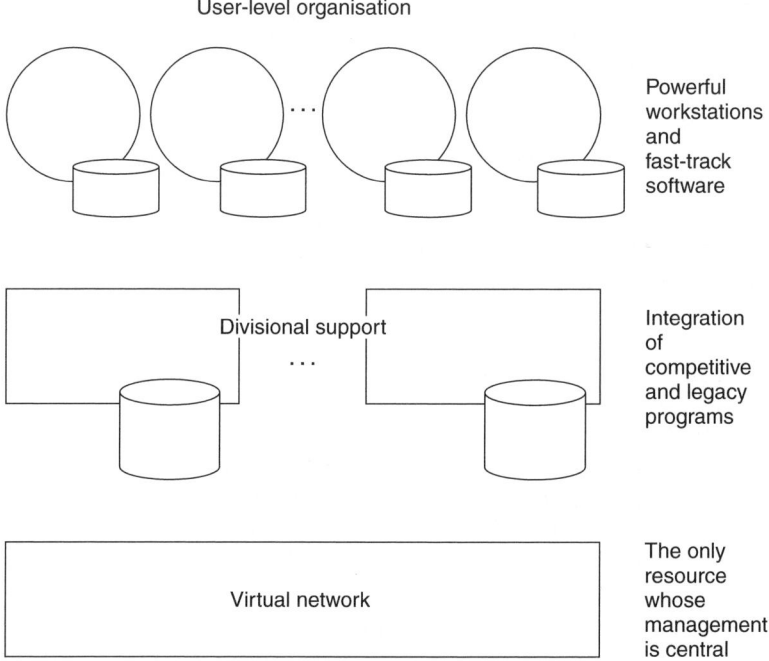

User-level organisation

Powerful
workstations
and
fast-track
software

Divisional support
. . .

Integration
of
competitive
and legacy
programs

Virtual network

The only
resource
whose
management
is central

Figure 13.1   Organisational re-engineering of communications, computers and software
resources

With respect to downsizing, re-engineering is a more sweeping approach to
cost reduction than method and time studies, standard costs (see Chapter 12),
or a simple reorganisation by switching managerial duties. The focus is on
the business infrastructure. For instance, through re-engineering credit
institutions aim at:

- putting the different sacred cows on the organisation's endangered
  species list for slaughtering
- eliminating multiple interfaces between customers and the bank which
  add to the cost of doing business.

The overstuffed branch network is one of these sacred cows. Online banking
technology makes available less expensive and more flexible ways to deliver
financial products and services at an affordable cost. Not only organisations
which find themselves under stress but also a healthy, profitable institution
should regularly undertake re-engineering studies because they are essential
to competing successfully in the twenty-first century.

State-of-the-art IT and downsizing correlate. A network of computers, databases and communications engines permits the company to reach its clients and its suppliers online. It also makes feasible better control over labour costs. There is, however, a prerequisite: any and every banking terminal should not be just an extension of paper-based operations but, to the contrary, a vital part of the strategy of the financial institution put in place through re-engineering.

In other terms, there are major policy considerations in the selection and implementation of a new system solution. Policy directives should stress the vital importance of both organisational design and system design, outlining the chief characteristics of both and their contribution to the novel solution which is emerging – including its usefulness to the clients but also to the company's own managers and professionals, as well as to the bottom line.

Along this frame of reference, re-engineering is a prerequisites to the cost-effectiveness of the investments being made in terms of better customer service and more sophisticated decision supports (see Chapter 14). This is written in appreciation of the fact that the demands on today's business leaders are fundamentally different than they were even a decade ago.

- Technology has transformed organisations into networks.
- Larger companies are increasingly made up of people running small business units.

This transformation cannot be effectively conducted without thorough re-engineering. Computers and suppliers are now seen as stakeholders – which is in itself an innovation, changing the business landscape and even knocking market leaders out of position for failing to better understand the evolution of market activities. From this particular viewpoint, re-engineering is the activity of staying relevant by always evolving to meet the changing times.

Among specific factors underpinning this particular view of re-engineering is the reduction of product development cycles, significantly cutting down product design time and cost, increasing the likelihood of success through real-time customer input, and positioning our organisation for future growth by organising for innovation.

Take dynamic inventory management as another example. Classically, in the past, companies operated by forecasting long-term demand, mass-producing goods to fulfil such anticipated demand, and then shipping the inventories on to the customer. Known as the 'push model', this has the dis-advantage that production decisions are based on projections which might be right or wrong – not on actual customer demand. This means that companies often end up with too much or the wrong inventory.

By contrast, the 'pull model' technology (which requires organisational re-engineering, and even a cultural change) uses explicit demand signals directly from the customer. Also known as the *virtual customer* approach, this fast-reaction cycle reduces capital requirements by enabling the company to respond quickly enough to demand signals.

- Parts inventory may be replenished according to forecasts but assembly is based on customer demand.
- Given the accuracy of the pull system, companies get a major competitive advantage.

Re-engineering capitalises on the fact that the internet lowers the cost of telecommunications and other services, while it helps in creating a closer relationship with business partners.[1] It also makes feasible a new market research method known as *voice-of the-customer* for:

- identifying new product opportunities
- improving the design and engineering of products, and testing ideas
- capitalising on market wishes early in the process when less time and money is at risk.

Re-engineering carried out primarily for innovation should put in place a fast analytical framework for understanding how products and markets evolve over time, which parts of the value chain will be most influenced by developments in customer needs, and what dominant technologies are most likely to emerge. This places the integration of organisation and strategy at the centre of the re-engineering effort, but also requires steady capitalisation of real-time, online management, including data-mining for market opportunity detection and online rebalancing of productive resources, as well as of the processes needed to support them.

3. Without appropriate testing, re-engineering and downsizing are in no way 'sure bets'

Like any other activity, re-engineering has fakes. One of them is outsourcing IT in the name of re-engineering and downsizing but without the proverbial long, hard look. Quite often, albeit not always, this is a melodramatic gesture deprived of the basic preconditions for success and without really accounting for the likelihood of, as well as the reasons behind, downsizing fiascos. The ten top reasons for failures in re-engineering are:

1 Top management does not stand solidly behind the job.
2 Company politics don't allow to reach results.
3 Objectives are not clearly stated.

4   Successive steps in the redimensioning effort are ill-studied.
5   Nobody is really in charge of the project.
6   Those doing the downsizing job don't believe in it.
7   Changes in the project are made mid-stream.
8   Transition milestones are fuzzy or contradict one another.
9   Transition time is too long and still extendable.
10 The skills being used are average, and there is no system of merits and
    demerits.

All or part of the ten factors outlined in this list can be found in practically
all projects which hit the skids. They are common failures to re-engineering
and downsizing as well as to outsourcing agreements. These reasons lie in

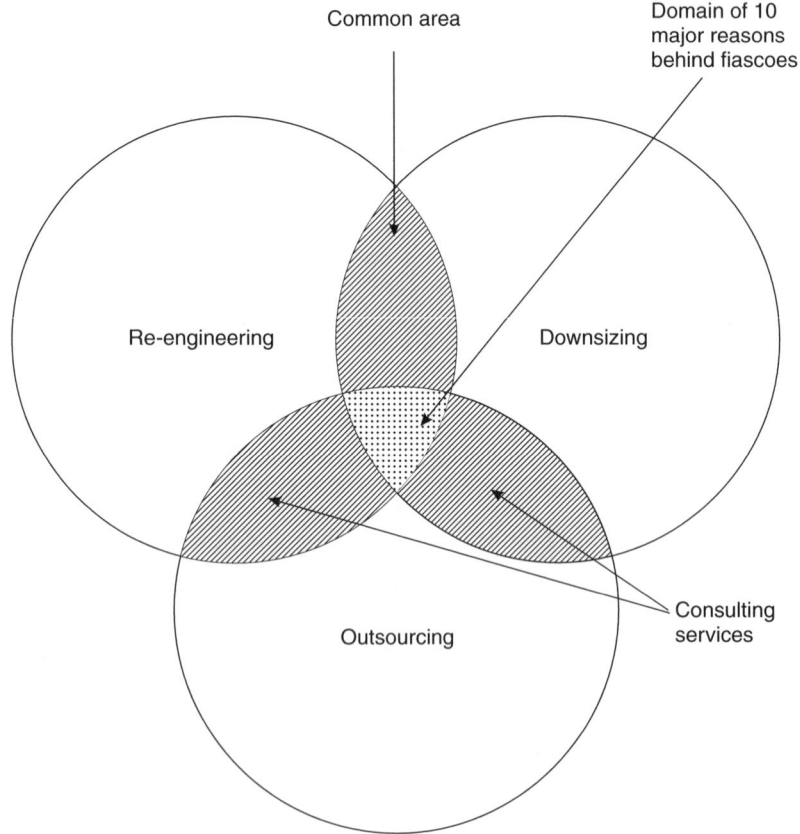

Figure 13.2   Re-engineering, downsizing, outsourcing and all activities beyond daily
routine are subject to contrarian forces

the grey area of overlap between activities relating to organisation (see Chapter 9), structure and the provision of services which are outside the daily routine. Figure 13.2 brings to the reader's attention the overlaps involving re-engineering, downsizing and outsourcing.

In my professional experience I have found mismanagement and company politics to be the most potent factor for failure of re-engineering projects – that's why I have put them at the top of the list. Not only do downsizing projects fail because internal company politics get in their way but also budgets run at high multiples of what they should be as if conflicting interests were bribing the project members to show no results. No wonder that if and when they are attained deliverables are substandard.

Incompetence and mismanagement tend to amplify one another. The runaway budget of the European Commission building is a good example. Belaymont, the 13-story European Commission headquarters in Brussels, had to be renovated because of asbestos and other defects. The original budget was $149 million – already too high. Then came a 691 per cent budget overrun. The time-plan for the completion of this glorious project was 1990 to 1992. Work started in 1995, with some five years delay. By 2001, 72 months down the line, it was still far from being completed, and financial control had gone out of the window. With costs running like a torrent, a new estimate was made and it put the restructuring and renovation price at $1.03 billion.

It is not only the bureaucrats of the European Union, alias Common Market, who are big spenders of other peoples' assets. Banks, too, spend an inordinate amount of money on expenses which should have been tightly controlled. As we saw in Chapter 12, their cost-to-income ratio (overheads) can run from about 44 per cent to over 73 per cent because of galloping mismanagement and the fact nobody is really in charge of cost control.

- Under these conditions, talking of re-engineering is really nothing more than cosmetics; it's an effort to keep the critics at a distance from the turf.
- A similar statement is valid about re-engineering projects involving the wholesale outsourcing of services, particularly in IT. The only sure thing to be obtained from such contracts will be the added costs.

Company politics and mismanagement are not the only reasons for major costs (and delays) associated with re-engineering. In the fourth quarter of 2001, a wounded AT&T recorded a $1-billion restructuring charge, primarily due to cutting 10,000 jobs: 5000 in 2001 and another 5000 by the end of 2002. On the heels of that announcement, AT&T also said that it had signed a $2.6-billion, five-year agreement with Accenture, the consultancy, to improve productivity, sales and customer service operations at its consumer unit.[2]

These sort of contracts are not uncommon; their magnitude, however, sees to it that most likely the only one to benefit from outsourcing re-engineering will quite likely be the consultancy. Years of experience have taught me that not only targeting through precise goals but also a *testing plan* should be the alter ego of every outsourced service. No words are strong enough to underline the importance of a written testing plan for everything being outsourced. In connection with information technology, for instance, this must set forth:

- objectives
- testing environment
- testing tools
- methodology
- schedules
- financial resources
- human resources
- fall-back.

Failure to plan for and conduct thorough testing reduces the likelihood of success and sees to it that nobody really is in charge. Lack of design reviews and tests also creates serious remediation problems. Failure to properly identify and correct outsourcing problems as they appear is sure to threaten the safety and soundness of both outsourcers and insourcers.

Because of being business partners, both insourcers and outsourcers should be keen to establish a testing programme.

- This must observe all prerequisites for assurance of deliverables which characterise a successful outsourcing agreement.

Companies which hope to succeed in their outsourcing need to appreciate what the issues are from an integrative perspective, including those affecting their business partners. For this reason they should plot a strategy to overcome present and foreseeable roadblocks by becoming aware of lessons learned by companies that have 'been there'. For instance, one of the basic requirements in testing IT outsourcing deals is to understand: what is meant by *due diligence*; how a *back-up strategy* will work; what to do if the *insourcer defaults*; and what happens with *operational risks* all along the contract's life-cycle. Also,

- whether the insourcer observes IT standards, including those of an open architecture
- or, the outsourcer will eventually find himself locked into parochial solutions which damage his competitiveness.

Re-engineering projects and outsourcing agreements which disregard standards reach dead ends. The observance of standards plays a particularly important role when we look at outsourcing from the perspectives of longer-term compliance and cost control. Part of the problem with standards lies in

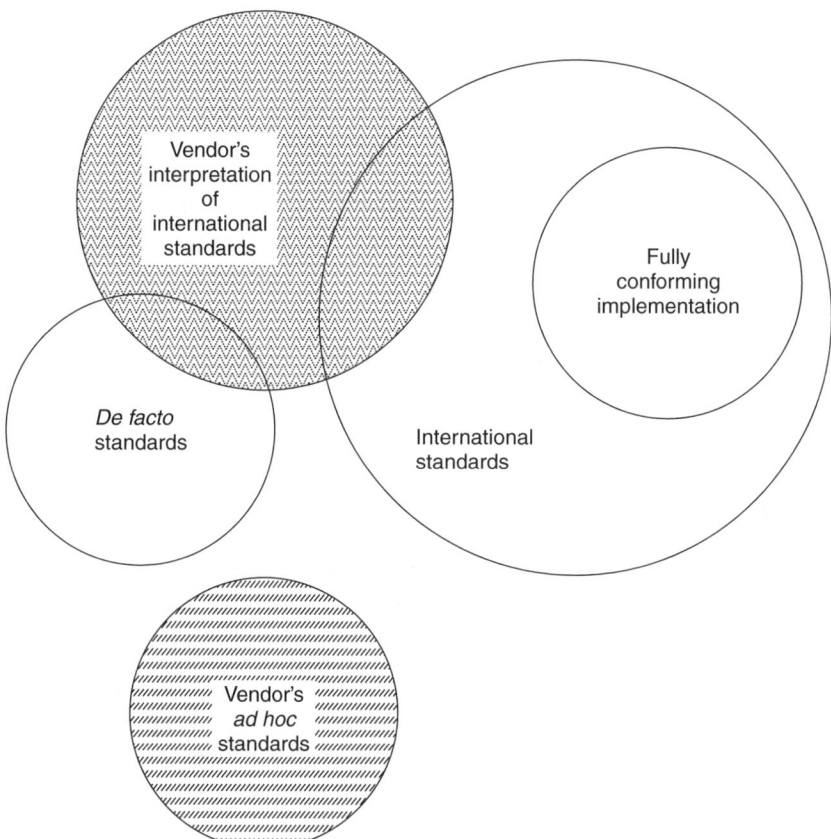

Figure 13.3 The integration of international standards, usual deviations and *de facto* or *ad hoc* solutions

the fact that, in a dynamic business field like IT, there exist no unique set of standards. The pattern is that described in Figure 13.3, which involves both established standards and many deviations which more often than not side-track the re-engineering and the outsourcing effort. For all these reasons testing is a wise strategy followed by most well-managed companies both in the planning phase and at specific milestones during the project's life-cycle.

4. The budget for outsourcing and for re-engineering must be tight

Companies which are successful in their business provide good examples which help to mould a policy, rather than other companies having to rein-vent the wheel. As every person who has been successful in business and industry knows from personal experience, *large supplies encourage large usage*.

Therefore, checks and balances should be at the source of the money supply chain – the *budget*. I will take KKR, the investment bank, as an example.

One of the sources of investment profits on which Henry Kravis and George Roberts of KKR have counted in their career was *increased efficiency*. Down to basics, increased efficiency means doing more with the same budget, or doing the same that was done but with less money. The rule of Kravis and Roberts is that every big company is hidebound by:

- excessive overheads
- creeping bureaucracy.

Headquarters staffs, for instance, are classically too large. 'I call them people who report to people,' Kravis remarks. 'Companies build up layers and layers of fat.' Because of these experiences based on their findings in the companies KKR buys and re-engineers, the virtues of *cost cutting* became almost a theological point for Roberts and Kravis.

Re-engineering, downsizing and outsourcing is an all-in-one business for Kohlberg, Kravis, Roberts. That's their forte. They are busy in acquisitions, including big-size ones like Nabisco; they downsize companies to make them more efficient; and they act as insourcers of management services to companies which they acquire and restructure (though not necessarily in IT).

Cost-cutting is thought to be a general strategy for mergers and acquisitions (M&A), but this is not the case. Many M&A are made for reasons of big ego, rather than costs. A true cost-cutting strategy can be expressed in one simple sentence: 'Pursue big-name clients but keep your own overheads small.' Safeway is a case in point, and a good example on inefficiency.

As KKR dug into the Safeway finances it found confidential figures that were the grocery chain's secret shame – and the delight of Kravis and Roberts. As profitable as the food chain was overall, huge chunks of its territory were operating deep in the red. Safeway was pursuing a strategy common to many big public companies:

- quietly draining cash from its strong business
- subsidising its inefficient operations which were never chopped off.

Associated to this is, of course, a matter of culture. Few managements have heard of Stern's solution or, if they did hear, really appreciated the wisdom of it. In his retirement from the helm, H.J. Stern advised the investment bankers of KKR, whose services he employed, to sell his firm: 'A company isn't like an oil well, where all you have to do is hold a pan out and collect the oil. It's like a violin. And I'm not sure my sons have what it takes to play the violin.'

Henry Kravis, George Roberts and their people know-how to play the violin. After the buyout, both themselves and their senior executives would storm tough the companies they acquired, taking once-unthinkable steps to increase the enterprise's economic value. They would deal with the highly contagious lack of leadership from tip to bottom, and give precise goals to those executives who were retained.

KKR acts as an insourcer of a different kind than the typical model, and the careful reader would wish to keep this reference well in mind. Many people erroneously think that all KKR has really done is to take over companies, but they forget that none of these deals walked in the door because of the company's name, or was turned around just by magic. Most of these deals had major problems in getting completed and all required innovative financing structures as well as new efficiencies at top-management level.

- Each turnaround has taken a lot of time, thought and effort to bring about.
- A financial track record does not just happen without a great deal of work, worry, thought, planning – and luck.

The policy which I have followed in my practice in re-engineering and restructuring poorly managed companies is presented through the three-dimensional frame of reference in Figure 13.4. Zero budgeting provides a new start for financial outlays; open internal control channels assure compliance and allows steady comparison of results to plans; attention is paid to both cashflow and profits to promote financial staying power.

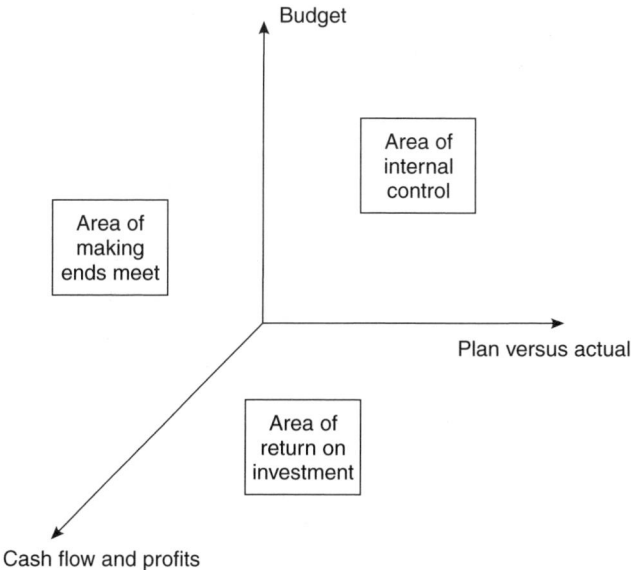

Figure 13.4 A three-dimensional frame of reference for successful re-engineering projects

This is a demanding task because of the reasons we have seen in section 2. In many cases the old management resists change or, alternatively, says that it was undermined in its efforts. But careful analysis quite often documents that this is far from the truth. The old management had undermined itself by not staying up on market developments, not looking after efficiency, and not watching like a hawk every dollar or pound being spent.

It takes very intelligent and sensitive people to run a modern company. And it is wrong to believe that the outside world does not know the difference regarding the fairest and best way to handle problems. 'A person without problems is decadent,' one of my professors taught me at UCLA. Problems keep the mind active, provided we care about their solution. In KKR's case this care is shown by the efficiency of the firms it put its hands on. Uninvolved in the sweaty details of making a company work, for which they hire knowledgeable managers, Kravis and Roberts:

- help set effective business strategies
- analyse and monitor financial reports
- pride themselves on a rigid financial discipline.

Organisations unable to steadily improve their efficiency are self-destructing. As the discrepancy between their profit-making and money-losing vehicles mounts, raiders move in, chop the management, take over the firm and turn it around. Alternatively, they cut it to pieces and sell it, if and when profit from the pieces is greater than from the company kept as one unit.

The principle always is that transitions involve effort, even pain, but failure to make transitions results in an even higher pain and cost. An enterprise can go out of business and die if it cannot make changes – and the same is true of any organisation, including empires, as well as of individual people. Like Alice in Wonderland, one has to run fast to stay in the same place.

5. Cost awareness improves the strategic advantages gained with computer systems

All IT investments and outsourcing agreements should be in compliance with the strategic plan established by *our* company's board, as well as in compliance with the prevailing rules and regulations. One of the best definitions of compliance comes from the late 1990s. In connection with the year 2000 problem (Y2K) the Bank of England defined compliance in a rigorous way:

To be Y2K compliant you must be able to work any date in the 21st century.

This definition has blown out half-baked technical approaches like 'windowing', which divided the century in two halfs: 1–50 and 51–100 years, and other fast and dirty solutions. It is wise to recall that as the twentieth century came to a close practically everybody claimed in the abstract: 'We are Y2K compliant'. The crucial question is: is this a factual and documented statement? Even if it were today, for how long may it be true? Similar questions can be asked regarding cost/effectiveness.

The principles established and followed by Kravis and Roberts are a first-class guideline regarding information technology. They are also the artithesis of what is most often done. Since the 1950s, computer services have been notably unsuccessful in contributing to profits because computer users have steadily overlooked the necessity of assembling and exploiting good cost information. Only a few companies appreciate that:

- it is essential that we know the costs associated to IT and make judgements based on this knowledge
- it does not really matter if computers and communications services are insourced or outsourced. What matters is to be in charge.

We need to know the IT costs of all our services to calculate profit and loss from each profit centre (see Chapter 12), as well as to bend the cost curve which otherwise tends to increase as a function of time. In theory, technology permits us to offer new and innovative services while curtailing paperwork, and also helps in the way we develop new banking products and services: from conception to production and delivery. In practice this happens only when:

- technology is very well managed
- it supports our company's strategic plan.

A topmost subject in achieving this goal is accuracy and quality of service provided in a cost-effective way. This must be a basic, steady objective while specific criteria for return on investment (ROI) on technology expenses can vary with the organisation. Speaking of its internal return on investment study, a leading organisation was to mention that its IT philosophy was embodied in one short phrase: *efficiency of investment* (more on this in Chapter 14).

The analysis of an efficient investment begins with a method of measuring employee productivity. Computers or no computers, unless we can measure productivity in a dependable manner, it is hard to demonstrate how we will improve it. For instance, when in the early 1990s Bankers Trust restructured its IT operations, with a very significant budget behind the relaunch, it put managerial and professional productivity as the number 1 goal in terms of ROI. Figure 13.5 explains how senior management explained the IT objectives the company's technologists had to reach.

While these references are valid throughout business and industry, they are particularly significant in an environment where labour costs dominate. For instance, every financial institution is facing substantial investment decisions

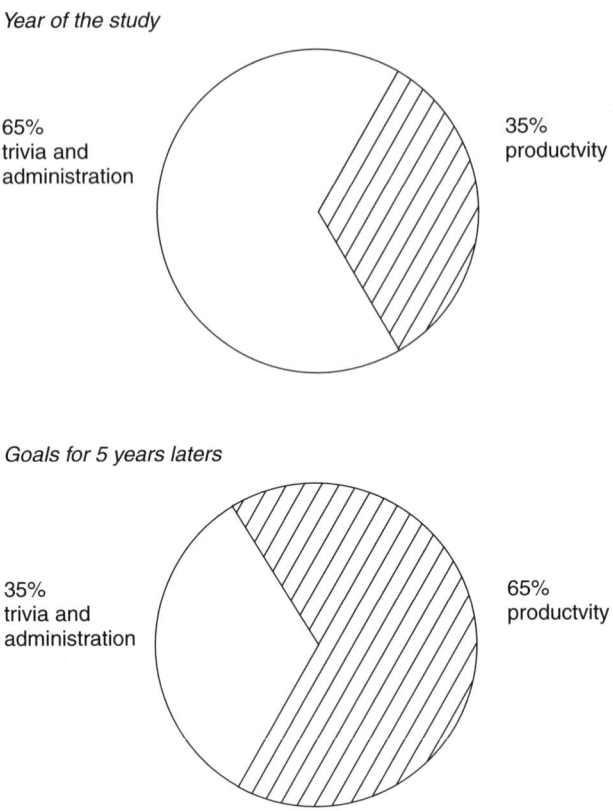

Figure 13.5   Doubling managerial and professional productivity can justify significant IT investments

in order to keep pace with the rapidly increasing overhead and its impact on the bottom line. But this does not mean writing blank cheques. Cost awareness, expense control and precision in pricing are necessary both of:

- the infrastructure of computers, communications and software
- the customer-oriented products and services which must be competitive in order to sell.

Management accounting methods can be very helpful only when they develop and are able to be ahead of the curve in the business environment. If the assumptions are reasonable, it is worthwhile to develop scenarios which offer a valid means for experimentation on volumes, costs and prices. All three factors are involved in a system able to reach the clients at their place of work and their home. We must focus on the longer term in connection with the computers and communications investments which we do and plan to do – without leaving the need for short-term benefits on the back burner.

Whether the solutions we seek are developed inhouse or are contributed by an insourcer, the longer-term view is necessary to assure continuity in the way *our* company communicates with its customers and suppliers. This includes the means by which it internally enters, transmits, processes, stores, combines and generates information flows. *Targeted spending* should be a policy. By contrast, today much heavy spending is undertaken in order not to be left behind in a race which:

- lacks clear targets
- does not benefit from return on investment criteria.

It matters little if the IT services are insourced or outsourced as long as they serve in the most cost-effective manner strategic objectives. This means that they can and do contribute in a significant way to *our* company's ability to become and remain a low-cost producer and distributor of products and services, as well as:

- enriching the information available to executives and professionals
- producing the needed documentation with accuracy and in realtime
- permitting *what-if* experimentation and examination of alternatives
- helping in management planning decisions as well as in internal control.

Such benefits require preparation and training, not just investments in hardware and software. As we have seen in Chapter 11, training should be lifelong and hands-on, providing a direct understanding on how to work with the evolving system and the tools being made available. Every employee of *our* firm must be able to appreciate the assistance technology provides in analysing business problems through increasingly more powerful tools. Computer literacy comes in stages. When this happens we talk of a totally different ball game in terms of return on investment.

In conclusion, high technology gives the best return when used by people who are active and not merely reactive; people for whom life is a perpetual learning, an incessant course of training. The ancient Greek word for training is *askesis*. The people who always strive to keep ahead of their time are the *asketics*. They put a lower priority on physical food because they find their fulfilment in logical food: the development of their mind. That is the attitude high technology requires to give results.

6. Charge-backs and the auditing of IT applications

Several references have been made to budgets, quality of deliverables and timetables. It is important for every entity not only to properly budget its IT operations but also to put in place a dependable system of charge-backs. Information technology is usually a service department and therefore senior management must be very careful concerning the money it spends, how it spends it and who is charged for use of the resources.

As has been already underlined, IT can be a profit centre (see Chapter 12) and hence make money through internal billing. Also, the company may market its information services aggressively to its clientele or other market participants. Practically, this can be achieved by charging at better than prevailing market prices for:

- computer processing
- telecommunications bandwidth
- software products and other services.

Charge-backs make users aware of IT costs, helping management realise that a lot of perhaps unnecessary IT expenditures are being made while computer resources are not being fully or properly utilised. End-users become much more aware of what is actually spent on IT within their own departments and as a result steps are taken towards better use of computer-based resources. Charge-back practices:

- help to assure that expenditures represent something meaningful to the inhouse users
- oblige the IT operations to accumulate cost data, reflect on it and swamp costs
- tell users what will be the price of an upgrade of current services, or alternatively inform them of cost savings possible through greater effectiveness.

Whether the support for IT services is inhouse or outsourced, making both the computer operations and the end-users aware of IT costs sees to it that they get interested in running a more efficient business. When users are billed for the utilisation of computers and communications resources, they become fairly reasonable on what they are asking for, and they go on alert when IT costs become excessive. This may happen because of:

- negligence on IT management's behalf
- ambitious projects which end by increasing budgetary outlays without corresponding results.

Cost awareness is the cornerstone of the good management of any resource. In the late 1980s, for example, the Union Bank of Switzerland built UBINET. This was a very sophisticated global network with reliability of 99.99 per cent. The service was excellent but user departments felt that the bill for telecom services increased too much.

In response to requests by the user departments for cost reduction, a study was done which co-involved five international carriers and their costing structure. This was not easy because, as documented through this study, no two carriers have the same pattern of tariffs; but it was do-able through simulation. The board then decided that the charge-backs of UBINET:

- should be 10 per cent below the average price demanded by the five carriers
- both the quality of service and the reliability obtained at a higher price should be maintained.[3]

If the IT user departments get and continue getting a free service, not only the costs would most likely run out of control but there always will be some people who demand the moon. By contrast, *if* a cost structure is in place and what the users are getting is costed and charged back, *then*:

- users will become more cognisant of what they are asking for
- the producers of information services will have an incentive to watch their costs.

The only way to really make people understand that computer resources are expensive is to charge. Also, to improve user awareness, some computer centres take pains to update them on the various opportunities, priorities and costs, while at the same time disseminating information so that users become better acquainted with the new offerings.

At the same time, for good management's sake and in order to gain the end-users' confidence, IT costs, quality of deliverables and the observance of timetables must be audited. This is true of quality, costs and timetables. For instance, in a bank audit made in mid 1998 were found 500 Y2K bugs in 3000 mission-critical programs. Seventeen more bugs were identified during internal integration testing. Another finding was that, on the average, correcting one of the instructions had program-wide repercussions, with an impact on seven other instructions in the average. The testing process itself came under scrutiny, and the analyst discovered risks in testing and been problems arising from the complexity of the testing environment. Another lesson learned from this experience was that:

- *if* a program is complex
- *then* every single line of code has to be looked at.

Outsourcing is no magic answer to this situation because errors are also made by vendors. In the late 1990s, Oracle came out with a new DBMS version which was Y2K compliant. It tested perfectly with one exception: every year in the twenty-first century was a leap year. The bug has been corrected, but:

- this is still a good example of the sorts of failure which can happen
- even the experts in software development and maintenance are prone to errors.

IT audit must address system level reliability as well as the reliability of each component unit. No chain is ever more reliable than its weakest link. A few years ago, because of a total computer failure, the Federal Reserve bailed out the Bank of New York with a $20 billion loan. The loan cost the bank $50 million. In a 1998 speech, Dr Alan Greenspan said that if the loan could not have been supplied, or if other banks simultaneously had the same problem, the entire banking system could have become unstable.[4] While minor information outages are common, meltdowns can be very expensive and highly risky. This is the core of the problem with IT. Solutions must be innovative, timely, reliable, high quality and cost-effective. It sounds like running after five hares at the same time. An IT project at Bank of America, back in the late 1980s, characterised this mission as changing the wheels of a car while it runs.

14
Return on Investment and IT's Impact on Outsourcing Agreements

1. Introduction

For the large majority of companies, spending on information technology is one of the chapters which has been growing all the time, and has done so for nearly fifty years. The pace has been accelerating. Since 1999 investments in technology by American banks alone exceeded $45 billion, or roughly 0.5 per cent of gross domestic product (GDP), to the tune of $1 to $2 billion by major credit institution (big bank.)

Even if the 2001–2002 time-frame brought a deceleration in technology spending, what we are talking about is a huge amount of money. What is return on investment (ROI)? No answer can be given a priori. My experience with ROI in IT is that we can expect good return on investment *if*, and only *if*, we are *really* using technology to our advantage:

- as a strategic weapon against competition
- for cultural change within the company
- to swamp costs and keep them low
- to innovate our product line, making it more appealing to clients
- to enter new markets and enlarge our base of operations.

The careful reader will appreciate that neither of these five bullets is directly connected to outsourcing or its avoidance. Seeing these goals through is strictly the responsibility of any insourcer. Notice as well that the fulfilment of strategic plans and a faster pace of innovation have replaced other, older objectives in the implementation of IT, like personnel reduction in production and distribution of products and services.

Modern technology allows to reach our clients online and link them better to the products and services of *our* company; but few firms – only those truly well managed – take advantage of it in that way. This is precisely why an a priori answer to the question of ROI with IT is only possible in a tentative sense and, for each company, it has to be documented with

appropriate hard evidence. What is more, few boards and senior managements are aware of the risks taken with IT which have a major impact on
ROI. These are largely of three kinds:

- project input
- project results
- vendor choice, including that of the insourcer.

Risks with project input are those of non-fitness of IT policies to corporate
strategy, lack of senior management involvement, use of lower-grade skills in
applications development, continued employment of legacy systems, absence
of design reviews and defective technology transfer from insourcer to our
company. A typical example of failure with project input is that of concentrating too much at the bottom of the pyramid (shown in Figure 14.1), as
most IT projects continue to do.

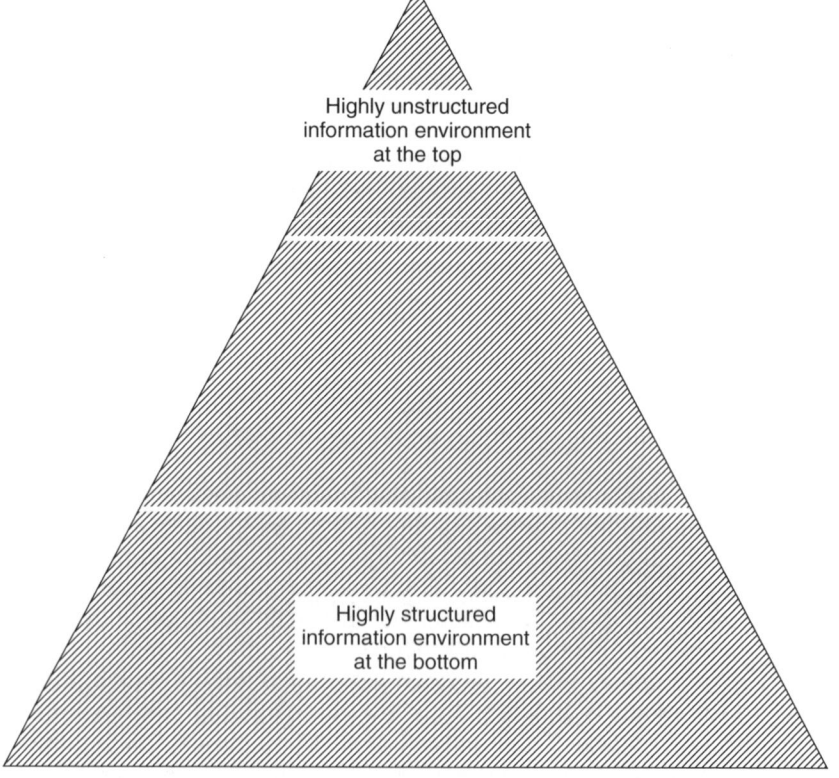

Figure 14.1   The better return on information technology can be found by addressing
the challenges of the unstructured environment

Computer illiteracy among board members and senior executives amplifies this problem. Able solutions to twenty-first century IT challenges typically combine real-time computing, multimedia approaches, knowledge-enriched tools and Internet interactivity. Such solutions, for instance, enable product development teams to obtain rapid and inexpensive customer input in all stages of the product design process – the virtual customer approach:

- assisting users to tune their own virtual products
- identifying important features and tradeoffs
- testing concepts and components quickly and inexpensively.

Once again, the definition of this return on investment strategy and its implementation is the responsibility of *our* company's CEO and his immediate assistants. It is not something to be relegated to an insourcer. An insourcer, however, can contribute knowledge and skills in facing risks connected to wanting functionality, low quality, lack of robustness, high cost or delays in deliverables.

Inevitably, *our* company's management must face risks, with insourcer(s) and other with vendor(s) choices. These revolve around too much dependence on the vendor, use of software behind the state of the art, hardware solutions behind those of competitors, an obsolete methodology, or languages incapable of facilitating end-user programming, and a variety of other problems. IT outsourcing is full of challenges, as this short list indicates.

2. Assistance in innovation and benefits from fast response time

The Introduction has made the point that the more return on investment in IT, the better is its contribution to strategic goals, innovation, competitiveness and productivity. Therefore, it has been a deliberate choice that prior to talking of ROI *per se* it would be appropriate to bring to the reader's attention to how to craft a winning strategy in industrial sectors that face rapid technological change.

Starting with the fundamentals, advanced IT solutions are those which can be effectively used to develop and steadily update a road map of dynamic evolution. This means modelling a dynamic value chain, incorporating competitive product and process technologies, and identifying emerging market opportunities, whose understanding can help position *our* organisation for future growth.

Closely associated with the above is the identification of new application areas in which optimisation problems need to be handled in real-time in order to promote our company's ability to solve problems ahead of its competitors – for instance, online detection of marketing challenges, decisions on pricing, balancing returns with risks and controlling the level of exposure being assumed.

The range of issues identified in the preceding paragraph documents that winning solutions must be both managerial and technological. Competitive pressures see to it that value-added features are part of further refinements *our* strategy. Without doubt, within a sophisticated information society IT must add value to our services.

This is a goal which has been sought with inhouse IT developments with various degrees of success. The key question therefore is: can an outsourcing – insourcing relationship significantly improve on past results? In other words, which is its projected strategic value? A focused answer to this query is important because the able use of technology helps to prepare for economic activity shifts:

- from adding low value on materials
- to adding high value on services.

The emphasis on value differentiation brings along the need for architectured solutions for system projects. These become increasingly vital to the successful harnessing of IT, including factors affecting real-time interactivity. Examples are the globality of networks, reliability of round-the-clock operations and factoring-in of response time. Dr Michael Stonebraker and Dr Wei Hong, of the University of California, have proposed the following algorithm for return on investment optimisation:

Cost function = Resource consumption + W • Response time (1)

where W is a judgmental factor, valuing response time over the cost of resources. *If* end-user time is expensive, *then* W can be equal to 5 or more. By contrast, for clerical work W may be equal to 1. Every time the response time increases, so does the system cost, and this translates to a significant decrease in return on investment.

Behind the Stonebraker-Hong algorithm lies the fact that we terminalise managers, professionals, clerks and secretaries to help them speed-up and improve the quality of their work – not to disgust them with slow-response computers. One of the reasons end-users get disenchanted with computer resources put at their disposal is their long time to give a response. In principle, response time should be subsecond.

Companies looking to outsource their IT tend to forget about response time prerogatives. Insourcers, too, don't pay enough attention to it. Yet experiments done at the University of California document that the cost function in equation (1) can be instrumental in determining the success of a system solution. It also assists in resource allocation – from the purchasing of new equipment (hardware and software) to its usage. It is a simple and very effective equation, which guides one's hand in answering queries such as:

- How powerful a system will be needed?
- How much throughput will be required?
- What kind of software should be provided?
- How much end-user training should take place *now*?

Whether we talk of inhouse systems services or of IT outsourcing, configuration decisions will have to be made fairly frequently because use loads change. Stonebraker has advanced another important principle. It states that every time the number of processes exceeds the number of processors, response time zooms. This is a most critical design parameter which, to my knowledge, is not being given the attention which it deserves in outsourcing agreements. Few outsourcers appreciate that:

- the costs charged by the insourcer should not be evaluated in only one dimension: outlays
- two other dimensions are also most important, along the frame of reference shown in Figure 14.2.

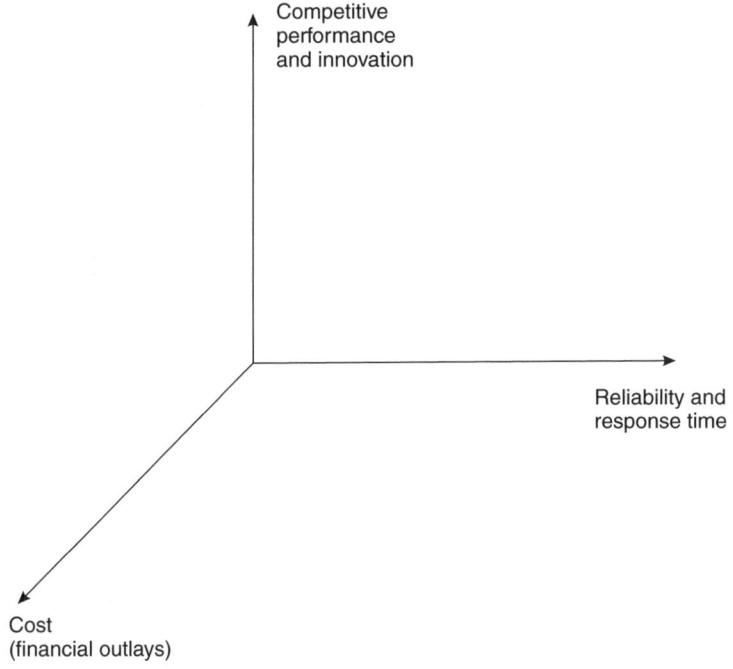

Figure 14.2   In terms of return on investment, the aftermath of IT outsourcing should be evaluated along a 3-D frame of reference

Reliability, as well as its counterpart, system availability, and response time correlate. Downtime reduces most significantly managerial and professional productivity, apart from damage because of lack of decision support. Figure 14.3 shows how fast the average downtime per week

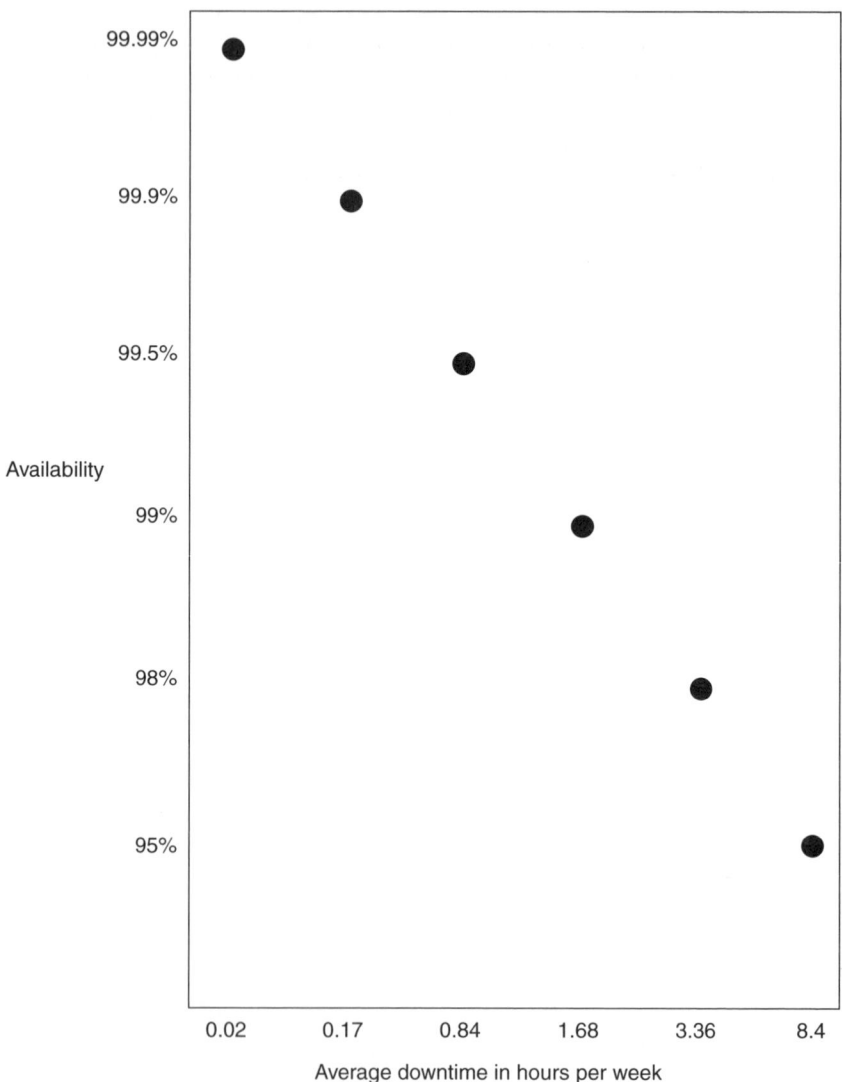

Figure 14.3 Translating availability percentages into hours lost (assuming a 24 hours per day, 7 days per week operation)

increases with a reduction in availability of online computers and communications resources.

In terms of reliability and systems availability relating to hardware and software woes, a great deal can be learned from past failures and related studies. The Bank of Boston, for example, evaluated the aftermath of a Year 2000 (Y2K) failure. Its tests have shown that in connection to Y2K:

- short-term interrupts resulted in inconvenience in service
- a one-day disruption was a major inconvenience but posed no lasting problem
- but a two-day disruption required contingency planning made well in advance
- a three-day disruption called for considerable damage control, in spite of contingency measures.

The Bank of Boston study also demonstrated that after three days the situation was alarming. *If* a bank cannot recover in four days, *then* the fifth day and thereafter will be impossible to recover – and to resume its work. Few outsourcing agreements cover the likelihood of such failure and therefore they fail to provide a fail-safe solution.

Taken together, these examples help in explaining why classical computer science found it difficult to manage reliability risk or to reach specific return on investment goals. It is also estimated that today, in spite of very large investments in technology, some 70 per cent of important management functions still have no computer support. The time has come to correct this failure and by so doing significantly improve ROI in IT.

In conclusion, to provide for reliable value-added services which help in attaining strategic goals, IT systems should be considered as vital connecting links among current solutions to operational problems. Return on investment is improved by using increasingly more intelligent systems components. No insourcer and no vendor is going to provide the best approach to meet in a global sense *our* company's customer-specific requirements. Therefore, every user organisation has to take its responsibilities all the way from system design to costing.

- The former should aim to increase utility and effectiveness.
- The latter should provide qualitative and quantitative expression for control over the cost of doing business.

As Chapters 12 and 13 have underlined, there is a steady need for examining IT costs associated with the services being provided, properly allocating incurred expenditures to the recipients of information services, and making sure that obtained results not only cover the cost but also leave a good margin for profits. Our way of costing IT products and of computing return on investment should be made more accurate and more focused all the time, and simpler and more comprehensible to end-users and, therefore, better appreciated.

3. The need for increasing management's awareness of return on investment

The first basic principle is that in any company and in any project *return on investment* should be a steady policy, not a oneoff affair. The second principle concerns the focus which is necessary on both detail and total figures. This work must be focused; it should never be detached. H.G. Wells wrote some seven decades ago that as he got more mature he realised the 'dissatisfaction' of the detached, uncoordinated work some writers were doing. 'There is a quantitative element in real affairs,' Wells said. 'Doing something does not amount to very much unless you do enough.'[1]

Well's dictum fits hand in glove every entity's return on investment policy. A good way of examining how involved management is, is to ask: do we know-how to appreciate the strengths and weaknesses of our company? of our business units? of their people? of their products? of their markets? of their technology? *If* the answer to each of these queries is 'yes', *then* the next crucial questions are:

- Can we classify these strengths and weaknesses in terms of severity?
- Can we do so steadily, in a documented manner, with accuracy and at reasonable cost?

A critical element in the process of evaluating return on the investments which we make is the ability to develop a method to reveal the desired facts about our activities and their aftermath. For financial purposes the method we adopt should emphasise the importance of capital turnover as well as of profit margins in calculating return on investment.

- ROI is never an abstract notion. The returns are always connected to the business we do and its outcome.
- The benefits we derive from our investments in the IT (or any other) channel should always be derived from the objectives we pursue.

With both inhouse and outsourcing solutions, the calculation of return on investment in IT is neither a purely financial job nor a purely statistical job. Its able execution is akin to that of interactive computational finance. Graphs must display the efficiency of unit performance in function of IT supports and investments, a technique of presentation which emphasises the value of detailed, disciplined controls in the operation of a business.

Reference was made in Chapter 13 to the role played by company politics. Any senior study of return on investment is bound to encounter detractors.

The bureaucracy will surely be against it, because it pinpoints the waste. But there might also be other issues, such as emergency problems which have been put on the backburner. These include:

- overruns on appropriations
- runaway inventories
- cash shortages and other reasons which mediate against return on investment studies.

Only the board and the CEO can fence the different detractors. The pillars on which should rest the evaluation of return on any investment are shown in Figure 14.4. Organisations are made up of people, and people should be accountable for the investment decision they make whether these concern IT, outsourcing or any other issue (more about this later).

Contrarians might argue that not all IT investments turn out to be as intended. This is, however, no excuse for poor performance. Whether the reason behind adversity is human or material, what is really exposed is the lack of control and co-ordination in the firm. At the same time, in the course of an effort to meet specific goals or emergency problems, new, more powerful, methods of financial co-ordination and control should be effectively applied.

In tier-1 companies, financial methods are so refined today that what I am saying may seem routine. However, because this is not the case for the majority of companies, it is necessary to stress the points made above. Management control is improved by organising and presenting data on ROI based on facts. Return on investment is, in essence, at the core of running a business.

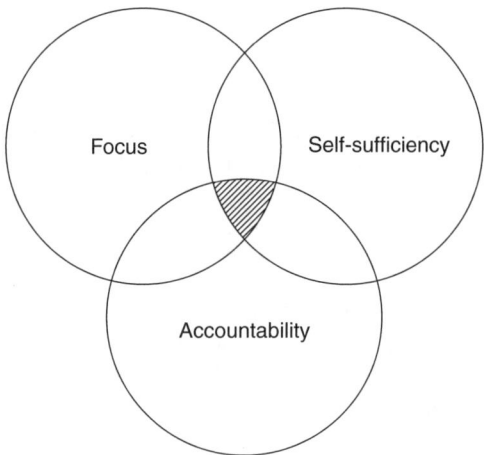

Figure 14.4 The three pillars on which rest the evaluation of return on investment

At any time, senior management must not only evaluate financial requests but also reconcile the total amount of such requests with available funds. Therefore, whenever and wherever I found myself confronted with return on investment problems, I recommended a thorough analysis of the operation and comparison with outside competitive solutions. The point I wish to relate with this reference is that before to techniques comes the general principle of:

- rate of return
- discounted cashflow.

Both are measures of the worth of a business. Its travails with derivatives left aside, Bankers Trust was a well-managed institution, particularly so in IT. The technology budget at Bankers Trust was closely connected both to company strategy and to investment guidelines. During the late 1990s:

- 22 per cent of the annual non-interest budget was invested in technology
- ten years earlier, in the 1980s this share stood at 10 per cent, but return on investment criteria were always present.

Indeed, since the late 1980s, at Bankers Trust a policy set by the board demanded 22 per cent ROI on all IT investments, except the R&D budget which stood at about 10 per cent of IT expenses. This left a healthy 20 per cent ROI on *all* IT money, and it also set the stage for a significant R&D fallout. RAROC and Magellan are two examples.[2]

Other IT policies by Bankers Trust are also worth recording. For every payroll dollar the bank saved because of the able use of IT, it invested 40 cents in technology. This left a hefty 60 cents in profits. The Mellon Bank had a similar policy. As Dr George DiNardo, of Mellon, once suggested: 'We are bankers and we do investments. If IT assures us a 22 per cent ROI, we will invest in IT.'

This idea of using ROI as a fundamental investment criterion should be applied to all management problems, obviously including outsourcing. Able solutions which make return on investment transparent to everybody not only improve a company's financial position but end by increasing the accountability of everybody in the organisation:

- establishing crisp criteria for selection
- placing each operation on its own foundation
- making each person feel that they are a part of the whole
- assuring the responsibility for results becomes a company principle.

Never underestimate the bearing of return on investment on financial control. The relation between net return and invested capital of each operating unit is the true measure of efficiency, irrespective of the number of other business units contributing to the end results. Well-focused studies have brought into perspective that the most solid way to success is to:

- delegate the ROI job to people who are open to change and who have no embedded interest in keeping around sacred cows
- start the ROI tests where you suspect a low profitability ratio and/or higher risk quotient
- gain experience, avoid attacking as a first try those posts with the higher or lower quartile of business turnover, and
- always pre-establish the criteria for a decision on success or failure of the ROI effort, while making the results of ROI studies known to everybody in the organisation.

In conclusion, return on investment in IT is so much better when we are fully aware of costs *and* when we answer in the most able manner end-users' needs. Notice that these may be different from customer needs. Both must be handled well. End-user needs within the organisation often suffer because the internal IT department too frequently loses contact with them. ROI is not only a very good financial evaluator but also a good device to bring internal IT – or outsourced IT – back to the track of its basic duties.

4. Structural change is one of the channels of return on investment

We should always be keen to learn from the rare success stories in information technology. Some years ago, for example, Barclays Bank restructured its risks archives. It shut down its main customer systems for a weekend to cut over to a new distributed system accommodating 25 million customer accounts, and thereafter this new system seamlessly replaced three incompatible legacy procedures and their programming support.

In London some analysts said that Barclays spent at least £100 million ($144 million) on the upgrade, but Barclays answered that the benefits derived from the restructuring of its customer system outweighed by far the costs. Like risk and return, cost and return is an integral function which should not be piecemeal.

Return on investment should be based on facts, and therefore on tangible results. Over and above that, outside the ROI equation there are also intangibles to consider; for instance, speed and quality of service, which cannot be easily quantified, as well as the ability to improve the quality of deliverables to the client base. Notice, however, that no solution (even the best) is good for ever.

This is evidently true of organisational studies and of structural issues. The careful reader will remember the reference made in Chapter 9 to the need for having and maintaining a lean organisational structure.

A reminder is given in Figure 14.5. In the early 1980s, Citibank justified the major financial allocation for Project Paradise (a total system solution to office automation) through the ability to increase the span of control from five people (on average) to eight. This cuts with a sharp knife the fat of management overhead.

Other overheads, however, are beyond the company's control, and may impact on ROI. Therefore, any serious study on return on investment cannot forget the cost of labour and government overhead. Today, on average, the hourly cost per worker is $18 in America, $17 in France and $28 in Germany. To this must be added the so-called social costs. Also, in terms of government overhead (per cent of population working for different government agencies) among G-7 countries France fares worst. In per centages, this government overhead is:

- 11.0 in Luxembourg
- 12.0 in Holland
- 14.4 in England
- 15.7 in Germany
- 17.8 in Italy
- 25.0 in France.

The more bureaucrats work for the government, the more prone will this government be put to iron bars in the wheels of change – even to turning back the clock. Look at the 35-hour work week in France. Implemented in 1999 by a socialist-communist coalition, the 35-hour week had this particular distinction: it angered everybody – management, workers and labour unions.

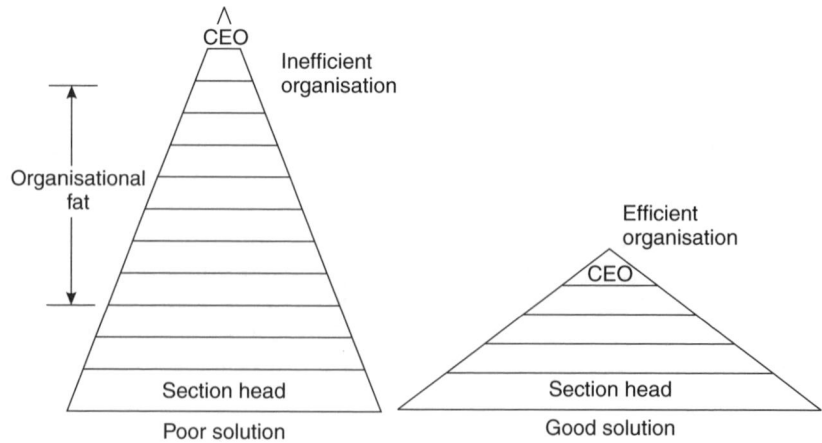

Figure 14.5 A large span of control leads to a flat and cost-effective organisation

Companies, too, look at tomorrow's society through the rear-view mirror. Some years ago, a study by the Pacific Stock Exchange examined the IT practices of the banking industry in California, and it found that three failures had happened with IT almost simultaneously and in defiance of any good sense.

- More paper was in circulation than before computers were implemented.
- Managerial requirements had been only partly answered.
- The reconciliation of payments paper remained simply manual.

Findings like these are what I encounter all the time through my own professional practice. They are a direct result of the fact that companies use brute force instead of intelligence in the implementation of IT. When I make reference to 'intelligence' I mean goals, problem definition(s), procedures, software developments and knowledge-enriched approaches to attain problem solutions.

Spending large sums of money on IT has become a sort of tradition, independent of any ROI. Many, too many, companies fail to appreciate that budgets must be allocated only when they have a clear idea of what benefit will be derived. This is also the golden rule for outsourcing: Cost – benefit must be king.

Among poorly managed companies, long term, large IT projects continue to be implemented as an act of faith rather than a critically assessed investment which follows structural change. At times, cost – benefit analyses are being massaged to look positive, so that large capital outlays can be made. One survey I saw recently claimed that:

- while 65 per cent of participating companies were able to quantify IT's contribution to their business
- most boards of CEOs intuitively believed their investment in IT were 'absolutely necessary', irrespective of ROI.

To a very substantial extend, these findings confirmed my own experience. Large organisations spend billions on technology every year, yet they don't particularly care for ROI. They are not even close to employing leading-edge tools. In the mid 1990s a study by Ernst & Young and *American Banker* said that:

- 84 per cent of banking software was designed for mainframes, while over 75 per cent of bank computer programs were still written in Cobol
- 80 per cent of the software used by the financial industry was over six years old, and only 37 per cent of supported locations are networked.

How did these issues fare in the seven years that elapsed? Networking has definitely improved by a wide margin, thanks largely to the Internet.

Among tier-1 banks, software has been renewed, largely because of action undertaken to face the Y2K problem, and the push the Federal Reserve, OCC, FDIC and OTS gave in this direction.

But inefficient Cobol programs are still in majority and mainframes are still around in big numbers. These issues improved slightly in the US and only marginally in Europe. Credit institutions are still in love with their mainframes and they don't seem capable of abandoning the obsolete Cobol culture. Under these conditions:

- restructuring is thrown out of the window
- ROI goes along with it.

Clumsiness in IT budgeting and ROI can do plenty of harm. All processes are subject to slow rot, and those that are not properly controlled are the first to get out of tune. If the solutions which we implement to measure ROI are inconsistent or retrograde, then we will quite likely also have troubles. Even if the chosen solution is good, we may have problems if we let the bureaucracy obstruct the chosen course of action or make it irrelevant.

This can be stated in conclusion: return on investment should be a management preoccupation all the time. We cannot afford to keep on spending on information technology if there are no measurable results. Cost control must be applied to every line of business, but costs alone give only one side of the story. What really interests us is cost – benefit. Steady vigilance and the will to get tangible results are the necessary ingredients of any return on investment study.

5. Infrastructural interdependencies with IT outsourcing

Beyond what has been stated in sections 3 and 4, any outsourcing project should account for infrastructural interdependencies which are critical in all applications involving computers, communications and electric power. Infrastructural interdependencies enlarge the frame of reference of IT applications in terms of systems availability. They also make outsourcing an integral part of any information technology solution.

- Telecom equipment uses computer facilities and requires electrical power.
- Electrical power systems depend on distributed control facilities supported by computers.

All systems involving information technology require a sophisticated infrastructure because of interdependencies and the associated risks. Today this infrastructural interdependence is largely software based, and this leads many experts to think that the one-sided emphasis on applications programs is misplaced. It is necessary to examine critically all software routines commanding the correct functioning of:

- outsourced services
- their deliverables.

This is an integral part of the outsourcer's responsibilities. In their origin, failures to account for infrastructural interdependencies are not too different from failures to spot the roadblock to better, more sophisticated computer applications. Infrastructural failures include: too heterogeneous equipment, incompatible operating systems (OS), scant attention to requirements for disaster back-up, and absence of written, contractually established requirements for timely response to end-user needs.

Infrastructural failures happen both with inhouse solutions and with outsourcing. The latter case is more serious because it makes co-ordination more difficult since the resources being misused or misplaced are outside the company's direct control.

In my professional practice I never stop being surprised by how often most entities fail in investigating new advances in computer applications for inhouse development and carry this deficiency to their outsourcing programs, too. Hence, they stay laggards or they relegate new advancement to an insourcer – whether these are applications-oriented or infrastructural. Computer illiteracy at top-management level is, to a substantial extent, responsible for this state of affairs, and the management of these companies are not in the habit of asking the necessary critical questions about IT budgets and ROI. Here, in a nutshell is, the procedure which I suggest.

ROI homework

- Spell out the assumptions made in terms of ROI.
- Define the deliverables (functionality, quality, timing, cost).
- Establish the constraints (what, when and why).

Budget

- Compute the outsourcing budget.
- Justify the outsourcing budget.
- Compare it to the inhouse budget.
- Do frequent post-mortems.

Infrastructural issues

- Identify the corrective steps to be taken.
- Examine which outsourcer has had experience with them.
- Visit the companies which applied those solutions.
- Evaluate the deliverables in terms of their impact on your company's problems.

Management control

- Carry out frequent design and performance reviews.
- Evaluate plan versus actual (functionality, quality, timing, cost).
- Spell out consequences if goals are not achieved and apply contractually specified demerits.

These four groups of criteria, and the guidelines which underpin them, are valuable with all outsourcing solutions. They should be enriched by a battery of tests so that the weak point of insourcers are detected before a financial commitment is made. As an example, the following is an evaluation scenario based on identified weak points of an insourcer's proposals. The references to identified insourcer deficiencies come from a recent project.

Company A

1 No integrated office functionality.
2 Mainly old legacy routines.
3 No cross-product DBMS solution.
4 Proposed services unable to support projected amount of work.
5 Documentation left much to be desired.
6 Weaknesses in handholding that is, keeping close to the customer and his wishes.

After this list of weaknesses was identified, insourcer A said it would work to correct them, but after five months no results were available.

Company B

1 Limited options in software products.
2 Incompatibility between its programming languages and 'ours'.
3 No open vendor policy possible.
4 Proposal has been inflexible, costly and risky.
5 Back-up was judged to be substandard.
6 The insourcer had high personnel turnover.

Company C

1 Proposed solution incompatible with 'our' policies on security.
2 No successful interfacing with 'our' legacy routines.
3 Emulation approach was weak, though company was committed to improving it.
4 Too many heterogeneous DBMS were in use.
5 Telecommunications offer was good, but too limited for our ongoing needs.
6 Poor coexistence of insourcer's gateways and 'our' gateways.
7 Weak help-desk and system support.

Company D

1 Restricted and unattractive architecture.
2 Different heterogeneous software products incompatible with 'ours'.
3 Lower software sophistication than competitor insourcers.
4 Few supported functions were attractive.
5 Limited technical skills.
6 No valid back-up approach.
7 Very limited marketing/support skills.

One of the critical variables in the evaluation of insourcer proposals is their use of open systems versus closed proprietary approaches. Open systems beat closed proprietary systems in the marketplace. In the 1990s Sun Microsystems was able to get the edge over other companies because its architecture was based on the open standards of Unix and Ethernet. It also took the upper ground versus Digital Equipment Corporation because it sourced disk drives and other components from other companies in Silicon Valley, while DEC tried to build as much as possible inhouse.

At the same time, however, better marketing and better distribution can beat better technology. In the 1950s, IBM took the computer market away from Univac because it focused on leadership in marketing. Covering itself through an ingenious applied science and training program it was selling machines which were not yet ready to deliver rather than letting its customers and prospects in the hands of Remington Rand. Customers went for products that were not yet available rather than for those available but poorly marketed.

6. The synergy between return on investment and streamlined organisational solutions

The late 1990s and early twenty-first century have seen a resurgence of interest in organisation and architecturing. The winners have been those companies able to realise that new technologies are more likely to complement old technologies than replace them. The technology of the Internet did not displace its predecessors completely. It provided, and will continue to provide, a higher-up layer which properly used enhances competitiveness.

In a fairly similar manner, a company which does not appreciate the synergy existing between a streamlined organisational solution and return on investment is in conflict with business reality. Indeed, information technology investments is a good example of how closely ROI and organisational studies correlate, and of what can be gained by capitalising on both of them.

To appreciate the sense of this reference, let's start with the premise that more often than not technology can be a mixed blessing. Sophisticated systems that are inserted into poorly organised companies may reduce rather than raise productivity and profitability. This is why information systems planning should become a strategic concern in practically every corporation.

Success greatly depends on how well the prerequisite organisational study which prepares the ground for new IT implementation (see Chapter 9) has been done. Another important element to be found in serious studies is that the technology in which we are investing should be itself cost-effective. This is easier to accomplish in the US, because competition sees to it that the cost of equipment (for equal power) is much lower than in Europe.

The statistics in Figure 14.6 come from a study by the German Bundesbank[3] and cover the 1991–99 time-frame. Equipment prices necessarily reflect themselves in all outsourcing agreements. Though this study compares American and German references, the Bundesbank suggests that there are similar differences between the United States and other member states of the European Union (EU). Prerequisites to an efficient cost – benefit analysis are to:

- determine the activities on which managers and professionals spend their time
- provide a solution to them tailored to these activities and their effective performance
- follow up to ascertain if they really use the functions supported by the system and how efficiently these are employed (see also section 2).

It would be redundant to underline that the activities of each manager and each professional must be themselves thoroughly studied. For instance, in a banking environment one of the professional duties which stands high in the ROI pyramid is relationship management. Other examples include new product development, derivatives trading and risk management.

While it is itself a most important duty, classical accounting stands low in the ROI evaluation scale because a great deal of what comes into this job has already been computerised – except, of course, creative accounting, which should not be practised in the first place. *If* however we get out of bread-and-butter transactions to activities such as the:

- evaluation of creditworthiness
- analysis of customer profitability
- matching disbursements with cashflow.

then we are back in the high ROI domain. This is particularly true with the many aspects of analytical accounting because we increase the effectiveness of our managers and professionals, and/or save their time. To be factual and documented about return on investment we must therefore focus on the use of time by highly paid persons, through more sophisticated system. This, too, should lead to a restructuring study (see section 5).

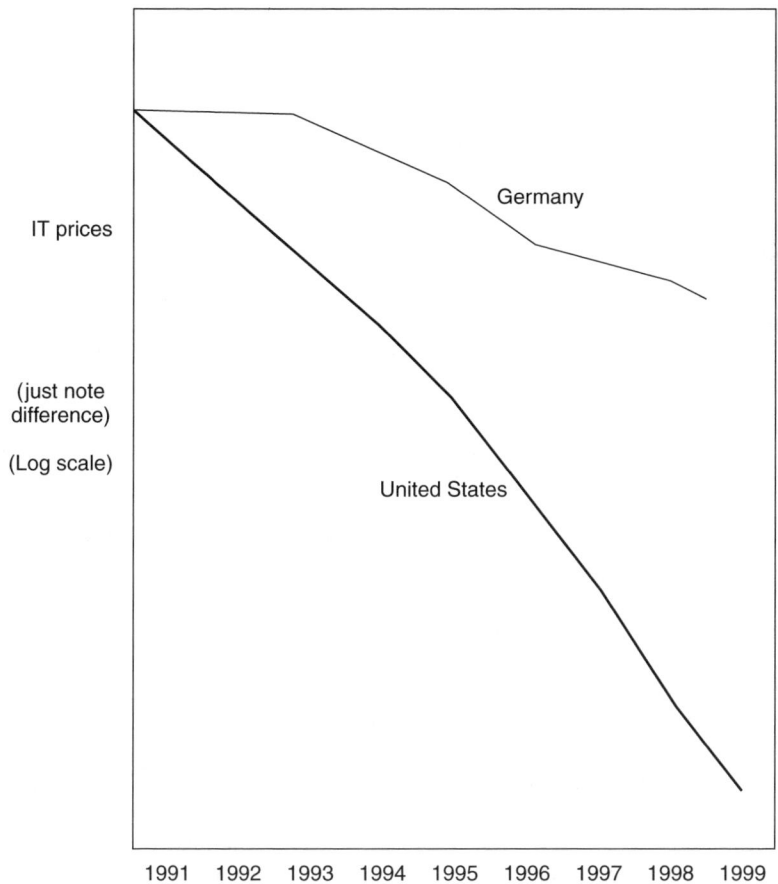

*Statistics by Deutsche Bundesbank

Figure 14.6   The rapid drop in prices of IT equipment in the United States versus germany (1991 = 100)*

When we measure productivity, let's always recall that work expands to fill the amount of time available for its completion. Work also expands to fill the capacity of the equipment which is available. If the right organisation work has been done, the technological solution we provide amplifies a wide range of executive communication and control capabilities. This is the reason why high-technology influences many operations which remained immune to classical data processing.

If outsourcing helps a company which has lagged behind to take advantage of these facts, *then* it might worth its salt. A similar reference is valid regarding the use of knowledge engineering.[4] Short of significant improvements, for the majority the return on technology investments is abysmal. A report by a consultancy points out that in America there is increasing polarisation between:

- those entities leading the high-technology wave
- the rest of the lot with less ambitious programs, which are unable to get a bang out of their bucks.

As this study suggests that if current patterns continue, the gap between leaders and laggards will widen rather than narrow. Down to basics, it does not so much matter how much money a company is spending in technology. What really matters much more than the absolute level of a budget is how well the money is used to produce tangible benefits. One should always remember that:

- return on investments is not a matter of cold numbers, but of a dual qualitative and quantitative evaluation
- a factual and documented *qualitative* answer must be given to the question: 'Why is the return on investment with technology spending?'

Part and parcel of this qualitative answer is how *we* are using such investment to our advantage. This means as a strategic weapon; for cultural change in *our* firm; to innovate *our* product line; to enter *new* markets; to control *risks*; to cut personnel costs; and to reach *our* clients online. As we have already seen in this chapter, these are bottom line questions well-run companies never fail to bring into perspective.

In conclusion, when we examine the ROI of a system solution – whether this is inhouse or outsourced – we should always keep in mind that technology provides results only when we actively manage our investments. Deficient organisational chores, patchwork-batchwork and old-hat online approaches no more fit the bill. Some years ago, Paul Strassmann made a study which proved that because of antiquated concepts:

- there is no correlation between spending big money on information technology and business performance
- productivity is flat in many service companies and in the manufacturing industries, because entities fail to take the long, hard look.

We should never 'assume' that information technology sees to it we are getting our money's worth with a profit because this is 'inevitable'. That's a false premise. Instead, our goal must be critical evaluation of *all* IT investments. Some of the leading questions are:

- Do we consider our investment in technology too low or too high?
- Have we analysed which one, men or technology, is the most expensive?

- Do we know-how fundamental is our company's study of *reducing costs*, and *improving serviceability* by substituting technology for men?

In short, can we explain to ourselves in no uncertain terms how successful has our company been in the past in reaching higher *productivity*, better *profitability*, and a pace of *innovation* that appeal to our clients? – and to new clients? Do we know-how well and how far our investments, including technology investments, support our bottom line? How sure are our findings? Will we write an all-or-nothing option of $1 billion on these findings?

Epilogue

The first and foremost, responsibility of enterprise management is to drive innovation and economic growth, enabling new ideas to flourish, novel approaches to develop and advanced technologies to show their potential. In every marketplace, entrepreneurship underlies the competitiveness and prosperity that characterise a free-market economy. Entrepreneurship is promoted by the competition a free market brings into place.

Intended for practitioners in business and industry, this text is designed for entrepreneurs; corporate officers in finance, IT, and procurement; and systems specialists who would like to develop or strengthen a climate of innovation and competitiveness in their companies and in their markets. Outsourcing and insourcing have been examined as two of the pillars of the process of change that characterises the economy of the twenty-first century.

Based on an extensive research conducted in the United States, the United Kingdom and Continental Europe, this book has brought to the reader the methods and tools of companies that taught themselves how to use advanced technology for integrated enterprise management. In many of these companies their goal has been achieved by putting in competition two strategies that sometimes contradict, but most often complement, one another:

- Outsourcing information technology and/or other activities such as R&D and manufacturing
- re-engineering the inhouse processes, including re-educating human resources, improving current methods and using technology to sharpen the management tools.

Because many firms are now developing policies for outsourcing IT and other basic functions, the text has looked into this issue from the dual perspective of the *outsourcer* and of the *insourcer* – bringing forward issues appealing to both. Rather than focusing on technological details, the text described enterprise management needs and explained how the reader can use technology to meet new requirements while keeping in perspective:

- the risks and rewards associated to outsourcing and insourcing in the New Economy of the twenty-first century
- ways and means of sustaining competitive advantages through technology and methodology while keeping costs in control
- the value and the pitfalls of outsourcing compared to internal IT, R&D developments and manufacturing processes

The virtual company in the New Economy greatly expanded the outsourcing of services. Still, there are serious problems to be faced when companies outsource and outskill their core functions, as documented through case studies in this book. It is always wise to keep in perspective both the benefits and the risks companies face when they attempt to differentiate themselves through new technology, whether inhouse or outsourced.

Offering advice to managers considering the wisdom of outsourcing some of their business functions means explaining how they should research the pros and cons, refocus attention on crucial aspects of competitiveness, and force their company to reconsider the best way to perform the work internally before outsourcing it. The book brought to the reader's attention basic questions such as:

- Why is a company outsourcing?
- What is it *really* outsourcing?
- Which are the core activities it should not wish to outsource?
- Is management ready to be in charge of the outsourcing process?

The book also aimed to help the reader determine projected cost – benefit and analyse how to get the most from an outsourcing arrangement. All people involved in competitive entrepreneurial environments must learn how to turn ideas into successful business ventures, increasing the opportunities of their organisation and expanding its area of activity. Key to this effort is to appreciate ways and means that produce tangible results.

The careful reader will have noticed that the executives who were interviewed on outsourcing have different enthusiasms on this subject. People whose companies were best prepared for outsourcing agreements commented that the person who believes in a process for that process's sake, is a hopeless fool. Contractual agreements, including those for outsourcing and insourcing, must express serious intent and not be an excuse for just doing something or for getting rid of one's responsibilities. 'I will go anywhere provided it is forward,' David Livingston once said. Is the contemplated outsourcing agreement a forward step?

Notes

Chapter 1

1 D.N. Chorafas, *Liabilities, Liquidity and Cash Management. Balancing Financial Risk*, Wiley, New York, 2002.
2 D.N. Chorafas, *Managing Operational Risk. Risk Reduction Strategies for Investment Banks and Commercial Banks*, Euromoney, London, 2001.
3 D.N. Chorafas, *Managing Risk in the New Economy*, New York Institute of Finance, New York, 2001.
4 *MIT Report*, February 2000.
5 D.N. Chorafas, *Understanding Volatility and Liquidity in Financial Markets*, Euromoney Books, London, 1998.
6 D.N. Chorafas, *Internet Supply Chain. Its Impact on Accounting and Logistics*, Macmillan – now Palgrave, Basingstoke, 2001.
7 MIT, 'Innovation in the New Millennium', conference programme, March 2002.

Chapter 2

1 *Communications Week International*, 4 March 2002.
2 D.N. Chorafas, *Agent Technology Handbook*, McGraw-Hill, New York, 1998.
3 24/7 stands for 7 days the week, 24 hours per day business operations.
4 'Outsourcing for Financial Services', conference organized by IIR, London, 11–12 December 2001.
5 An example is General Electric's experience during the 1990s, exemplified through its implementation of Six Sigma. See D.N. Chorafas, *Integrating ERP, CRM, Supply Chain Management and Smart Materials*, Auerbach, New York, 2001.
6 D.N. Chorafas, *Alternative Investments and the Management of Risk*, Euromoney, London, 2002.

Chapter 3

1 D.N. Chorafas, *Integrating ERP, CRM, Supply Chain Management and Smart Materials*, Auerbach, New York, 2001.
2 Dimitris N. Chorafas, *Stress Testing*, Euromoney, London, 2002.
3 D.N. Chorafas, *Reliable Financial Reporting and Internal Control: A Global Implementation Guide*, John Wiley, New York, 2000.
4 D.N. Chorafas, *How to Understand and Use Mathematics for Derivatives*, Volume 2 – *Advanced Modelling Methods*, Euromoney Books, London, 1995.
5 Which should not be confused with same symbol used for volatility.
6 *European Automotive Design*, June 2001.
7 *Business Week*, 1 April 2002.
8 Dimitris N. Chorafas, *Stress Testing*, Euromoney, London, 2002.

Chapter 4

1 D.N. Chorafas, *Internet Supply Chain. Its Impact on Accounting and Logistics*, Macmillan – now Palgrave, Basingstoke, 2001.
2 D.N. Chorafas, *Integrating ERP, CRM, Supply Chain Management and Smart Materials*, Auerbach, New York, 2001.
3 *Business Week*, 13 March 2000.
4 D.N. Chorafas, *Management Workstations for Greater Productivity*, McGraw-Hill, New York, 1985.
5 *Forbes ASAP*, 30 November 1998.
6 *Forbes ASAP*, 30 November 1998.
7 Dimitris N. Chorafas, *How to Understand and Use Mathematics for Derivatives*, Volume 1 – *Understanding the Behavior of Markets*, Euromoney, London, 1995.
8 *The Economist*, 28 November 1998.
9 *Business Week*, 8 February, 1999.
10 *Communications of the ACM*, February 2002, Vol. 45 No. 2.
11 *Business Week*, 1 April 2002.
12 D.N. Chorafas and Heinrich Steinmann, *Expert Systems in Banking*, Macmillan – now Palgrave, Basingstoke, 1991.
13 *Financial Times*, 8 July 1999.

Chapter 5

1 *Business Week*, 1 April 2002.
2 Another example of a wrong outsourcing control is the Sainbury case study in Chapter 2, section 5.
3 *Information Strategy*, July/August 1997.
4 *Information Strategy*, October 1997.
5 D.N. Chorafas, *Modelling the Survival of Financial and Industrial Enterprises. Advantages, Challenges, and Problems with the Internal Rating-Based (IRB) Method*, Palgrave Macmillan, Basingstoke, 2002.

Chapter 6

1 See also an article on social charges in France in *Business Week*, 22 April 2002.
2 *EIR*, 18 January 2002.
3 *Communications of the ACM*, November 1999, Vol. 42 No. 11.
4 *Business Week*, 21 January 2002.
5 *Business Week*, 24 September 2001.
6 D.N. Chorafas, *Agent Technology Handbook*, McGraw-Hill, New York, 1998.
7 *The MIT Report*, June/July 1996.
8 *Business Week*, 21 May 2001.
9 George Anders, *Merchants of Debt*, Basic Books, New York, 1992.

Chapter 7

1 *Business Week*, 22 April 2002.
2 D.N. Chorafas, *Integrating ERP, CRM, Supply Chain Management and Smart Materials*, CRC/Auerbach, New York, 2001.

3 *Business Week*, 21 January 2002.
4 *The MIT Report*, April 2001.
5 *Business Week*, 24 September 2001.
6 *Communications of the ACM*, October 2001, Vol. 44, No. 10.
7 Dimitris N. Chorafas, *Stress Testing, Euromoney*, London, 2002.
8 See D.N. Chorafas, *Statistical Processes and Reliability Engineering*, D. Van Nostrand Co., Princeton, NJ, 1960.
9 *Financial Times*, 7 February 2002.
10 R. Brian Woodrow, An Applied Services Economic Center (ASEC) Seminar, *Progress* No. 32, The Geneva Association, December 2000–January 2001.
11 *Communications of the ACM*, January 2002, Vol. 45 No. 1.
12 MIT Innovations in the New Millennium, Conferences on Technology and the Corporation, 2002.
13 D.N. Chorafas, *Internet Supply Chain. Its Impact on Accounting and Logistics*, Macmillan – now Palgrave, Basingstoke, 2001.

Chapter 8

1 D.N. Chorafas, *Enterprise Architecture and New Generation Information Systems*, St Lucie Press/CRC, Boca Raton, FL, 2002.
2 D.N. Chorafas, *Enterprise Architecture and New Generation Information Systems*, St Lucie Press/CRC, Boca Raton, FL, 2002.
3 *Communications of the ACM*, January 2002/Vol. 45 No. 1.
4 *Communications Week International*, 4 February 2002.
5 11 and 12 December 2001, organized by IIR.

Chapter 9

1 A.P. Sloan, Jr, *My Years With General Motors*, PanuBooks, London, 1963.
2 Sam Walton, *Made in America. My Story*, Bantam Books, New York, 1992.
3 A.P. Sloan, Jr, *My Years With General Motors*, Pan, London, 1963.
4 *Business Week*, 24 May 2001.
5 C. Williams-Ellis and A. Williams-Ellis, The Tank Corps, George Newnes, London, 1919.

Chapter 10

1 See D.N. Chorafas, *Commercial Banking Handbook*, Macmillan – now Palgrave, London, 1999.
2 Sun Tzu 'L'Art de la querre' (*The Art of War*), Flammarion, Paris, 1972.
3 Alfred P. Sloan, *My Years With General Motors*, Sidgwick & Jackson, London, 1965.
4 Frank Partnoy, *F.I.A.S.C.O. The Truth About High Finance*, Profile Books, London, 1997.
5 Alfred P. Sloan, *My Years With General Motors*, Sidgwick and Jackson, London, 1965.

Chapter 11

1 *Business Week*, 11 March 2002.
2 *Communications of the ACM*, December 2000/Vol. 43 No. 12.

3   *Le Monde*, 8 March 2002; *Canard Enchainé*, No. 4246, 13 March 2002.
4   Alfred D. Chandler, *Inventing the Electronic Century. The Epic Story of the Consumer Electronics and Computer Industries*, Free Press, New York, 2001.
5   *The Economist*, 3 November 2001.
6   *Wall Street Journal*, 27 July 2001.
7   D.N. Chorafas, *The Management of Philanthropy in the 21st Century*, Institutional Investor, New York, 2002.
8   Henry Kaufman, *On Money and Markets. A Wall Street Memoir*, McGraw-Hill, New York, 2000.
9   *The Manager*, November/December 1995.

Chapter 12

1   *Business Week*, 15 November 1999.
2   Ralph Barnes, *Motion and Time Study*, John Wiley, New York, 1952. A *therblig* study is typically done using a watch which indicates fraction of a second, filming the manual words and subsequently analysing it. This achieves high precision in the time study.
3   *Business Week*, 28 October 1996.
4   *The Economist*, 2 March 2002.
5   *Business Week*, 23 October 2000.
6   D.N. Chorafas, *Integrating ERP, CRM, Supply Chain Management and Smart Materials*, Auerbach, New York, 2001.
7   J.B. Caouette, E.I. Altman, P. Navayanan, *Managing Credit Risk*, Wiley, New York, 1998.

Chapter 13

1   D.N. Chorafas, *Internet Supply Chain. Its Impact on Accounting and Logistics*, Macmillan – now Palgrave, London, 2001.
2   *Communications Week International*, 4 March 2002.
3   D.N. Chorafas and H. Steinmann, *Intelligent Networks*, CRC Press, Boca Raton, FL, 1990.
4   *Communications of the ACM*, June 1998.

Chapter 14

1   H.G. Wells, *The Outlook for Homo Sapiens*, London, 1942.
2   D.N. Chorafas and H. Steinmann, *Database Mining*, London and Dublin: Lafferty, 1994.
3   Deutsche Bundesbank, Monthly Report, May 2001.
4   D.N. Chorafas and Heinrich Steinmann, *Expert Systems in Banking*, Macmillan – now Palgrave, Basingstoke, 1991.

Index

ABN-Amro, 275
Accenture, 25, 41, 44, 297
accounting standards, 47
agency costs, 54, 98
agents, 28, 201
Alcatel, 40
alternative investments, 44
analytical thinking, 222
Amazon.com, 75, 85, 92
American International Group, 281
AOL-Time Warner, 74
AT&T, 25, 26, 117, 155, 297
applications service provider, 6, 8, 110
audit committee, 47

backoffice, 271
balance-sheet uplifting, 40
Banca di Roma, 115, 175
Banco Ambrosiano, 115, 116
Bang & Olufsen, 20
Bank for International Settlements, 212
Bankgesellschaft Berlin, 115
Bank of America, 89, 90, 136, 308
Bank of Boston, 315
Bank of England, 198, 302
Bank of New York, 30, 308
Bank of Wachovia, 254
Bank One, 118, 119
Barclays Bank, 70, 319
Barings, 54
Basle Committee on Banking
    Supervision, 30, 49, 184
BMW, 146
behavioural characteristics, 230
Bell Telephone Labs, 15
Boeing, 80, 81, 123, 124
brand name, 85
Broadband internet, 14
BroadCom, 28
Bundesbank, 326
business-to-business, 17, 19, 21-3
business-to-consumer, 21, 23

business continuity management, 198
business process operations, 8, 9,
    106, 110
business service provider, 6, 9

Cambridge University, 255
CampusWorld, 260
Canadian Imperial Bank of Commerce,
    176, 178, 179
Cantor Fitzgerald, 185
Carnegie Mellon University, 260
catastrophic events, 185, 187
cell-based manufacturing, 154, 155
certified public accountant, 8, 140
chargebacks, 306, 307
Charles Schwab, 73, 90, 91
chronological age, 215, 216
Chrysler, 268, 269, 278, 279, 280
Cisco, 19, 21, 125, 130–2, 150–2, 246
Citibank, 114, 115, 132, 320
Clearing House Interbank Payment
    System, 186
cognitive complexity, 222, 227, 230
collaborative filtering, 169
Columbia University, 260
Commerce Bank, 284
compliance, 33
computer aided design, 133
computer illiteracy, 173, 311, 323
Confirm project, 116
consumer-to-business, 21
consumer-to-consumer, 21, 23
contingency planning, 45
core functions, 33
cost center, 273, 274
cost control, 266
Covisint, 22
creative accounting, 29, 39, 47
credit risk, 196
Credit Suisse, 91
Credit Suisse First Boston, 196
custody, 6, 9, 10

Daimler-Chrysler, 22
database management system, 174
Dell Computers, 19, 92, 155
derivatives, 3, 18, 40, 226
design reviews, 139, 140, 310
Deutsche Bank, 119, 183, 184,
   275, 284
Digital Equipment, 129, 325
distance learning, 255, 256, 260
double sourcing, 35
downsizing, 292, 293
Dresdner Bank, 284
Drysdale, 54
dynamic financial analysis, 82
dynamic pricing, 81

earnings before interest and taxes, 12
e-Commerce Advisory Commission, 24
EDS, 115
Enron, 40, 152
Enron Energy Services, 159
enterprise architecture, 166
enterprise management, 11, 57,
   85, 330
Ernst & Young, 321
European Commission, 14
European Union, 14
event analysis, 134
experimental design, 54
external profit center, 210
external utility, 9

fast-flow replenishment, 80
Federal Deposit Insurance
   Corporation, 31
Federal Reserve, 283, 308, 322
Fidelity Investments, 110, 281
Financial Accounting Standards
   Board, 40
Financial Services Authority, 108, 109
fund accounting, 10
Federal Reserve, 32
Ford, 22, 85, 196

General Bank of Luxembourg, 115
General Electric, 15, 17, 18, 22, 71, 102,
   141, 157, 208, 287
GE Capital, 72, 73

General Motors, 19, 122, 204, 205,
   225, 232
German Federal Banking Supervision
   Office, 164
Gillette, 275
globalisation, 3, 249, 254
gross domestic product, 14
Group of Ten, 14

Honda, 210
human resources, 97, 215, 241, 248

inductive reasoning, 220
infomediaries, 20
information infrastructure, 14
information outages, 308
information technology (IT), 10, 14,
   32, 43
IT budget, 42, 322, 323
IT costs, 281
insider trading, 67
insourcing, 5, 6, 8, 9, 12, 25, 32, 33, 35,
   38, 39, 45, 46, 81, 87, 97, 101, 102,
   108, 114, 125, 140, 142, 144, 147,
   149, 160, 167, 175, 181, 183, 213,
   249, 271, 281, 283, 286, 287, 298,
   310, 311, 313, 324, 330
intellectual age, 215, 216
internal audit, 111
internal control, 31, 33, 111, 164, 198
internal profit center, 210
internal utility, 6, 19
IBM, 22, 106, 155, 174, 325
Internet, 19, 24, 71
Internet commerce, 20, 23, 25, 75,
   84, 85, 94, 168
Internet economy, 23
Internet investing, 91
Internet learning, 254
Internet service provider, 259
Internet Tax Freedom Act, 24
Internet time, 75, 77, 79, 80, 83
intrinsic time, 79
IX Europe, 175

JP Morgan, 115, 116
JP Morgan Chase, 9, 118
just in time, 80, 123, 147

Kidder Peabody, 54
knowledge artefacts, 28, 162, 187, 201
knowledge workers, 251
KKR, 136, 300
KPMG, 111, 136, 259

law of photon, 3
legacy approaches, 207
legacy software, 47
legacy systems, 177
legal risk, 100, 108, 185
life-long learning, 58, 245, 246, 250, 252–4
Lloyd's TSB, 39
London School of Economics, 260
lone wolf, 6
Lucent Technologies, 15

management, 15
management accounting, 304
management control, 317, 324
management risk, 64, 185
Manhattan project, 109
market risk, 196, 197
Marks & Spencer, 149
MIT, 11, 21, 97, 123, 134
MIT Media Lab, 163
MIT Project Oxygen, 163
materiality, 69
Merrill Lynch, 110
merits/demerits, 246
metamanaging, 26, 28
Microsoft, 91, 106
Microsoft's Carpoint, 93
Mitsubishi Motors, 210
mobile commerce, 24
mobility of knowledge, 163
Monte Carlo Investment Forum, 281
Moore's Law, 3
Morgan Stanley, 185

Nanyang Technological University, 255
National Air Traffic Services, 172
National Westminster Bank, 31
NatWest Markets, 31, 54, 56
net interest margin, 212
New York Board of Trade, 185
New Economy Value Research Lab, 88
New York Stock Exchange, 73

Nissan Motors, 267
NASDAQ, 153
Northwest Airlines, 181

office automation, 40
Office of the Controller of the
   Currency, 32
Office of Thrift Supervision, 32
offshore outsourcing, 154, 156
Olivetti, 40
on the job performance, 243
operational risk, 31, 45, 49, 51, 52, 54,
   55, 57, 59, 60, 68, 69, 99, 164, 166,
   182, 185, 187, 196, 197, 298
operating characteristics curve, 61, 63
operating system, 174
organisational competence, 192
organisational obsolescence, 200
Organization of Economic Cooperation
   and Development, 122
out-of-control outsourcing, 152
outsourcing, 4, 5, 6, 9, 11, 25, 29, 30,
   35, 37–9, 45, 46, 51, 54, 68, 81, 87,
   97, 99, 100, 102, 104
overhead, 272, 275, 278, 279, 297
overhead costs, 82

Pacific Stock Exchange, 321
pattern of production, 143
Pechiney, 64
peer-to-peer agreements, 105
per cent defective, 62
Perot Systems, 115
personality characteristics, 221,
   229, 236, 238
personnel development, 244
Pinnacle, 117
profit centre, 273, 274, 280,
   281, 303
progress review, 139
Project Paradise, 320

quality control, 287
quality control program, 45, 57

real-time reporting, 70
research and development (R&D),
   120, 121

re-engineering, 81, 292, 293, 295–7,
300, 330
reliability engineering, 158
Renault, 268
Renault-Nissan, 22
reputational risk, 47
request for information, 37
request for offers, 38
response time, 314
return on assets, 212
return on investment, 126, 178,
203, 214, 303, 309, 312, 315,
316, 319, 328
risk analysis, 31
risk self-assessment, 50
risk management, 31, 111, 217,
219, 231
risk profile, 31
Royal Bank of Canada, 138, 141

Safeway, 300
Sainsbury, 40, 41, 44
scenario analysis, 198
September 11, 185
service level agreements (SLAs), 5,
109, 182
shareholder value, 12
Six Sigma, 287
Sloan School of Management, 88
small and medium sized enterprises,
144, 146
Softbank, 15
Southwest Airlines, 285
span of attention, 194
span of control, 193, 195
span of knowledge, 194
span of management, 193
spatial perception, 226
standard costing, 269, 293
Stanford University, 260
Statement of Financial Accounting
Standards, 40
Store Finance, 41
strategic information system, 87
strategic planning, 217
stress tests, 157, 160
SudAviation, 123, 124
Sun Microsystems, 325

supply chain, 19, 20, 71, 105
Swissair, 65, 66
Swiss Bank Corporation, 115, 175
system availability, 314, 315
Systemhaus, 116

targeted spending, 305
TIAA/CREF, 64, 65, 211, 276
technical transfer, 37
technology budget, 317, 318
technology risk, 185
telecommunications outsourcing, 179
Therblig, 269
Toyota, 107, 143, 144, 149, 196, 210
Type I error, 61
Type II error, 61

Unilever, 110
Union Bank of Switzerland, 306
Unisys, 67, 136
US Air Force, 223, 224
US Airways, 285
US Department of Commerce, 160
Univac, 325
University of California, 312
UCLA, 35, 64, 302
University of Chicago, 260
University of Pennsylvania, 260

value differentiation, 13, 312
venture capital, 126
verification outsourcing, 140, 142
virtual company, 26–8, 47, 331
virtual customer, 123, 170, 295
virtual customer initiative, 22
Virtual University, 259
visistraction, 227
Visteon, 20
Vodafone, 15

Wal-Mart, 149, 155
Wharton Direct, 260
work sampling, 269
World On-line International, 76
World Trade Organization, 144
worst-case scenarios, 198

zero budgeting, 301